Contemporary Issues in Art Education

Yvonne Gaudelius and Peg Speirs,
EDITORS

Prentice
Hall

Upper Saddle River, New Jersey 07458

Library of Congress Cataloging-in-Publication Data

Contemporary issues in art education/Yvonne Gaudelius and Peg Speirs, editors.
    p. cm.
  Includes bibliographical references and index.
  ISBN 0-13-088688-2
    1. Art—Study and teaching (Elementary) 2. Art and society. I. Gaudelius, Yvonne. II.
Speirs, Peg.
  N350 .C66 2002
  372.5—dc21

                                                                  00-140087

VP, Editorial Director: Charlyce Jones-Owen
AVP, Publisher: Bud Therien
Editorial Assistant: Wendy Yurash
Managing Editor: Jan Stephan
Production Liaison: Fran Russello
Project Manager: Marianne Hutchinson (Pine Tree Composition, Inc.)
Prepress and Manufacturing Buyer: Sherry Lewis
Art Director: Jayne Conte
Cover Designer: Bruce Kenselaar
Marketing Manager: Sheryl Adams

This book was set in 10/12 Giovanni-Book by Pine Tree Composition, Inc.,
and was printed and bound by Courier Companies, Inc.
The cover was printed by Phoenix Color Corp.

©2002 by Pearson Education, Inc.
Upper Saddle River, New Jersey 07458

Printed in the United States of America
10 9 8 7 6 5 4 3 2 1

ISBN 0-13-088688-2

Prentice-Hall International (UK) Limited, *London*
Prentice-Hall of Australia Pty. Limited, *Sydney*
Prentice-Hall Canada Inc., *Toronto*
Prentice-Hall Hispanoamericana, S. A., *Mexico*
Prentice-Hall of India Private Limited, *New Delhi*
Prentice-Hall of Japan, Inc., *Tokyo*
Pearson Education Asia Pte. Ltd, *Singapore*
Editora Prentice-Hall do Brasil, Ltda., *Rio de Janeiro*

To my family, especially Nigel and Julia
      —*Yvonne Gaudelius*

*In memory of Margaret Mary Evanson,
my mother and first art teacher*
                  —*Peg Speirs*

3 Children must learn they are the future!

3- issues based approach - help solve world problems!

5- creating art for purpose of social change

12- def. of art criticism
13- Freire Pedagogy of the Oppressed

Contents

Preface

This book is a collection of essays that are framed around social issues, art, and teaching. Using an issues-based approach, the authors provide a valuable resource for teaching issues-based content, especially as these issues are explored through contemporary art and visual culture in the classroom.

The focus of the text is on contemporary issues such as those involved in our understandings of identity, the political, the social, the body, difference, and the environment. These important issues are being addressed in the art-world, in critical theory, and in art education. The authors present ideas for educators at all levels who want to incorporate an issues-based approach to teaching. This book combines theoretical perspectives with tangible and practical strategies for generating content and pedagogical approaches. While primarily written for pre-service elementary teachers, *Contemporary Issues in Art Education* will prove extremely useful to general classroom teachers and art educators at all levels, whether they are teaching in the K-12 or the college classroom.

This anthology is divided into three parts. In the first, **Theoretical Frameworks**, the chapters provide an overview of a variety of theoretical perspectives that include a focus on postmodern, feminist, multicultural, popular and visual culture, and community issues. The chapters in **Content,** the second section, center on aspects of creating issues based curricula, issues of identity and difference in the elementary classroom, visual culture and popular media, and artistic issues in the elementary education classroom. In the final part of the book, **Pedagogical Strategies,** the authors examine issues surrounding the relationship of pedagogy to content, the application of specific pedagogical strategies, and assessment and evaluation in issues based curricula.

The writings that we have included are those that address contemporary issues in both theoretical and practical terms. One of the aims of this anthology is to provide elementary pre-service teachers and art education pre-service teachers with a complex of conceptual frameworks dealing with contemporary issues such as identity, the political, the social, and the environmental and connect these issues to the work being done by contemporary artists and critical theorists. In addition, the chapters encourage connections between contemporary experiences and past experiences, between students' lives and the concepts under discussion, and between a variety of critical contexts.

It is very important to us that readers make connections between the materials that they are reading, the information that they are gathering and their own lives and experiences. In order to facilitate this, each chapter begins with a series of questions and explorations. We encourage readers to take the time to think about these questions, write responses to them, and to use them as a framework within which to read the chapter. We follow each chapter with a similar list of questions that ask readers to re-consider their initial personal reflections in light of the understandings that they have developed from their reading. We also provide a list of additional resources for further investigation of the issues that each chapter presents.

The authors in this book are highly respected within the field of art education. They provide thoughtful approaches to a realm of complex ideas encompassing artistic, social, political, and educational issues. While many of the ideas that are being dealt with are complex, the language used throughout the book is direct and straightforward. Readers will develop an understanding of a variety of ways to teach about such issues in the classroom, how to draw upon the contemporary artworld, and a sense of the critical frameworks within which we need to explore such issues.

Yvonne Gaudelius
Peg Speirs

Acknowledgments

We would like to thank everyone who contributed to this book. Putting the book together became an enriching collaborative experience. It began as a conversation in a hotel room between the two of us and led us on a journey that developed both between the two of us as coeditors and between us and each of the authors whose ideas are represented in this book. It was, and remains, tremendously encouraging to us that so many art educators are concerned with the ways in which we can use works of art to approach the teaching of issues. It was especially heartening that the authors joined us in seeing the elementary classroom as being of paramount importance to an issues-based approach to teaching. In light of this, we wish to express our deepest gratitude to all of the authors who contributed to this book.

We give special thanks to Mary Wyrick, Shirley Hayes Yokley, B. Stephen Carpenter, and Billie Sessions for their contributions to our list of artists included in the appendix to this book. We would especially like to thank Glen Speirs for his critical assistance in the early stages of this project. We also thank the following reviewers of our manuscript for their helpful suggestions: Nancy Vanderboom Lausch, Grand Valley State University; Jack A. Hobbs, Illinois State University (retired); Stephen LeWinter, University of Tennessee-Chattanooga; Susan Shoaff Ballanger, Truman State University; and Jean L. Langan, Miami University.

Finally, we would like to thank our colleagues, the staff, and the students at The Pennsylvania State University and Kutztown University for their ongoing support and encouragement throughout this process. The belief that Wendy Yurash and Bud Therien of Prentice Hall showed in the importance of this project, and the assistance that they gave us was crucial to the completion of this book. The contributions of our families cannot be understated—we thank them for the help, of all forms, that they provided throughout the bringing together of this book.

Introduction

I n recent years, exposure to contemporary art and theory has caused many of us to rethink our approaches to teaching art at the K–12 and the college level, as well as in museums and community art centers. Just as art has changed over the years, so too has art education changed. These shifts include our rethinking of approaches to the methods through which we teach as well as the issues and ideas that make up the content of our lessons. Traditional theories such as a child-centered approach or discipline-based art education once held firm ground to support art education practice. However, these theoretical foundations are inadequate when we teach, discuss, and interpret content-rich contemporary art works, especially since these works are layered with meanings and often explore contemporary social and political issues. Current theories such as those found in postmodern approaches, critical pedagogy, feminist theory, and cultural studies are now being used as frameworks for understanding and interpreting art, developing curricula, and guiding pedagogical practices in the classroom. Also of crucial importance in contemporary art education in the elementary classroom is the link that emerges between these issues and ideas and the lives of our students. The issues that daily surround us cause us to reexamine and critically reflect upon what and how we are teaching and what our students, be they elementary or college students, are learning.

Why do We Take this Approach to Art Education?

The focus of this book is on contemporary art, contemporary issues, and teaching in the elementary classroom, a combination that we refer to as an issues-based approach to the teaching of art. The contemporary issues and artworks that we are dealing with intersect with education on a number of levels. First, such an approach affects the understandings that we bring to the foundational theories upon which we base the teaching of future teachers. As mentioned briefly above, an issues-based education looks to contemporary theory as one point of departure from which we can develop a foundation for education. While there a number of different theoretical perspectives that this may encompass, these theories share a desire for equity and for understanding differences. In addition, they work away from presenting universal understandings about the meanings and purposes of art and education.

Issues-based education also changes the content that we bring to the classroom. In this book we have loosely defined an issue as an idea about which at least two distinct points of view can be held and articulated. This approach to content seeks to include diverse perspectives and understandings of the ways in which knowledge is constructed and used. The many knowledges that students

an issue is

1

bring to the classroom are valued, as are their everyday lives and experiences. Such a view does not seek to present objective knowledge that transcends individual experiences but looks to the specifics of our lives and understandings.

Finally, issues-based education changes the approaches that we bring to teaching. Just as content is no longer fixed and objective, so too the methods that we use to construct knowledge with our students become more open, situated, and inclusive. In the classroom the teacher is no longer the sole authority, dispensing irrefutable facts and assigning meanings. Instead the boundaries between the teacher and the students become blurred, universal methods become contextualized strategies, and our pedagogies become a form of critical discourse through which we engage and learn with our students.

We believe that an issues-based approach to the teaching of art is where our energies need to be channeled for our future survival in a world where the daily decisions that we make are impacted by and have an impact upon the social issues that surround us. Believing that an issues-based approach for teaching art should begin when children are young, this book is our effort to document a shift in art education theory and practice. We examine current trends in order to propose a theoretical framework and a structure for developing content and pedagogy that offers teachers an opportunity to move beyond traditional teachings in art. Over the last fifty years, art education theory and practice have been influenced primarily by the formalist, child-centered, and discipline-based approaches[1] (DBAE) that have had an impact on theory and practice in the field. We propose that an issues-based framework supports and expands these approaches and offers a more inclusive framework for the teaching of art. It must be made clear that we are by no means suggesting that an issues-based approach replace any or all other ways of teaching and understanding art. However, through an issues-based approach we present a theoretical framework for art education that challenges, expands, and rewrites the limits of what already exists.

Schooling as Socialization

Why should teachers consider an issues-based approach for the teaching of art at the elementary level? Schooling is a socialization process (Spring, 1991; Shor, 1992; Shor and Freire, 1987). School is one of the primary worlds in which children come into contact with people other than their own families. As a part of their socialization in school, children learn to act, interact, and react when they encounter people who are different from themselves or ideas that are different from their own. As evidenced by many of the chapters in this book, issues of difference emerge in an issues-based approach and provide opportunities for learning. In an issues-based approach to art education any issue of difference may be brought to the foreground. This may include, for example, issues of culture, race, gender, class, ethnicity, ability, religion, sexual orientation, age, and community. Contemporary art offers us an important source from which critical and meaningful explorations of contemporary issues and ideas can take place.

Social issues need to be understood on two levels. The first comprises larger, more general categories such as poverty or violence; the second includes more specific understandings of the issues being explored. Social issues affect every living person in the world either directly or indirectly. How we choose to deal with them as individuals has an impact on how they are dealt with on a larger scale. Social issues become cause for legislation that regulates our everyday lives in both positive and negative ways. These issues affect every person as participating critical members of a society. For our society to be truly just and democratic, children need to learn that how they act, interact, and react to the social issues that surround them will determine the kind of society we will live in.

Children need a critical consciousness in order to function as members of society. Schools, and the educators who teach in them, are an important arena within which we can develop such criticality. As such, it is the responsibility of teachers to help children develop critical understandings. Comprehension, communication, problem solving, and critical thinking skills are primary in the development of the child in an elementary classroom and can be taught through a variety of school subjects including art. As you will read throughout this book, art provides avenues for many kinds of learning. As art educators, we know that all of our students will not grow up to be professional artists, but we would like them all to grow up to be creative and critical thinkers actively participating as members of a just and democratic society, no matter what their vocation. When they become adults, we want our students to freely engage in dialogues about issues that surround their lives, make good decisions for themselves and others, and contribute to the well-being of society. We want our students to walk away with the varied knowledges and understandings that they need to help create, maintain, and function within a society. Studying art through an issues-based approach in the classroom is one place to learn how to explore issues through the engagment of students and teachers in dialogues that fuel our sense of agency in the world, beginning with our own attitudes and beliefs. Visual art can help to both initiate and support this dialogue. An issues-based approach to teaching art to children enables students to study art in the context of social issues. Through this children can develop critical agency to help them interpret, create, and critique the visual culture that surrounds them.

Issues as Content and Context

Social, political, and cultural issues have become subjects to address in the teaching of art because they create contexts within which we can teach art, interpret art, and make art. Contexts provide frameworks for understanding.

lived experince?

They encapsulate a period of time, a space, a place, an idea, a set of beliefs, or an interaction. Too often art at the elementary level is perceived by elementary teachers to be a series of make-and-take activities, devoid of any meaning in relation to students' lives or the learning that is taking place in the elementary classroom. When art is used only as a recreational time-filler or revolves around holiday themes it demonstrates the lack of awareness that teachers have for the potential of art at the elementary level. Framed within a social, political, and cultural context, issues-based art learning can be directed in a variety of ways and can be easily integrated into other subject areas. Through art, many of the authors in this book address a variety of issues, guide teachers in how to choose issues to teach about, and offer ways to teach art and issues.

Teaching art through an issues-based approach exposes children to issues that give them reason to interact with the world around them as well as look deeply into themselves as the issues connect and intersect with their lives. As teachers we may ask our students how they might address these issues creatively and artistically. We might also ask how students can address these issues through their everyday lived experiences. What we are teaching children is that art can be used for a number of different purposes. Addressing issues is one purpose that links directly to all members of a culture. In addition, art offers us a form of critique and a way of engaging with issues.

Some educators might argue that social, political, and cultural issues do not belong in an elementary classroom because they carry particular agendas and disrupt the status quo. This position is based on the assumption that traditional course content is neutral, when in fact it is always political. Ira Shor (1992) reminds us that it is a misconception to view any classroom as politically neutral when it "tacitly endorses and supports the status quo" (p. 12). No matter who we are, where we teach, what, how, or whom we choose to study, political beliefs and biases are reflected in our choices and attitudes and our conceptualization of teaching and education. What teachers choose to include in their classrooms has often been predetermined for them by "experts" who decide what students need to know. Such information is standardized and often devoid of any contextual particularities. It is made available through national standards, in textbooks, through videos, and as art reproductions for classroom use.

Decisions made by experts also support biases that promote certain areas of content over others. When we closely examine what is included in such content, omissions surface with regard to race, class, and gender as well as additional social factors. Some teachers may be more aware of this dilemma than others and make efforts to include content beyond preselected texts, artworks, and curricula. However, this is a challenge even at the college level. As Georgia Collins (1995) reminds us, "art at the university level emphasizes the concepts, skills and values of the masculine identified Western art tradition" (p. 50). Art from different cultures, and art by women and artists of color has not been standard content in many university art courses.

contextual particularities

Such choices have been even less available at the elementary school level. It is equally problematic when, for example, African-American artists are included in the curriculum only during Black History Month or women artists are included only during Women's History Month. Such inclusion does little to shift the canonical and theoretical foundation upon which art education is based. Instead an issues-based approach suggests that teachers ask, for example, fundamental questions about the nature of the canon and the nature of the choices we make in our curricula and our classrooms.

Art in the context of social issues offers teachers flexibility, a broad range of subject matter and potential choices, and a wide range of possibilities upon which to build curricula. Another reason to develop an issues-based approach for the teaching of art is that many contemporary artists deal with social issues as content in their art works and create art for the purpose of producing social change. To be able to understand such artworks we need to understand the social issue(s) that are being addressed by these artists. Contemporary art opens the arena for discussing content that deals with issues that surround us, including our students, on a daily basis.

Many educators consider the content of an issues-based approach desirable and necessary yet find it difficult to use because they lack experience with it in the classroom. In this book art educators make issues and art accessible and practical for both the students and teachers in the elementary classroom. Integrating art with other subject areas, issues of identity, the use of narrative and storytelling, connecting art learning with everyday life, issues of the body, understanding how knowledge and meaning are constructed, ecological issues, building art-centered curricula, recognizing differences, interpreting contemporary art, and connecting with local communities are some of the examples of what an issues-based approach to art can offer elementary teachers.

Through the numerous examples discussed in this book and from our own experiences we find that elementary students eagerly participate in an issues-based approach to art because it makes meaningful connections to their lives. Using an issues-based approach, art is no longer an abstract concept but an empowering strategy, a way to critically communicate ideas or issues in different ways to different audiences for different purposes and to learn about ourselves in the process. Young children who participate in an issues-based art curriculum contribute to thoughtful dialogue, develop a sense of connectedness with the world around them, and a sense of self. In making connections with their lives, students think about themselves in meaningful ways in relation to what they are learning and to different contexts outside of the classroom. As such there is a blurring of boundaries between public and private knowledges and between the learning that takes places outside of school and that within the school. We believe that an issues-based approach to teaching art is a move towards a more equitable and democratic kind of education, one that will benefit all of our students no matter what direction or career goals they might choose for themselves, and benefit all members of society as well.

Contributors to this anthology, contemporary art educators from around the United States, Canada, and Australia, approach the teaching of art at the elementary level from multiple perspectives and present art in ways that expand traditional notions of elementary art. By using an issues-based approach we have the capacity to consider multiple ways to view art as a part of the school curriculum, alternative ways to view students, teachers, and their relationships with the local community, different pedagogical strategies to teach art, a critical selection of content to include in the curriculum, strategies to incorporate issues into teaching and learning, contexts as a part of understanding art, non-school sites for learning, and issues of difference.

The Traditions of Art Education

Before we proceed to the chapters and activities in this book, we shall introduce and discuss the traditional formalist, child-centered, and discipline-based approaches that have, in combination, long been the foundation of much of art education. Many of the authors in this book make reference to these traditions and it is important that readers have a basic understanding of the focus of each approach, recognize the differences between them, and understand the limits of each. In addition, we include overviews of other topics that have had an impact on art education in important ways and are referred to by some of the authors. These topics include: liberatory pedagogy, critical pedagogy, and social reconstructionism.

Before we begin these discussions we ask you to think about the art education that you received, especially in elementary school. What did you learn? What types of activities did you engage in? Did you ask critical questions about art or the world? What was the focus of your art education? Did you look at and talk about works of art? As you read the brief descriptions that follow, you may recognize your own experiences of art in elementary school.

Formalism

Immanuel Kant's eighteenth-century theory of aesthetic response serves as the philosophical underpinning of formalism. Over the next two centuries aestheticians, art critics, and theorists fueled formalism's development and sustainability. Kant's theory is based on aesthetic judgement, how people respond to works of art, how they interpret art, and how they judge it based on nothing but the work itself (Reese, 1980). Kant believed that when people view artwork without any personal or outside influences or contexts they make the same determinations about the work (Barrett, 2000).

Arthur Wesley Dow (1899) later introduced the elements and principles of design; formalist qualities in art developed from looking at the commonalities of artworks. A formalist approach considers line, color, shape/form, texture, space, value (the elements of art) and pays attention to how they are organized or arranged through balance, emphasis, proportion, movement, rhythm, repetition, pattern, contrast, variety, and unity (the principles of art). Combined to create a composition, Dow offered the art world visual qualities that could be used to determine what makes a work of art successful. The elements and principles of design are still considered by many to be the visual language of art.

In the early part of the twentieth century, art critics Clive Bell and Roger Fry promoted the idea of "significant form," which established the basis for the use of the term formalism when we talk about viewing works of art. As Marcia Eaton (1988) explains it, "formalists emphasize intrinsic properties of the object or event itself, not what it represents or expresses. When we look at a work of art, we should not attend to *what it represents* but to *how it presents*" (p. 79). Within the constructs of formalism, content in a work of art is irrelevant. A more recent proponent of formalism is Clement Greenberg who used the formal principles to champion the paintings of the abstract expressionists in the United States in the 1940s and 50s.

Critics into the 1960s and 1970s continued to support this path until artworks appeared that required more than a formalist approach to understand them.[2] In looking at these artworks an understanding of their content as well as the contexts surrounding them were and are necessary for interpretation. Some art critics today still use a formalist approach when writing about art but many others have embraced other criteria and contexts through which to interpret what they see. This change in direction in how we come to understand art reflects the shift from theories of modernism to those of postmodernism, a difference that is echoed when we look at modernist and contemporary art.

Modernist art can be recognized as a style that is based primarily on formalist philosophical and aesthetic ideas. Although modernism is seen as a historical period or milieu, scholars do not agree upon the exact dates that it began and ended. Formalism is a very influential aesthetic theory[3] within the history of modernist art. In contrast to this, contemporary art, in other words art that is being currently produced, cannot be categorized as following a particular style. While many contemporary artists deal with social, cultural, and political issues in their work, they also pay attention to the formal elements and principles of the artwork. Those of us who come from a tradition of Western art history have learned to look at and value artworks based upon the artist's use and manipulation of the formal characteristics. What postmodern theory and contemporary art has enabled is a broadening of this interpretive framework.

Postmodern theory challenges the idea that everyone sees and understands the world in the same way and encourages us to accept multiple ways of understanding, making, and teaching art by critiquing the restrictive practices of modernism and exposing its limitations. As a theoretical framework, postmodernism offers infinite possibilities for more inclusive ways of participating in the world artistically and socially. However, modernism and the aesthetic theory of formalism has influenced the face of art and the teaching of art for most of the twentieth century, and is still embedded in many elementary art curricula under the guise of teaching about the elements and principles of design.

Formalism holds art to particular standards and qualities that have been agreed upon as visually acceptable by people who are considered authorities in art. A formalist response does not consider the political ramifications of such action. It also does not include factors that could broaden the definition of art beyond its formal qualities, and as such, sets up criteria for dismissal when examining works that move/exist beyond this narrow set of parameters. A formalist approach to the teaching of art promotes certain visual and aesthetic qualities that viewers (teachers and students) come to expect in any art work and contributes to attitudes that form judgments as to what is and is not art, and what is and is not good art.

Formalism provides one set of criteria that can be used when making artworks or when viewing contemporary artwork, but within a postmodern framework there exist other criteria. The content of the art work and the contexts surrounding it (personal, historical, social, aesthetic, and cultural) all contribute to meaning and our understanding of art. Many art teachers at the elementary level consider it their responsibility to incorporate formal principles in their teaching of art to children. While we understand the value of formal principles and of studying the visual and aesthetic qualities in works of art and in the art education curriculum, we question the sole emphasis that is often given to this approach. We are not proposing the exclusion of formal principles when teaching art to children, but rather, we are proposing a shift in emphasis. Formal and aesthetic qualities will remain in the curriculum but they do not need to be the central focus for every lesson. In an issues-based approach, formal principles can still be discussed but such a discussion will occur within the context of how the formal qualities of an artwork are used.

The Child-Centered Approach

The name Viktor Lowenfeld is synonymous with the child-centered approach[4] for teaching art. From the 1940s and continuing long after his death in the early 1960s, Lowenfeld's legacy to art education places the child, and a child's interests, abilities, and expressive needs in a central position in the teaching of art. From a child-centered perspective, art is primarily a means of expression that changes as children grow. The child is viewed as an individual whose artistic expression is a reflection of where the child is developmentally and how she/he relates to the environment. The child controls and manipulates materials as a creative expression of the self. A child-centered approach is grounded in developmental psychology and presents a theory of child development in art. Art education that is based upon this foundation uses the child's developmental stage as the precept for creating curriculum.

Within a child-centered approach, children should be provided with materials so that they may intuitively express themselves without any adult imposition of taste or artistic standards of importance or beauty. According to Lowenfeld, adult standards are irrelevant to a child because art means something different to the child than it does to the adult. Lowenfeld believed that adults who intervened and suggested ways to improve the work "prevent[ed] children from using art as a true means of self expression" (Lowenfeld and Brittain, 1975, p. 8). In child-centered art education, children's art should not be evaluated by the quality of the product, but rather growth should be measured by the creative process of the individual child expressing thoughts, feeling, and interests.

The difference between a child-centered approach to art education and a formalist approach is in their relationship to the process and the product. A child-centered approach concerns itself with the process of art making. What children learn from the process is more important than the end product. The process includes a child's thinking, feeling, perceiving, and reacting to her/his environment. A formalist approach concerns itself with the end product and the ways that an artwork can be measured and judged through formalist criteria.

A child-centered approach promotes active participation, sensory experiences (using all five senses), self-identification with the experience expressed in the artwork and the materials used to create it, and self-expression through visually expressing the feelings, emotions, and thoughts of the child. As was the case with the formalist approach, the content of the artwork is irrelevant except to the extent that the child can identify with it. However, it is important to note that while a formalist approach concerns itself with how an artwork presents itself, a child-centered approach concerns itself with how the art is created. The way the art is expressed is of utmost importance but that does not mean technical perfection. Rather, Lowenfeld argued, it is important for children to express themselves, their thoughts and ideas, at their own levels of development. How a five-year-old child expresses a relationship to the environment, how she/he sees and experiences it through the senses and understands it in relation to her/his own life, is different from the expressions of a fifteen-year-old adolescent. Each child's expression is different, based on her/his level of development and relationship to the environment. The adult's job is to encourage, stimulate, and "make meaningful the relationship" between children and their environment (Lowenfeld and Brittain, 1975, p.11), working within the children's frame of reference. Lowenfeld believed that if children were left alone to their own devices, they would not need any special stimulation for art making.

Based on his study of children's drawings, Lowenfeld determined that children pass through different stages of natural development in relation to their art making. Each stage follows in sequence beginning with the Scribbling Stage where toddlers (ages 2–4) make random marks on paper. Over time these marks become more controlled, leading to attempts at representation in the Pre-schematic Stage (ages 4–7). In the Schematic Stage (ages 7–9) children show repetition of form and symbols in describing their environment. A base line develops and objects are arranged across the bottom of a page. When children reach the Stage of Dawning Realism (ages 9–12), symbols are still used rather than representational drawing, but detail becomes important and children recognize themselves more in relation to others. The Pseudo-naturalistic Stage (ages 12–14), or the stage of reasoning, occurs when children become aware of their natural surroundings and consider such details as proportion, depth, or color gradation in their drawings. Lowenfeld thought that children's natural artistic development ends around age fourteen and that it is at this age that students should be helped in developing their artistic skills. Some art educators have since modified these categories and given them looser interpretations but still view children's artistic growth as stages through which they progress. Others have challenged the notion of children's natural development.

Art production is primary in a child-centered approach. The child-centered approach invests its philosophy and theory in the effect of the creative process on the child through art making and the sensitivity derived from art experiences. Anything outside of the child's experience and expression is not considered appropriate stimulation or influence. Imposing adult images on a child is thought to inhibit growth by causing the child to become dependent on them for imitation. Art educators such as Marjorie and Brent Wilson (1982) have questioned the idea that children independently create their own concepts of the world in their art making and put forward the idea that children freely incorporate ideas and imagery in their artwork from media, popular culture, and other artworks. The Wilsons remind us that before children attain the skill of reading written text, they read visual symbols (pictures and images) that provide them with a symbolic means for understanding reality.

Discipline-Based Art Education

A major shift in art education theory and practice surfaced in the mid-1980s when scholars in the field promoted the idea that children can indeed learn from an art world constructed and inhabited by professional art critics, aestheticians, art historians, and artists. Emphasis moved from a focus on the child to a focus on art as a subject for study. Positioning art as an integral part of the general education curriculum and viewing art "as a subject with content that can be taught and learned in ways that resemble how other subjects are taught in schools" (Clark, Day, and Greer, 1987, p. 131), art educators developed discipline-based art education (DBAE) as an approach for teaching art. By focusing on works of art, DBAE integrates content from four art disciplines—aesthetics, art criticism, art history, and art production. By studying works of art through these disciplines, students develop critical-thinking skills and inquiry processes. DBAE is built on a framework that supports the idea that more than art production is necessary for art learning and that art can relate to other subjects in the school curriculum.

DBAE is a comprehensive approach to art education in an effort "to transform the way students create and understand art" (Wilson, 1997, p. 10). With support from the Getty Education Institute for the Arts and instituted in elementary, middle, and high schools around the U.S. as an educational reform to improve arts education, DBAE challenges existing practices, positions art at the core of the school curriculum, involves teachers and administrators in the planning process, connects with the art community, and has contributed to the reorganization of elementary school curricula. Considered by some art educators to be a workable solution for problems that plague art education and education, DBAE has also faced challenges and criticism from within the art education community. Some art teachers in the public schools who held deeply embedded beliefs about the importance of art content such as the elements and principles of design (Wilson, 1997) and the ways art should be taught also expressed dissatisfaction with DBAE's diminished emphasis on studio time for art production. Other art educators critically examined DBAE practice and called attention to a variety of omissions and assumptions that supported its practice (Collins and Sandell, 1988; Delacruz and Dunn, 1995). Art education continues to modify itself in response to these criticisms. Educational reform movements such as multiculturalism, feminism, and democracy in education developed alongside DBAE, both challenging and informing its practice.

As a fairly recent development in art education, DBAE is still being refined, redefined, and reinterpreted by scholars as well as teachers in the schools and some of the most recent rethinkings are included as chapters in this book. Moving from broad generalizations such as "requir[ing] a balanced art curriculum that emphasizes content from the four art disciplines," (Clark et al, p. 133) teachers are now encouraged to create "holistic and integrated models for artwork-centered instruction" (Wilson, 1997, p. 15) that also provides understanding of the art disciplines as "the means through which art objects are created and studied and not the primary content" (p. 17). In the following paragraphs, we introduce each art discipline in order to gain an understanding of the differences that exist between them, although in practical application there may be considerable overlap.

Art production is the studio component of a discipline-based approach and is what many of us think of when we think of elementary art teaching. However, since art production within the DBAE model is combined with aesthetics, art criticism, and art history, the scope of production is usually broader than the artmaking found in project-based art classrooms. Art production can take many forms, in relation to two-dimensional works such as drawings or paintings, three-dimensional artwork such as sculpture or ceramics, installation art where work is created within a particular environment, conceptual works that require viewer engagement to be realized, and performance art. Form can be understood as not having clearly recognizable subject matter, such as abstract art, or it may look very much like what it represents, such as art categorized as realistic. Form is how an artist "presents subject matter (or excludes it) by means of a chosen medium" (Barrett, 2000, p. 66). Medium is the material that has been used by an artist to create the artwork such as oil paint on canvas or limestone from which a sculpture was carved. Media (plural) can also include non-traditional art materials such as organic matter or the human body (as in performance art.) Subject matter can be explained as "the persons, objects, places, and events in a work of art" (p. 64). Therefore an artwork might best be understood as comprised of basic components—subject matter, medium, and form—put together in a variety of combinations for different reasons, purposes, ideas, and effects.

Commonly recognized as the philosophy of art, *aesthetics* is a branch of philosophy comprised of different aesthetic theories that help us make judgments about art (Barrett, 2000). Aesthetic theory describes our beliefs about art based on a set of principles or facts that become a framework to explain, justify, or define what we understand art to be. When we think about art and the concepts, practices, and issues surrounding it, we formulate positions or arguments for what we believe and support them with reasons and/or evidence. Aesthetic theories[5] become criteria for judging works of art. Some examples of different aesthetic theories are briefly mentioned below but it is important to understand that some of these theories have well-developed histories and traditions that go back hundreds, and in some cases, thousands of years.

Philosophers have been contemplating aesthetic issues for centuries although the use of the word "aesthetics" did not surface until the eighteenth century (Eaton, p. 4). Aesthetic theories affect our decisions about art whether we are conscious of them or not. Formalism, described earlier in this introduction, is an aesthetic theory that positions form, that is, how the work presents itself, as the criterion of judgment. The belief that art should look like what it represents is the basis of a realist aesthetic theory. Instrumentalism views art as serving a larger purpose such as guiding or changing human behavior, and positions art as an instrument for social change. Expressionist aesthetic theory is based on having the feelings portrayed by the artist being similarly felt by the person viewing the work. These aesthetic approaches certainly do not exhaust aesthetic possibilities, but they are generally recognized and acknowledged broad categories and serve as a basis for understanding aesthetics. The authors deal with some of these theories explicitly and implicitly in this book.

Art critic and art educator Terry Barrett defines *art criticism* as "language about art that is thoughtful and thought out, for the purpose of increasing understanding and appreciation of art and its role in society" (Barrett, 2000, p. 25). Art criticism is based on the assumption that art has meaning, and that an interpretation, whether it is verbal or in written form, is the expression of that meaning. Art criticism is an investigative process that helps us see critically and look more deeply into artworks, most often beyond the formal and aesthetic qualities. This reveals more than just the work itself and helps us find meaning and understand the significance of the artwork.

Investigation into the contexts surrounding the work, information about the artist, the intention behind the work, connecting the artwork to our own experiences, looking at other work the artist has created, and deciding criteria for judgment are all components in understanding the work and interpreting its meaning. We most often find examples of art criticism in newspapers, magazines, or art journals, venues in which critics write about a particular art exhibition or about an individual artist's work, often as a first introduction of the artwork to an audience. Criticism usually deals with contemporary artwork that is currently being exhibited, although critics also write about artists of the past whose works may be currently exhibited.

Unlike art criticism that deals with the immediacy of the contemporary art world, *art history* deals with art over extended periods of time—years, decades, and centuries—and is increasingly cumulative, building a history that chronicles art of the past. Art history positions art within a historical context that includes social, religious, economic, and scientific contexts, the artist's life, political events, and technological developments taking place at the time the work was created. Art history helps us understand that art changes as the result of what is going on in the world (Gardner, 1975). Art historians classify art over periods of time in chronological order according to styles, influences, and place of origin so that we may understand art in relation to other artworks that may be similar or different. Art historians add their own interpretations and layers of meaning to artworks contributing to the body of literature known as art history so that we may understand an artwork and its meaning not only within the context of the time it was created but also to understand an artwork and its meaning over time.

Educational Theories

In addition to the three traditional approaches to art education discussed previously, the following educational theories are important in order to provide a context for many of the chapters in this book. Although the authors offer explanations of the concepts or ideas, anyone reading about them for the first time may require more explanation. Through these brief comments we hope to provide a broader context about the educational theories that underpin many of the chapters.

Liberatory Education

The term liberatory pedagogy[6] is often associated with Paulo Freire, a Brazilian educator who in 1970, introduced a radical education theory through a book titled, *Pedagogy of the Oppressed*. Working with illiterate adults as his students, Freire developed literacy methods that were grounded in a liberatory education theory, an approach that rests upon a vision of social transformation. In liberatory pedagogy, self-awareness is an empowering strategy for experiencing the world critically. Criticality can be understood as not accepting the world at face value but instead recognizing and challenging oppressive practices, behaviors, or ways of thinking in order to create alternatives. Provided with tools to participate in a dialogic relationship with others, including the teacher, students move from the position of passive acceptance to become active participants in the learning that is taking place in the classroom.

Different from traditional education, liberatory pedagogy reexamines the roles of the teacher and students. Freire refers to traditional education as the "banking model" of teaching, in which "knowledge is a gift bestowed by those who consider themselves knowledgeable upon those whom they consider to know nothing" (p. 53). Instead, according to Freire's educational theory, "the teacher is no longer merely the-one-who-teaches, but one who is himself taught in the dialogue with students. . . . They become jointly responsible for a process in which all grow" (p. 61). Liberatory pedagogy is built upon a foundation that considers the relationship of teaching to the content of learning. Several authors in this book make mention of Freire's educational theory as informing the practice of teaching art.

Critical Pedagogy

Critical pedagogy, a more recent development in educational theory, has been influenced by the writings of Freire as well as other radical thinkers such as Gramsci, Marx, Marcuse, the Frankfurt School of critical theory, and Bourdieu. Some contemporary theorists whose names have become synonymous with critical pedagogy are Henry Giroux, Stanley Aronowitz, Peter McLaren, and Michael Apple. Grounded in critical theory and liberatory pedagogy, critical pedagogy emerged in the mid-1970s as a response to traditional educational theory. Rather than continuing to reproduce what already exists, critical pedagogues analyze schooling within the larger contexts of society, such as the political, historical, and social, and examine teaching for its ideological content and functions (Brady-Giroux, 1989) for the purpose of social transformation. Critical questions such as "Whose interests does this form of education serve and why?" become the basis for critical teaching in order to reveal power structures and consider other possibilities.

Critical pedagogy positions education as a political discourse and teachers as reflexive, critical practitioners who take active responsibility in questioning what they teach, how they teach it, and the larger goals to which they are teaching. Critical pedagogy also takes into consideration factors external to classroom work, namely the larger environment within which teachers teach such as economic conditions and institutional structures. Several authors in this book make reference to critical pedagogy in their chapters.

Social Reconstruction

Social reconstructionism is an attempt to influence the development of society, generally in opposition to or in modification of the status quo. It was first recognized as a utopian movement that came out of the social reconstruction movement of the Great Depression in the 1930s (Freedman, 1994). Proponents of social reconstructionism try to reconstruct society based on particular criteria.

During the reconstruction period of the 1930s, the emphasis within art education shifted from self-expression and art in isolation from life to the study of art in society and viewing art as an integral part of life (Efland, 1990, pp. 203–204). The economic pressures of the depression contributed to this change (Efland). Social reconstructionism in education and in art education is a self-enlightened acknowledgment of responsibilities for the well-being of the society in which the educational process is embedded. Contemporary reconstructionist emphases grew out of the civil rights and feminist equity movements of the 1960s and 1970s and, in the artworld, as a reaction to the exclusivity and social disengagement symptomatic of formalist modernism.

Current social reconstruction theories do not necessarily lay claims to utopianism but are trying to model a more equitable society. Because "what and how we choose to teach can either reinforce traditional social patterns of power and submission or bring them into question and loosen their hold" (Hicks, 1994, p. 149), social reconstructionism inevitably reflects a political awareness. Multiculturalism, feminism, disability rights, and environmental awareness are examples of the political concerns implicit in contemporary social reconstructionist theories.

Visual Art and Visual Culture

Many contemporary art theorists and art educators are locating visual art within the larger framework of visual culture. Visual culture includes all forms of visual imagery from a variety of sources such as television, the Internet, magazines, advertising, cartoons, comics, and product packaging. The traditional boundaries that once separated "art" from "non-art" (visual culture) become blurred when, for example, visual artists use media strategies to capture public attention and advertisers use fine art to sell their products. Many authors in this book make reference to visual culture in general and cite specific examples of how it is used within the context of teaching art. We believe that, in a culture that is bombarded with visual imagery on a daily basis, it is important for children to learn how to critically negotiate a visually saturated world.

Plots and Stories

With every book come decisions about the narratives that are structured through the chapters. The organization that the writings are placed within constructs stories. Such stories help us conceptualize a different way to think about the teaching of art in the elementary classroom. It is our belief that the teaching of art is not prescriptive, but rather that it represents a dynamic process that moves in multiple directions offering multiple possibilities for translating theory into practice and adjusting that practice to different situations, students, content, and ways to teach art. The chapters in this text affirm our belief. The book is divided into three sections, *Theoretical Frameworks*, *Content*, and *Pedagogical Strategies*. The placement of a chapter into a particular category is not meant to suggest that the chapter offers ideas that are pertinent only to that section of the book. Nor is the arrangement of chapters meant to indicate that these writings are mutually exclusive. All of the authors deal with theoretical frameworks, content, and pedagogical strategies but for each author the emphasis differs. For example, while the main focus of a chapter might be an examination of a pedagogical strategy, the author's ideas are based within a theoretical framework and will present content, both of which overlap with the other sections of the text.

The first section, *Theoretical Frameworks*, provides future and current teachers with foundations to draw upon while they are in the classroom teaching art to children. The issues addressed in this section are not necessarily issues to take into the classroom to teach as subject matter to elementary children, but should be considered as perspectives or lenses through which future teachers can frame their teaching of art to children. The second section, *Content*, becomes more specific by guiding teachers in their selection of content, developing skills to find content, and suggesting ways to integrate art content into an elementary curriculum. In the third section, *Pedagogical Strategies*, the authors offer concrete examples of ways that content can be approached with students and provide lessons and examples of different ways to teach art. The pedagogical strategies are the application of theoretical frameworks and content even if this is not explicitly stated.

At the beginning of each chapter we have a section called *Questions and Explorations*. These are designed to critically and personally engage readers with the materials they are about to read. The questions at the end of each chapter, *Conclusions and Further Questions*, serve to raise key points addressed by the author and relating the chapters to other ideas and issues. In addition, the *Resources and Suggestions for Further Reading* at the end of every chapter provides a list of resources that can assist readers in further explorations of the issues discussed in the chapter.

This book draws upon a variety of theories, strategies, suggestions, artworks, and issues that address complex ideas. These are made accessible to audiences with different levels of experience with relation to art and teaching throughout the chapters. The book is written for anyone interested in teaching art to children. It is our hope that it will be used by elementary and art education pre-service teachers, teachers already in the field, graduate students, and university faculty members who are interested in an issues-based approach to the teaching of art. Because of the breadth and depth of material covered, this book can be used at any time throughout a teaching career, serving as a resource for contemporary artwork, issues, ideas, and approaches for teaching art at the elementary level. We recognize that boundaries that once separated art-education majors from elementary-, early childhood-, and special-education majors at the university level are now dissolving and that faculty are faced with teaching and/or developing courses that can accommodate multiple interests. We also recognize that many preservice teachers in education only have one course to prepare them for teaching art at the elementary level. We believe this book will establish strong foundations for teaching art to children. As you will read in the upcoming chapters, it is our goal to expand the vision of art learning in schools.

Endnotes

1. It could be argued that there are more than three major directions but we based our determinations on the predominance of literature in the field of art education.
2. We are speaking in generalizations here. Up until this time, critics dismissed or ignored works of art that did not fit formalist criteria, and this often included works by women and artists of color.
3. Realism, expressionism, contextualism, instrumentalism, originality, and craftsmanship are other criteria for judging art. See Terry Barrett (2000), Thomas Anderson and Sally McRorie (1997), Marilyn Stewart (1997), and Elizabeth Garber (1992) for information on these criteria.
4. In an attempt to briefly define a child-centered approach, the information from this section is drawn from chapters 1 and 2 in Lowenfeld's *Creative and Mental Growth*, 3rd edition, (New York: Macmillan, 1957) pp. 1–37 and chapters 1 and 2 in Viktor Lowenfeld and W. Lambert Brittain's *Creative and Mental Growth*, 6th edition, (New York: Macmillan, 1975) pp. 3–58.
5. See footnote #3 for additional readings on aesthetic theories.
6. According to David Lusted (1986), pedagogy may be understood as "a concept [that] draws attention to the *process* through which knowledge is produced" (p. 2). He also goes on to describe it as an interactive trilogy of how one teaches, what is being taught, and how one learns (p. 3).

References

Anderson, T., & McRorie, S. (1997). A role for aesthetics in centering the K–12 art curriculum. *Art Education, 50*, (23), 6–14.

Barrett, T. (2000). *Criticizing art*. Mountain View, CA: Mayfield.

Brady-Giroux, J. (1989). Feminist theory as pedagogical practice. *Contemporary Education, 61*(1), 6–10.

Clark, G., Day, M., & Greer, W.D. (1987). Discipline-based art education: Becoming students of art. *Journal of Aesthetic Education 21*(2), 129–151.

Collins, G. (1995). Art education as a negative example of gender-enriching curriculum. In J. Gaskell & J. Willinsky (Eds.), *Gender in/forms curriculum: From enrichment to transformation* (pp. 43–58). New York: Teachers College Press.

Collins, G., & Sandell, R. (1988). Informing the promise of DBAE: Remember the women, children, and other folk. *Journal of Multicultural and Cross Cultural Research, 6*(1), 55–63.

Delacruz, E.M., & Dunn, P.C. (1995). DBAE: The next generation. *Art Education* 48(6), 46–53.

Dow,. A.W. (1899). *Composition: A series of exercises selected from a new system of art education. Part I.* Boston: J. M. Bowles.

Eaton, M. M. (1988). *Basic issues in aesthetics.* Belmont, CA: Wadsworth.

Efland, A. (1990). *A history of art education.* New York: Teachers College Press.

Freedman, K. (1994). About this issue: The social reconstruction of art education. *Studies in Art Education 35*(3), 131–134.

Freire, P. (1970). *Pedagogy of the oppressed.* New York: Continuum.

Garber, E. (1992). Feminism, aesthetics and art education. *Studies in Art Education, 33*(4), 210–225.

Gardner, H. (1975). *Art through the ages* (6th ed.). New York: Harcourt, Brace, Jovanovich.

Hicks, L.E. (1994). Social reconstruction and community. *Studies in Art Education, 35* (3), 149–156.

Lowenfeld, V., (1957) *Creative and mental growth.* (3rd ed.) New York: Macmillan.

Lowenfeld, V., & Brittain, W.L. (1975). *Creative and mental growth* (6th ed.). New York: Macmillan.

Lusted, D. (1986). Why pedagogy? *Screen, 27*(5), 2–14.

Reese, W.L. (1980). *Dictionary of philosophy and religion.* Atlantic Highlands, NJ: Humanities Press.

Shor, I. (1992). *Empowering education.* Chicago, IL: The University of Chicago Press.

Shor, I., & Freire, P. (1987). *A pedagogy for liberation: Dialogues on transforming education.* South Hadley, MA: Bergin & Garvey.

Spring, J. (1991). *American education: an introduction to social and political aspects,* 5th ed. New York: Longman.

Stewart, M. G. (1997). *Thinking through aesthetics.* Worcester, MA: Davis Publications.

Wilson, B. (1997). *The quiet evolution: Changing the face of art education.* Los Angeles, CA: J. Paul Getty Trust Publications.

Wilson, M., & Wilson, B. (1982). *Teaching children to draw: A guide for teachers and parents.* Englewood Cliffs, NJ: Prentice Hall.

Section I
Theoretical Frameworks

Introduction

Theory helps us make sense of our day-to-day experiences as we construct explanations of why we do what we do. Theory is generated from lived experience and derived from existing theories. As bell hooks describes it, theory can help us imagine a different world and embody, name, and experience our lives and our world (hooks, 1994). Poet Audre Lorde locates artmaking as a primary way of theorizing, arguing that art helps us develop an architecture upon which we can dream different, more equitable worlds (Lorde, 1984). Theories provide us with a grounding and with a support system even while we may move in different directions. Theory helps us expand our ideas by adding to what we already know. It also provides us with tools to challenge existing ideas in order to consider alternative ways of thinking and living. Theories enable us to construct critical settings from within which we can examine the world we live in.

All of the chapters in this book are based upon and present theoretical frameworks, constructs that help guide the authors as they support their ideas and directions and provide readers with possibilities for teaching and learning in the elementary classroom. In this section, theoretical frameworks are more explicitly addressed. They serve as examples of the ways that theory can be translated into the teaching of art and furnish us with lenses through which to see and understand what we are experiencing in our worlds. The theories foregrounded in this section include critical pedagogy, postmodernism, phenomenology, and performance pedagogy, and help us address issues such as community-based art education, personal identity, teaching in non-school settings, and multiculturalism. Using different theoretical frameworks some authors raise similar issues but offer different approaches to address them. The chapters in this section provide future teachers with theoretical foundations for teaching art to children. The ideas discussed will help teachers inform their practice of teaching.

Graeme Sullivan introduces visual culture and some of the concepts involved in postmodernism to broaden the discourse of art education. As he applies postmodernist theory to art education he points out the validity of identifying and critiquing multiple contexts of making and assessing classroom art and contemporary art. Visual culture becomes a source of art content that helps us see and understand contemporary art in relation to everyday life. Sullivan introduces the work of contemporary artists who tell us about their artwork in their own words, revealing insights and intuitions that give us a sense of how their ideas turn into visual forms, informing the practice of art learning.

Joyce Barakett and Elizabeth Saccá suggest narrative and storytelling as a way to reveal the dilemmas that students and teachers have experienced in their everyday lives and/or continue to face. This allows readers to reflect upon their own lives and learn something new about themselves and others through ensuing dialogue. Barakett and Saccá foreground issues of voice, lived experience, and empowerment by using liberatory education theory as well as critical pedagogy as theoretical frameworks to support their approach to art education. As empowering strategies, storytelling and narratives provide opportunities for those sharing their stories to critically examine what they say and consider a language of possibility for the future.

Ed Check offers us a narrative of his own experiences as a teacher, student, and artist, sharing his discoveries and struggles with integrating his identity into teaching and learning. Check suggests that as teachers we should approach the teaching of art from the context of our lives, fueled by our own personal experiences, so that we and others may learn from them. Check infused real life issues into his teaching in an attempt to bridge the gap between school and life, causing him to seek alternative approaches for teaching art. By sharing his current approaches with students, Check shows us that for meaningful teaching and learning to occur in the classroom teaching should not be a disembodied practice.

The issue of identity continues to weave through the chapters of several authors who consider personal and cultural identities of the students and teachers as vital sources that contribute to the learning in the classroom. Using a multicultural theoretical framework, Andra Nyman suggests that teachers can help students develop their identities through the study of contemporary artists and artwork from different cultures. Such an approach can help students understand how culture and other social factors affect and influence the development of who they are, what they believe, what they create, how they do it, and why. Nyman situates her chapter around the personal growth of students through the content from a culturally based curricula. She asks that teachers acknowledge the differences in students and include culturally diverse content that will encourage a tolerance of differences. Nyman, in a theoretical sense, and Flávia Bastos, more specifically, offer teachers ways to develop and utilize the cultural identities of both students and teachers for learning through art.

Bastos promotes the study of local art from the community for the purpose of revitalizing the cultural identities of students and teachers by paying attention to everyday life and seeing it in a new way. Like Barakett and Saccá, Bastos is interested in raising the critical consciousness of students, however, she approaches this through the study of locally-produced art. Supported by a community-based art education framework (CBAE) laced with the emancipatory practices of liberatory pedagogy, Bastos sees the study of local art in school as a step towards critical participation in a community whereby value systems, social-economic structure, and institutions can be examined and questioned for the purpose of social change.

Debra Attenborough also works towards developing school and community relationships. Attenborough offers the educational programming of museums and galleries as alternative sites for learning, reminding teachers that learning can also take place in non-school settings. Attenborough tours us through the programs of two community arts organizations that successfully adapted their programming to the current educational needs of local schools, offering integrated programs with art as the basis for learning other subjects. The arts organizations formed partnerships with local schools so that teachers and museum educators work together to develop workshop programs that coincide with learning in the classroom. Attenborough critically examines the role of education in traditional galleries/museums and seeks ways to develop more socially responsive relationships that are relevant to the needs of the local community, especially with schools.

The relevance of art education to the lives of students and to the communities in which we live and teach continues as a theme throughout the chapters. Several authors stress that issues related to everyday life should be a part of the learning taking place in the elementary classroom. When teaching and learning are connected to our everyday lives, the educational experience becomes more meaningful and relevant for both teachers and students.

Paul Duncum asks that teachers recognize and acknowledge the real-life issues that surround children which influence how we should see them and, in turn influence how we should teach them. Childhood is not the perfect, socially constructed image we hold of it, and children's identities are quite complicated. Duncum uses a postmodern framework to dismantle the myth of childhood as being a state of innocence and reconstructs it as a complex and fragmented identity that is comprised of multiple discourses and ways of seeing.

Kristin Congdon, Marilyn Stewart, and John White provide teachers with a strategy to understand how identities are socially constructed and composed of multiple discourses in order to understand how identity influences a teacher's curricular choices. The authors pose a series of questions and provide a chart to map our identities using different social factors, such as age, race, ability, gender, and religion, positioned as differing, yet overlapping, social communities to which we belong. As a result of the synergy of these communities, we come to know ourselves, our students, and the assumptions, beliefs, and values that guide our curricular decisions. This awareness becomes an opportunity for growth.

Charles Garoian suggests that children perform their identities in the elementary classroom as part of the learning process. Inspired by the autobiographical content of performance art, Garoian infuses teaching in the elementary classroom with the cultural identities, memories, and bodies of students. Children perform identity as a critical act when the content of their lives intersects with the academic assumptions of the classroom. By drawing upon personal attitudes, values, beliefs, and experiences and comparing them to what is learned in school, students are afforded opportunities for critical thinking and participating in a dialogue that challenges academic assumptions in order to create new ones.

Debra Koppman asks that teachers return to the state of wonder we experienced as children, suspending our beliefs and preconceptions, so that we may once again use our senses to experience art. Koppman questions the current emphasis in art education on understanding art from linguistic and analytic perspectives and proposes phenomenology as a teaching methodology and approach to art criticism. She offers phenomenology as a tool to challenge our existing frameworks for experiencing the world and expand our vision to consider other possibilities. Grounded in historical and cross-cultural relationships between art and spirit, Koppman combines art with a sense of the sacred so that teachers and students may experience the poetry of art.

References

hooks, b. (1994). Theory as liberatory practice. In b. hooks, *Teaching to transgress: Education as the practice of freedom* (pp. 59–75). New York: Routledge.

Lorde, A. (1984). Poetry is not a luxury. In A. Lorde, *Sister outsider: Essays and speeches by Audre Lorde* (pp. 36–39). Freedom, CA: The Crossing Press.

CHAPTER 1

QUESTIONS AND EXPLORATIONS

1. Where do you think that artists get their ideas?
2. Find an example of an artwork that you find interesting and that you enjoy looking at. What idea(s) do you think that the artist is trying to communicate?
3. Where do children get their ideas for artworks?
4. Do you think that the works that children produce are or are not art? Explain your answer.
5. What types of ideas and objects do you include when you hear the word "art?" What characteristics do these share? How do they differ?
6. Describe the art education that you have experienced, both within and outside of a school context.

Ideas and Teaching: Making Meaning from Contemporary Art

Graeme Sullivan

There is something exciting about ideas when they take shape. Artists make ideas happen when they create images and objects. Those who respond to art make ideas happen when they write about the things they see. Teachers make ideas happen when they excite students about art. The way art happens continues to change but remains one of the most important ways humans achieve individual, social, and cultural understanding. The elementary classroom, like society itself, is a complex field of ideas and influences that shape the way art is made and learned. A challenge facing elementary teachers today is to make sense of how contemporary art can help their students make meaning from and through art.

Historically, art comprises paintings, sculptures, drawings, prints, crafts, architecture, and the like. At different times and in different circumstances various ways were used to categorize art such as fine arts, graphic arts, plastic arts, high arts, popular arts, and so forth. Today there is a realization that these categories rely as much on cultural, social, or ideological distinctions as they do on technical processes. For instance, the tendency to label the art of indigenous cultures as "artifacts" and display them exclusively in museums of natural history in the first half of the 20th century served to marginalize the significance of these artworks and of those who made them.[1]

Art is a form of individual and cultural expression that influences the way we see ourselves. Whether used to heighten our sensory awareness; as an agent of personal or social meaning; as a form of political commentary; as a means of religious or spiritual consciousness; as an imaginative solution to a practical problem; or as a technological tool, the purposes to which art is put are many. These include expression, communication, education, patronage, entertainment, and commerce.

Art and Visual Culture

As a result of the present day interest in working within a more inclusive view of how we learn about art, the term *visual culture* is used to describe all those things that affect our sense of sight (Mirzoeff, 1999; Walker and Chaplin, 1997). Art embraces all the areas of individual and cultural activity that influence the things we make and the way we view them. This means that art is not only a representation of a creative idea that is given some material form, but includes all the processes, products, and practices we use to come to know about art. Further, these kinds of artistic experiences are influenced by the way our visual culture is composed of images that are constructed by others that reflect different ideas, views, values, and beliefs. Therefore the study of art within visual culture involves not only learning about artworks themselves, but also how others make, view, and understand art. The range of visual forms created and encountered, and the diversity of individuals and cultures that abound, means that art learning will at times include different disciplines, media, and technologies.

Whether knowingly or unknowingly, we are part of a visual world. The different ways art functions in visual culture reflects the scope of the human imagination, yet how we make meaning from these images is determined not only by what we see but also by what we bring to the experience.[2] Whether seen in school or on the street, in a magazine or on television, in a museum or on the Internet, the visual images used to assist human interaction are constructed in particular ways. While we see things through a personal lens colored as much by bias as by knowledge, the forms of visual culture are also filtered through the ideas and intentions of others. How we might extract meaning from visual information is informed in part by those who make art, and further extended by those who help us interpret the ideas and images that influence what we see, and how we see (Berger, 1972; Carrier, 1987).

The content of art in elementary schools has mostly been drawn from experiences centered on the students' world and the life of the imaginative mind. Later changes in emphasis saw curriculum content move to embrace the world of art and the quest for the appreciative mind. The complexity of art within the current world of visual culture suggests there is a need to teach for the kind of understanding that comes from a critically informed mind. Visual culture can, therefore, be seen as a source of art content that warrants inclusion for within the image blitz of today it is often difficult to distinguish the valued from the vulgar. The ability to exercise control over the pervasive nature of the visual environment and the capacity to make choices about how one responds to contemporary art requires a critical eye and a commonsense approach. Linda Weintraub suggests,

> The bewilderment that often accompanies encounters with contemporary art exists because we check our real-life sensibilities at the museum coatroom. But the same events that control our lives are catalysts for change in art. Thus, if we view today's art from the perspective of everyday life, our receivers will be tuned to the artists' transmissions. (1996, p. 11)

Anyone who is receptive to the responses of young children to exhibitions of contemporary art will invariably be surprised, informed, and at times challenged by their insightful and commonsense critiques (Barrett, 2000). Yet there remains a tendency to assume that the complexity of postmodern issues means that these ideas are irrelevant in the elementary school setting. This seems strange to me for the affinity one finds among the ideas of young children and their capacity to entertain diverse, contradictory worlds is striking.

This discussion about art and visual culture from a postmodern perspective can help as this gives the educator access to an array of tools for inquiry. Rather than argue that postmodern critiques generate a mood of mindless relativism, a more positive attitude reveals that there is much to be gained if we see the postmodern "crisis" as one of opportunity. Postmodernism acknowledges a world of multiple realities and discloses places of privileged histories (Nochlin, 1988; Pollock, 1988). It challenges the myth that claims space for certain individuals at the center of the universe and instead positions the person off-center as part of a changing cultural condition.[3] Rather than accept the singular vision of the authorial voice, postmodern theorists draw attention to a more intriguing set of frames through which to view things. For example, while postmodernists argue against the relevance of absolute truth or grand, universal themes, they advocate forms of local knowledge characterized by multiple perspectives and cultural diversity. To deny the pervasive impact of personal perceptions and cultural canons is to remain blinkered to other probabilities. The responsibility of the educator is to be able to sift the valuable from the vacuous and to construct art programs that reflect the breadth of contemporary cultural practices and capture the depth of students' creative and critical capacities.

The Idea is Elementary

In taking up the postmodern challenge facing art education, Brent Wilson states,

> We have been reintroduced to the notion that works of art are the carriers of ideas as well as means of expression, that art reflects society perhaps even more than it reflects individual artists, and that art is a carrier of convention every bit as much as it is the invitation to creativity. (1992, p.106)

It is instructive to consider that artists, both young and old, share the capacity to give form to ideas. While the outcomes and conventions that shape our understanding of adult art and child art are qualitatively different, there are some parallels. Art learning at all ages involves surrounding ideas and exploring them using imaginative thinking and forming processes. Different perspectives are invoked that are informed by individual, social, cultural, and contextual conditions. Creative practice is evident in artistic ideas, images, and actions and what is created not only carries the signature of the individual but bears the imprint of the setting and the circumstance. The challenge for the teacher in the elementary classroom is to be aware of the multiple frameworks that shape art learning. For when children make art it is created and viewed according to a set of institutionally determined conditions much in the same way the work made by artists is interpreted within the prevailing climate of artworld practices.

The elementary classroom is a coalition of instincts, energies, and actions that carry a diversity of developing voices. Yet what we know about the learning life of children is only slowly coming into sharper focus. The history of inquiry into children's artistic development does not comprise a research regime that builds on a robust accumulation of knowledge. While our developmental theories continue to lack explanatory power, the descriptive patterns that are found in these theories reflect some agreement about features of artistic growth. Consensus suggests we are moving beyond an inevitable route to realism and that "drawing realistically" is a means rather than an end in artistic development. Art learning, it is argued, follows less linear pathways that feature multiple "repertoires" of artistic choice whereby students select from among a range of media, activities, and intentions (Kindler and Darras, 1997; Wolf and Perry, 1988).

Present views suggest that artistic development may be seen as a consequence of a diversity of informing factors that are culturally grounded, socially mediated, and individually constrained. The use of a greater range of research approaches in studying how children make meaning from experience indicate that children clearly know more than we originally thought (Donaldson, 1978; Harris, 1998). At certain times the constraints that influence a child's response to a task are going to include filters such as language, a facility for action, materials at hand, and a range of situational and cultural factors. Drawings, paintings, clay models, or constructions will remain inadequate indicators of learning if they are seen in isolation. Rather than view children's ideas as naive, a more useful position is to consider what they do and say to only be a partial reflection of what they know. Ideas offer rich potential for learning in the elementary classroom if children are not only encouraged to think about ideas, but to draw them, make them, speak them, write them, and enact them. This is a cognitive capacity that children share with others who make art, write about it, and teach it.

Viewing art learning as a cognitive coalition of ideas, media, language, human processes, and cultural cues allows us to ignore the rhetorical question: should art emphasize the process or the product? To maintain that art learning is restricted to the psychological process of thinking in a medium, or is a product that results from the disciplined inquiry of thinking in a language, denies the rich ensemble that surrounds art practice. A more plausible position is to describe art learning as "thinking in a setting."[4] This approach locates sites for learning within the various social, cultural, environmental, and situational influences that shape students thinking. This is a "transcognitive" activity that involves a strategic interaction among students, their art, the teacher, and the classroom situation, with each playing a role in helping co-construct meaning. Transcognition is a process wherein the individual and others are parallel and necessary agents of mind that inform each other through imaginative thinking strategies such as problem solving, metaphoric association, and critical reflection. This interaction occurs over time as purposes are mediated by situational factors such as personal intentions, artistic problems, and classroom demands. This is a picture of a learning world that looks strikingly similar for artists of all ages.

In a move towards an elementary art education where ideas are negotiated and given form it becomes clear that a description of content is not the main determinant shaping curriculum. The content of art will continue to draw on the histories, disciplines, individuals, cultures, and technologies that inform us about the changing landscape of human imagination. What has changed, however, is the way we learn from this content. What is at hand these days is a greater range of ways of surrounding and investigating information. These give teachers and learners greater opportunity to construct meanings.[5] Just as qualitative research has opened up new approaches to study complex phenomena, the diversity of art practice offers imaginative ways to investigate the content of art. Content therefore is not a description of subject matter to be learned, but information which is negotiated, reviewed, and reconstructed. This view of learning is grounded in constructivism[6] yet the particular artistic character surrounding the way new ideas are shaped gets its impetus from contemporary ideas about art.

If there is a point of agreement among contemporary cultural theorists it is the idea that artworks contain much more information than we might suspect.[7] The notion that an artwork is an object that signifies a certain view or idea had its genesis in the way the artist was seen as a genius. This somewhat linear model that saw the artist's idea carried through the artwork to a passive viewer is now abandoned in favor of a more inclusive view. The creative processes and practices used to make contemporary art certainly offers new and provocative ideas and images. Today, art may exist in many forms, as much an idea as an object; animated, enacted, or installed; documented, displaced, or hung on a wall. These forms, however, are given broader meaning by the way they are used (or not used) by viewers for personal response, public discussion, and cultural debate. In this way it can be seen that artworks are ideas embodied in objects or events and that these undergo continual remaking as the relationship between the artist, the viewer, and the cultural conditions change.

The way an artwork can be seen to carry information that not only resides within the object itself but also by what emerges from its interpretation has important implications for the elementary educator. Consider, for instance, the interpretive demands at play when a child's artwork has to be assessed. If one accepts that an artwork is at once an example of a response to a task demand, an individual representation of an idea, a form that carries traces of how decisions were made and technologies used, and a basis for dialogue to be opened up with others, then the array of assessment options is greatly increased. As such, it is a legitimate practice to assess the child's artwork in terms of how it reflects his or her artistic decision making as this is evident in the work itself. On the other hand one can assess the piece on an "intertextual" or comparative basis relative to other classroom examples or documented outcomes such as statements of standards. Then again, the way the artwork is seen as a product created in response to the direct or indirect influence of the classroom, and within the institutional setting of the school, allows the teacher to take into account the many contextual factors that might be important to consider in making an assessment.

What Contemporary Art Teaches

The various conditions that shape how children learn art in the elementary classroom are similar to the way different personal, social, and cultural factors influence contemporary art practice. To appreciate what the contemporary artist and the elementary teacher have in common is to accept that the classroom setting, the children, and the teacher, are part of a creative coalition of ideas, intentions, and actions. Like the contemporary artist, the elementary teacher is faced with the challenge of working within certain cultural and institutional constraints in the quest for human development. This suggests that there is much to be gained by looking closely at what contemporary artists do, and what others have to say about what artists' create.

Research about contemporary art practice that includes direct contact with artists and their work reveals how an artwork can be seen as a "site of possibility" for making art, thinking about art, and teaching art. The artists' commentaries that follow give some sense of the rich array of ideas that bubble beneath the surface of contemporary art practice. They are from several artists who also happen to be graduate students at Teachers College, Columbia University who come to the program with rich and varied backgrounds in contemporary art practice.[8] The comments are extracts from interviews conducted as part of a course where students are encouraged to use their studio experience as the basis for developing their professional profile as researchers and art educators. The ideas the artists talk about get enacted in the artworks they create and the related forms of discourse they produce. For these contemporary artists, the process of producing art for public display is an educational act that continually opens up new possibilities for art learning and art teaching.

Lori Kent (b.1962): Seeing the Special in the Ordinary

Lori Kent is an artist who teaches us about the importance of those image bits not normally noticed. Her work captures those fragments of place and time mostly known to the very young or the very old. She explains,

> What I find more interesting than the total landscape itself is the individual elements themselves. And this can take the macro landscape down to the micro, it can call attention to something banal, or reconstruct bits by digging in the dirt of the past. One of my works, *Mississippi River*, is a photo which is about how you can look in that river, a river that is very important in the lives of people in the area I'm from, and you get lost, all the way up to your peripheral vision because it's such a wide, slow moving river. I sewed a piece of mirror mylar onto the photograph. I just like the idea of literally being able to see yourself in it. It's about looking with curiosity and reverence, and with humor. Humor is a very effective means of communication about serious things. I also see it as the antithesis of cynicism. It's not only in my artwork but how I negotiate in the world. You can say things through humor you can't normally say, and that's like art. So my challenge as an artist and educator is to express how art can communicate unseen things.

Pamela Lawton (b.1959): The Art of Storytelling

Through her printmaking and artist's books Pamela Lawton teaches us how to make our human stories visual. She explores her rich African-American traditions of culture and community in a way that sheds light on individual identity through shared ideas and experiences. She explains,

> When I was little I found out my grandmother kept a diary everyday. She had been doing it from the time she was eighteen. She would pull them out and say, "Well, this is what happened on the day you were born." And my great grandfa-

ther wrote down a lot of oral histories. And he built a lot of furniture and when he retired he built dolls houses, the Smithsonian has one. When I thought about my family history, I thought of all these people who did things with their hands and I feel like I'm carrying on a tradition, just in a different format.

Telling stories orally comes alive for me rather than just reading a journal. It's a hands-on thing. Telling the story, talking with the person, it's a different experience, it has a human trace. I feel that when I'm working with wood, working with the grain and then against it. So the stories I tell in my woodblock prints are autobiographical. By participating in these collective memories it makes the past come alive. The process of creating artist's books allows me to return to the handcrafted method of storytelling using visual narrative and it allows me to think about my African-American history, about my identity, and about my art.

Lisa Hochtritt (b. 1962): Making Surprising Connections

Lisa Hochtritt is an artist who uses objects in ways that can't be fully planned as new possibilities emerge during her public art collaborations. She talks about materials as having histories that may be partly known yet their future

Figure 1.1 Pamela Lawton. *Learning from the Past.* 1998. Woodblock print. 22″ × 28″. (Photograph: Aphrodite Désirée Navab)

can only be inferred. Here she teaches us how the unpredictability of art practice can mirror the uncertainty of art teaching. She talks about some of her ideas in the following extract.

> *Lisa:* I like to create things to share and give away. It's not to help people think differently, but just to let them know that other things exist. And it's the interaction with others that is the most interesting thing that spurs what I do. I like the idea of planning an art project, and once it's done, it's done. The process is significant, but it's just this trip down the highway. But when I have an idea it usually comes via a very circuitous route. It can be sparked by anything, an image, a pattern of movement, something that can be taken into another form, into another layer. Then I could turn it back in on itself, maybe add another element. But the final form is a surprise. Things are not always as they seem.
>
> *Graeme:* How do you configure the artistic relationship among the old, the used and the new?
>
> *Lisa:* I like the idea of recycling as that plays a large part in my work because I try to reuse things. I see things and I know I can use them for something, even if I don't know right then and there. I'd like to think things have a story and I can continue that story. It's the whole idea of the journey of other materials, looking at the progress of where this physical thing has been and to see what I can do to maybe alter that path, to change what it can become.

Lori Don Levan (b. 1957): Challenging Perceptions

The photographs of Lori Don Levan are grounded in her lived experience and teach us about those who cannot or choose not to fit within a mythical view of what it is to be "normal." Her photographic self-portraits give elegant reassurance to anyone who has been singled out as being different. She explains,

> The self-portrait has been very important subject matter for me. My work is created from a feminist point of view where I explore body image and the large-sized female form along with cultural, social, and artistic constructs of female beauty. By combining art historical and contemporary references in the photographic image, I am able to re-construct and re-present alternative possibilities of seeing and understanding the female form where the marginalized body can become a new vehicle for understanding beauty in all of its complexity. Since I am a fat woman, I am able to explore issues concerning beauty and body image through lived experience. Through my efforts as an artist it is my hope that I will contribute to a dialogue that encourages new ways of seeing and understanding the lived experience of people who have been marginalized by a process that thrives on misinformation and moral judgment. The photographic image is a part of everyday life, easily recognized and taken for granted, yet, it can be used as a transformative tool when challenging the status quo.

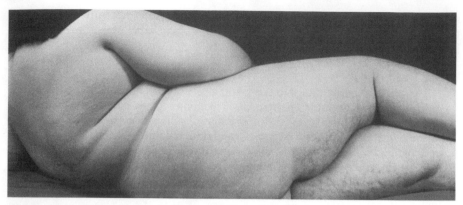

Figure 1.2 Lori Don Levan. *Bodyscape Series I, #1.* 1996–97. Black and white photograph.

Hugo Ortega (b.1965): Making Meanings in Art

Hugo Ortega is an artist who makes use of whatever materials he finds around him to construct his assemblages and sculptures. His work uses the symbolic power of visual images to communicate different ideas. In the following extract Hugo responds to interpretations made by two art critics about his work and teaches us how the artist and viewer can draw highly plausible but quite different meanings from art.

> *Raquel Tibol (Art Critic):* In Hugo Ortega's composition we do not see the flower that the hummingbird nibbles. The place where the nectar should be has been invaded by metallic elements and imprisoning twine, a metaphor for the annihilation of freedom.
>
> *Ana Olivia Galindo (Art Critic):* The goal of this piece, *Tribe of the Shields*, is to achieve uncorrupted art where the symbol and aesthetic sense are a singular reality: a political statement that lets us see how Hugo Ortega is directly affected by the political, economical, and cultural arena in Mexico. He cannot ignore it, he is part of that reality. They [hummingbirds] represent two alternatives, two different readings for the fate of Mexico: the hummingbird on the right is forever trapped by a mesh that covers him completely, locked by a lead security seal. The one on the left, though dead, is still a promising image. The hummingbird is dead but free.
>
> *Hugo Ortega (Artist):* Raquel Tibol is analyzing and placing meaning on this piece in relation to her own experience of living in a city infested with crime and insecurity. There is no doubt that this was part of my reality, but it is not the meaning or concept that generated the piece. Ana Galindo also mentions political, cultural and economical situations. It seems they need to validate the work by placing it in a bigger scene, in its comment on society, on culture, on crisis. She is able to notice the rigidity of the hummingbird, very few persons did.

Figure 1.3 Hugo Ortega. *Tribe of the Shields.* 1998. Wood, paint, twine, lead, nails, mesh, photographs. 12″ × 16″. (Photograph: Aphrodite Désirée Navab)

Aphrodite Désirée Navab (b.1971): Re-Picturing Photography

Aphrodite Désirée Navab uses her photography to explore a personal journey that draws on her Iranian heritage. While her work teaches us that art practice can be used to reveal private stories, she also critiques assumed cultural roles and accepted ways of working by challenging the language surrounding the use of photography.

The series of black and white photographs, *Tales Left Untold*, were torn. Torn memories from a wandering woman's walk into the West. They are portraits of the self and of the other. They are both portrayals and betrayals, tales of dislocation, location, and relocation. Tales of longing and belonging. She at once composes and poses, conceals and reveals. Exiled, she is pushed to play her part as the Persian, pushing roots into unfamiliar soil.

> Photography is a construction or re-presentation of reality or imagination like any other artistic medium; it enjoys no privileged relationship to reality. Just as we need to deconstruct the photograph itself I believe we also need to critique the language we use to describe photography. To start with, in place of the verbal construction "to take a photograph," why not simply say, "to *make* a photograph"? When a photographer must "aim" or "point" and then "shoot," how can she avoid feeling like a predator, and how can the subject avoid feeling the

Figure 1.4 Aphrodite Désirée Navab. From the *Tales Left Untold* Series. 1999. Black and white photograph.

vulnerability of a target? This is not a mere issue of semantics. Through making more mindful choices in how we talk about photography, we will create a much larger scope of potentialities for what the process entails, how it is experienced by its participants, and how we teach it.

Conclusion

Art involves thinking about ideas and making them happen in ways that enhance what is known and unknown by capitalizing on what Barbara Stafford (1996) calls the "intelligence of sight" (p. 4). The value of this kind of imaginative thinking has long been acknowledged. Artists and young people are versatile in using insights and intuitions to bring ideas to fruition in ways that might initially appear strange or novel but in retrospect can seem entirely appropriate and delightful. Notwithstanding the more obvious constraints, the ability to think up imaginative ideas is a capacity shared by all. There is nothing "childlike" about seeing things with a fresh eye, assuming that existing knowledge can be an asset or a liability, or using a rule or convention to spur creativity. For the six artists who talk about their work in this chapter ideas may arise on the spot, in planning, while making something, as a result of reflection, or through meanings offered by others. These significant others could include elementary teachers, art specialists, students, and parents, as well as artwriters and cultural commentators. After all, when art is made, displayed, and discussed it gives us ideas about how to think and learn in new ways.

Endnotes

1. See the museum projects of Fred Wilson. He reinstalls permanent collections in a way that questions the basis on which the art of minority cultures is represented. In his 1992 exhibition at the Maryland Historical Society, *Mining the Museum*, he rearranged museum objects to display slave shackles alongside silver metalcraft to highlight stories omitted from "official" historical accounts (Corrin, 1994).

2. In psychology, the way we process information is seen to be filtered through perceptual schemata which direct and modify what is seen (Neisser, 1976), or via *cognitive scripts* which refer to individual ways of seeing that are a function of conceptual structures such as intellectual proclivity and prior experience (Nelson, 1986). An influential idea about how we interpret things that has its source in postmodernism and literary theory is the concept of *framing*. Here, we interpret objects or events as "texts" that are "read" by decoding the text itself and the surrounding contexts and genres as these influence what we see (MacLachlan & Reid 1994).

3. The way identity is blurred is captured in the *New Yorker* cartoon that shows a dog at a computer terminal saying, "On the Internet, nobody knows you're a dog." See also Sherry Turkle, (1995), *Life on the screen: Identity in the age of the Internet.*

4. This idea is based on research conducted by the author that explores the ways contemporary artists think, act, and respond to a range of influences that inform their art practice. See Graeme Sullivan (1996), *Critical interpretive inquiry;* and *Critical influence* (1998).

5. I am reminded of an incident several years ago when Gloria Steinem was being interviewed and she was asked, now that she had turned 50, how she solved problems. She thought for a while and said, "you don't solve problems, you surround them." Teaching and learning art is very much about coming up with imaginative ways to "surround" problems, issues, and ideas.

6. The central thesis of constructivism is that learners are active players in the way knowledge is sought, accessed, and used. Meaning, therefore, is constructed as prior experience is transformed into new understanding through learning experiences that challenge and build on existing conceptual structures. Current views of constructivist learning give prominence to the role social and cultural practices play in shaping individual learning (Moll, 1990; Newman et al. 1989).

7. The idea that objects carry rich potential for learning is, of course, not new. For example, for many years art educator Ken Marantz and others (Marantz et al. 1992; 1994) have argued that picture books are powerful sites for art learning. As works of art, picture books offer opportunities for learning that encompass the full range of visual and verbal experience.

8. The commentaries are from several artists enrolled in a graduate course I teach where they are encouraged to theorize their art practice and to develop approaches to art-based research that serves personal interests and addresses changing professional and art-educational needs. I am indebted to them for their permission to use their comments and artworks in this chapter.

References

Barrett, T. (2000). Studies Invited Lecture: About art interpretation for art education. *Studies in Art Education 42*(1), 5–19.

Berger, J. (1972). *Ways of seeing.* London: Penguin Books.

Carrier, D. (1987). *Artwriting.* Amherst: The University of Massachusetts Press.

Corrin, L. G. (Ed.) (1994). *Mining the museum: An installation by Fred Wilson.* New York: New Press.

Donaldson, M. (1978). *Children's minds.* New York: W.W. Norton & Company.

Harris, J. R. (1998). *The nurture assumption: Why children turn out the way they do.* New York: Touchstone.

Kindler, A. M., & Darras, B. (1997). Maps of artistic development. In A.M. Kindler & B. Darras (Eds.), *Child development in art* (pp. 17–44). Reston, VA: National Art Education Association.

MacLachlan, G., & Reid, I. (1994). *Framing and interpretation.* Melbourne: Melbourne University Press.

Marantz, K.; Hammond, H.; Howard, P.; Packard, M.; Shaw, J.; Wilson, M. (1994) *The picturebook: Source and resource for art education.* Reston, VA : National Art Education Association.

Marantz, S., & Marantz, K. (1992). *Artists of the page: Interviews with children's book illustrators.* Jefferson, NC: McFarland.

Mirzoeff, N. (1999). *The introduction to visual culture.* New York: Routledge.

Moll, L. C. (Ed.). (1990). *Vygotsky and education: Instructional implications and applications of sociohistorical psychology.* New York: Cambridge University Press.

Neisser, U. (1976). *Cognition and reality: Principles and implications of cognitive psychology.* San Francisco, CA: W.H. Freeman.

Nelson, K. (1986). *Event knowledge: Structure and function in development.* Hillsdale, NJ: L. Erlbaum Associates.

Newman, D., Griffin, P., & Cole, M. (1989). *The construction zone: Working for cognitive change in school.* New York: Cambridge University Press.

Nochlin, L. (1988). *Women, art, and power and other essays.* New York: Harper & Row.

Pollock, G. (1988). *Vision and difference: Femininity, feminism and art history.* New York: Routledge.

Stafford, B. M. (1996). *Good looking: Essays on the virtue of images.* Cambridge, MA: The MIT Press.

Sullivan, G. (1996). Critical interpretive inquiry: A qualitative study of five contemporary artists' ways of seeing. *Studies in Art Education 37*(4), 210–225.

Sullivan, G. (1998). Critical influence: A visual arts research project with Jayne Dyer and Nikki McCarthy. CD-ROM. Sydney: University of New South Wales.

Turkle, S. (1995). *Life on the screen: Identity in the age of the Internet.* New York: Simon & Schuster.

Walker, J. A., & Chaplin, S. (1997). *Visual culture: An introduction.* Manchester, UK: Manchester University Press.

Weintraub, L., Danto, A., & McEvilley, T. (1996). *Art on the edge and over: Searching for art's meaning in contemporary society 1970s–1990s.* Litchfield, CT: Art Insights Inc.

Wilson, B. (1992). Postmodernism and the challenge of content: Teaching teachers of art for the twenty-first century. In N. C. Yakel (Ed.), *The future: Challenge of change* (pp. 99–113). Reston, VA: National Art Education Association.

Wolf, D., & Perry, M. (1988). From endpoints to repertoires: New conclusions about drawing development. *Journal of Aesthetic Education, 22*(1), 17–35.

CONCLUSIONS AND FURTHER QUESTIONS

1. What might be the benefits of teaching art in a postmodern way, that is, through multiple conceptual and contextual frameworks?
2. What types of issues might elementary students explore in their artworks?
3. How does Sullivan suggest we view contemporary art? Why?
4. What can children learn from studying the work of contemporary artists?
5. What are some ways that an artwork can be viewed? How does this affect assessment? What does Sullivan mean when he discusses assessing a piece of artwork on an intertextual basis?

RESOURCES AND SUGGESTIONS
FOR FURTHER READING

Laura E. Berk. *Child development,* 2nd ed. Boston, MA: Allyn & Bacon, 1991.

Norman Bryson, Michael Ann Holly, & Keith Moxey (Eds.). *Visual culture: Images and interpretations.* Hanover, NH: University Press of New England, 1994.

Jessica Evans & Stuart Hall (Eds.). *Visual culture: The reader.* London: Sage, 1999.

Judith Rich Harris & Robert M. Liebert. *The child: A contemporary view of development.* Englewood Cliffs, NJ: Prentice Hall, 1991.

Chris Jenks (Ed.). *Visual culture.* London; New York: Routledge, 1995.

Anna M. Kindler (Ed.). *Child development in art.* Reston, VA: The National Art Education Association, 1997.

John Matthews. *The art of childhood and adolescence: The construction of meaning.* London; Philadelphia, PA: Falmer Press, 1999.

F. Philip Rice. *Child and adolescent development.* Upper Saddle River, NJ: Prentice Hall, 1997.

Christine Thompson (Ed.). *The visual arts and early childhood learning.* Reston, VA: The National Art Education Association, 1995.

John A. Walker & Sarah Chaplin. *Visual culture: An introduction.* Manchester, UK; New York: Manchester University Press, 1997.

Marjorie Wilson & Brent Wilson. *Teaching children to draw: A guide for teachers & parents.* Englewood Cliffs, NJ: Prentice Hall, 1982.

CHAPTER 2
QUESTIONS AND EXPLORATIONS

1. What do you think is meant by the statement "different types of knowledge?"
2. Describe the different types of knowledge you have encountered and explain how and where you learned this knowledge?
3. What is the role of the teacher in each of the types of knowledge that you have listed? What is the role of the student?
4. What do the words "culture of silence" and "language of possibility" mean to you?
5. Write the story that you would tell if you were asked to describe teaching as a narrative.

Narratives Empowering Teachers and Students: Educational and Cultural Practice

Joyce Barakett & Elizabeth J. Saccá
with contributions by
Deborah Baverstock-Angelus, Margaret
Seewalt, and Valerie Stephenson

Amy: When we try [to talk about Black issues], people have their own conversations and talk over your voice. . . .

Steven: If anything [bad] happened, they'd call all the Black kids first. . . . I wish I could have done something. . . . Who could I go to? There was nobody to talk to. (Stephenson, 1999a, p. 75)

Margaret: This latest surgery had stolen most of my eyesight. . . . My life as a photographer had come to a final stop. (Seewalt, 1999b, pp. 27–28)

Betty: What made me really unacceptable to the white teachers was that I made friendships with the natives. (Baverstock-Angelus, 1999, p. 64)

Each of these people faces a dilemma. The dilemma is between their own well-being and the way our society functions. Each tells us of the beginning of critical consciousness.

Their stories address dilemmas commonly faced by teachers and students. People's stories help them develop critical consciousness, a concept advanced by Brazilian educator Paulo Freire. Stories also help us generate the language of possibility and empower teachers and students to address our dilemmas and change education.

Critical Consciousness through Stories

Amy and Steven, cited above, describe how they were silenced. Margaret, faced with loss of her vision, is silenced. She doubts her value as an artist and questions her own voice. Betty confronts silence where there could be dialogue among native and non-native people.

Amy and Steven are among the fifteen to twenty-five year-old Black students in focus groups who tell their stories of elementary and secondary school. Valerie Stephenson (1999a) notes that these students were always a minority in their classrooms; often they were the single members of their race in a group. They explain the pressures placed upon them to keep silent. Silence that becomes the norm is what Paulo Freire (1970) calls a "culture of silence" that reflects one's subordinate position. In telling their stories, these students break from this culture of silence and create a new discursive space where they discuss and value their subjective experience. They object to being categorized according to race and gender, and to being considered "lesser than" (Stephenson, 1999a, p. 96). She illustrated this point in her research presentation (1999b).

> Allison: *Teachers just don't have the time to give us the motivation to excel . . . I guess they figure they have so many students to deal with. And especially if there's only one or two of us in the classroom, they just don't have time to focus on us . . . time as devotion from their hearts to want to give to this child.* (p. 73)
>
> Roxanne: *In elementary school, somebody said the forbidden word [nigger!] to somebody and . . . of course . . . a big uproar . . . FIGHT! . . . The principal came to class and said, "You shouldn't say that because it was not nice." It was not like he made us recognize each other to be individuals of equal worth.* (p. 76)
>
> Cynthia: *I told her [the advisor] what my goal is—to go into teaching. I wanted to be a teacher and she kept telling me it would be better if you did this and this . . . and it had nothing to do with education . . . it was like lower and lower and lower, . . . you know . . . maintenance types of stuff.* (p. 37)
>
> Barbara: *From my experience I know not to ask my teachers anything. Just from what happened in the past. If I wanted to do something, like go back to the Sciences, I would not ask my teachers. I would not! (Vehemently).*
>
> Interviewer: *Why not?* (p. 82)
>
> Barbara: *I am not stupid. I am not a child. I know what's going on around me.* (p. 81)
>
> David: *They are teachers, man. They should be building your self-esteem.* (p. 74)
>
> Roxanne: *I think it was the people in authority who made my [school] life difficult.* (p. 73)

> *Nathalie: Sometimes, sometimes I wish I were somebody else, somebody OK! This sounds really bad, but I wish I were somebody white because that person does not have the problems we have . . . not only in school but when you go applying for jobs . . . they see your colour first before they see anything, even gender and this has an effect on whether they employ you or not . . . and it is the same thing in school. (p. 40)*

Freire, well known for his listening that empowers others, emphasizes the power of this kind of dialogue. Dialogue can foster empowerment and influence future thoughts and actions.

Giroux (1989), following Freire, encourages the kind of reflection that occurred in Stephenson's focus groups. He advocates the self-examination of attitudes, values, and beliefs, in an approach he calls critical pedagogy. He encourages students and teachers to question domination by powerful groups and the ideologies that control our social institutions. His basic premise is that schools are not democratic institutions and that they reproduce the labor force and dominant ideologies of society.

In Stephenson's focus groups, students criticize people for jumping to false conclusions about them based on their race. This is an example of the language of critique that Giroux sees as focusing on the economic and political relations (such as racial policies) that characterize the educational system.

Language of Possibility

Giroux (1988) would also like us to go beyond the language of critique to develop a language of possibility. For example, in breaking the culture of silence and creating new discursive spaces, members of Stephenson's focus groups move from the language of criticism to the language of possibility as they talk about their school and then their futures.

Looking specifically at the women students and the seriousness of their concerns, Stephenson says, "Yet these young women do survive within the school system. 'Why, and how do they do it?' I wondered. So I asked, 'Why do you feel that you need to stay in school, to put up with the injustice?'" (p. 52) Rejecting these categorizations based on race and gender, these students develop their own "language of possibility," as the following excerpts by Stephenson (1999b) indicate.

> *Roxanne: Education is a first step, to get . . . to achieve your goal, to fulfill your dreams. When I'm on top [I'll be able to say] . . . you know what . . . you did this to me, you did that to me, and look where I am. If you want to fight, come now! [But] If I start arguing and fighting now, I will be so preoccupied with that, people will start passing me and I'd still be fighting over this . . . When I could get the degree and come back. (pp. 52–53)*
> *Barbara: The degree is a lever. (p. 53)*

Amy: Without it they'll think all Black people are dumb, ignorant . . . the way they expect us to be. (p. 53)

Roxanne: The paper is proof that I am qualified, neither Black nor female. (p. 53)

Barbara: Black guys get their eyes off the goal. (p. 55)

Melissa: There are some guys who react violently . . . Oh! I don't want to take this garbage . . . This pisses me off and this is how I react and they [authority figures] go "Oh my gosh! Look at the Black guy. He just did this. Get him out of school . . ." They lose track of their goal and it becomes harder . . . I guess we have to keep quiet if we want to stay here . . . to get where we want to be going. (pp. 55–56)

Primarily, the young Black women embrace academia as a milieu in which to demonstrate their sense of self-worth. To accomplish this, they construct a special personality, the main attributes of which are possibility thinking, resolve, and resilience (Stephenson, 1999a). Possibility thinking is generating positive alternatives for their futures; this thinking influences how they look at situations and address conflict. Resolve is the will and deliberate choice to succeed and to stay focused on the goal. Resilience is the ability to recover from setbacks and trauma such as being treated in a discriminatory manner.

Developing Knowledge

According to Giroux (1989), this language of possibility leads to the development of different forms of knowledge. Margaret Seewalt (1999b), whose life has been altered by her loss of vision, describes her struggles with her personal voice, and, like focus group members, she discusses her development of the language of possibility. She also develops new knowledge from this difficult situation. At a conference, she (1999a) presented the following description taken from her thesis.

Before I started writing my thesis, one of the struggles I encountered was my own personal voice. I wondered how I could use this voice as an educational tool, until I heard Steve Thunder-McGuire tell his personal stories at Concordia University. I was listening to his story and I realized that I was learning from this experience. The story and his personal voice were teaching tools for me, and my personal voice. It was at this time that I actually gave my personal experiences credibility.

(MY)STORY
        Eight years ago, I suffered from a medical condition called glaucoma and uveitus coreitus, leaving me with impaired vision, losing the total vision in my right eye and my left eye has only 20%–30% of vision. Being unable to see things clearly I rely on landmarks to guide me through the city. The details I once was able to admire are completely gone. The world, which I exist in, has a continuous haze covering it. (p. 1)
        I have been a photographer for nearly twenty years. After losing my eyesight I felt that my life was over as an artist, but as an educator I found myself bound and deter-

mined to start retraining myself within my daily life, not yet understanding that art is also a tool for education. (p. 28)

As I continued on my journey trying to understand my new existence, I found myself aching to pick up a pen and paper and start drawing, but I still did not have the confidence for this. Looking at art books and trying to figure out where I stood in my life as a sighted artist, I remembered thinking back to my painting class. My professor had told me about great artists who were also visually impaired. I was also told that Monet's style of painting derived from his impaired vision. This gave me the encouragement I needed to try drawing.

My roommate Maila decided to take me to a drawing studio, the nude. I was intimidated by the entire experience. For one thing I couldn't see a thing from sitting at the tables and the lights were so bright I needed to keep my sunglasses on. But I was taken by the hand and put on a chair about five inches from the model, and the lights were turned off so I could remove my glasses. Here I sat in a dimly lit room trying to draw the nude. I could smell her essence and hear her breath. Although not being able to see all of her, I allowed myself to fall into her breathing patterns. Through this experience I found myself allowing my hand to draw what it felt and not what I imagined drawing . . .

For the first time, I did not let my memory of the nude body become the main focus for my drawing, and my drawings became free and full of movement—loose and gestured. When it came time for everyone to view my work, another artist stated, "This is the proper way to draw the model; you are to be in the model's space in order to draw them correctly." And he touched my arm and said, "This is some of the best work I have ever seen you create." I felt honored and respected as an artist. (pp. 32–33)

During this time I decided to take a trip to Hamilton to visit a friend. While I was there she continued to remind me about taking photographs . . .

While I was on the train ride back to Montreal, I found myself reflecting on the experiences of the past two months. I sat looking out the window watching the landscape pass me by. How serene it looked and felt to me. As I continued watching the passing of homes, towns and farms, I realized that this was how I saw things. People used to ask me all the time, "What do you see?" I could never answer this question with words, for they never understood the concept, but I could answer it with images. (p. 36)

Up until now, since I am a photographer, the camera was my eye. I realized that I could not use the camera anymore in this way, for I could not see the subject/object clearly through the lens. When I returned to Montreal, I went to the darkroom to develop the rolls of film. I realized at this point that I had a hard time recognizing what was on the negatives. Not only am I once removed, but I have been twice removed. And now I am three times removed for the only time I am sure of what I photographed is when I have blown-up the negative through the enlarger. The enlarger, instead of the camera, has become my eye. (p. 37)

Seewalt reflects on connections and understanding developed through stories.

Storytelling as a part of the creative experience allows me to understand and reflect on the artwork that I have created. When an artwork represents me through my memories of these experiences, it allows me to share with others and create an understanding of the present. To ignore these experiences is to deny memory, and, therefore to live in a non-imaginative world. (p. 11)

Seewalt refers to Bachelard's (1969) claim that we must accept our imagination and reflect on our own experience in order to live in an inhabited space. In a research presentation, Seewalt (1999a) credits several sources for finding her own voice: writing her own story in a class assignment, readings, and listening to a storyteller who served as a catalyst. She extracted these from her thesis (1999b).

> I continuously refer back to Steve Thunder-McGuire and Marilyn Zurmuehlen on the importance of lived experiences, and art-making as a foundation for myself as artist/educator. This reflective practice opens up a dialogue between the artist and the art being made, but it also creates a dialogue between the teacher/student, the student/art, and teacher/artist. Going back and remembering as teachers our first art experience gives teachers an understanding of their students. It also helps teachers to relate to, and understand, their own art process. (p. 12)
>
> Telling (my)story, has enabled me to understand myself as an artist and an educator. According to McGuire (1985) as an educator my responsibility is to "give students their possibilities in a world." (p. 66)
>
> Zurmuehlen (1990) suggests that 'studio art' is created from our outer-image experience which in turn is presented through an inner-image and then produced back into an outer-image, as art. This inner and outer process is the exploring and recalling of our memories and early experiences; through this process we create art. (p. 40)

The link between Steve Thunder-McGuire and Marilyn Zurmuehlen and Seewalt is essential in Seewalt's process of empowerment. Through stories, people see connections—connections among their experiences and the experiences of others, and connections between experience and underlying social values. Recognizing these connections is essential in developing empowerment.

Recognizing the connection between self and society is also essential in the process of liberatory education. As Shor and Freire (1987) write:

> [E]ven when you feel yourself most free, if this feeling is not a social feeling, if you are not able to use your recent freedom to help others to be free by transforming the totality of society, then you are exercising only an individualist attitude towards empowerment or freedom. (pp. 109–110)

In the introductory quotation that began this chapter, Betty, interviewed by Deborah Baverstock-Angelus (1999), recognizes the connection among nonnative and native people. This is also the connection her co-teachers do not recognize.

> When I got to northern Quebec, I suddenly realized that this was an ideal place to raise a child, mainly because there wasn't any pollution, and it was a very small community. It was like a big sandbox for him and he was in heaven . . .

> *My sister, who lived there, had told me a bit about the area . . . The school was not equipped with very much. Their audio-video facilities included one overhead projector. We didn't have a television or other video equipment. They only got television in the community the year before I arrived . . .*
>
> *When I first arrived, most of the teachers at the school were non-natives, except for the kindergarten teacher. The pedagogical advisors were also white . . . Unfortunately, teachers prejudged the students. They didn't think they were bright, or talented, or even capable of learning in an academic fashion. So it was the teachers' biases and inexperience that made it difficult for them. (pp. 63–64)*
>
> *I didn't get along too well with my colleagues. My view on things did not make me socially acceptable to the non-natives. The teachers would often have potluck suppers. I went one time, and all the teachers did was back-stab the people they knew and they would talk very prejudicially about the native people. They would say things like, "The natives smell." They complained about the living conditions. They talked about the problems of doing their shopping, about having to wait for the cargo plane. After that, I stopped going to the pot-lucks. What made me really unacceptable to the white teachers was that I made friendships with the natives . . . There was a lot of hatred for non-natives. I managed to get accepted by the natives, at least some of them. But the other teachers resented me. They felt I was ostracizing them, so in return they would ostracize me. It got to the point that because I wasn't going to their potluck dinners, they stopped inviting me. The funny thing about it was that although they thought they were punishing me by ostracizing me, I felt kind of relieved. I didn't like making excuses for not showing up. (pp. 64–65)*
>
> *I endeared myself to the natives because I tried to incorporate their culture into my programs. For example, I was the first person ever to put their native language in the Christmas Concert. It was overwhelming to see the reaction of the parents, especially the elders. Also, I created materials to use with the "bush kids" that incorporated their native language. Bush kids are kids who spend many months in the bush with their family, hunting and participating in their traditional way of life. When they come back to the village and come back to school, they're really out of it. First of all, it's like coming from a small community to a big city; coming from the bush into their community is a culture shock. They have very little understanding of English, maybe just a few words. They're at a loss just for being out of class for so long, and they haven't kept up. To help them, I created teaching materials that incorporated some Cree words. For instance, a tent is mitchua—so I would have a text and a drawing of a tent. The text might read: "Sandy came out of the mitchua." That really caught their attention. When I asked a child to read it out and he read the word mitchua, he gave me the look, the expression, that gives a teacher true satisfaction. (pp. 65–66)*

Teachers and students generally play subordinate roles in educational settings; traditional and institutional authority is rarely questioned. In this context, native and Black students are further disenfranchised by racial prejudice. To resist this domination and to exercise power in the schools, students and teachers need to develop critical consciousness, voice, and a language of possibility—all of which provide the underpinnings for developing knowledge and changing society.

Discussion

The authority we would like to foster is the authority of both teachers' and students' voices, that is, the acknowledgment that they are important sources of knowledge. Increasingly, students, educators, artists, and writers are recognizing their responsibilities as active agents in opposing the traditional patterns of domination in educational training and research processes.

The narratives presented by Margaret Seewalt, Deborah Baverstock-Angelus, and Valerie Stephenson illustrate how examining lived experiences through stories can help students and teachers reflect on their own experiences and create new knowledge in the process. We see students and teachers reflecting on their experience, recognizing their own subjectivities and acquiring voice. The Black students in the focus groups use critical language to assess their situation, and move on to use the language of possibility to embrace a more hopeful future in which society accepts them in new roles. Seewalt, facing her loss of sight and people's expectations about vision, recognizes the importance of her own voice when she hears Steve Thunder-McGuire's story. She develops a new way of experiencing and new knowledge of the world. Betty saw possibilities of building connections and empowerment where other teachers had not.

Through stories, people speak for themselves. Sharing narratives can lead to questioning ideology and politics that control teachers and students, countering the master narrative. In fact, many stories are based on challenges to authority. In this process of questioning, one may see other alternatives and develop the language of possibility.

Children arrive in classrooms eager to paint and tell their stories, including stories of their aspirations and encounters with authority, social conventions, trauma and social problems. Built into some of these stories are their questions regarding social justice. Many adults attempt to protect children from these difficult subjects by placing taboos on them as subjects of art and discussion. Therefore, teachers interested in addressing social consciousness and helping children develop the language of possibility need to let the students know that they may discuss these subjects and address them in their art work in classrooms. Classic examples of this type of art and discussion include Sylvia Ashton-Warner's (1963) teaching from key words based on children's personal stories and elaborated in their art; Elwyn Richardson's (1964) integration of stories, printmaking and pottery; and Robert Cole's (1967, 1971, 1977a, 1977b, 1986) in-depth discussions with children from socially diverse groups. They help readers understand the choices children face, and they help children articulate and solidify the possibilities for their lives.

Marilyn Zurmuehlen (1987) describes the intersection of art and life. She encourages teachers to "seek occasions" where their students "may construct personal contexts" (1986, p. 36), as in the art classes she describes in her book *Studio Art: Praxis, Symbol, Presence* (1990). Christine Thompson

(1999, 2000) documents children's reflections and their development of what we are calling language of possibility through their freely chosen art and stories.

When children are "free" to choose, Anne Dyson (1997) writes,

> teachers can find their content downright dangerous (i.e., filled with the complexities of power and identity, of gender and race).
>
> "Innocent" children, adults may feel, should be free from such complexities, free to play on paper and playground. But children's imaginative play is all about freedom from their status as powerless children. Tales about good guys and bad ones, rescuers and victims, boyfriends and girlfriends allow children to fashion worlds in which <u>they</u> make decisions about characters and plots, actors and actions. Thus, for children, as for adults, freedom . . . is experienced as an expanded sense of agency, of possibility for choice and action. (p. 166)

Through this language of possibility, teachers and students can assert their sense of agency, changing power and politics of schools so that their democratic actions can be more effective. Their voices, once heard and joined with the voices of others, can address change at educational and social levels. These narratives show us how individuals can change their circumstances and, ultimately, their relations within society.

References

Ashton-Warner, S. (1963). *Teacher*. New York: Simon & Schuster.

Bachelard, G. (1969). (M. Jolas, Trans.). *The poetics of space*. Boston, MA: Beacon Press.

Baverstock-Angelus, D. (1999). *Using teacher narratives for reflection, representation and reforms in teacher training programmes*. Unpublished master's thesis, Concordia University, Montreal, Quebec, Canada.

Coles, R. (1967). *Children of crisis: A study of courage and fear*. Boston, MA: Little, Brown.

Coles, R. (1971). *Migrants, sharecroppers, mountaineers: Children of crisis, Volume 2*. Boston, MA: Little, Brown.

Coles, R. (1977a). *Eskimos, Chicanos, Indians: Children of crisis, Volume 4*. Boston, MA: Little, Brown.

Coles, R. (1977b). *Privileged ones: The well-off and the rich in America: Children of crisis, Volume 5*. Boston, MA: Little, Brown.

Coles, R. (1986). *The political life of children*. Boston, MA: Atlantic Monthly Press Edition.

Dyson, A. H. (1997). *Writing superheroes: Contemporary childhood, popular culture, and classroom literacy*. New York: Teachers College Press.

Freire, P. (1970). *Pedagogy of the oppressed*. New York: Continuum.

Giroux, H. (1988). *Teachers as intellectuals: Toward a critical pedagogy of learning*. Westport, CT: Bergin & Garvey.

Giroux, H. (1989). Schooling as a form of cultural politics: Toward a pedagogy of and for difference. In H. Giroux & P. McLaren (Eds.), *Critical pedagogy, the state, and cultural struggle* (pp. 125–277). New York: State University of New York Press.

McGuire, S. (1985). Narrative interpretation: Personal and collective storytelling. In M. Zurmuehlen (Ed.), *Working papers in art education*. Number 4, (pp. 65–69). Iowa City, IA: University of Iowa Press.

Richardson, E. S. (1964). *In the early world*. New York: Random House.

Seewalt, M. (1999a). Research presented in the session "Storytelling and empowerment in teaching art," conducted by Elizabeth J. Saccá and Joyce Barakett at the meeting of the Association québécoise des éducatrices et éducateurs spécialisés en arts plastiques, St. Hyacinthe, Québec.

Seewalt, M. (1999b). *(RE)visualization: A pedagogical journey through black and white photography*. Unpublished master's thesis, Concordia University, Montreal, Quebec, Canada.

Shor, I., & Freire, P. (1987). *A pedagogy for liberation: Dialogues on transforming education*. South Hadley, MA: Bergin & Garvey.

Stephenson, V. (1999a). *Equal to the challenge: Reconstructing ways of thinking, knowing and doing, Re: the schooling years of young black women in Metro-Montreal*. Unpublished master's thesis, Concordia University, Montreal, Quebec, Canada.

Stephenson, V. (1999b). Research presented in the session "Storytelling and empowerment in teaching art," conducted by Elizabeth J. Saccá and Joyce Barakett at the meeting of the Association québécoise des éducatrices et éducateurs spécialisés en arts plastiques, St. Hyacinthe, Québec.

Thompson, C. M. (1999). Action, autobiography, and aesthetics in young children's self-initiated drawings. *Journal of Art & Design Education, 18* (2), 155–161.

Thompson, C. M. (2000). Children as artists, critics, and teachers. Paper presented at the meeting of the National Art Education Association, Los Angeles, CA.

Zurmuehlen, M. (1986). Reflecting on the ordinary: Interpretation as transformation of experiences. *Art Education, 39* (6), 33–36.

Zurmuehlen, M. (1987). Context in art: Meaning recovered and discovered. *Journal of Multi-Cultural and Cross Cultural Research in Art Education, 5* (1), 131–143.

Zurmuehlen, M. (1990). *Studio art: Praxis, symbol, presence*. Reston, VA: National Art Education Association.

Authors' Note

Joyce Barakett and Elizabeth J. Saccá contributed equally to the research. Contributions by Deborah Baverstock-Angelus (MA Education), Valerie Stephenson (MA Education) and Margaret Seewalt (MA Art Education) comprise edited excerpts from their theses completed at Concordia University and excerpts from their theses as they presented them at a professional meeting.

Correspondence concerning this article should be addressed to Joyce Barakett, Education Department LB-549–7, Concordia University, 1455 de Maisonneuve West, Montreal, Quebec H3G 1M8 Canada, and Elizabeth J. Saccá, School of Graduate Studies S-201, Concordia University, 1455 de Maisonneuve West, Montreal, Quebec H3G 1M8, Canada.

CONCLUSIONS AND FURTHER QUESTIONS

1. Think of a situation in which you faced a dilemma. How did dealing with your dilemma help you develop a language of possibilities?
2. Did this language of possibility lead you to develop a different form of knowledge about yourself based on lived experience?
3. What is the relationship between the language of critique, the language of possibility, possibility thinking, resolve, and resilience? How do these lead to different forms of knowledge?
4. How do the authors help us understand critical pedagogy as a theoretical framework for teaching? What makes this form of pedagogy critical?
5. What is a critical consciousness? What is significant about developing one? How is it different from consciousness?
6. Explain what Freire means by a "culture of silence." Have you ever been made to feel silenced? Describe the context in which this occurred.
7. What kinds of exchange take place when narratives are included as a part of learning? Who benefits and how? In what ways can narrative be used in the elementary classroom?

RESOURCES AND SUGGESTIONS
FOR FURTHER READING

Stephen J. Ball (Ed.). *Foucault and education: Disciplines and knowledge.* London; New York: Routledge, 1990.

Mary Beattie. *Constructing professional knowledge in teaching: A narrative of change and development.* Toronto; New York: Ontario Institute for Studies in Education; Teachers College Press, 1995.

Carol Becker. *Zones of contention: Essays on art, institutions, gender, and anxiety.* Albany: State University of New York Press, 1996.

Susan Cahan & Zoya Kocur (Eds.). Contemporary art and multicultural education. New York: New Museum of Contemporary Art: Routledge, 1996.

Diane DuBose Brunner. *Inquiry and reflection: Framing narrative practice in education.* Albany, NY: State University of New York, 1994.

Michel Foucault. Power/knowledge: Selected interviews and other writings, 1972–1977. Colin Gordon (Ed. & Trans.). New York: Pantheon Books, 1980.

Paulo Freire. *Pedagogy of hope: Reliving pedagogy of the oppressed.* Robert R. Barr (Trans.). New York: Continuum, 1994.

Coco Fusco. *English is broken here: Notes on cultural fusion in the Americas.* New York: The New Press, 1995.

Henry A. Giroux & Peter McLaren (Eds.). *Between borders: Pedagogy and the politics of cultural studies*. New York: Routledge, 1994.

Joe L. Kincheloe & Shirley R. Steinberg (Eds.) *Unauthorized methods: Strategies for critical teaching*. New York: Routledge, 1998.

Joe L. Kincheloe. *Toward a critical politics of teacher thinking: Mapping the postmodern*. Westport, CT: Bergin & Garvey, 1993.

Lucy Lippard. *Mixed blessings: New art in a multicultural America*. New York: Pantheon, 1990.

Audre Lorde. The transformation of silence into language and action. In *Sister outsider: Essays and speeches by Audre Lorde*. (pp. 40–44). Freedom, CA: The Crossing Press, 1984.

Trinh T. Minh-ha, *Woman, native, other: Writing postcoloniality and feminism*. Bloomington, IN, Indiana University Press, 1989.

Joy S. Ritchie & David E. Wilson. *Teacher narrative as critical inquiry: Rewriting the script*. New York: Teachers College Press, 2000.

Jontyle Theresa Robinson. *Bearing witness: Contemporary works by African American women artists*. New York: Spelman College and Rizzoli International Publications, 1996.

Kathleen Weiler & Sue Middleton (Eds.). *Telling women's lives: Narrative inquiries in the history of women's education*. Philadelphia, PA: Open University Press, 1999.

Carol Witherell & Nel Noddings (Eds.). *Stories lives tell: Narrative and dialogue in education*. New York: Teachers College Press, 1991.

CHAPTER 3

QUESTIONS AND EXPLORATIONS

1. What kind of approach(es) did your teachers use to teach art in the elementary classroom? Do you believe it was effective? How do you feel about art as a result of these experiences?
2. How do the ways that you were taught art influence your thoughts and feelings about yourself as a future elementary teacher teaching art?
3. How does your identity as a teacher intersect with other aspects of your identity? How might your students' identities intersect with your identity?
4. What parts of your identity do you think are the most important at this given moment? Why?
5. Does identity shift depending on time and context? Have you ever experienced such a change? What caused this shift?
6. How do our identities play into our role as a teacher?
7. How is sexual identity treated in our culture? In school settings?

In the Trenches

Ed Check

Ten Years of Elementary Teaching

I taught in a rural elementary school district for ten years. I commuted 120 miles (round-trip) to school each day. I was expected to teach 780 students a week at three schools from a cart. Twenty-eight art classes per week: on Fridays, I taught seven fifty-minute classes. I had one small closet/office to store art supplies at each school. At one school, I shared a closet with the music teacher.

Most of the faculty and support staff was female. There were six males among the three schools. Art, music, physical education, and library were considered "specials." Teachers normally left the classroom to correct papers or do lesson planning during this time. I dealt with over forty different faculty and staff personalities each week, some kinder than others. I also was responsible for weekly lunch and playground duties. I exhibited students' work at all three schools. Initially, I was responsible for providing back drops for the Christmas pageants. I also scheduled annual field trips to a local art museum.

At the time I was teaching (1980–1989), these seemed like normal teaching conditions. Now, I gasp, wondering how I did it all.

My university art education really didn't prepare me to teach art well. I learned strategies to "dumb-down" everything to elements and principles of design (Wachowiak, 1977). All my ideas for student projects came from books, and the student results looked like the examples in the books. I was told, "kids have short attention spans and can't handle much." My principal echoed that advice, as he required me to make sure that the kids took home a project every week.

My end-of-year evaluations stressed classroom management and control. My principal remarked how neatly a student had filled in a practice sheet for mixing colors. He noted that another student's sheet was very messy and not good. What he failed to notice was that the messy student understood color mixing and the neat student's sheet was incorrect. I noticed that children's studio projects took on a mytho-poetic quality—they seemed more about pseudo-creativity, expression and imagination than anything real. And that fit perfectly into my principal's notion of art: he wanted pretty childlike things hanging in the halls. It bothered me that much of what we did seemed merely to be filling in between the lines—whether we were painting or making animal sculptures. I felt that I wasn't challenging the students. More importantly, I didn't know how because I wasn't taught how. Art was fun. It had little to do, in my opinion, with creating change or transforming lives.

My elementary school world was really an adult world with a kid's look. Unintentionally, I treated my students as second-class citizens: rarely, did I ask for their input. They were there to follow my directions. I made most of the decisions, and from what I can tell, did most of the work and learning. That's what I regret about my teaching. I didn't know that there were other ways to teach about art. As a result, many kids left their childhoods—the realities of them at least—at the school door. Because of that, there were art and life lessons that could never be learned in my classes.

I never really felt confident as an art teacher. Even though the other classroom teachers were impressed with what the children were making, I felt something was missing. I only knew how to make more of the same thing: more paintings, more watercolors, more collages, or more drawings. I tried expanding the art curriculum. I added art history, story-telling, and writing. But the learning was still disconnected, detached from the real world. My principal kept pressuring me to produce weekly art products.

I engaged in shouting matches with my principal. I felt like I was being dumped on. I felt devalued and abused. I was constantly told my schedule was easy compared to the student contact time classroom teachers had. One way I took care of myself during those early years was to make art. I made wood collages using scraps from my dad's shop. I started to attend state art conferences and even gave presentations. I also started working toward a Masters in Art Education. Though inconvenient, I took night classes. I treasured the time I spent with other artists. My thesis was about a disembodied aesthetic education model for teaching—just another way to distract from the real issues in my world.

I recall an advanced graduate oil class. I painted window scenes—interior landscapes looking to the outside. My instructor advised me to look at David Hockney's work. I seemed to be striving toward a minimalist abstracted style, similar to Hockney. I found out Hockney was gay. It made me feel a little less isolated. This was the mid-eighties. It was ironic in a way, because a man I was dating had zero-converted that summer.

I liked most of the people I worked with. Many of the classroom teachers disconnected art from the real world. They were afraid of art; afraid of their own art skills. They were afraid to do anything where they could not control the outcome. Every year, I consented to make life-sized body tracings for Mrs. White's second grade class. This was an activity she could have done herself, but clearly she did not trust her skills. She taped the finished images in the student's seat for open house.

Another second grade teacher asked if I would construct a bulletin board with space ships made by her students. Consenting, to keep good faculty relations, I later asked some of her students to put together the display. Delighted, they spent four days thinking and designing the showcase. When the display was finished, it was obvious that second grade hands had constructed it. When their teacher saw the display, she was displeased.

What saved me during my elementary teaching years was that I continued to make art and I never tired of the students. They were amazingly resilient and inspired me. As I think back, I wish I would have let them make more decisions. Too much of my time was wasted on seating charts, discipline, delegating duties—not on making art and taking risks.

When I resigned my position to go back to graduate school full-time, I left behind a brand new art room that I helped design. It was a large room and even had a library corner. But I was exhausted. Teaching ten years had taken its toll.

Remembering My Childhood

I was born a second generation Polish-American, into a devout Polish-Catholic and working-class family in 1956. My mom's education stopped abruptly at the eighth grade. She was forced to quit school to work in a factory to provide money for her family (circa 1930s). She became a homemaker and raised six children. My dad was raised on a farm and had a sixth grade education. He was a carpenter by trade and later in life bought out his brother's small home building business.

As a child, I used to bike to my dad's shop to drop off his lunch box. Though I loved building things with wood, I preferred the action and activities in our house. I hadn't realized that at the time, I had chosen domesticity over adventure, femininity over masculinity.

I kept pretty much around the house. I especially liked being in the kitchen. I would help my mom with dishes, cleaning, baking, shopping and other chores. I especially liked it when my mom's sisters would visit. They canned, cooked, and baked together. All three of them talked about their childhoods and relatives.

When I think about my formal childhood education experiences, the first response that comes to my mind is rage. I'm still angry at my hometown school systems because little of what I learned and experienced worked for me as a gay kid from a working-class background. I was never taught much about my working-class background much less anything queer. Silence, misinformation, invisibility, and shame characterized the methodology and curriculum that I experienced.

When I was five years old, I persuaded my mother to borrow a neighbor's brownie dress for me to wear. I biked all over the neighborhood. After that day, people in my neighborhood started to refer to me as "Nancy." This discrimination would turn violent as I got older. As a result, I quickly learned to shutdown and withdraw. I disconnected for safety. I avoided anything that had to do with the feminine or female. These things were anathema to being a boy.

I loved to draw cityscapes. I constructed my own HO-scale city in my basement furnace room. I spent years down there creating architecture and stories. I also liked to play with dolls and cross-dress. I often played with my younger sister.

School reflected little of what was going on in my life or what was going on outside school. On the street, we were talking about kissing, where babies came from, and sex. In school, we talked about current events, but in a de-politicized and sanitized way. I figured out that school wasn't the place to talk about what I was really thinking or feeling. Not seeing my reality mirrored at school, I became detached. Needless to say, school didn't prepare me for the realities of my life: death, sex, disease, love, or work.

I did not have much art in elementary school. I recall my fourth-grade teacher not liking my salt map of the United States. I also remember Sister Mary Carla's sixth-grade class taping large collages in the halls. Elementary school was neat, clean, and cold. It was where I learned to disconnect from my body (Foucault, 1979).

Graduate School

After teaching ten years at the elementary level, I got out. I tired more from the effects of the structures of schooling than teaching kids. I liked being around kids. But, I needed a more hospitable climate for my own interests and my emerging sexuality. One colleague said she was glad that I found a way to get out. We often talked about the job abuse and fatigue we experienced. Graduate school provided me the opportunity to learn new information and teaching strategies. I was exposed to people and ideas that connected teaching and art to real life issues. I wondered, "Why wasn't I taught this in the first place?"

I recall a life-altering incident in a graduate theory course. During class introductions the instructor introduced herself as a lesbian. She spoke about her struggle to integrate the personal and professional in her research and teaching. Caught by surprise, I introduced myself as a gay male struggling to connect my identities as artist, gay male, and teacher. I had never talked about sexuality in an educational setting prior to that. It was exhilarating.

From that moment on, I knew it was possible to incorporate my life into my teaching. As a teaching assistant, I experimented with various ways to include the students' lives into learning about art. I requested non-art major students to develop a semester project that wove together political, personal, or professional interests that they chose.

My teaching started to evolve as a lively interactive process (Ellsworth, 1997). It was a work-in-progress. I took risks and experimented. I created semester work-in-progress projects. At the end of the course, we would present work done to date. One female student investigated the cultural and historical assumptions behind shaving and women. She wrote to various companies for information about ad campaigns and used a first-person narrative as her presentation format. Throughout her presentation, she shaved one leg. Many students were startled. I was too. We were all trying to make connections between her performance art and learning/teaching. It was serious, real, and exciting. Another semester, a male student talked about his interest in baseball architecture. He showed slides and compared and contrasted differences in baseball architecture throughout the twentieth century. Relying upon personal experiences, he used his visits to major ballparks every summer as a context for his investigation.

My changing pedagogy still belied the realities of my life. I continued to disconnect my body and mind. Sexuality was shaming and confusing for me. Talking about sexual identity issues was dangerous—inappropriate at best. I learned from the courage of my students. One female student shared her fears about doing her semester project about AIDS. She debated all semester if she would focus on AIDS as her topic. She was torn between talking about a subject that impacted her life and respecting the privacy of her fiancé's grief (his brother had recently died of AIDS). She negotiated a respectful way to give her presentation and not offend her fiancé. She cried, retelling how she mustered the courage to confront her fiancé and her own fears and tell her story.

For my part, I volunteered at a lesbian, gay, and bisexual social resource agency and learned first-hand, how other marginalized people created meaning and sanity in their lives. In my dissertation, I was able to examine disparate parts of my life—gay, aesthetic, and nurturer. I was supported by faculty and friends and, at least in theory, my dissertation and graduate school experiences provided me with the confidence to rethink ways to teach.

University Professor

Graduate school life was quickly brought to a halt with my arrival at a conservative university. In a way, I got slammed back into silence. I initially shut down. I second-guessed any impact I might have on students in such an environment.

I recall the first art education class I taught. Early in the course, I asked students to bring in some art and talk about it. It seemed like a great way to introduce ourselves and connect as artists. I decided to do the same. I explained how my art explored the tension I experienced between being a gay teacher and artist. I described my art heroes and mentors: David Wojnarowicz (1991), Suzanne Lacy (1985), Jonathan Silin (1995), etc. The class was silent. A few students dropped out. A few others suggested that my comments (i.e., my life) were inappropriate in an educational setting.

At first, I internalized the shame of that day—trying to infuse real life issues into the curriculum. And for some time felt I had disappointed my students. I later found out that my introduction was what some students had been waiting for—for years. They knew the power of art and truth-telling. They also sensed that there were other ways to teach and impact kids. What I continue to learn about teaching is that I rarely know when I am connecting with students and for what reasons. I owe it to myself to be as truthful as I can be. This does not mean that being myself and trusting my vision does not involve frustration, rejection, or isolation. It always has.

Later that first semester, we watched *Common Threads*, an award-winning documentary about the AIDS Quilt. I used it as a contemporary example of people dealing with important issues through the medium of quilt making. As we watched the video, I became physically and emotionally moved. During our break, I cried. I cried about the tension in the class, the loss of friends to AIDS, the difficulty of bridging the gap between school and real life, and the difficulty of being myself in class.

It was during the next semester that a student made everyone leave the art room as he prepared for his end-of-semester presentation—a performance piece critiquing the control and regulation of bodies in culture. Upon re-entering the semi-darkened room, each of us received a slip of paper with writing. Dressed in white, he walked on the tops of tables, blindfolded at first, and without saying a word, gestured to individuals to read their sheets of paper. He made us repeat our words, first singly, then in groups. Then simultaneously. Toward the end, we were all shouting our verses.

He described his performance as his way to examine the silence of real truths in teaching. He critiqued what schooling had become for him—a loud silence. As we talked about the performance, we realized we had broken every rule usually enforced in school: talking softly, one person at a time, being courteous, etc.

Lessons for Teaching

I wish my undergraduate experiences would have exposed me to collaborative models of teaching and multicultural content. In spite of that, one issue remains constant to this day: the role of the elementary teacher is innately connected to the historical role of women in society (DeSalvo, 1989). By that, I mean patriarchy and misogyny. Women (and men) continue to be systematically marginalized at the elementary level. Teaching duties and responsibilities are disproportionately huge to the value this work receives in the culture and the pay. That's the reality I experienced and continue to see and hear from elementary teachers. The culture continues to ignore and abuse the vast majority of its elementary teachers. We need to address what we call "normal" teaching schedules at the elementary level. The current paradigm does not serve students or teachers well.

Within such environs, control is one of the few ways to survive—that's what I found as a teacher. Unfortunately, that's what still exists. Recently, I visited a former student now first-year teacher. He was frank about his fears of not only being himself in a school culture that valued conformity and order, but his reliance on classroom discipline to stay sane.

This semester, I am working with a group of art education students who will be teaching at an at-risk and minority elementary school for ten weeks. The school has no art teacher. Already, the students are wondering how to teach a lesson in forty-five minutes. How is that possible? I suggest there are ways but I am quick to remind them of the insanity of the situation. I encourage and challenge them to think of other ways to teach. The model I was taught and used as a teacher did not work for me and will not work for them.

So, we experiment.

Listening to students is an important part of my pedagogy. Saying my truths and witnessing to theirs helps build community and integrity (Felman and Laub, 1992). It is these interactive and interdependent relationships that have helped teachers survive in the classroom to this day. But we need to do more than survive. School should be a space where teachers grow alongside students as co-learners.

It has taken me twenty-one years of teaching experiences to realize how cultural sexism and misogyny get enacted in schools. High schools get more money. Art isn't important. One local elementary teacher teaches 480 students on a $200 budget.

I continue to struggle with personal ghosts, loss of control, success, failure, and fear. It's a long list. I recall that I was taught that a good teacher controls the classroom. That's how you get kids to learn. Yeah, that's also how you survive.

Teaching and life experiences have demonstrated to me that children and teachers learn best in supportive, safer and saner environments. But then, kids and elementary teachers are not considered important commodities in this culture. If they were, we wouldn't be having this discussion.

References

DeSalvo, L. A. (1989). *Virginia Woolf: The impact of childhood sex abuse on her life and work.* New York: Beacon Press.

Ellsworth, E. (1997). *Teaching positions: Difference, pedagogy, and the power of address.* New York: Teachers College Press.

Felman, S., & Laub, D. (1992). *Testimony: Crises of witnessing in literature, psychoanalysis, and history.* New York: Routledge.

Foucault, M. (1979). *Discipline and punish.* (A. Sheridan, Trans.). New York: Vintage Books.

Lacy, S., & Labowitz, L. (1985). Feminist media strategies for political performance. In D. Kahn and D. Neumaier (Eds.), *Cultures in contention* (pp. 122–33). Seattle, WA: The Real Comet Press.

Silin, J. (1995). *Sex, death, and the education of children: Our passion for ignorance in the age of AIDS.* New York: Teachers College Press.

Wachowiak, F. (1977). (3rd ed.). *Emphasis art: A qualitative art program for the elementary school.* New York: Thomas Y. Crowell Company.

Wojnarowicz, D. (1991). *Close to the knives: A memoir of disintegration.* New York: Vintage Books.

CONCLUSIONS AND FURTHER QUESTIONS

1. How familiar is Check's description of teaching elementary art? In what ways, if any, does it resonate with your own experiences of art as a student or a teacher in elementary school?

2. In what ways does Check describes his early years of teaching? How effective was the approach that he took? For whom was such an approach effective?

3. What did Check come to realize was missing from his teaching? What did this lead him to do now in the classroom that he did not do before? What made Check discover these things?

4. What did Check do to make art more meaningful for his students and teaching more meaningful for himself?

5. How is Check's teaching like a work-in-progress? Would your conceptu-
    alization of yourself as a teacher change if you were to describe your
    teaching in this way?
6. Check describes the role of the elementary teacher as being connected
    to the historical role of women in society. Why does he make this con-
    nection? How does this idea affect your identity as a teacher?
7. What is the larger issue that Check raises with regard to elementary
    teachers and children?
8. How did Check's college students respond to his honesty about his
    identity as a gay teacher? How do you respond to people who may be
    different from you? How will that affect your performance in a class-
    room?

RESOURCES AND SUGGESTIONS
FOR FURTHER READING

Debra Chasnoff. *It's elementary: Talking about gay issues in school.* San Francisco: Women's Educational Media, 1996. (78 minute long videotape.)

The Gay, Lesbian, and Straight Education Network works to end anti-gay bias in K–12 schools through a network of 85 chapters. The aim of the Network is to create an affirming environment in schools for all students. (www.glsen.org)

The Gay, Lesbian, and Straight Teachers Network. *Reaching out to lesbian, gay, and bisexual youth.* Coral Gables, FL: The Gay, Lesbian, and Straight Teachers Network, 1997. (21 minute long videotape.)

Madeleine R. Grumet. *Bitter milk: Women and teaching.* Amherst, MA: University of Massachusetts Press, 1988.

Harmony Hammond. *Lesbian art in America: A contemporary history.* New York: Rizzoli, 2000.

Karen Marie Harbeck. *Gay and lesbian educators: Personal freedoms, public constraints.* Malden, MA: Amethyst, 1997.

Inclusive curriculum: The silent minority comes to the classroom is a curriculum guide produced by the Los Angeles chapter of the Gay, Lesbian, and Straight Education Network intended for grades pre-K through 12. (www.glsenla.org)

William J. Letts IV & James T. Sears (Eds.). *Queering elementary education: Advancing the dialogue about sexualities and schooling.* Lanham, MD: Rowman & Littlefield, 1999.

Arthur Lipkin. *Understanding homosexuality, changing schools: A text for teachers, counselors and administrators.* Boulder, CO: Westview Press, 2000.

Adam Mastoon. *The shared heart: Portraits and stories celebrating lesbian, gay, and bisexual young people.* New York: William Morrow; Lothrop, Lee & Shepard Books, 1997.

William F. Pinar (Ed.) *Queer theory in education.* Mahwah, NJ: L. Erlbaum Associates, 1998.

Kenneth Plummer. *Telling sexual stories: Power, change, and social worlds.* London; New York: Routledge, 1995.

Tackling gay issues in school, produced by the Connecticut chapter of the Gay, Lesbian, and Straight Education Network offers a great deal of information on classroom activities, in-service workshops. It also includes a collection of fact sheets. (www.outinct.com/glsen)

Dan Woog. *School's out: The impact of gay and lesbian issues on America's schools.* Boston: Alyson Publications, 1995.

CHAPTER 4

QUESTIONS AND EXPLORATIONS

1. Describe the elementary school that you attended. As you write your description, think about the size of the school, where it was located, and the various aspects of the heritage and backgrounds of the students and teachers.

2. Write a description of your personal history, background and heritage. How did your elementary schooling intersect with this personal history?

3. When you were a child, how did you view people who were different from you and your family? How do you view them now?

4. What artists and artistic traditions did you learn about in your elementary art education?

5. What kinds of changes do you think are taking place in schools? Why are these changes happening?

6. Find three images or descriptions of elementary schools from popular culture? How are schools represented in these images?

Cultural Content, Identity, and Program Development: Approaches to Art Education for Elementary Educators

Andra Lucia Nyman

The elementary classroom offers an environment that can foster creativity, independence, self-awareness, self-expression, and an understanding of the visual world. Education through art can provide opportunities for exploring one's creativity, for communicating ideas, and enabling students to express themselves through the use of materials, processes, and tools. The teacher who is teaching about art can foster students' perceptual skills by encouraging them to look closely at their environment, to achieve fluency in the language of art, and use technical skills to communicate their own ideas and feelings (Nyman, 1996).

Rapid change in the demographic makeup of schools in the United States has occurred during the last ten years. One need only talk with teachers to understand that this change has affected curricular decisions and instructional approaches. For example, in one metropolitan school system in Atlanta, there is a high school in which 176 languages are represented; in another nearby elementary school, 140 flags are flown to represent those students' heritages or countries of origin. These are only two of the schools in an area of the country that has seen tremendous growth in recent years. This trend is occurring in many major cities in the United States today, further reinforcing the need to prepare teachers to teach towards the inclusion of culturally diverse content and towards tolerance for others' beliefs, customs, and heritage.

With the influx of increasing numbers of students from diverse ethnic and cultural backgrounds in our schools, the role of art in the curriculum is also changing. Traditional goals of art education included providing children with opportunities for self-expression and engendering an understanding of the history of Western art. Contemporary art instruction now demands the incorporation of content that includes art works created by artists who represent the diverse cultures of our nation and the world.

The elementary teacher is, through art, in a unique position to nurture the development of the child's understanding and awareness of other cultures and their traditions thereby encouraging students to become culturally, perceptually, and aesthetically aware. Artist, educator and writer Amalia Mesa-Bains (1996) wrote that "recognizing the cultural resources and experiences students bring to the classroom and connecting these resources and experiences to our instruction is key" (p. 32). Recognizing that art can also be a rewarding and successful experience for students with limited language skills, a teacher can also use art to provide opportunities for nonverbal learning. Common experiences can be used to link students from varying backgrounds while the integration of diversity into the curriculum can provide opportunities for intercultural teaching by linking social content, shared histories, significant contributions by individuals, and multiple perspectives (Mesa-Bains, 1996).

Teaching children about artists from global cultures, as well as racial and ethnic groups in this country, can provide insights that may enhance students' visual awareness as well as assist them in communicating their own feelings and ideas. Teaching through art can indirectly effect social change as students gain awareness of and appreciation for cultures other than their own. If schools are to make education relevant for all students and assist students in overcoming prejudice, racism, and the lack of equitable economic opportunities, teachers must strive to include content that is inclusive of many heritages. This can better occur when students learn about the cultural and social contexts of art works, and, in turn, develop a more humanistic understanding of themselves and others (Bersson, 1987).

Although the goals of education have become more globally and culturally oriented, educators still face the questions: How do we meet the individual needs of the child? How do we kindle children's imaginations? How do we help children to learn about their own identities, heritage, and roles in an increasingly complex society and "shrinking" world?

Culture and Cultural Context

The questions concerning how teachers will help students to (a) learn about themselves, (b) become creative individuals in an everchanging society, and (c) develop their own identities, demand that one understands the roles that a person's background, cultural heritage, and environment play in the development of the individual. The meaning of terms such as culture and cultural context must be clearly understood if teaching about the art of contemporary artists, as well as those from globally oriented traditions, is to be successful.

Art educator June King McFee's description of *culture* provides teachers with a working definition and framework for the development of curricula that are culturally based. McFee (1995) states that "culture includes a group's values, attitudes, belief systems, social structures, concepts of reality, cognitive styles, ways of knowing, motivating, categorizing and making order, creating symbols, environments, technologies and art" (p. 187). Why is it important to teach these seemingly unrelated bits of information? Because it is through understanding the complex relationships of these "bits" that one can understand a culture and its art. It is, therefore, important for the elementary teacher to approach the study of art from an inclusive stance which not only recognizes this complexity but also demonstrates to students that many ideas and differing viewpoints are allowable (Magee and Rozewski, 1998). Students can learn how artists have expressed their own responses to the world through their art. They can also learn to accept many viewpoints as valid and understand how art reflects an individual's or group's values, beliefs, customs, and traditions. Multicultural art education can enable students from various backgrounds to generate ideas and symbols that reflect their own cultural beliefs, experiences, and environments (Anderson, 1991).

The other important term, *cultural context*, delves more deeply into the fabric of society and social practices. The cultural context of an artwork may include information about the artist's ethnic background, personal or family history, political or historical contexts, and other factors that may influence the aesthetic decisions made by the artist (or in the case of a functional object, by the maker). It is through recognizing the context in which the artwork was created that a fuller understanding of the artist's motivation, expression of ideas, and technical approach to that artwork can occur.

Personal and Cultural Identity

Teaching about art through this approach recognizes the importance of one's community, family, peers, values, and ideas in the formation of one's identity (Neperud and Krug, 1995). The question of what identity is and how it is formed is a complex matter, debated in psychology, education, anthropology, sociology, and other fields.

In his text, *The Saturated Self,* Kenneth Gergen (1991) describes how the complexities of Western culture influence the definition of each individual. He summarizes the effects that the advents of communication and technology have played in defining who we are. Tracing the development of transportation and communication innovations that have occurred over the past century, he describes the effect of technological advances related to rapidly expanding modern forms of communication, transportation, print media, and film, which have increased our contact, knowledge, and relationships with many people across geographic distances. Gergen credits recent technological developments such as computers, electronic mail, satellites, faxes, fiber optics, cellular communications, and other innovations as contributing to a "swirling sea of social relations" (p.61). All of these factors contribute to the changing nature of our relationships with others and with the development of our beliefs and identities and play a role in a process of socialization which is lifelong (Gergen, 1991).

Teachers can assist students in forming their own identities, to stay afloat in this swirling sea of social relations, through clarification of one's knowledge and understanding of their origins, beliefs, cultural mythology, family traditions, languages, and those political, social, and historical factors which shape each student's development as an individual. Teachers can help students to discern how perceptions of other's lives can be inaccurately reflected in the media, and assist them in becoming critical consumers of the technological images that face them everyday. Teachers can help students to interpret and assess the ideas and images that they see depicted in popular culture and develop tolerance for beliefs unlike their own, in order to avoid the formation of prejudice and discrimination toward people of other cultures.

How, then, can teachers use art to help students understand the varying viewpoints of those around them? How does art reflect the identity and beliefs of the artist who created the artwork? How does art help students understand how an artist's cultural heritage and identity are related? The formation of an artist's identity is characterized by changes which result from the influences of one's heritage(s), community, education, art training, and place of origin (Lippard, 1990). These influences are not static and, together, create the boundaries and characteristics of one's culture. Freedman and Hernández (1998) describe the nature of culture as one that is constantly changing. Cultural identity and redefinition occur within national boundaries as people construct their identities by selectively adapting or rejecting practices and beliefs of their own cultural heritage or the society surrounding them (Freedman and Hernández, 1998).

How then can the study of art teach students about other cultures? One viewpoint supports the belief that art, culture, and aesthetics are interrelated, and that art is associated with the maker's values and with meanings "which are relationally situated within social, economic, religious, technological, political, historical, and cultural contexts" (Neperud and Krug, 1995, p. 165).

How can an elementary teacher encourage students to discover and appreciate the "sources" of identity of others? Laurie Hicks calls for an approach she names "coalition education" (Hicks, 1991, p. 23) which is based on Maria Lugones' (1987) idea of the world traveler who finds themself in another person's world, gaining understanding of that person's world, and contrasting that person's identity with one's own, while developing understanding of ourselves. Hicks describes the importance of using art to help students to explore other peoples' worlds and their perspectives, in order to learn respect for differences, to "build coalitions" (p. 23) with those who are different than themselves in order to avoid marginalizing others and, thereby, encouraging cooperation and understanding.

Culturally-based Program Development

Teachers who elect to build their curriculum around the art created by artists of many cultures may benefit by understanding the following terms. *Culture*, in sociological terms can be described as ideas, traditions, products, and language, many of which are passed from generation to generation within human societies.

The term, *diversity*, is often used to describe the population make-up of our schools. In *Teaching Young Children in Multicultural Classrooms*, Wilma Robeles de Meléndez and Vesna Ostertag (1997) state that

> [D]iversity, as observed in the social context, contains a variety of social factors that exert an influence, either singly or interactively, on the individual's behavior. These social factors are nationality, race/ethnicity, religion, social class, gender, exceptionality, and age. (p. 58)

Their three-phase model for including multicultural content in culturally based curricula involves the development of a strong rationale and personal conviction for teaching about the cultures of their students and others. This approach requires that the teachers do research and engage in an introspective process to teach about a diverse range of viewpoints and cultures and engender tolerance and understanding for others. In the second phase, teachers explore different approaches, materials, and models in designing their curriculum. The third phase involves constant revision of the curriculum based on the teacher's reflection about the goals and success of the approaches used.

It is clear that transforming education to reflect a more relevant and culturally inclusive model is a complex process. Prior to the 1990s, resources and commercial materials for teaching about art from a non-western or global context were limited or non-existent, and art educators were called upon to develop comprehensive curricular resources (Delacruz, 1992). Today, resources and culturally based curricula are available and accessible. However, it is important that teachers understand *how* to approach teaching about a diverse range of cultures. The critical importance of this step has been supported in the writings of Lanier (1987), Gablik (1989), Congdon (1987), Feldman (1980), Klein (1998), McFee (1998), Neperud and Krug (1995), as well as others.

Jacqueline Chandra (1994) and Patricia Barbanell (1994) describe strategies for inquiry methods that are culturally sensitive. Chandra (1994) describes the use of iconology, iconography, and social art history. The first two approaches focus on the study of the meanings of images which leads to discovery of the underlying ideas as suggested by motifs, symbols, forms, stories, and allegories and places importance on discussion about the meanings of the subject matter derived from the cultural context of the image or object. This social art historical approach takes into account the economic, political, religious, scientific, and social backgrounds of the artwork as reflective of a specified time in history (Chandra, 1994).

Barbanell (1994) provides an overview of art education curricular content based on the five-level approach offered by James Banks. Barbanell offers examples of art lessons which illustrate the five levels of Banks's hierarchy: (1) the cultural contributions approach; (2) the additive approach; (3) the infusion approach; (4) the transformation approach; and (5) the social action approach (Banks, 1988). Teachers infusing content using the contributions and additive approaches can foster student's development of understanding on an appreciation level. Educational theorists support the use of transformative and social action approaches to help students develop deeper understandings of the diversity and complexity of world cultures, to gain understanding of universal human themes, develop their abilities to analyze content, and engage in dialogue about the artist's life and intentions (Barbanell, 1994). Barbanell believes that "by understanding the social context of art and the importance of artist as social activist, students can develop abilities to take action with and through their art"(p.31).

Conclusions

Through a multicultural educational approach, students can be taught to value art and to understand the role of the arts throughout the history of humankind. The arts help students develop their abilities to appreciate and interpret art of other cultures and to learn about people of the past through exposure to reproductions, to art works in museums and galleries, or through discussions about contemporary artists and art works. Art history can also provide the student with a source of information about the world and can be incorporated into the curriculum through relating the information to real-life occurrences and through approaches which utilize role play, museum experiences, and interdisciplinary approaches (Johnson, 1992). The artwork created by elementary-level students can gain special significance when teachers relate content and processes to subjects in the history and social studies curricula taught in the regular classroom (Johnson, 1992). But this approach is not nearly enough. Teachers must seek to empower students to look closely at their own and others' cultural contexts and to gain an understanding of how art can provide a "voice" for each person regardless of their backgrounds or circumstances. One need only look to political situations in Bosnia, the Middle East, Northern Ireland, Tibet, and other global regions, not to mention those in our own country. It is imperative that this process occur in our classrooms at a time in civilization that demands the development of sensitivity towards and acceptance of ideas and beliefs of others in order to enable our children (and our children's children) to learn to coexist peacefully.

References

Anderson, K. (1991). Multicultural art education. *School arts, 90*(6), 10.

Banks, J. A. (1988, Spring). Approaches to multicultural curriculum reform. *Multicultural leader, 1*, 3–4.

Barbanell, P. (1994). Many views, one reality. *Journal of multicultural and cross-cultural research in art education, 12*, 26–33.

Bersson, R. (1987). Why art education is neither socially relevant nor culturally democratic: A contextual analysis. In D. Blandy & K. G. Congdon (Eds.), *Art in a democracy* (pp.78–90). New York, NY: Teachers College.

Chandra, J. (1994). Exploring cultural concepts through art: A crosscultural comparison. *Journal of multicultural and cross-cultural research in art education, 12*, 15–25.

Congdon, K. (1987). Occupational art and occupational influences on aesthetic preferences: A democratic perspective. In D. Blandy & K. G. Congdon (Eds.), *Art in a democracy* (pp.110–125). New York, NY: Teachers College.

Delacruz, E. M. (1992). Reconceptualizing art education: The movement towards multiculturalism. In A. N. Johnson (Ed.), *Art education: Elementary* (pp. 55–75). Reston, VA: National Art Education Association.

Feldman, E. B. (1980). Anthropological and historical conceptions of art curricula. *Art education, 33*(6), 6–9.

Freedman, K. J., & Hernández, F. (1998). *Curriculum, culture and art education: Comparative perspectives.* Albany, NY: State University of New York Press.

Gablik, S. (1989, January). Deconstructing aesthetics: Toward a responsible art. *New art examiner, 32–35.*

Gergen, K. J. (1991). *The saturated self.* New York, NY: Basic Books.

Hicks, L. E. (1991). The politics of difference in feminism and multicultural art education. *Journal of multicultural and cross-cultural research in art education, 9*, 11–26.

Johnson, A. N. (1992). *Art education: Elementary.* Reston, VA: National Art Education Association.

Klein, H. (1998). Beyond prejudice: Facing multiculturalism. In R. J. Saunders (Ed.), *Beyond the traditional in art: Facing a pluralistic society* (pp. 40–41). Reston, VA: National Art Education Association.

Lanier, V. (1987). Misdirections and realignments. In D. Blandy & K.G. Congdon (Eds.), *Art in a democracy* (pp. 175–183). New York, NY: Teachers College.

Lippard, L. R. (1990). *Mixed blessings.* New York, NY: Pantheon Books.

Lugones, M. (1987). Playfulness, "world"-traveling, and loving perception. *Hypatia, 2,* (20), 3–19.

Magee, L., & Rozewski, T. (1998). Strategies for deciding which cultures to include in a multicultural art curriculum. In R. J. Saunders (Ed.), *Beyond the traditional in art: Facing a pluralistic society* (pp. 73–76). Reston, VA: National Art Education Association.

McFee, J. K. (1995). Change and the cultural dimensions of art education. In R. Neperud (Ed.), *Context, content, and community in art education: Beyond postmodernism* (pp. 171–192). New York: Teachers College.

McFee, J. K. (1998). *Cultural diversity and the structure and practice of art education.* Reston, VA: National Art Education Association.

Mesa-Bains, A. (1996). Teaching students the way they learn. In S. Cahan & Z. Kocur (Eds.), *Contemporary art and multicultural education* (pp. 31–38). New York: The New Museum of Contemporary Art and Routledge.

Neperud, R. W., & Krug, D. H. (1995). People who make things: Aesthetics from the ground up. In R. Neperud (Ed.), *Context, content, and community in art education: Beyond postmodernism* (pp. 141–168). New York: Teachers College.

Nyman, A. L. (1996). Art as a key element in the development of understanding. In C. Henry (Ed.), *Middle school art: Issues of curriculum and instruction.* (pp. 29–33). Reston, VA: National Art Education Association.

Robeles de Meléndez, W., & Ostertag, V. (1997). *Teaching young children in multicultural classrooms.* Albany, NY: Delmar Publishers.

CONCLUSIONS AND FURTHER QUESTIONS

1. What is culture according to Nyman? How does this definition fit within your approach to understanding culture?

2. Nyman takes a contextualist approach to studying art from different cultures. How does this approach improve our understanding of cultures different from our own?

3. What happens if we view art from different cultures within a Western aesthetic framework?

4. Nyman identifies three goals for education. Briefly explain each of these goals and describe why each is important.

5. What is meant by the words "cultural context?"

6. How can teachers help students understand themselves as well as understand others? Why is it important for teachers to do this?

7. How should elementary teachers approach studying art from different cultures?

8. How can art provide opportunities for learning about our own and about different cultures? Why is it important to include different cultures in our curricula?

RESOURCES AND SUGGESTIONS
FOR FURTHER READING

Judith P. Butler. *Gender trouble: Feminism and the subversion of identity.* New York: Routledge, 1990.

Georgia Collins & Renee Sandell (Eds.). *Gender issues in art education: Content, contexts, and strategies.* Reston, VA: The National Art Education Association, 1996.

F. Graeme Chalmers. *Celebrating pluralism: Art, education, and cultural diversity.* Los Angeles, CA: The Getty Education Institute for the Arts, 1996.

Michelle Fine, Lois Weis, Linda C. Powell, & L. Mun Wong (Eds.). *Off white: Readings on race, power, and society.* New York; London; Routledge, 1997.

Kerry Freedman & Fernando Hernández (Eds.). *Curriculum, culture, and art education: comparative perspectives.* Albany, NY: SUNY, 1998.

Elizabeth Garber. Teaching art in the context of culture: A study in the borderlands. *Studies in Art Education, 36* (4) 1995: 218–232.

Carol Gilligan. *In a different voice: Psychological theory and women's development.* Reissue edition. Cambridge, MA: Harvard University, 1993.

Carol Gilligan, Nona P. Lyons, & Trudy J. Hanmer (Eds.). *Making connections: The relational worlds of adolescent girls at Emma Willard School.* Cambridge, MA: Harvard University Press, 1990.

Sylvia & Kenneth Marantz. *Multicultural picture books: Art for understanding others.* Worthington, OH: Linworth, 1994.

June King McFee & Rogena M. Degge. *Art, culture, and environment: A catalyst for teaching.* Dubuque, IA: Kendall/Hunt, 1980.

Robert J. Saunders (Ed.). *Beyond the traditional in art: Facing a pluralistic society.* A Report on the United States Society for Education through Art (USSEA) Symposium, 1991, Columbus. Reston, VA: National Art Education Association, 1998.

Ella Shohat (Ed.). *Talking visions: Multicultural feminism in a transnational age.* New York, Cambridge, MA: New Museum of Contemporary Art & MIT Press, 1998.

Richard Smith & Philip Wexler (Eds.). *After postmodernism: Education, politics, and identity.* London: Falmer Press, 1995.

Charleen Touchette. Multicultural strategies for aesthetic revolution in the twenty-first century. In Joanna Freuh, Cassandra L. Langer & Arlene Raven (Eds.), *New feminist criticism: Art, identity, action* (pp. 182–215). New York: HarperCollins, 1991.

1. Describe the images that come to mind when you hear the word "community." What factors determine membership in a particular community?

2. What communities do you see yourself as belonging to? Describe what makes you a part of these communities.

3. What is the relationship between personal identity and community membership?

4. How does schooling play a role in the development of community?

5. In what ways do communities remain stable and/or change over time? What factors shape the nature of a community?

6. What local art are you familiar with in your community? Do you or any of your friends, neighbors, family or community members produce art? If so, describe the types of art that they make.

Making the Familiar Strange: A Community-Based Art Education Framework

Flávia Maria Cunha Bastos

The term community-based art education (CBAE) has gained increasing popularity in the field of art education. As a broad orientation, CBAE describes art education practices that are attentive to possible relationships between the arts and communities. Numerous art educators have recommended CBAE and, simultaneously, promoted their unique understandings and interpretations of it. CBAE has been used as an umbrella term, encompassing diverse art education practices and theories aimed at a close relationship between art education and communities.

In this chapter, I propose a change-oriented CBAE framework that draws on local community art and culture. Such an approach is an outgrowth of my work with three elementary school teachers in Orleans, Indiana (Bastos, 1998). Working in an economically disadvantaged rural community, these teachers showed knowledge of how local culture, art, and heritage can empower teachers and students to revitalize their cultural identity and examine their possibilities in society. Fundamentally, this work clarified the emancipatory character that CBAE practices have the potential to assume. The community of Orleans and its art are very different from the art of Brazilian urban communities I know well. However, it seems true in both instances that the study of locally-produced art can awaken people to riches, contradictions, and meanings ingrained in their own culture.

Learning about Community and Culture

Valuing the intrinsic connections between art and daily life underpins a democratic framework for art education because it requires recognizing a variety of art practices, such as gardening, embroidery, decorative painting, or pottery, and the diverse people who make them. Within such an orientation, CBAE can focus on the art readily available in the community surrounding the school, refuting the usually "hostile reaction to a conception of art that connects it with the activities of a live creature in its environment. The hostility to association of fine art with normal processes of living is a pathetic, even tragic commentary on life as it is ordinarily lived" (Dewey, 1934/1980, p.27).

A broad-based conception of art is not pervasive. On the one hand, we continuously seek to categorize and define different types of art. On the other hand, boundaries between categories of fine and folk art have become blurred, as such labels no longer help us understand art works. Into this tension, CBAE contributes a conception of art in which several categories of art making—for example, traditional and contemporary folk art, local crafts, women's art, vernacular art, popular arts, and so on—are equally valued as intrinsic to a community's culture.

Art educator June King McFee (1991) commented that many art education approaches consider art forms hierarchically; that is, high art (i.e. drawing, painting and sculpture) as contrasted with low art (i.e. furniture making, ceramics, and sewing). Segregated views of art tend to correspond to stratified views of society (Tucker, 1996). An art education that is based on encompassing a variety of art frameworks challenges narrowly defined categorizations, inspiring participatory visions of art and society. The importance of studying art produced in local communities lies in the possibilities for students and teachers to gain insights into multiple aspects of life surrounding them, including economics, politics, education, and culture. Education, and art education in particular, would be at fault if it overlooked the importance of both (a) preparing teachers to identify, examine, and critically teach locally-produced art and (b) educating students to interpret and appreciate it. Furthermore, locally-produced art interpretation can inform participation in the local community and society at large, and perhaps fulfill Paulo Freire's educational utopia of affecting social change.

Paulo Freire

My interest in community-based art education derives from the work of the Brazilian educator Paulo Freire. His educational philosophy was firmly rooted in a commitment to liberation from domination and to fundamental social change. According to Freire, education is a political process that either reinforces an inequitable status quo through control of consciousness or seeks to change it through critical reflection. Consequently, education's ultimate mission is fulfilled in the promotion of critical consciousness, which is a referent for change.

Stressing that as conscious beings men and women are not only in the world but with the world, Freire's literacy methods are based on the notion that the act of learning to read and write starts from a very comprehensive understanding of the act of reading the world, something that human beings do before reading words (Freire, 1987). Only humans "are able to achieve the complex operation of simultaneously transforming the world by their action and grasping and expressing the world's reality in their creative language" (Freire, 1995, p.68).

Approximations between reading a text and interpreting other creative languages, such as art, are not new, but they acquire unique connotations from Freire's perspective. Critical interpretation of a written text unveils the context in which the text was produced and the life circumstances of both its authors and interpreters. Freire's broad notion of literacy connects reading and writing to an awareness of our own historical existence in the world and to our ability to question, and affect change.

Brazilian art educator Ana Mae Barbosa (1992) presented a notion of visual literacy that bears similarities to Freire's ideas. Barbosa proposed that visual literacy can lead to cultural identity and social integration. The interrelated skills of reading and producing images allow individuals to interpret their own cultures. In addition, a knowledge of history and art promotes an awareness of citizenship. By becoming knowledgeable about different art traditions, including those germane to their local communities, learners can contextually understand art forms in relationship to a society's functioning, values systems, historical influences, and economic tensions. Education, for both Barbosa and Freire, is a political process of awakening one's consciousness of belonging historically and culturally, which then leads to critical reflection and participation. In economically inequitable societies such as Brazil, art production reproduces the class conflicts of society at large. Therefore, bridging the gap between elitist and indigenous art forms, or the art of the rich and the art of the poor, depends upon understanding why and how these traditions came to be valued differently. Expanding art notions that include non-mainstream art forms are inclusive and correspond to democratic views of society.

Freire focused on the learner's position in and with the world as providing the conditions of interpretation. Therefore, attention was paid to the context surrounding the learning act. For example, the people in Freire's *culture circles*[1] were asked to survey their farms and villages and to collect the names of tools, places, and activities that were of central importance in their lives. This examination of familiar objects aroused learners' critical reflectiveness and prompted a dialogue about their life circumstances. A narrative about a culture circle described a situation during the literacy campaign in Santo Tomé and Príncipe in Africa during the 1970s. This account's vivid impact stresses the importance of knowing one's community, and alludes to the power of artistic representations for critical reflection.

> We visited a culture circle in a small fishing community called Monte Mario. They had as a generative word, the term bonito (beautiful), the name of a fish, and as a codification[2] they had an expressive design of the little town with its vegetation, typical houses, fishing boats in the sea, and a fisherman holding a bonito. The learners were looking at this codification in silence. All at once, four of them stood up as if they had agreed to do so beforehand; and they walked over to the wall where the codification was hanging. They stared at the codification closely. Then they went to the window and looked outside. They looked at each other as though they were surprised and looking again at the codification, they said: "This is Monte Mario. Monte Mario is like this and we did not know it." (Freire, 1987, p.67–8)

Through this visual codification these participants could achieve some distance from their world and they began to recognize it. Recognition when defined in this way is an act of active critical consciousness, yielding new meanings to familiar phenomena. For we never simply see: we see as, in terms of, with respect to, in the light of. These fishermen, in the light of their village's representation, recognized themselves. Such a recognition experience suggests that CBAE practices could be catalysts of change through the examination of locally-produced art. Studying art from students' own cultures, community-based art education can enhance students' abilities to understand and critically analyze their culture through the study of its art. My vision of CBAE, as inspired by Freire's pedagogy, is of an educational project committed to raising students' critical consciousness through the study of locally-produced art.

Making the Familiar Strange

Frequently, the art germane to our immediate life circumstances is invisible to us. Interpretations that enable bringing locally-produced art into a focus are powerful because they can yield critical consciousness not only about art itself, but also about the context of art production and the value systems reflected in it. Such interpretations are most needed in community contexts perceived as disenfranchised because they alter perceptions and generate recognition and ownership. *Making the familiar strange* describes that process of appreciation and is encapsulated in the following conversation with these three elementary teachers.

> Sinuous dirt roads led to Leah Morgan's country house. I followed Debbie Edwards through clouds of dust that intensified the heat. As we passed through groves of shady trees, I heard birds singing, and I framed countless snapshots of country life. Fields and barns, butterflies and flowers, hay, horses, and cows were composed and re-composed in a hundred mental photos. I wanted to discuss my latest ideas with the teachers, Leah Morgan, Debbie Edwards, and Ann Bex.

Bastos: One time I was asking Leah why she teaches local art. She said she wanted to make students aware that things Orleans people make are art and to promote a connection to their local community.

Bex: Last night when I was reading my interview, I saw that. One thing we try to do at school is to point out, "Grandma makes quilts, Grandma crochets, and that is beautiful."

Morgan: Traditionally in our Western European society, it has been taught to us that sewing, crocheting, and quilting—the things your mom does—aren't art.

Edwards: Those are made out of necessity, at one point.

Morgan: Yes and no. Necessity, but also a need to create. A need to create something beautiful that was also functional.

Bastos: I am after your personal histories. How did you become aware of the art that surrounds you in the community?

Morgan: My mom was always making something. She made all our clothes. She could make them better than we could buy them in the store. We thought it was kind of poor and disgraceful. Later on, maybe ten years ago, I met this one girl that was in my class, and she said, "I was always so jealous of you because of your clothes." I said, "Why?" "You always had the nicest things that your mom made," she explained. I was never really appreciative of them. I wanted my clothes from a store box. You could see something in a magazine and she could make it. All we ever had, were clothes that she made. Jeans and coats were the only things we bought. She would also make little stuffed animals and they were not appreciated because, in those days, people wanted store-bought things. It was a different age. If it was homemade it wasn't good, store-bought was better. But she was always making something, which I did not consider art then, whereas now, it was art.

Bastos: When did you begin considering that art? What happened?

Morgan: Well, people would say, "You are so artistic, where did you get that from?" "Well, I don't know," I would answer.

Bex: Now you know.

Morgan: Maybe in the last ten or fifteen years, as I got older, I considered her making of things more of a creative process. From taking classes at the university too, I am broadening the spectrum of what art is. (Bastos, 1998, pp. 1–3)

Interpretation is a fundamental aspect of change-oriented CBAE. It is the process that enables re-visiting the art that is important to a community. The Indiana teachers participating in this conversation, similarly to Monte Mario's fishermen, were somewhat oblivious to the community, art, and culture surrounding the school. Because of its familiarity, and because of its contradictions, everyday life is largely invisible to those who live it. Erickson (1986), stressing the value of attending to everyday phenomena, invited educators to "make the familiar strange," strange enough to be noticed (p. 121).

Erickson's expression became emblematic of the myriad of interpretative processes associated with community-based art interpretation. The notion of *making the familiar strange* can metaphorically describe the process by which members of a community gain insight about their own culture through the examination of locally-produced art.

By surveying and analyzing phenomena and objects indigenous to their communities' culture, the fisherman and the teachers engaged in a critical activity. *Making the familiar strange* describes interpretation performed by insiders and is a first step towards a growing awareness of the cultural identity that each of us holds. It invites historical and political engagement, and reflectiveness upon the possibilities for change. It can lead to understanding human authorship in people's cultures and the value systems that are supportive of those authorship choices (Hamblen, 1990). Furthermore, as a framework, *making the familiar strange* can add to current art and education discourses in its potential to deal with gender, social class, and ethnicity issues as they affect communities.

Multicultural Education and Art Education Developments Informing CBAE

While the influence of multicultural education in many art education practices is widely discussed, relationships between multiculturalism and CBAE development require further examination. CBAE can be understood as an outgrowth of multicultural art education concerns and practices. As multicultural art education practices seek to respect students' heritages and traditions, creating a diverse and equitable classroom, community-based art education draws on local art, culture, and experiences to design curricula. In its various forms, CBAE has proposed concrete ways to deal with the relationship among art, schools, and communities. Similar to the various existing orientations to multicultural education, there are a variety of approaches to CBAE that are dependent on different educational orientations. More specifically, each teacher's CBAE orientation is shaped by his or her views of art, culture, and community (see Figure 5.1).

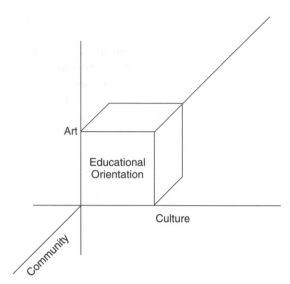

Figure 5.1 CBAE's core aspects: Community, culture, and art.

Working with the three Orleans's teachers I mentioned earlier, it became clear that CBAE practices enacted in real classrooms represented a different set of priorities, views, and concerns. In order to understand these variations I combined Sleeter and Grant's (1994) five approaches to multicultural education[3] and Marché's (1998) three orientations to CBAE practice[4] in a framework (see Figure 5.2). The five orientations to multicultural education describe increasingly encompassing ways to deal with diversity and equity issues in education, which parallel the expanding CBAE orientations of (a) taking from (←), (b) learning about (→), and (c) acting upon (↔) communities.

Sleeter and Grant's discussion of the five approaches to multicultural education revealed educational practices presented in an expanding fashion, in which ideas, concepts, and practices of previous approaches were assimilated, modified, or rearranged in the next approach presented. Similarly, the three orientations proposed by Marché gradually built upon each other. For example, to act upon the community, teachers and students need to have learned about the community previously and to have taken information from the community in order to understand it.

In fact, the Orleans teachers I came to know represented three distinct educational orientations. None of them engaged in change-oriented CBAE practices. Although I did not find teachers who subscribed to social reconstruction ideals, as represented by Paulo Freire, one teacher's views and classroom practices suggested directions in which CBAE practices can develop. Leah Morgan offered such an inspiration because not only has she made the

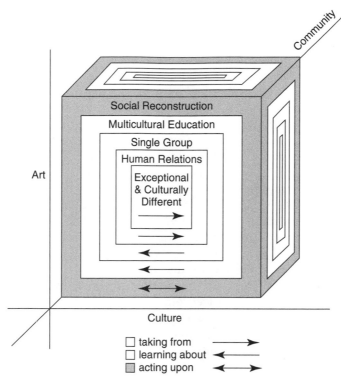

Figure 5.2 Conceptual framework.

familiar strange, but also systematically sought to engage students in a similar process. Leah Morgan's art teaching is emblematic of the potential re-signifying connections between school and communities through local art.

Leah Morgan: A Local Art Teacher

Born in Cadiz, Kentucky, Leah Morgan has lived in Indiana most of her life. She lived and attended school in Orleans. A pen and ink drawing of the old grade school building hung behind her desk, a modest, small, hand-colored drawing. "That was my first pen and ink," said Morgan (personal communication, February 4, 1997). The new Orleans Elementary School building was her other drawing on the wall. Leah Morgan's teaching targeted realistic goals:

> I don't see myself producing artists. I don't see that as my goal here in this community. It's not a high art community, where there are a lot of artists around. And there are not a lot of job opportunities for these kids, even if they are artists in this community. . . . I don't want them to think that just certain people can

do [art]. . . . I just want them to be willing to try new things. (Personal communication, February 4, 1997)

Opening the School to Local Artists

Morgan's knowledge of local artists' networks sprang from her intimate connection to the community. Bringing local artists to the school, she invited a
woodburning artist, Nancy Eagan, to conduct a three-day workshop for art
students. Orleans's newspaper, the *Progress Examiner*, featured Eagan's photograph on the front page of the February 21, 1996 issue. As a result, Eagan felt
praised and recognized by students and community. "Even my son who is
good at woodburning, well, even my son was surprised to learn something
new from me. There was a lot about woodburning he didn't know" (N. Eagan,
personal communication, June 21, 1997).

According to Morgan, although students enjoy learning about local art,
"It is hard to get the local people to come in." The relationship between local
artists and school was marked by distance. When she invited community
artists, parents in most cases, she frequently listened to excuses, "I'm not really trained in this, and I don't feel comfortable speaking in front of people."
She interpreted their refusals as fear of criticism or of appearing uneducated:
"They are afraid their work isn't good enough." They may feel uncomfortable,
she pondered, because "they think I am an art authority and I am going to
look down on them." However, the gap between local artists and school van-
ished as soon as artists came in and felt comfortable. "They say, 'Well, I won't
be able to talk for one hour. I might be able to talk five or ten minutes.' Then
they get started, and the kids ask questions, and they talk a lot longer"
(L. Morgan, personal communication, February 4, 1997).

Bridging Art and Community

Morgan's teaching about community art was motivated by her students' interests in combination with locally available resources. A unit based on a local
furniture factory grew out of a fifth-grader's interest in industrial design:

> He made a chair out of *papier-maché*. I was impressed with the chair. Since we
> have a chair factory and one of the students' parents is management, I talked to
> him about developing something. The Monroe County School Corporation had
> a grant open. It was a School-to-Work grant, distributed through the vocational
> school in Bedford. It was a special grant to tie together classroom work for mid-
> dle school students to actual jobs and occupations. You could work with a busi-
> ness, or community service, or something else getting kids into careers. So, we
> developed the unit from there. (Personal communication, February 4, 1997)

Exposing students to a well-established business in the community, Morgan
explained that "a high percentage of students may work there" (personal com-

munication, February 4, 1997). The $500 grant proposal described the central aspects of the project:

> One of the main industries in our community is Paoli Chair and Desk Company. Many people in our community work at this manufacturing plant. This includes the relatives of several of our students. . . . The intent of our project is to introduce sixth grade students to thinking about the chair as an art form, a piece of furniture, a product, and an occupation. . . . The target outcome will be problem-solving by students in groups or teams to create a chair design and model chair of their own. We hope this project will meet the needs of Paoli, Inc. by sharing their need for employees with our students and challenging them to seek career choices. This project will be ongoing and repeated with each sixth grade annually. . . . Through photo displays and newspaper articles, we will let our school and community know the value and purpose of this project. Finished student chair designs and models will be displayed in our school, community, and at the chair factory. (L. Morgan, grant proposal, December 4, 1996)

As part of the activities, Janet Slaughter, responsible for personnel at the factory, visited the school. She gave students practical information about completing job application forms, dressing code, interviewing, and invited students to participate in a simulated job interview.

> *Slaughter:* Have you ever worked with wood? Did some drafting, something like that?
> *Interviewee:* [Confidently] We made a chair in art. (Classroom observation, February 4, 1997)

Spontaneously, this student expressed that art projects were fully appreciated and perceived as real-life experiences. The students' chairs merged functional and artistic concerns. By making and exhibiting chairs, students experienced first-hand connections between art and functional objects. Morgan's goal to raise students' awareness of connections between art knowledge and the job market available in Orleans was achieved. As she suggested, more than creating artists, Morgan developed art education practices that had the potential to revitalize as well as to create new links between school and community through art.

Morgan's CBAE Practice

Morgan's views and understanding of Orleans local arts were grounded in her community membership. A sensibility to locally-produced art grew out of her close association and involvement with the community. In addition, Morgan's art training and practice broadened her definition of art, allowing her to review previous tenets. Not only knowledgeable about local culture, art, and history, she was committed to promoting students' awareness of locally-developed art activities and connections between art and community.

The furniture making project and Nancy Eagan's woodburning workshop illustrate Morgan's attempts at contextually meaningful art teaching. Embedded in these teaching practices was a concern for developing art curricula
based on locally-produced art. Therefore, implicitly, Morgan subscribed to
CBAE orientations that focused on acting upon communities. However, by
targeting art experiences directed to practical goals, she did not explore
locally-produced art's role in questioning a community's value systems,
socio-economic structure, or institutions.

Morgan's locally-produced art teaching could more directly and specifically discuss the status of rural Midwestern art as compared to fine art. Such a
discussion could impact students' understanding of rural communities' lower
status and inform action. Celebrating and valuing local art is an important aspect of CBAE that becomes even more powerful if it tries to unveil the mechanisms by which local art came to be under-appreciated. Schools, museums,
universities, local politics, and business influence local art, creating a context
that favors or hinders local art development. Morgan's own awareness of local
art was indebted to her university education. Therefore, calling attention to
locally-produced art, whether a forgotten quilt, a beautifully landscaped garden, or hay figures in the field can awaken people to their heritages and traditions, should be accompanied by an analysis of the contextual factors, value
systems, and institutions impacting the community.

Morgan valued and celebrated the community as it existed and did not
make use of art practice to critically examine it. Multicultural education,
rather than social-reconstruction tenets, informed her opening the fine arts
canon to honor Orleans artistic diversity (Katter, 1995). A common criticism
of multicultural education is teachers' avoidance of addressing structural and
social issues (Sleeter and Grant, 1994). A change-oriented CBAE orientation
combines art learning with unveiling the dynamics of power in a community.
In order to enact change-oriented CBAE practices, Morgan could explore the
social, political, and structural aspects at play in the local community and art.
Such development would depend on a view of education that, similarly to
Paulo Freire's, posits education as a political act. Accordingly, art education
would seek to understand the local people, their art and culture, and the possibilities available to them.

At this point, the outcomes of change-oriented CBAE projects in a community such as Orleans are merely conjectural. However, Morgan indicated
that revitalizing the links between schools and communities through local art
is not only meaningful to students and community, but it is also a required
step towards social-reconstruction practices. Accordingly, locally-produced art
study is at the core of educational practices that value community participation. Local art carries the seeds and traditions of a community, creates and
reflects contradictions and controversies, and constantly alludes to renewal
and change. Therefore, it seems reasonable to believe that through local art
study, students and teachers can make the familiar strange—strange enough to

be appreciated, criticized, and transformed. This renewed connection would be desirable not only in Orleans, Indiana, but certainly in the many communities within which we participate.

Conclusions

Originally conceived as an emancipatory tool for Brazilian peasants, Freire's social reconstruction ideas can prove meaningful to other communities. Encompassing in nature, ambitious in goals, and visionary in scope, Freire's educational utopia has inspired numerous educational projects. It followed from my heritage and experiences to draw on Paulo Freire to propose a framework for CBAE practice. The CBAE orientation presented in this chapter encompasses many previous art education and multicultural education developments. Intended as a persuasion, this framework posits the value of locally-produced art study and consideration for the myriad of social and cultural relationships enacted within a community as two sound pillars of contemporary art education development. I hope this proposition inspires further developments.

References

Barbosa, A. M. (1992, August). *The role of art education in the cultural and artistic development of the individual: Developing artistic and creative skills.* Paper presented at the UNESCO International Conference on Education, Geneva, Switzerland.

Bastos, F. M. C. (1998). *Making the familiar strange: Teachers' interpretations of community art.* Unpublished doctoral dissertation, Indiana University, Bloomington.

Dewey, J. (1980). *Art as experience.* New York: Perigee. (Original work published in 1934).

Erickson, M. (1986). Qualitative methods in research on teaching. In M. C. Wittrock (Ed.), *Handbook of research on teaching* (3rd ed.) (pp. 119–161). New York: Macmillan.

Freire, P. (1987). *Literacy: Reading the word and the world.* South Hadley, MA: Bergin & Garvey.

Freire, P. (1995). *Pedagogy of the oppressed.* New York: Continuum.

Hamblen, K. (1990). Local art knowledge: A basis for rethinking the art curriculum. *Arts and Learning Research, 8* (1), 66–79.

Katter, E. (1995). Multicultural connections: The craft community. *Art Education, 48*(1), 8–13.

Marché, T. (1998). Looking outward, looking in: Community in art education. *Art Education, 51* (3), 6–13.

McFee, J. K. (1991). Art education progress: A field of dichotomies or a network of mutual support. *Studies in Art Education, 32*(2), 70–82.

Sleeter, C. E., & Grant, C. A. (1994). *Making choices for a multicultural education: Five approaches to race, class, and gender.* Columbus, OH: Merril.

Tucker, M. (1996). *A labor of love.* New York: The New Museum of Contemporary Art.

Endnotes

1. *Culture circles* refer to the learning groups central to Freire's pedagogy; that is, a group of adults who are learning to read and write. The *circle* indexes the horizontal relationship between the teacher and students.
2. *Codifications* are part of Freire's methodology; most commonly they are a visual representation of the learners' existential situation. The codification functions as the knowable object mediating knowing subjects and the act of learning.
3. Sleeter and Grant's five approaches to multicultural education are (a) Teaching the exceptional and culturally different; primarily adopted by mainstream teachers who take their backgrounds and culture for granted and are trying to deal with backgrounds and cultures they view as different. (b) Human relations involve practices that focus on developing positive interactions between individuals and groups. (c) Single-group studies pay attention to a selected group, for example women, African Americans, people of the working class. (d) Multicultural education describes policies and practices that affirm human similarities and differences related to gender, race, class, disability, and so on. (e) Multicultural and social reconstructionist education addresses issues of structural inequality among diverse groups in society.
4. Marché's three CBAE orientations are based on the type relationship between school and community. (a) Taking from (←) describes an exploitative, hunting and gathering, interaction in which community is decontextualized to serve educational goals. (b) Learning about (→) involves studying and investigating the community to know its historical origins, arts, occupations, and celebrations. (c) Acting upon (↔) communities expands beyond human contexts to include the natural environment, students become social activists and interact with the community to understand it and preserve it.

CONCLUSIONS AND FURTHER QUESTIONS

1. In this chapter Bastos argues for "making the familiar strange." Explain what she means by this statement. Have you ever had an experience in which the familiar was made strange? If so, what did you learn through this?
2. How does Bastos's Community-Based Art Education (CBAE) approach expand upon the Discipline-Based Art Education (DBAE) approach to art criticism, aesthetics, and art history? Did your understanding of what art is change after reading this chapter?
3. What makes a CBAE approach to art a critical one? Why should we be interested in using critical approaches in our classrooms? How is critical activity instigated in a community-based approach to art education?
4. What would happen if local art were only considered by a formalist approach?
5. How can we expand traditional approaches to art teaching in order to enact a change-oriented practice?

6. Why are art educators making a call for change in the way we view and teach art?
7. Using the grant proposal in the chapter as a potential starting point, what kinds of connections can be made integrating community-based art education into other subject areas?
8. What do you want children to learn from locally-produced art? What does Bastos see as its potential?

RESOURCES AND SUGGESTIONS
FOR FURTHER READING

Alan W. Barnett. *Community murals: The people's art.* Philadelphia, PA: New York: Art Alliance Press; Cornwall Books, 1984.

Carol Becker (Ed.). *The subversive imagination: Artists, society, and social responsibility.* New York: Routledge, 1994.

Eva Cockcroft, John Weber, & Jim Cockcroft. *Toward a people's art: The contemporary mural movement.* New York: Dutton, 1977.

Trevor J. Fairbrother. *In and out of place: Contemporary art and the American social landscape.* Boston, MA: Museum of Fine Arts, 1993.

Nina Felshin (Ed.). *But is it art? The spirit of art as activism.* Seattle, WA: Bay Press, 1994.

Rita L. Irwin & Anna M. Kindler (Eds.). *Beyond the school: Community and institutional partnerships in art education.* Reston, VA: National Art Education Association, 1999.

Mary Jane Jacob. *Culture in action: A public art program of Sculpture Chicago.* Seattle, WA: Bay Press, 1995.

Suzanne Lacy (Ed.). *Mapping the terrain: New genre public art.* Seattle, WA: Bay Press, 1994.

Lucy R. Lippard. *Lure of the local: Senses of place in a multicentered society.* New York: New Press, 1998.

Ronald W. Neperud (Ed.). *Context, content, and community in art education: Beyond postmodernism.* New York: Teachers College Press, 1995.

Jane Remer. *Beyond enrichment: Building effective arts partnerships with schools and their communities.* New York: ACA Books, 1996.

Lynda H. Schneekloth & Robert G. Shibley. *Placemaking: The art and practice of building communities.* New York: Wiley, 1995.

CHAPTER 6
QUESTIONS AND EXPLORATIONS

1. Describe your most recent visit to a museum or gallery. What type of museum or gallery was it? Why did you decide to go to it? How long did your visit last? How did you feel when you entered the museum or gallery? Why did you feel this way? What was your favorite part of the museum or gallery?

2. What would you like to have had included as a part of your visit to the gallery or museum? How would this have added to your visit?

3. Name all of the galleries and museums within commuting distance of your home or school. If there is a museum in the town where you live, have you ever visited it? Why or why not?

4. What kinds of activities are available for the public at these galleries or museums? For school groups? If you have you ever attended any of these activities briefly describe your experience.

5. Describe the types of school experiences that you have had with galleries and museums. Would you think of taking your students on such a visit? Why or why not? What educational benefits might students receive from visiting a gallery or museum as a part of their elementary education?

There's More To It Than Just Looking: The Art Museum as an Integrated Learning Environment

Debra Attenborough

What if imagination and art are not frosting at all, but the fountainhead of human experience? What if our logic and science derive from art forms and are fundamentally dependent on them rather than art being merely a decoration for our work when science and logic have produced it." (Rollo May (1975). The courage to create. In Roger Clark's *Art education: A Canadian perspective* (1994), (p. 150).

Educators who are working within an art gallery or museum setting are continually striving to re-define not only their own concepts of the arts and arts education but also the role of arts education as it relates to the gallery/

museum and the learner within and outside of the school system. In *Art and Visual Perception* (1974), Arnheim gives us a view of art and mind that puts art at the heart of the educational process. He discusses how perception itself is a cognitive event and encourages us to realize that the creation of images in any medium requires skilled reasoning, invention, and imagination. Arnheim suggests that the senses play a crucial role in our cognitive life and that the arts; visual art, music, dance, drama, are "our culture's most powerful means for making life in its particulars vivid" (Eisner's forward in Arnheim's *Thoughts on Art Education*, 1989, p. 6). In this century, theorists in all areas of education, have realized the importance of seeing the whole picture, rather than examining each aspect of education as a separate entity. However, incorporating this into the traditional models of the nature of art galleries and museums is a relatively new phenomenon.

In this chapter I examine the role of education in traditional art galleries/museums and discuss why these existing roles no longer function in socially relevant ways. In addition, I would like to introduce some of the ways that the Niagara Falls Art Gallery and Rodman Hall Arts Centre in southern Ontario have tried to re-define what education should be in an art gallery/ museum and the relationship that the art gallery and museum can, and I would suggest should, have with the local community, in particular with the schools.

Education in the art gallery/museum has developed in some ways, apart from the ways early museums were established and run. "Early museum collections, were not intended for public display; they simply reflected the personal collecting interests of individuals. In 1845 the British 'Museum Act' permitted town councils to use public funds to establish and maintain museums," (Grinder and McCoy, 1985, p.11). There was a distinct change in the concept of American museums when artist Charles Wilson Peale founded one of the earliest museums in North America; his idea was to present "universal knowledge" and through this presentation to educate a general public (Grinder and McCoy, 1985). According to Alexander (1979), the American Association of Museums has defined [a museum as an] "organized and permanent non-profit institution, essentially educational or aesthetic in purpose, with professional staff, which owns and utilizes tangible objects, cares for them, and exhibits them to the public" (p. 5). However, this limited definition does not necessarily fit in with what we now realize are the varied kinds of museums, and new definitions are constantly being developed. Nor does it address the concept of education within the museum setting. It must also be very clear that there are a number of different kinds of museums, for example: the art museum, the natural history museum, the museum of science and technology, the history museum, the planetarium, botanical gardens and zoos. Each of these areas incorporate basic tenets of what make a museum (according to Alexander, 1979); that is, collection, conservation, research, and exhibition. Although introduced by Peale in 1786, education and interpretation in museums, particularly art museums, are basically products of the twentieth century.

The primary functions of the traditional art gallery/museum were originally those of collecting, preserving, and displaying. This being the case we must ask, how does education fit into this definition? Many of those who run museums have never fully agreed on what museums/galleries should teach, if they should teach at all, to whom they should teach, and for what ends? These questions are still evident although the importance of education is generally acknowledged in galleries and museums. Museum educator Elizabeth Vallance (1994) suggests that the function of art museums is to serve as a bridge or translator between art and the public. She continues to promote questions in education journals such as: "What should art museums be doing in their education programs?" and "what is the goal of art?" (p. 236). There are many answers to these questions depending on where you are located theoretically and also whether you are in the area of education within the gallery/museum setting or whether you are in a curatorial capacity. Whatever answers we give to these questions there is no doubt that these institutions have always included educational programming in some limited form or another, almost from the time they were established.

The idea of the museum as an agent of education has been pervasive, even though there continues to be an obvious tension between the original tenets of collecting and those of education. As an educator working in an art gallery/museum setting I often hear of curators who fear for the artwork by having too many people in the gallery space, or refuse to include expanded explanations of difficult artwork. According to Tomkins (1970), a basic early premise of educational activity common in art galleries/museums was, "the diffusion of a knowledge of art in its higher forms of beauty would tend directly to humanize, to educate and refine a practical and laborious people" (p. 16).

As a result of societal forces there has occurred a shift in museum policy to include more educational services and a greater involvement of the public. Change happened for a number of reasons: first, there is an emphasis on education in our society as a whole in this century; and second, there is a need for financial support from an ever-powerful public. This is particularly apparent in the cash-strapped museums of the 1990s. Real change in museum policy towards recognizing the importance of education occurred in the 1960s and 1970s when museums and galleries became more accessible and began to introduce educational programming through a variety of ways, including lectures, labels, catalogues, guided tours, and exhibitions which involved visitors both physically and intellectually. Grinder and McCoy (1985) describe this phenomenon as the "democratization of museums" (p. 15).

The restrictions on education departments and the effective influence of these educational areas in art galleries/museums are however, still very limited, even though education has proven successful both in terms of raising museum attendance and in bringing financial benefits to museums and galleries. Despite these successes the focus on the traditional aspects of collection and display are still obvious as we move into the new millennium. There is still a distinct division and often friction between curatorial and education departments in most art galleries, which makes the innovations happening at the two southern Ontario art galleries/museums previously mentioned all the more valuable.

The premise for art-based integrated learning is that all aspects of life are linked together through art. It is disruptive to disassociate art from other subject areas in life and in schooling. Integration of the arts with other disciplines is paramount, and art becomes the cement to re-form life into a unified whole. The arts are often not included in discussions of "what matters most" and "core knowledge" in education. Educator Maxine Greene argues, "it is difficult to accept a call for excellent teaching and 'teaching for America's future' that pays no heed to the awakenings the arts make possible. And the arts, of all forms, may awaken teachers-to-be from the 'anesthetic'" (Cornett, 1999, p. 2).

Throughout her writing in the 1990s, Greene has focused on the relevance of creativity, the arts, and the imagination. She suggests that the imagination is a means through which we can assemble a coherent world, and that through imagination and creativity (arts) we are able to give credence to alternative realities. Through Greene's assertions, we can see that the arts, in general, can provide a vast range of possibilities, an opening up of options. Using art as the basis for learning allows us, through arts experiences of our own, to broaden our horizons. According to Greene (1995) "at the very least, participatory involvement with the many forms of art can enable us to see more in our experience, to hear more on normally unheard frequencies, to become conscious of what daily routines have obscured, what habit and convention have suppressed" (p. 123). Elliott Eisner (1972) introduced similar ideas in *Educating Artistic Vision*, when he suggested that the prime value of the arts in education lies in the unique contribution the arts make to an individual's experience with and understanding of the world.

As Cornett (1999) notes, the J. Paul Getty Foundation has been a great advocate for the arts in the schools. In *The Power of Arts to Transform Education* (1993) the Foundation advocates that,

> The arts contribute to an overall culture of excellence in a school. They are an effective means of connecting children to each other and helping them gain an understanding of the creators who preceded them. They provide schools with a ready way to formulate relationships across and among traditional disciplines and to connect ideas and notice patterns. Works of art provide effective means for linking information in history and social studies, mathematics, science and geography, opening lines of inquiry, revealing that art, like life, is lived in a complex world not easily defined in discrete subjects. (p. 2)

The Getty has not only advocated for the arts in the schools, but in fact has gone to great lengths to encourage the acknowledgment of the arts in everyday life. This became an important aspect to my own practice as an arts educator.

I began my tenure in a small community arts centre in St. Catharines, Ontario, at Rodman Hall Arts Centre in 1981.[1] My focus was two-fold: to dispel the elitist atmosphere of the gallery setting and to bring the community into the gallery and create a place where people would feel comfortable and free to experience the arts in a variety of ways. I began this by introducing new programming into the gallery. This programming not only incorporated the traditional art classes for children and adults but it also included classes in yoga, tai chi, and ballroom dance among others. In 1995, attendance of traditional education programs was well under 1,000. In 1999, the number of adult participants from the community in Rodman Hall's variety of programmes was close to 20,000. Over 6,000 children attended children's classes (apart from school programming) in 1999. The elevated attendance is not only indication of the success of the programme, it is also apparent in the positive comments and feedback which I receive from people who now feel as though the art gallery is an important aspect of their lives. As these programmes developed successfully, my focus turned to the improvement of the school programs, and I was influenced by the fine work being produced in this area at the Niagara Falls Art Gallery, which is also located in southern Ontario.

The basis for the concepts presented at Rodman Hall and the Niagara Falls Art Gallery originated through the Ontario Ministry of Education and Training's 1993 regulatory document, *The Common Curriculum, Grades 1–9*, that envisioned integrated subject areas:

> An integrated curriculum also has the potential to alleviate the problems of curriculum overload and fragmentation. As society changes and the frontiers of knowledge expand, the curriculum is under pressure to accommodate new material. A curriculum organized along traditional lines becomes a constantly expanding body of knowledge that must somehow be fitted into a finite school day. By contrast, a curriculum that focuses on the relationships between subjects promotes learning that applies to several disciplines at the same time, and may allow teachers to streamline curriculum. (Ontario Ministry of Education and Training, 1993, p. 2)

The value of using art as the beginning for the integration of other subjects creates an atmosphere of acceptance, experimentation, and imagination. "To lack an education in the arts is to be profoundly disconnected from our history, from beauty, from other cultures, and from other forms of expression" according to Cornett (1999, p. 2). This became a starting point as I began organizing school programming that centered on the visual arts as integrated with a variety of other subjects in conjunction with exhibitions that were on display. The initiating factor was an exhibition of artwork by Dutch artist M.C. Escher (1898–1972) that Rodman Hall received from the National Gallery of Canada in 1997. In conjunction with this exhibition I developed a series of school workshop programs on Mathematics and Visual Art, with

Dr. Eric Muller, a mathematician at Brock University in St. Catharines. The response from the school board was phenomenal. Teachers were excited by the possibilities offered by these integrated workshops and during the two-month period the exhibition was on display the gallery was full of school children. These workshops incorporated integrating mathematics and visual arts for children from kindergarten through higher levels of high school. For younger children we worked with tangrams and special puzzles that were then translated into art objects. As the grade levels progressed, workshops included the introduction of making a set of tangrams, mobius strips, shape and color puzzles, and exercises working with art objects, which encompassed mathematical concepts such as area and perimeter. For higher-level grades, we used a number of concepts including working with wooden blocks and one, two, and three-point perspective in art.

At the same time the Niagara Falls Art Gallery was developing what they termed ABIL, or Art Based Integrated Learning, a series of workshops using art as the vehicle to explore the various disciplines. This cross-curriculum application of art concepts, tools and techniques not only helps participants gain fundamental skills and competence in visual art but was also the basis that assisted the learner with understanding the concepts, tools and techniques of the other subjects being studied. The Niagara Falls Art Gallery developed two different approaches in their workshop programs. The first was aimed at those teachers who looked at art as a separate discipline. In other words, teachers whose personal instructing method did little in the way of integrating art with the other subjects. They identified the following three reasons why art should be separated from the other disciplines: a teacher may have no art background, may follow the Ontario curriculum verbatim, or may take the traditional view that art has little or no relationship with any of the other disciplines.

The second approach was aimed at teachers who naturally integrate the various disciplines in their teaching style. For these teachers, the gallery offered a number of components that the teacher could choose from that integrated the student's work with what was being studied in the other subject areas. For example, the workshops in *Bugged By Insects* examined art concepts and techniques such as manipulation of media to create textures, but they also included items such as examination of fractions (mathematics), as well as camouflage and adaptation to the environment (science) (Smylski, 2000, p. 1).

The original concept behind these developments was discussed in arts education literature as early as the 1950s, however it was not until the 1990s that we actually saw some evidence of this thought in practice. It is apparent in the development of curriculum theory that there was a definitive shift of perception from the 1960s through to contemporary ideas. This is particularly evident in the work of Jerome Bruner, particularly in *The Process of Education* (1960). Throughout the past four decades, Bruner has acknowledged the changing field of educational theory. We have noticed a change from the Tylerian (1949) model of curriculum based on a linear evolution of organizing principles and structures to a more post-modern, integrated model of what curriculum should look like. Interestingly, educational discourse has picked up on these changing theories at a much faster rate then the gallery/museum world. This shift is evident in the idea of a holistic look at education, and the integration of many subjects.

Newsom and Silver (1978) suggest that,

> [N]on-artistic disciplines have discovered unexplored territories in the visual arts and have revealed the inherent capability of the visual arts to be all things to all disciplines, in short, it can well be argued that the study of art is the most fruitful interdisciplinary study available to the academic world at all levels from elementary through graduate school. (p. 23)

The curriculum should be concerned with a variety of life experiences for the child to find the information relevant, and each life experience has a visual aspect to it and can, therefore, be related to art in some way. From infancy we begin to learn with our senses, for those of us with the sense of sight, visual learning is a primary source of our cognitive life. We begin to make associations and learn new concepts through sight and images. Throughout our lives we are bombarded with visual images through the media as well as from many other sources. Arts specialists have always known that the arts provide alternative ways of knowing that occur apart from language, which entail teaching with, about, in, and through the arts (Cornett, 1999 p. 5).

Using art as one springboard for integrating the subjects that children will be exposed to during their school life will, necessarily, make the experiences of learning much more relevant. Rudolf Arnheim (1989), in *Thoughts on Art Education*, suggested that,

> Attention to the whole and to its constituent qualities is one of the important lessons the arts can teach. The fragmentation of content in forms that do not yield for the child a feeling for the whole are not likely to be particularly meaningful. Too much of the teaching and curricula in our schools has this disembodied, fragmented character. (p. 5)

Art is a way of breaching or bridging this kind of fragmentation.

Few changes take place in human behavior, including those changes that we call learning, purely on a thinking level. Perceptions and emotions set their own conditions for the process of change. In turn, perceptions and emotions are the stuff from which the arts are made, and are basic to creative behavior (Madeja, 1973). In my experience, hands-on, interactive art experiences can help people to see relationships and that all learners are capable of creative activities, not just those born with talent. There is more attention paid in galleries and museums to what Glaser and Zenetou (1994) call "shared cultural knowledge" and it's role in a pluralistic society. They also suggest that "museums should be further appreciated as repositories for this 'core knowledge' at a time when information has become overwhelmingly complex and standards for excellence have become diffuse" (p. 119).

Art is usually taught in North America as something rather precious, separate from education and from life. For example, we often see art as the Friday afternoon activity at a given school, or the reward for good behavior in other subjects. Pear Cohen and Straus Gainer (1976) suggest that rather than being separate, art is an integral part of life and can act as glue, enriching and binding together many aspects of human experience.

Many teachers feel that their personal strengths in education do not lay in the arts and as a result of this, they either ignore art or turn to the experts within their own community. It is in this role that the art gallery/museum can best serve the needs of their local schools. The visual arts can then provide both unconscious, informal, and formal ways of knowing through art.

The Niagara Falls Art Gallery and Rodman Hall Arts Centre each present a series of visual arts workshops, beginning at the pre-school level and continuing through to the end of high school. These workshops include a program of half-day and full-day hands-on workshops in drawing, painting, cartooning, sculpture, drama, music, mathematics, the environment, history, photography, science, and archaeology. All of these lessons are planned using the arts as both learning tools and unit centres. Teachers can choose workshops from a pre-arranged listing or request a specific consultation with education staff to produce a specialized workshop that is relevant to their unit of study. At each gallery the arts workshops are divided into levels with core and supplemental classes focused around the new curriculum areas, using art as the basis to teach any subject. Core and supplemental workshops are designed to support and supplement specific units of study in the classroom while students learn the basic art concepts and techniques.

One example from Rodman Hall's workshop program was the development of the ancient civilizations unit, centered on an Egyptian exhibition on loan to Rodman Hall from the Royal Ontario Museum in Toronto during the spring of 2000. This series of workshops was created based on the Grade 5 Ontario curriculum and therefore programming was centered on that particular age group. The educators at Rodman Hall developed a number of workshops that integrate history (the variety of Egyptian objects in the display) with art (the hands-on making of objects such as canopic jars out of clay, or mummies out of plaster casting), mathematics and engineering (the development and measuring of pyramids), language (hieroglyphs and the stories of ancient Egypt), family life, religion and funerary practices. In addition to the school-based workshop program, educational hands-on areas, similar to a discovery room in a children's museum, were set up where students could experience one-on-one, outside of the school setting, a variety of related activities such as: wrapping a mummy; applying Egyptian make-up, jewelry, headpieces and clothing; creating hieroglyphic cartouches; creating stone carving of Egyptian origin into plasticine and many other participatory activities. The purpose of a combination of all of these activity centres was to incorporate

the historical art and artifacts into a relevant and enriching personal experience for each student.

The importance of art as the primary agent through which students explore and comprehend language, history, mathematics, science, personal and
social studies in order to provide the opportunity to make connections is the
basis for these programs. Cornett (1999) suggests that,

> The arts play an integral role in integrating wholes and parts, and it is how liter-
> ature, visual art, drama, dance and music interact with science, social studies,
> math, and the language arts to support learning about important life skills, con-
> cepts, and themes that is the goal of integration. Traditional lines become mud-
> died in integrating the arts. Is it art or science as a child mixes color and discovers
> that blue and yellow make green? (p. 40)

The purpose of these innovative, non-traditional art education programs is to
present visual arts as one vehicle through which to explore and understand a
variety of other subject areas in the school curriculum. In addition they foster
and encourage the relationship between community arts organizations and
the school systems within a given community. Originally, both the Niagara
Falls Art Gallery and Rodman Hall Arts Centre offered a limited variety of programs. This was necessarily expanded upon, first by Niagara Falls, then by
Rodman Hall in an effort to work with the needs of teachers and to encompass aspects of the school curriculum into the programming. Prompted by the
community, both Niagara Peninsula galleries sought to develop and pursue a
number of these new initiatives.

The success of these programs is evident in the responses by the education community, and from schools and teachers in particular. For example, in
the1999–2000 school year the Niagara Falls Art Gallery hosted over 18,000
school children (with 6,000 on a waiting list), and Rodman Hall Arts Centre
hosted between 11,500 and 12,000 students (again with an extremely long
waiting list).

In Ontario, the curriculum is swiftly moving away from the Common
Curriculum of integrated learning made accessible during the mid-1990s to a
more discipline based focus with considerably less emphasis on integration.
Teachers find it necessary to bring in outside specialists to enhance the learning experience for students. It is in this role that we have found the programmes that we are presenting to be most beneficial.

What the most recent research in both curriculum theory and contemporary art education suggests is that students learn effectively when they are
engaged by rich and meaningful experiences. Using art as the basis for learning enables students to draw on their own past experiences to enrich their understanding of not only other subjects but also the connections that are
apparent throughout life itself.

It is important for educators to recognize the community resources that are available to them in their local gallery and/or museum. Teachers can make these connections on a number of levels. First, they can access their local or regional art gallery or museum in the traditional way. That is, to visit on a yearly, or bi-yearly basis and participate in whatever programming may be available through that institution. The second and more vital way of accessing this resource is to form a partnership with the educational staff of these organizations. This can be seen as moving away from the traditional focus of the gallery and museum as a place to exhibit artworks and artifacts and of education simply as a vehicle to interpret these objects. These partnerships, like the ones Niagara Falls Art Gallery and Rodman Hall have formed with local boards of education and specific schools, enable teachers to become an important aspect of the development of workshop programs, and allow the gallery or museum to become the teacher's aide and community resource that can be called upon to supplement what is being taught in the classroom. It is through the active input of both teachers and museum educators that students will gain the most benefit from an integrated program. The benefit for the museum and gallery is twofold, the gallery and museum becomes an integral part of the community and also by catering to the children of the region we are able to foster the involvement of future gallery and museum patrons.

Finally, what I have realized through the exploration of this view of integrated arts education is that art can provide focus or the center from which to view many other aspects of the world. It can provide learners with a way into a myriad of subjects, which makes those subjects much more approachable and accessible.

Endnote

1. Although I began working at Rodman Hall in the 1980s, it was not until the 1990s, when the direction of the arts center programs changed, that I was able to implement the ideas that I discuss here.

References

Alexander, E. (1979). *Museums in motion: An introduction to the history and functions of museums.* Nashville, TN: American Association for State and Local History.

Arnheim, R. (1974). *Art and visual perception: The new version.* Berkeley, CA: University of California Press.

Arnheim, R. (1989). *Thoughts on art education.* Los Angeles, CA: The Getty Center for Education in the Arts.

Bruner, J. (1960). *The process of education.* Cambridge, MA: Harvard University.

Clark, R. (1994). *Art education: A Canadian perspective.* Toronto, Canada: Ontario Society for Education through Art.

Cornett, C. (1999). *The arts as meaning makers.* Upper Saddle River, NJ: Merrill-Prentice Hall.

Eisner, E. (1972). *Educating artistic vision.* New York: Macmillan.

Glaser, J. & Zenetou, A. (Eds.) (1994). *Gender perspectives: Essays on women in museums.* Washington D.C.: Smithsonian Institute.

Greene, M. (1995). *Releasing the imagination: Essays on education, the arts, and social change.* San Francisco: Jossey-Bass.

Grinder, A., & McCoy, E. (1985). *The good guide: A sourcebook for interpreters, docents and tour guides.* Scottsdale, AZ: Ironwood Press.

Madeja, S. (1973). *All the arts for every child: Final report on the art in general education project.* New York: The JDR 3rd Fund Inc.

Newsom, B., & Silver, A. (Eds.) (1978). *The art museum as educator: A collection of studies as guides to practice and policy.* Los Angeles, CA: University of California Press.

Ontario Ministry of Education and Training. (1993). *The Common Curriculum, Grades 1–9.* Toronto, Canada.

Pear Cohen, E., & Straus Gainer, R. (1976). *Art: Another language for learning.* New York: Citation Press.

The power of the arts to transform education. (1993). Los Angeles, CA: J. Paul Getty Trust.

Smylski, B. (2000). *Community development through education. Context.* The newsletter of the Ontario Association of Art Galleries, Spring/Summer 2000. pp. 1–2.

Tomkins, C. (1970). *Merchants and masterpieces: The story of the Metropolitan Museum of Art.* New York: E.P. Dutton.

Tyler, R. (1949). *Basic principles of curriculum and instruction.* Chicago, IL: University of Chicago Press.

Vallance, E. (1994). Relearning art-museum education. *American Journal of Education 102*(2), 235–43.

CONCLUSIONS AND FURTHER QUESTIONS

1. Based on your experiences and Attenborough's descriptions, what were some of the traditional roles of art galleries/museums? Why have these functions begun to change?

2. What does Attenborough present as the premise for art-based integrated learning? What are the differences between integrated and interdisciplinary learning?

3. What are some of the reasons that she uses to argue for art as a part of a child's education?

4. In what ways do you see art education as a part of an integrated elementary curriculum? Explain why.

5. Discuss the ways that Attenborough describes the art gallery/museum as working with local schools? How are the arts used? Where does learning begin? What is the purpose of the programs? As a teacher, how might

you see yourself using the resources that a museum or gallery has to offer? How might such experiences help your students' learning?

6. What alternatives does Attenborough offer teachers who would like to connect with local galleries and museums? What is the teacher's role in the gallery/museum/school connection? What is the museum educator's role?

7. Attenborough provided us with the theoretical framework for using the art museum for integrated learning. How might this framework help us understand other non-traditional locations for schooling?

RESOURCES AND SUGGESTIONS
FOR FURTHER READING

Carol Becker. *Zones of contention: Essays on art, institutions, gender, and anxiety.* Albany, NY: State University of New York Press, 1996.

Carol Becker. *Different voices: A social, cultural, and historical framework for change in the American art museum.* New York, NY: Association of Art Museum Directors, 1992.

Susan A. Crane (Ed.). *Museums and memory.* Stanford, CA: Stanford University Press, 2000.

Douglas Crimp, *On the museum's ruins.* Cambridge, MA: The MIT Press, 1993.

Carol Duncan. *Civilizing rituals: Inside public art museums.* New York: Routledge, 1995.

Susan Hazelroth & Juliet Moore. Spinning the web: Creating a structure of collaboration between schools and museums. *Art Education, 51* (2), 20–24.

George E. Hein. *Learning in the museum.* New York: Routledge, 1998.

Ellen Cochran Hirzy, (Ed.). *True needs, true partners: Museums and schools transforming education.* Washington, DC: Institute of Museum Services, 1996.

Eilean Hooper-Greenhill. *Museums and the shaping of knowledge.* Leicester, UK: University of Leicester Press, 1992.

Rita L. Irwin & Anna M. Kindler (Eds.). *Beyond the school: Community and institutional partnerships in art education.* Reston, VA: National Art Education Association, 1999.

Ivan Karp, Christine Mullen Kreamer, & Steven D. Lavine (Eds.). *Museums and communities: The politics of public culture.* Washington, DC: Smithsonian Institution Press, 1992.

Suzanne Lacy. *Mapping the terrain: New genre public art.* Seattle, WA: Bay Press, 1995.

Audre Lorde. Poetry is Not a Luxury. In *Sister outsider: Essays and speeches by Audre Lorde.* (pp. 36–49). Freedom, CA: The Crossing Press, 1984.

Lisa Roberts. *From knowledge to narrative: Educators and the changing museum.* Washington, DC: Smithsonian Institution Press, 1997.

Alan Wallach. *Exhibiting contradiction: Essays on the art museum in the United States.* Amherst, MA: University of Massachusetts Press, 1998.

Stephen E. Weil. *A cabinet of curiosities: Inquiries into museums and their prospects.* Washington, DC: Smithsonian Institution Press, 1995.

CHAPTER 7

QUESTIONS AND EXPLORATIONS

1. What age groups and images come to mind when you hear the word "children?"
2. What memories do you have of your own childhood? What words and images would you use to describe yourself as a child?
3. Find three images of children from the media. What drew you to these particular images? What words would you use to describe these children? Who has created these images of children? For what purpose(s)?
4. What is the relationship between the idea of "a child" and that of "a student?"
5. What image do you hold of the students that you will come into contact with in your teaching? What words would you use to describe your future students?
6. How are children represented in differing forms of popular culture (for example, in children's books, in the news, in television shows aimed at children, or in television shows aimed at adults)?
7. How are children of different genders, races, classes, and abilities portrayed? What does this communicate about the nature of childhood?

Children Never Were What They Were: Perspectives on Childhood

Paul Duncum

Children, it is often said, are not what they used to be. I will suggest they never were. When I was an undergraduate training to become an art teacher I was taught that children are gullible and immature beings incapable of knowing what is in their best interests and requiring adult guidance and control. In this view, children were simply happy learners. But the media today offers images that are altogether more complex, fragmented, and often vile. Children starve en masse; they are used as soldiers, slave labor, and prostitutes; and they are even killed for their organs. Even among the Western middle class, children are routinely abused, emotionally, physically, and sexually. Children maim other children and shoot and kill their teachers. In the past, children's ignorance of sex and violence helped mark the distinction between children and adults, but now even what we like to regard as "normal" children have free access to information about sex and violence. Nowadays children seem to be well ahead of their years; indeed, they often seem not to be children at all.

What are we educators to make of the complex realities of children? How are we to conceive of the children under our charge? Do we experience emotional confusion and cognitive dissonance when we seek to maintain the idea of children as happy, innocent learners and yet acknowledge the often unpleasant realities of many children's lives? If so, how do we deal with the disparity? Art educators have long debated about the nature of art and how best to teach about it, but, by contrast, children have been regarded as unproblematic. We have tended to see children as natural, as given, in the nature of things, and therefore not subject to interpretation or debate.

This chapter is a contribution to re-examining the child in education. I will suggest that despite the long-held, popular view of children as innocent beings in need of adult guidance, children have instead always been subject to a variety of conceptions and often deeply disturbing ones (Jenks, 1996). Children never were what they were. I will suggest that in order to do justice to children it is important to acknowledge a variety of conceptions of childhood, and I will suggest some ways in which educators can contribute to the well-being of children in contemporary society.

Children and Childhood

It is important, first, to make the distinction between biological children and the concept of childhood, which is historically and socially determined. In what can now be seen as a modernist conception of childhood, children were regarded as possessing a unitary state. They were innocents. Any other conception, such as object of erotic desire, abused victim, or violent criminal, were seen as aberrations or deviations from the norm of innocence (Jenks, 1996).

The lack of a more complex understanding of "the child" in art education, and education as a whole, reflects, at least until recently, the general position of childhood in sociology. While eager to deconstruct gender, class, and ethnicity, sociologists found childhood too close to home (Jenks, 1996). Sociologists resisted interpreting it. Childhood seemed to be a pure, unmediated state.

Under the impact of the media, however, the idea of an essential innocence to childhood is now impossible to maintain. Highly aesthetic images of idealized children are commonplace; they can be found on cards, calendars, and posters, but they stand in marked contrast to other constructions. The nightly news brings images of starving children from the Third World. Television advertising offers images of children as often rabid consumers. Newspaper photographs show us brutal wounds inflicted on children's bodies. They show images of children who are soldiers, for example, from Africa, and factory workers and union leaders, for example, from Pakistan. From our own society they show images of smiling children who have been murdered by other children, whose equally happy faces are also sometimes reproduced. Such images are usually drawn from the genre of the school class photo or the family snapshot where children have learnt that the right kind of photographic behavior is to smile sweetly even if their school and family life are unhappy.

Postmodern theory and historical studies of children's lives underpin this variation in pictorial representation. Where modernist thinking is characteristically concerned with searching out an essential truth, postmodern theorizing tends to seek out complexity, with many, sometimes competing, truths. Through the ideas presented in postmodern theory we can see childhood inhabiting a range of social discourses such as education and health, but also war, international trade, labor markets, and crime, including prostitution and pornography.

This range of discourses denies any simple essence. Instead of a natural, unmediated state, childhood can be viewed as being constructed out of broad social, political, and economic pressures and process, some of which are discussed below.

What we need is a more complete view of children than that now found in art education. We need a view that does justice to children. In developing such a view it is crucial to understand the powerful historical, psychological, and social forces that help maintain the concept of childhood as a unitary state of innocence clearly separate from adulthood. The discussions I develop below about different perceptions of childhood each have the purpose of highlighting both the socially constructed nature of childhood and how, despite evidence to the contrary, we often still attempt to maintain childhood as a separate and special state of being.

A Historical Perspective

The idea of childhood as a time of happy innocence and openness to learning owes its origin to the Enlightenment of the 18th century and was foundational to the modernism of the 19th and early 20th century. Childhood was thought to embody what then seemed the possibility of endless social progress (Jenks, 1996). Such is the historical originality of this idea, and so dominant did it become, that some historians of childhood deny the existence of any conceptions of childhood much before this period (Cunningham, 1995). According to Rousseau and the Romantic poets such as Keats and Wordsworth, children were strangers to avarice and were imbued with such natural altruism and kindliness they could be entrusted to complete the as yet incomplete plans of adults. Children were viewed as goodness itself, so that in representing the future, the best of days always lay ahead. Childhood embodied no less than the promise of an endlessly brighter and enlightened future.

But it was not always so. Conceptions of childhood have long existed, but so foreign are they to the notion of innocence they were not always recognized by historians. In literature and art, and in theological treatises and statements of public policy, we see, starting from the Ancients, that there has existed a wide range of conceptions regarding childhood. These sources suggest that the fragments of contemporary childhood such as victim, threat, abused, erotic object, and so on, have well-established precedence (Cunningham, 1995). Consider the following examples: Today, child labor fuels labor markets in parts of the Third World, but the Industrial Revolution in the West was founded on child labor. During the Middle Ages, children had access to the adult culture of violence and sex (Postman, 1982). Hellenistic *putti* demonstrate that children were seen as erotic objects. Medieval religious tracts and American puritans alike stressed the sins of the child as strongly as their innocence (Shahar, 1990). And from early Christian times there are fictionalized accounts of childhood homicide which is sometimes directed at teachers (Chapman, 1975). Childhood turns out not to be as distinctly a different state as the ideology of innocence leads us to believe.

A Developmental Perspective

Much teaching practice is underpinned by the theory of developmentalism, which, in contrast to the historical perspective above, marks a clear distinction between children and adults (Stainton-Rogers & Stainton-Rogers, 1998). Developmentalism informs education, including art education, about what is good practice as to how children should be educated and prepared for adult life as well as identifying the policies that we provide to safeguard and promote children's welfare. Developmentalism stresses children's biological and psychological maturation. Children are seen as undergoing a psychobiological process of maturation eventually achieving a state of mature adulthood. Whether it is by Piaget or Freud, or their many successors, natural, biological processes are viewed as wired into the human organism which, through interaction with the physical and social worlds, inexorably unfolds. Because children are seen by developmentalism to be moving toward being adults, childhood is viewed as fundamentally different from adulthood.

A Psychosocial Perspective

Developmentalism is derived from psychology, and to understand its limitations on conceptualizing childhood, it is helpful to employ a perspective that combines psychology with sociology. Doing so helps us to see that a romantic, simplistic view of childhood is often maintained for powerful, personal reasons such as a desire to maintain childhood as an idealized state. It can help us see why giving up this idea can create cognitive and emotional confusion. And it helps explain why adult relations to childhood are fraught with paradox.

With its separation of childhood from adulthood, developmentalism appeals to teachers and to adults generally. A clear separation helps us define ourselves as adults. We invest much emotion in our children, not only because of our memories of our own childhood, but because we carry within us something of the child we once were (Holland, 1992). Psychology has taught us to see the child within us as a basic metaphor of our psychic being. This is sometimes called our "inner child." According to this view, childhood engages us because the child we once were always co-exists with our concept of ourselves as adults and we are frequently prone to draw upon this child that we have carried forward into our adult lives. We may be unwilling to closely examine concepts of childhood precisely because childhood describes not only biological children but because it also resides within us.

According to the psychoanalytical tradition, the world of the unconscious is the world of childhood, not actual childhood but a metaphor for a world of infantile pleasures, moral chaos, violence, and vulnerability. Equally it is a world of play, spontaneity, and imagination. For Freud, our idea of ourselves as an adult necessitates repressing the child within the adult. To be an adult means to be a rational and moral being able to work out problems rationally and to be in control of oneself. On the other hand, childhood represents all that is vulnerable, inept, clumsy, primitive, thus putting us at the mercy of emotions and subject to petulant or violent behavior. This view of childhood arose during the 19th century and intersected with other symbols of emotion and its unpredictability, notably through women, colonial peoples, and working-class masses. Each was defined as existing dangerously outside rationality. Even today, while cherished for its innocence, childhood often represents a lower, inferior state of being.

According to this perspective, adulthood requires repressing the inferiority of childhood. But suppressing the child within us is always a struggle (Holland, 1992). We try to resist behaving irrationally or being viewed as childish, immature, or infantile, but it is easy to regress. As children we learn ways to cope with events, and, frequently, when similar events arise in adulthood, we play out the same coping strategies that we acquired in childhood. Patterns of behavior learnt as children persist into adulthood and, instead of responding with the calm and thoughtfulness of adulthood, we respond with the frustration, sense of inadequacy, misplaced anger, and tears of childhood. As advocates of Transactional Analysis say, when adults are in the grip of feelings, their child has taken over; when their anger dominates their reason, their child is in command (Harris, 1970). Thus the child within us makes our adult status highly vulnerable. The achievement of adulthood is always precarious, always under threat. We are deeply fearful of behaving childishly, or being accused of doing so. And so we have devised measures to defend ourselves, such as curtailing unruly behavior amongst ourselves and physically separating children from adults.

The contemporary segregation of children from adults can be viewed as part of a pervasive adult desire to protect the status of adulthood (Holland,

1992). The desire to segregate children may be not only about controlling actual children, but controlling the child within us. As adults, then, we continuously strive to gain control over actual children, our own childhoods and even the very idea of childhood.

Many of what are popularly assumed to be the essential characteristics of childhood, such as spontaneity and playfulness, we frequently deny ourselves as adults. A sense of wonder, awe, and excitement in the face of new things, of limitless horizons stretching out before us, and of a seemingly boundless creative imagination—all of which we like to associate with childhood—we tend to curtail as adults. Such so-called childlike qualities are, of course, still present in adults and can be replayed, notably during leisure times, but the pressures of working life, including working with children, devalue these qualities in ourselves. The driven impetus of a materialistic and highly organized society offers few opportunities for childlike qualities among adults. Consequently, adults often construct ideal childhoods for themselves where childhood is viewed through the lens of a warm nostalgic glow. Where one's childhood has involved abuse or deprivation of some kind childhood as an ideal is oftentimes created with particular strength (Bradshaw, 1990).

Childhood becomes a mythical time when the characteristics adults deny themselves, or were denied in actual childhood, can be lived out as in a dream. What is denied the adult is still achievable in childhood. Adults feel pressure to preserve childhood for their own children while, for their own sakes, they seek to preserve a sense of their own early life. Childhood becomes an homage to the imaginary, a rich depository for all the qualities adults desire but believe they cannot indulge in for themselves. Our ideas about childhood as a singularly precious time are not then altogether about children or childhood. They tell us about ourselves as adults (Holland, 1992). While adults insist that childhood belongs to actual children, it is also a construct which fulfills a need to place fantasies and desires somewhere out there in reality (Hillman, 1992).

On the one hand, childhood is an idealized past, a projection of qualities many adults desire but deny themselves; on the other hand, regression to childish behavior is an ever-present fear for many adults. Much of the time most adults deny child-like qualities in themselves while dreading a return to childishness.

An Institutional Perspective

These psychological and social dynamics are manifest in our institutional practices, such as what we do in schools with children. Our roles as teachers help define childhood as a state of being separate from the characteristics of modern, adult society. Unlike many societies now and in the past, in our Western kind of society children neither work nor play alongside adults. Children have their own institutions, clothes, pastimes, even culture. They have different rights and responsibilities from adults, and our expectations of their behavior are markedly different from what we expect of ourselves. We have created a special world with children's rooms, toys, books, music, caregivers, doctors, and nurses; and children's play is quite segregated from the lives of working adults.

The boundaries between children and adults are maintained by institutions like the family, hospitals, and schools each with their own routines of operation. How does the ever-present need to deal with children obscure our views of children? Each institution imposes its views of childhood which act like self-fulfilling prophecies about their nature (Prout & James, 1990). For example, we routinely line children up outside classrooms before letting them in; in the artroom we routinely hand out materials one at a time. Such routines help ensure control and reduce confusion but also teach both teachers and children that control and efficiency are important. The wider social conditions under which control and time-on-task have become important are excluded from consideration. Ways of thinking about childhood fuse with routinized institutional practices to produce nurses, parents, classroom teachers, and art teachers, even children themselves, who think and feel about themselves using these ways of thinking. Children are thus subject to a range of discourses whose function is to both impose order and exclude other discourses.

A Contemporary Cultural Perspective

I noted earlier that childhood as a time of happy innocence and openness to learning was foundational to modernism where childhood embodied hope in a seemingly unlimited future. Today, the symbolic significance of childhood appears to be undiminished, but the significance of childhood appears to have been transformed.

According to many cultural observers, contemporary, postmodern conditions have seen the modernist hope in the future eroded and replaced by a sense of disorientation and disenchantment. For many, unbridled hope has at best been replaced by a cautious optimism and at worst by a deep skepticism about the future (Jenks, 1996). With an erosion of confidence in the future the concept of childhood appears to have been adopted for the better world that it evokes from days now gone.

Rather than abandoning the child who embodied modernity, postmodern times have reinvested the child with an equally powerful symbolic role where childhood has come to embody fond memories of past times (Jenks, 1996). At least this is a view proposed by some observers. They argue that although childhood as future hope can no longer be sustained, the child as nostalgia offers a sense of continuity with the past. A sense of continuity at least suggests a future. In this way childhood continues to embody the kind of optimism necessary to underpin social goodwill and cohesion.

The sense of disorientation and dislocation, which is often associated with postmodern times, finds a ready source of comfort in the image of the child. The certainty of trust and love that was previously invested in the traditional institutions of marriage, social class, and the church are now invested in childhood. Where society is experienced as unstable, childhood appears to offer not only a stable space but also unconditional love. While other relationships appear temporal, the characteristics of the child appear stable. Because the childhood seems grounded in biological and psychological predictability, everything that is desired but ephemeral in other relationships is directed towards children. Childhood becomes a hedge against the vanishing possibilities of love (Jenks, 1996). We now seek from children an unconditional love that protects us from an unstable and disorienting social reality. In postmodern times childhood has become a central bulwark against uncertainty and alienation. Where traditional sources of emotional comfort have broken down, children have become a major source of comfort and, consequently, of enormous symbolic value. Adults have readopted childhood as a site for reintegrating the social bond. If this cultural perspective is accurate it is surely no wonder that we persist, despite the evidence, in maintaining an unreconstructed view of childhood as essentially good and seeing all other views as aberrations of the singular truth of childhood. Undermine a belief in the redeeming qualities of childhood and what is left of a social structure already under enormous strain? On the other hand, consider that the view of childhood as singularly a time of innocence in search of knowledge is an illusion, a false myth that can only do real children harm. The ideology of innocence sets up expectations that real children cannot possibly hope to achieve so that they can only disappoint.

Dealing with Children Today

First, I believe we need to think in a more consistent way about children than we frequently tend to do. It is important to see them realistically rather than through eyes blinded by our own adult needs. The first step would be to consider that our ideas about children are constructed from historical processes and contemporary social pressures and to see children as possessing fragmented identities. We also need to see that while children are different from adults they are not as different as we often like to imagine. It seems important to keep our minds, and hearts, open to children as fragmented and much like us and thereby do them no injustice of thought or deed.

Secondly, within the classroom, images of children provide rich resources for discussing with children how they see themselves positioned and to discuss the extent to which they accept, negotiate, or resist inferred meanings. For example, I have found that while at first enjoying highly aesthetic images of babies and young children, grade six students feel very unhappy with the suggestion that their own younger siblings should pose in such images. What do children make of representations of themselves as rabid consumers? What do they make of themselves when asked to pose smiling for the camera as family members? What do they make of images of starving children and others maimed by war? So long as teachers hold the view that childhood is essentially innocent they will resist addressing the latter topic. But if they acknowledge that children are regularly exposed to violent images that often involve children, working through the fears aroused in children by such imagery becomes an important task for education. Children need time and mature adults to debrief and unless they can do so at home, they need to do so in the classroom. Dealing with the realities of children offered through imagery gives new meaning to the artroom; it means dealing with pictures of children's deepest concern, themselves.

Thirdly, as implied above, it is important for art educators to extend beyond conventional art images of children to engage with the images of a consumer culture and mass communications media; for example, Internet advertisements, travel brochures, television dramas, and photojournalism. Today, images of children can be found on coffee mugs, tea towels, calendars, and date books. They help sell products and promote causes. Such consumer-orientated images are the most immediately assessable for most children. Examining them does not mean abandoning art images however. Many mass media images of children, especially those that show childhood as a blessed state, owe more to the history of art images than the reality of contemporary children. In examining media images of innocent childhood, then, it is very useful, for example, to compare the highly idealized children by artists from the 19th century.

Fourth, art educators may wish to consider that they adopt a broader public role than their traditional concern with classroom instruction. This is because any claim we can make to professional status rests on our expertise regarding both children and images. With images of children our two professional concerns intersect. It may be considered impingement upon us to speak out in public forums about images that we see as dehumanizing to children. What could be more central to our task as educators than to address how children are visually represented in contemporary society?

References

Bradshaw, J. (1990). *Homecoming: Reclaiming and championing your inner child.* New York: Bantam Books.

Chapman, G. (1975). *The child Jesus.* London: Adey Horton.

Cunningham, H. (1995). *Children and childhood in Western society since 1500.* London: Longman.

Harris, T. A. (1970). *I'm OK, You're OK.* London: Pan Books.

Hillman, J. (1992). Abandoning the child. In C. Jenks (Ed.), *The sociology of the child: Essential readings* (pp. 97–114). Hampshire, UK: Gregg Revivals.

Holland, P. (1992). *What is a child? Popular images of childhood.* London: Virago.

Jenks, C. (1996). *Childhood.* London: Routledge.

Postman, N. (1982). *The disappearance of childhood.* New York: Delacorte Press.

Prout, A., & James, A. (Eds.) (1990). *Constructing and reconstructing childhood: Contemporary issues in the sociological study of childhood.* London: Falmer Press.

Shahar, S. (1990). *Childhood in the middle ages.* London: Routledge.

Stainton-Rogers, R., & Stainton-Rogers, W. (1998). Word children. In K. Lesnik-Oberstein (Ed.). *Children in culture: Approaches to childhood* (pp. 178–203). London: Macmillan.

CONCLUSIONS AND FURTHER QUESTIONS

1. What images of children and childhood does Duncum present us with? How does he interpret these images? How does he differentiate between children and childhood?

2. Why does Duncum ask us to challenge the myth of childhood?

3. After reading Duncum's article, collect three images of children from the popular media. What considerations affected your choice of images now that you have read Duncum's chapter? How do these images correspond with those that you initially chose?

4. What does Duncum suggest that is contrary to popular long-held beliefs about children?

5. What characteristics of childhood could/should we retain as adults and teachers of children? Why is it important?

6. What images of childhood do you think are most frequently held in the elementary classroom?

7. What does the author suggest that teachers do in the classroom? What kinds of images does he suggest teachers use? Why?

8. What do the child and images of childhood offer contemporary culture?

RESOURCES AND SUGGESTIONS
FOR FURTHER READING

Laura E. Berk. *Child development,* 2nd ed. Boston: Allyn and Bacon, 1991.

Alan A. Block. *I'm only bleeding: Education as the practice of social violence against children.* New York : Peter Lang, 1997.

Norman Bryson, Michael Ann Holly, & Keith Moxey (Eds.). *Visual culture: Images and interpretations.* Hanover, NH: University Press of New England, 1994.

Jessica Evans & Stuart Hall (Eds.). *Visual culture: The reader.* London: Sage, 1999.

Judith Rich Harris & Robert M. Liebert. *The child: A contemporary view of development.* Englewood Cliffs, NJ: Prentice Hall, 1991.

Chris Jenks (Ed.). *Visual culture.* London; New York: Routledge, 1995.

Anna M. Kindler (Ed.). *Child development in art.* Reston, VA: The National Art Education Association, 1997.

John Matthews. *The art of childhood and adolescence: The construction of meaning.* London; Philadelphia, PA: Falmer Press, 1999.

Nicholas Mirzoeff. *An introduction to visual culture.* London; New York: Routledge, 1999.

F. Philip Rice. *Child and adolescent development.* Upper Saddle River, NJ: Prentice Hall, 1997.

Christine Thompson (Ed.). *The visual arts and early childhood learning.* Reston, VA: The National Art Education Association, 1995.

John A. Walker & Sarah Chaplin. *Visual culture: An introduction.* Manchester, UK; New York: Manchester University Press, 1997.

CHAPTER 8

QUESTIONS AND EXPLORATIONS

1. What influences the choices that we make as teachers with regard to curriculum planning and implementation? As you think about your answer, consider both conscious and unconscious influences.
2. How are our individual identities constructed? Write about the various aspects of your identity and explain how they help make you the person that you are.
3. How are our community identities constructed?
4. How does your identity determine the curricular choices that you make?

Mapping Identity
for Curriculum Work

Kristin G. Congdon, Marilyn Stewart,
and John Howell White

At the outset, it appears to be a simple proposition—teachers bring values, beliefs, and trusted practices to their work as curriculum developers. Most educators are familiar with what has been called "the hidden curriculum." This is the notion that any plan for teaching and learning carries with it assumptions about what is important and that these assumptions guide more than the identified content. Educators' assumptions also guide the ways in which school days are structured, spaces for learning are designed, textbooks are selected, children are addressed, and other educational decisions are made.

As teachers, we do well to remember that the decisions we make on a daily basis are value-laden. Beliefs about children, the enterprise of schooling, the subjects we teach, and the instructional practices we employ are only some of the beliefs that undergird our selection of content, the means we choose for its delivery, and the practices we sanction within the school community. It is also important, however, to recognize the sources of these beliefs.

Teachers, as do all people, exemplify and actualize the beliefs and values that emerge from their active participation with the world. Our individual identities are constructed through our interaction within overlapping and intersecting communities to which we belong. In addition to living in a local community—our city, town, or neighborhood, for example—we are members of what we loosely refer to as "shared-interest" communities. If one is a member of a softball team, for example, one belongs to a larger recreational community of people who play or watch softball. Part of our identity consists of membership in this recreational community. The assumptions, beliefs, and values we hold as a result of our membership in a variety of such communities converge within the culture and work of the school. When we, as teachers, engage in curriculum planning and implementation, we bring, in varying degrees, these deeper level assumptions, values, and beliefs to our work.

Community influences persist and typically go unrecognized in curriculum decision-making. We rarely think of how our geographic community membership, for example, affects the choices we make in designing curriculum and teaching. How do assumptions stemming from one's life within an urban community differ from those related to living in rural or suburban settings? Assumptions, values, and beliefs associated with our age, family structure, politics, and economic communities similarly guide our choices, although we rarely consider these influences.

When we begin to think carefully about the ways we define ourselves in relation to our community relationships, we go beyond simply accepting the obvious proposition that curricular decisions are value-laden. This became evident in two professional development institutes held during two consecutive summers at Kutztown University entitled, "Inquiry, Community, and Curriculum." We presented an activity in which the participants—art specialists, elementary classroom teachers, secondary subject area teachers, and a few administrators—"mapped" their identities. We asked the participants to recognize how private experiences move them to public action and how their constructed identities influence their curricular decisions. Believing that the creation of art is like the creation of curriculum, in that the community influences converge in both practices, we also suggested that participants consider the underlying power of community influences in their art-making as well as their educational processes.

The Mapping Identity Project

The Mapping Identity Project consists of using a Project Guide, divided into two parts, to complete a large "map"—a ring of two concentric circles divided into separate boxes for each shared-interest community (see Figure 8.1). In Part One, participants follow a series of prompts in the Project Guide that encourage reflection upon individual community memberships. The participants consider identification with and relationship to religious, gender, geographic, family, age, economic, political, recreational, aesthetic, racial/ethnic, occupational, and health communities. The kind of self-reflection required to complete this initial phase of the mapping exercise helps participants come to an awareness of self as much more complex than day-to-day experience typically provides. We have found that participants take this initial

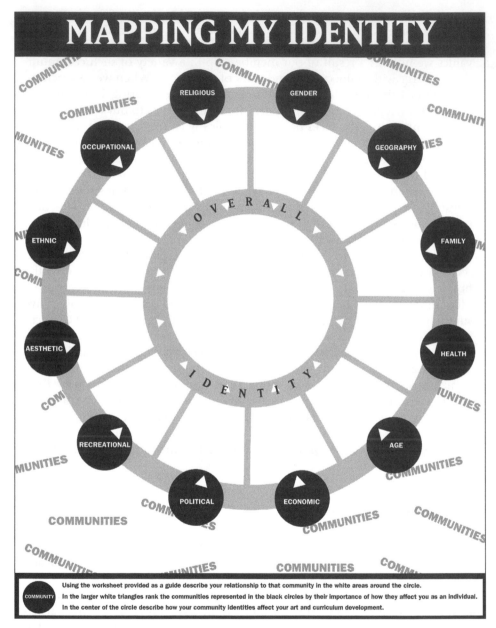

Figure 8.1 Identity Map.

charge very seriously. Most report that they have not previously reflected upon these questions and that the experience of doing so is poignant and, in some cases, life-changing. Part Two prompts participants to review their shared interest community memberships and rank those memberships' importance in relation to their impact upon them as individuals. For instance, a teacher might rank her or his gender identification as the most important factor in construction of identity, followed by political, ethnic, occupational, and other community relationships. Finally, participants consider how their community identities impact the decisions they make in their curriculum work (and art-making, when appropriate).

The Mapping Identity Project can serve as both an instructional tool and an artwork. The map may be enlarged, printed on poster-board, and worked on with paint, markers, collage, etc. It also may be used to prompt reflection in journals or sketchbooks or responses in essay form.

MAPPING MY IDENTITY PROJECT GUIDE

Part One

Use the following prompts to guide your responses in the outer ring of your identity map:

Religious Identity/Community

- I consider my religious identity to be what?
- I share it, or do not share it, with others because why?
- I consider myself as an isolated or an active religious community member because?
- I would prefer to explain my religious identity in a different way (for instance, I am a privately spiritual person; I consider religion a lifestyle, etc.).

Gender and Sexual Identity/Community

- Most of, some of, very few of my choices in life are influenced by my gender/gender identity and/or sexual identity.
- Most of, some of, very few of my teaching decisions are influenced by my gender/gender identity and/or sexual identity.
- My gender/gender identity and/or sexual identity affects my relationship with my male/female students.
- My gender/gender identity and/or sexual identity has had an impact on my choice of career because?
- I most often choose to spend leisure time with friends of the same? opposite? sex because?

Geographical Identity/Community

- When people ask me where I am from, it is easy or hard to answer because?
- I consider my home to be?
- I am a rural or urban person because?
- I need or do not need to have a sense of roots in a particular place or geographical community because?
- I express my geographic roots to others by my (politics, community work, gardening, accent, clothes, etc.).

Family Identity/Community

- Family is of great significance, somewhat significant, not at all significant to me because?
- I choose to or do not choose to spend leisure time with members of my family because?
- My definition of family is?

Age Identity/Community

- I consider myself young, middle-aged, old because?
- Aging is hard or easy because?
- I like to or do not like to spend time with others my own age because?
- Generational things I identify with that are age specific are (certain music, clothing, politics, experiences such as going to school in the 60s, etc.).
- If I were the opposite sex, I'd think of aging differently because?

Economic Identity/Community

- Economically, I consider myself to have low income, moderate income, or high income?
- I consider myself to be poor, middle class, or wealthy?
- I do or do not think one's economic situation is an appropriate topic for discussion in this context or many others.
- I am comfortable or uncomfortable with my economic status because?

Political Identity/Community

- Politically speaking, I consider myself to be (conservative, liberal, Republican, radical, apolitical, Democrat, etc.) because?
- My political identity comes mostly from my (family, growing up in the 80s, personal experience, religious identity, etc.).
- I think our political values inform most of what we do, or I would prefer not to make politics too much of an issue in education, or "let's tip-toe around political issues, please," because?

Recreational Identity/Community

- In my spare time, I (work out at a gym, spend time with a gardening group, engage in politics, read, relate to the world of cyberspace, etc.).
- I belong to a recreational community in the following ways (read the same magazines, have a similar language, wear the same kinds of shoes, bowl at the coolest alleys, etc.).
- I don't take time for recreation because?

Aesthetic Identity/Community

- You can or cannot tell who I am by the way I dress.
- My outward appearance is representative of the above other communities to which I belong.
- I spend a lot or a little energy, money, and/or time on shoes, tee-shirts, jewelry, etc. because?

Racial/Ethnic Identity/Community

- My ancestors are mainly (Spanish, Italian, African-American, Amish, etc.).
- I consider myself to be (White, Black, mainstream, mixed, I don't like being asked this question, etc.).
- I consider my ethnic identity a heritage that is informed by my biological heritage or my cultural experience because?
- This part of my identity is important or relatively unimportant because?

Occupational Identity/Community

- I consider myself to be first and foremost an artist, a teacher, a student, an art educator, or something else.
- I like this part of my identity, I am ambivalent about this part of my identity, or I want to change this part of my identity, because?
- The rest of the world respects my occupational identity or does not respect it because?
- Members of my occupational community respect or do not respect their identity because?

Health and Body Identity/Community

- My physical attributes greatly affect or do not affect the way I see myself and the way others see me because?
- My physical and mental health play an important role in the ways that I view the world because?
- Members of my health and body identity communities recognize and communicate their shared experiences with one another in what ways?

Other Identity/Community

The categories listed above are provided to encompass some reoccurring issues and themes that have affected many different people. Remember that this is not an exhaustive or even an essential list, but rather a good place to begin. It is important that as an individual or as a group member you examine other significant relationships. For example, the guide was changed to include family identity at the suggestion of some individuals working with it. Before proceeding, consider whether the above categories adequately represent the major interest communities to which you feel attached. If not, consider what you mean by the area identified then add it to your list. Develop a few questions directed toward this specific dimension of your life.

Part Two

Overall Identity

We find that it is not only valuable to identify community memberships, but also to prioritize them. Prioritization can confirm valuable relationships, reveal undervalued relationships, and provide a more realistic view of relationships previously thought to be important.

- If I were to rank the importance of all the communities I belong to in the way they affect me as an individual, the ranking would look like this: (for example, 1. Political, 2. Racial/Ethnic, 3. Occupational, etc.)

Consider the following questions to reflect upon the ways that your community identities affect your curriculum planning:

- How would I rank the effect of my community identities on the kinds of art works that I show my students? Take a moment to consider examples from each area.
- How would I rank the effect of my community identities on the kinds of learning activities that I promote in my lesson plans? Take a moment to consider examples from each of your identity communities.
- How would I rank the effect of my community identities on my relations with other teachers and the field of teaching in general? Take a moment to consider examples from each of your identity communities.

Using the Mapping Identity Project

Completion of the map provides a deeper understanding of one's engagement in professional work. We have found the exercise to be useful with teachers at varying levels in their careers and in a variety of contexts. Because identities shift with continued participation in the world, the exercise can be repeated at various points throughout one's teaching life. We also encourage those who use the mapping exercise to add communities to the process. As with any map, the terrain may change, and new maps must be made.

The Mapping Identity Project can be valuable for individuals working alone to develop curriculum, and it is also useful when teachers plan together. The mapping process helps members of the group to be more aware of individual and collective perspectives. This awareness helps to establish a more open and embracing atmosphere during the curriculum planning and, presumably, the implementation process.

We have found that teachers readily value and explore ways in which mapping their own identities as teachers can be translated into instructional practices to be used with their students. An identity map is a tool for guiding and reflecting upon learning by both teachers and students.

Past institute participants have shared with us ways that they have adapted the exercise for use in their classrooms. In some cases, teachers used the identity mapping exercise to help students carefully consider their shared-interest community memberships as groundwork for approaching the study of art. The self-reflection process provided students with a better understanding of their identities at work while viewing and making artworks. Teachers have found that the process can be used to develop ideas related to the creation of art works. For example it can be used as a tool to generate an initial idea, to provoke thought in the midst of working on a project, to consider how another person might interpret the work, and to critique and reflect upon the final stages of the work.

Some of the teachers also used a variation of the mapping exercise to consider art made by others. After investigating the work of particular artists, for example, students attempted to complete the identity map by taking on the voice of the artist studied. Such an approach highlights the important notion that art-makers are real people, with influences stemming from real-world experiences.

Identity Maps and the Interpretation of Artworks

Artworks emerge from communities of interest and are interpreted by viewers, including students, who in turn have their own shared-interest communities. Needless to say, as time goes by, the interactions among all of these voices becomes a vibrant and interesting mix.

To use the identity map in the process of interpreting artworks, a teacher can have students review a collection of artworks and select one artwork to investigate. Recognizing that this initial selection will inevitably reflect a student's community identity, the teacher can then ask students to consider how they made their choices in light of the identity map categories. In a large class discussion, the teacher and students discuss each category in relation to how they made their selection. The students can then prioritize the importance of the categories in relation to their choices and discuss their prioritization in small groups.

With their attention directed toward their chosen artwork, students can then use their identity maps as a guide to consider the communities of interest that have affected the development of their selected artwork. For example, they might ask, "What is the religious identity of the work?" They offer reasons for attributing the specific identity to the work. Pushing toward art history, a teacher might ask students to consider the religious identity of the culture within which the art work was produced. The complexity of interpretation becomes clear as the student sees that there might be differences among the religious identity of the work, the religious identity of the artist, the religious identity of the culture within which the artwork was produced, and the students' own religious identity. In addition, they might consider the religious identities of past critics and historians who have shaped our understanding of the work(s).

Using the identity map as a tool for interpretation can provide students and teachers with a means of understanding that, in addition to artworks, texts, conversations, classroom practices, and other cultural phenomena are all developed out of communities of practice. Teachers may not only guide the interpretation of artworks but also guide the interpretation of groups of works, exhibition spaces and museums, objects and events from popular culture, and interpretations of art writing and art books. Ask yourself, "Does my favorite textbook have a cultural or community identity?"

Conclusion

For many practiced teachers, working with students comes easily and seems to be a natural outgrowth of their lives. Good teaching includes reflective practices that provide teachers with a means to gain fresh insights into their work. Identity mapping is one way to accomplish this. It provides a means to intentionally reconsider the social and cultural dimensions of our lives that we bring into classrooms.

Authors' Note

Our thanks to Professor Elaine Cunfer, Communication Design Department, Kutztown University for her design of the Worksheet.

CONCLUSIONS AND FURTHER QUESTIONS

1. What do the authors mean by community? What kinds of frameworks support the authors' use of community? Explain. What is the relationship between community influences and curricular choices?

2. Why is it relevant for teachers in the classroom to know this about themselves? How can a discovery of identity help us in the classroom?

3. Complete Part I and II of the "Mapping Identity Project." Did your understanding of your identity change from the description that you wrote before reading this chapter? In what ways? What did you discover? What did others in your class discover? Once we discover this about ourselves, how can we relate this to the differences among our students?

4. What are the community identities of your students? Who are your students with regard to race, gender, ethnicity, etc.? How do your community identities affect your choices for your students' learning? Do you consider the community identities of your students when making choices?

5. How can an identity map be used in the elementary classroom? What might we learn about ourselves and our students by completing identity maps? What problems or limitations might arise from attempting to map our identities in an elementary classroom?

RESOURCES AND SUGGESTIONS
FOR FURTHER READING

Alicia de Alba. *Curriculum in the postmodern condition.* New York: Peter Lang, 2000.

Michael W. Apple. *Power, meaning, and identity: Essays in critical educational studies.* New York: Peter Lang, 1999.

Louis A. Castenell, Jr. and William F. Pinar (Eds.). *Understanding curriculum as racial text: Representations of identity and difference in education.* Albany, NY: State University of New York Press, 1993.

Henry A. Giroux. *Living dangerously: Multiculturalism and the politics of difference.* New York: Peter Lang, 1993.

Cameron McCarthy & Warren Crichlow (Eds.). *Race, identity, and representation in education.* New York: Routledge, 1993.

William F. Pinar (Ed.) *Queer theory in education.* Mahwah, NJ: L. Erlbaum Associates, 1998.

William F. Pinar (Ed.). *Curriculum: Toward new identities.* New York: Garland Pub., 1998.

William F. Pinar. *Understanding curriculum: An introduction to the study of historical and contemporary curriculum discourses.* New York: Peter Lang, 1995.

William A. Reid. *Curriculum as institution and practice: Essays in the deliberative tradition.* Mahwah, NJ: L. Erlbaum Associates, 1999.

CHAPTER 9

QUESTIONS AND EXPLORATIONS

1. Where do our identities come from? Do they remain the same over time and in different contexts? Explain.
2. What is included in a person's cultural history? How does this conjoin with learning in the classroom?
3. What do students gain by having their cultural and historical identities included as a part of classroom learning?
4. What kind of opportunities for self-expression should we provide children when making art? How is the idea of self-expression related to that of identity?
5. Describe ways in which you have explored and expressed your identity. Have you ever used art as a means of understanding your identity?

Children Performing the Art of Identity

Charles R. Garoian

a, b, c, d, e, f, g, h, i, j, k, l, m, n, o, p, q, r, s, t, u, v, w, x, y, z
alphabet cards stretch clear across the front of the classroom pinned above the front wall, to the left hangs a polyester American flag on a black wooden pole mounted at a 45° angle

a green chalkboard, framed with aluminum, covered with numerical symbols, formulas, figures 1, 2, 3, 4, 5, 67+32=99, $\sqrt{2}=1.414$, $a^{2}+b^{2}=c^{2}$, 3×13=39, 50% of 10=5 like the transmutations of an alchemist, they aspire to mystic truths

worn black felt erasers line the ledge covered with white dust
adjoined with fragments of broken and used chalk—testimonies to ruminations, calculations, and articulations lost

large colorful posters tacked along the bottom of the chalkboard and along the entire front wall of the room, each instructing a proper breakfast diet prior to school: orange juice, milk, two pieces of toast, two eggs, two strips of bacon, and hash brown potatoes a large golden oak desk stands at the head of the room, its top symmetrically lined with a felt pad surrounded by textbooks, a cylinder of sharpened pencils, erasers, pens, papers, and a roll book

smaller desks regimented in a grid five across and six deep, stand like sentinels on steel legs with esoteric texts, images, graffiti etched into their wooden surfaces, like ancient pictographs they lack any pictorial coherence

a musty aroma of bananas, peanut butter, body odor permeates the room as if the abandoned site of some pagan rite or sacrificial altar

the room is lit with four banks of florescent lights, one makes a hypnotic buzzing sound as it continually blinks on and off, on and off, on and off, on and off

acoustic tiles line the ceiling, some water-stained, others missing, with dangling mobiles made of coat hangers, their crayoned paper birds swaying to and fro in the thermals of this suburban tropical zone

the east wall entirely windowed, its threadbare curtains tightly drawn, illuminates natural light; the view and traffic sounds from the adjacent street reverberate in the room

a silver steam radiator stands on iron legs below the windows its inner organs gurgling and hissing at random intervals

a tarnished copper fire extinguisher hangs askew on the wall, ready should disaster strike along side a make-shift sign that reads DO NOT TOUCH

a stained white porcelain sink at the rear of the room, half filled with murky water, its drain clogged, its faucet dripping, a lesson in depletion of resources ignored

reproductions, posters line the corkboard next to the entrance images of George Washington, Albert Einstein, Martin Luther King, Susan B. Anthony, and Bill Clinton gaze back at the viewer like medieval icons, whose worship aspires to notions of a civilized life

a lit fresh-water tank purrs, its aerator sending bubbles to the surface as exotic fish swim among a menagerie of plastic flora and fauna, and a miniature pirate's treasure chest

a collection of rocks, aligned on the weathered window sill, follow a geological order from igneous to metamorphic to sedimentary, an intense refraction of light from adjacent crystals reflecting off the walls alludes to the presence of some entropic process

crinkled tempera paintings pinned above the sink as if in a commercial gallery or museum, their images obsessively repeat the same turkey, pilgrim, Indian, turkey, pilgrim, Indian, turkey, pilgrim, Indian

a single door serves as both entrance and exit to the room, made of steel it is secured with three deadbolts all keyed differently

a 1972 edition of the *World Book Encyclopedia*, its blue cloth covers tattered, is shelved along the side wall, with miscellaneous books piled on top

labeled potted plants simulate a hot house at the end of the counter their leaves dropping from a root bound condition

the linoleum floor tiles sparkle from the window's reflected light as their newly waxed surfaces expose black scuff marks near the threshold— the doorway, and under each of the desks

a dysfunctional pencil sharpener, screwed to the closet door, its grinders jammed with fragments of lead, its cover missing, with a pile of shavings strewn on the floor

a variety of colored coats hang in desolation on tarnished brass hooks in the closet above brown paper bags reeking of mayonnaise, mustard, and baloney each in their cubby hole with an assigned name

Christine, Martin, Suzanne, Kirk, Daren, Johnny, Billy, Sharon, Carlos, Cindy, Juanita, Jason, Stephanie, Victoria, Georgi, Charles, Christopher, Kate, Victor, Tyler, Betsy, Sherrie, Karen, Michael, Cynthia, Linda, Guillermo, Francois, Hiroshi, Catherine, Joyce, Shaquanna, Joe, Carmen, Bonnie, Alan

on the back counter, like a planet frozen in orbit, a *Rand McNally* globe stands propped on its metallic gold axis next to a faded atlas of the United States of America pinned to the wall

Where are the children? Where is the teacher? Where are their bodies? I offer this soliloquy of an empty classroom as a metaphor to suggest an approach to teaching that acknowledges and includes teachers and children's cultural identities and bodies as intellectually significant to the process of learning. In traditional school environments where emphasis is placed on historically and socially determined ideas, images, and behaviors, children learn to perform the academic knowledge imparted by their teachers who are also performing it. Exclusively school curricula and the teacher's lesson determine what they say and do. The questions children ask in school are those that they have learned how to ask from their teachers. The activities in which they engage are by the teacher's design or by the teacher's choice of curriculum through which culture is being transmitted. What about the ideas, questions, and activities which they bring from their respective cultural experiences, personal memories, and cultural histories? Are they not significant content to consider in the classroom?

Classroom environments, where the content of learning is solely determined by the teacher's knowledge, consider children's memories and cultural histories worthy of little regard. Even if children are physically present, their identities are absent. Like the classroom in my soliloquy, children are considered empty vessels waiting to be filled with school knowledge. Classroom environments devoid of children's memories and cultural histories presume that this knowledge is insignificant when compared with the prevailing assumptions that they have to offer. By comparison, children embody the values, attitudes and beliefs of their cultural environments, ones that include their families, neighborhoods, communities, and schools. Such personal knowledge may seem intellectually incongruous with school knowledge, but their conjunctions and interconnections can provide multiple perspectives and interpretations about what and how children learn in school. Who they are, where they come from, and what they desire represent personal identity considerations that are important to knowledge construction in the classroom.

Children's identities are constructed artifacts. By re-membering, re-considering, and re-presenting who they are children learn that identity is "not fixed but in continual formation."[1] From birth and throughout adult life, their social and cultural experiences determine who they are, how they think, behave, and the choices that they make in the world. On the one hand, learning under these circumstances is desirable because the knowledge that children gain provides them with the ability to function in the world. On the other hand, if learning is to foster creative and political agency, the ability to become instrumental citizens, it requires that children participate in culture as critical learners. Engaging in a critical dialogue with school, for example, assumes that children challenge academic assumptions from the perspectives of the aggregate memories and histories that they have acquired throughout their lives. The disclosure of subjective content in the school in this way enables children to understand, appreciate, and shape the complex and ever-changing character of knowledge and how it can be used to create new cultural assumptions and new identities.[2]

Thus, the purpose of creating and performing identity in the classroom as art is not for children to romanticize the past, to revel in nostalgia, or to trivialize learning activities in school. On the contrary, it is meant to encourage critical reflection as they compare and contrast their memories and cultural histories with the academic knowledge that they learn in school. The performance of identity as art finds its historical and theoretical roots in the work of performance artists Rachel Rosenthal, Suzanne Lacy, Guillermo Gómez-Peña, Tim Miller, Holly Hughes, and others whose live autobiographical works expose, examine, and challenge the dominant culture's stereotyping of identity according to race, ethnicity, gender, sexual orientation, and class distinctions. Unlike the conventional materials and techniques of the visual arts, and the prescribed narratives and actions of theater, the principle medium of performance art is the artist's body and its identity. The performance artist uses her/his body as an artifact to perform the narrative material of its memory and cultural history to resist cultural assumptions and stereotypes. Accordingly, performance art teaching is an inclusive practice that enables children's creative expressions of identity in the classroom and their appreciation of cultural difference as a critique of cultural domination.

As I stated previously, when teachers allow a conjunction to occur between children's cultural experiences and the academic content of their curriculum, they create opportunities for intellectual dialogue and debate. For example, school activities that enable children to create and discuss images and ideas that express their cultural identities, introduce content that is otherwise hidden, unknown, or taken for granted by curricular assumptions that are socially and historically constructed. The tension between children's knowledge and experiences and the academic assumptions taught by the teacher represents a radical form of teaching, provoking creative thoughts and inciting creative actions in children.[3] "Play," a creative strategy that children use to learn by, is important to consider under these circumstances. As they "play" with a diversity of ideas, images, and actions in their minds and with their bodies, they learn to explore, experiment, and invent ways of interconnecting their experiences in school with those outside of school.[4] This "interplay" between children's personal knowledge and that which is imparted by the teacher represents a dynamic observable act that can be examined, critiqued, and debated in the classroom. In such instances, the value that they assign to their personal perspectives, and to those of others, fosters a culturally diverse community of learners.

Paradoxically, the opening soliloquy describes a classroom deprived of children's voices, yet its construction is predicated on my own aggregate memory of the public school classrooms that I attended as a child, later taught in as a public school teacher, and those that I visited as a parent. The significance that I have given to the empty classroom metaphor comes from my personal experiences as a child where the academic knowledge that I learned in school overwhelmed and suppressed my cultural identity, never once giving it credence. Thus, the soliloquy represents an expression of my identity as it relates to my schooling experiences. Children's performances of identity enable them to expose, examine, and critique their memories and cultural histories within the context of the classroom. They are able to view their histories within the larger context of the school, the culture, and history. When given intellectual credibility in this way, such content can serve children as a means of dialogue with and challenge to the academic assumptions they learn in school in order to create new assumptions. The purpose of this process is not to diminish the importance of school, but to involve children in a process of critical citizenship and education by engaging them in a democratic debate about its academic assumptions. This debate can take place with their peers and with their teachers and between themselves and their families, neighbors, and community members. Personalizing academic knowledge in this way gives children ownership in the school's curriculum and in society.[5] Moreover, by performing identity children participate in an intercultural exchange of ideas in and out of the classroom that develops into an atmosphere of understanding and appreciation for cultural difference rather than oppression.

The art classroom is one school environment where children's identities can come into play with academic assumptions as they learn to create and engage with art forms by expressing the content of their lives. In doing so, they learn how to "perform the art of identity" as a critical act. Although art is commonly considered a discipline in which children can engage in self-expression, the "self" is often overlooked or denied. Lessons that require children to produce the *same turkey, pilgrim, Indian, turkey, pilgrim, Indian, turkey, pilgrim, Indian* as in my soliloquy, tend to treat art making as a stereotypical and clichéd activity that is far removed from the conditions and circumstances of their personal lives. For the "self" in art to have any relevance, its expression of content must originate from the children themselves. Art making is self-expressive when it enables them to create new images, ideas, myths, and identities based on their personal memories and cultural histories. Art activities that are limited exclusively to the use of materials and techniques, art historical knowledge, and cultural clichés dismiss the critical content that students can introduce from their personal lives to create art forms that are relevant to their personal lives. Teaching the critical art of identity requires opportunities for children to complement and challenge the academic assumptions of art history with autobiographical knowledge that they bring from their cultural backgrounds. Such content can serve as a powerful source for children's art forms and their overall intellectual development.[6]

Autobiography is essential for children's performances of identity because it exposes, authorizes, and validates subjective content in the classroom that is unique to their cultural experiences in life. As children tell and perform about the past and present, they reflect back on it and construct it as they see and understand it from their critical personal perspectives. The expression of identity in this way enables their social and political agency in school because they learn to see themselves in relationship to academic ideas, images, and activities and to engage them in a critical dialogue. By participating in this process children learn how their cultural histories agree or disagree with the dominant historical assumptions that are taught in school and, in doing so, it authorizes them both to learn and challenge those assumptions. The following art lesson provides an example that teachers can use to encourage children to use autobiographical content to create identity performances in the classroom. The lesson involves children in creating an artwork that represents a significant experience in their lives through visual and verbal forms of expression and through the movement of their bodies.

To begin the identity performance lesson children are first given materials with which to create a visual artwork that represents the ideas, images, and actions of a significant experience in their lives. Their artworks may take the form of a drawing, painting, ceramic vessel, sculpture, collage, montage, assemblage, photography, or any other genre in the visual arts. The language through which the children express their significant story in the artwork will consist of visual analogies and metaphors about their life's experiences that can be read and interpreted by their classmates.[7] After "writing" their visual stories, the children participate in an oral discussion to read and interpret the visual language of their artworks in order to identify and conceptualize their meanings. The teacher should record the children's comments to use later in the lesson. Both the creation of the artwork and the oral discussion that follows are part of a sequence of activities that will culminate in an identity performance in which the children's artworks serve as its "script" and their visual analogies and metaphors as its "notations."

In the next part of the lesson, the children translate the notations in their artworks into words, sounds, body movements, or a combination of these that they can use in order to animate the visual ideas and images in their artworks. This is where the teacher's record keeping is crucial because it reminds the children of the previous readings and interpretations of their artworks. This next layer of analogy and metaphor enables children to use their bodies as an object, material, or instrument in order to create a live performance. In doing so, they learn to explore and experiment with words, sounds, and body movements that signify the visual images and ideas in their artworks. Questions such as the following can encourage children to read their artworks as scripts for performances that involve their bodies in movements to animate their identities in the classroom: If you were to assign *words* to the train in your photograph, what would you choose? If the color red in your painting were to make a *sound*, what would it sound like? If the house in your drawing were to *move*, what would it look like? In responding to these questions, children will use words, sounds, and movements as analogies and metaphors to represent the visual images and ideas in their artworks.

This improvisational process complements the multiple ways that children conceptualize and play in the world. Play, which is usually reserved for recess time and given little intellectual significance, becomes a way of learning in the classroom. Through this playful process children learn how disparate words, sounds, body movements, and visual images can coexist and complement each other to represent the complex characteristics of their identities in new ways.[8] What this strategy illustrates is the ability of the human mind to play with disparity, to interconnect unrelated ideas, images, and actions, to create new analogies and metaphors that link them together. Once the children have identified the words, sounds, and body movements that represent the meanings in their artworks, they compose, construct, rehearse, and perform a "live" artwork before their classmates. As in the previous example, after each performance has ended a discussion is held for children to read and interpret the images, ideas, and actions in their performances and how they relate to the analogies and metaphors in their visual artworks. Throughout this performance process, children's memories and cultural histories are being presented, re-presented, and validated in the classroom.

For the identity performances to gain further credibility in the classroom, they can be extended into another academic subject. In doing so the intercultural content of children's personal histories, having once been placed in the unfamiliar context of the art lesson, are now placed in yet another academic discipline. Once again the conjunction of these two areas of content raise questions about their disparity that children can improvise with to create new analogical and metaphorical links between them and their personal histories. This play between their identity performances and the various disciplines in the school teaches children how to create both intercultural and interdisciplinary links between their respective cultures and the academic culture of the school. In doing so, the identity performances challenge the discipline- and culture-specific assumptions of academic knowledge by opening the classroom to the multiple perspectives of the children.

What are the possible ideas, images, and movements that can emerge when children's stories are performed in the context of a history, arithmetic, geography, or a science lesson? After learning addition and subtraction, for example, children may conjoin these arithmetic principles with their identity performances to represent what it means to add or subtract something or someone from their lives. In doing so, they learn to interpret and incorporate these numerical concepts as analogies and metaphors that represent inclusion (adding) or exclusion (subtracting) in their performances. As children conceive of the ideas, images, and actions in their identity performances that are similar to the arithmetic principles, they create analogies. When they cross-designate the two, they create metaphors. The creation of meaning in this way is synonymous with the creation of identity in that the form and content of arithmetic engages in a critical dialogue with that of children's lives. In doing so, arithmetic not only informs their lives, but they inform the perception and representation of arithmetic.

Although the concepts of analogy and metaphor may be too complex for children to understand, teachers can explain its linguistic characteristics by asking them to "perform stories," "to bring objects and materials from home, or to make things in the classroom" that "remind" them of the arithmetic principles. Re-minding enables re-membering, re-considering, and re-presenting personal memory and cultural history within the new context of the arithmetic lesson.[9] Arithmetic images, ideas, and actions in their performances represent analogies and metaphors that re-mind them of past experiences. After each identity performance, a class discussion can ensue in which all the children participate by interpreting its relationship to the arithmetic principles being taught by the teacher. Such opportunities provide children with the means by which to create links between the discipline of arithmetic and their personal lives. The interplay between these two areas of knowledge reveals new insights about arithmetic and new ways of perceiving and conceptualizing the past. As children perform the art of identity in this way, the objectified concepts taught by the teacher take on a subjective character that validates personal knowledge and constitutes their creative and political agency in school.

Endnotes

1. For a more developed discussion about memory and cultural history as pedagogical performance, see Charles R. Garoian, *Performing pedagogy: Toward an art of politics* (1999). Albany, NY: The State University of New York Press.
2. Ibid.
3. Shoshanna Felman refers to this form of pedagogical provocation as a "crisis" in learning. A comprehensive discussion of this concept is provided in Shoshanna Felman & Dori Laub, M.D., *Testimony: Crises of witnessing in literature, psychoanalysis, and history* (1992). New York: Routledge.
4. For more information on the educational significance of play see Johann Huizinga, *Homo ludens* (1950). New York: Beacon.
5. For further information about critical citizenship and civic education, see Richard Pratte, *The civic imperative: Examining the need for civic education* (1988). New York: Teachers College, Columbia University.
6. James E. Young discusses the use of image and narrative in autobiographical representations in his article entitled "The holocaust as vicarious past: Art Spiegelman's maus and the afterimages of history" (Spring 1998), *Critical Inquiry,* 666–699.
7. For more on this topic see Lakoff & Johnson's *Metaphors we live by* (1980). Chicago: The University of Chicago Press.
8. See James E. Young (Spring 1998, cited above) regarding how commixing of images and texts triangulates meaning and provides multiple representations and readings of history.
9. Re-membering is a concept that Vivian Patraka discusses more fully in "Spectacles of suffering: Performing presence, absence, and historical memory at U.S. holocaust museums." In E. Diamond (Ed.), *Performance and cultural politics* (1996, pp. 89–107). New York: Routledge.

CONCLUSIONS AND FURTHER QUESTIONS

1. Why does Garoian begin his chapter with a long soliloquy? What meanings did you get from this introduction?

2. Explain the rationale that Garoian gives for including cultural histories and memories in the curriculum. Were your cultural histories and memories included as a part of your elementary experiences? Do you recall times or incidences when you wish that they had been?

3. In the introduction to this book you read about a child-centered approach to teaching and using art in the classroom. How does Garoian's idea of the performance of identity expand upon this approach?

4. What is meant by the idea of a performance of identity? How is the body viewed in this context? What does a performance of identity enable children to do?

5. Why is autobiography an essential component of children's performances of identity? What is the first link to the child in creating a performance identity lesson?

6. What kinds of interdisciplinary connections can be made to performance art?

7. How do analogies and metaphors play into teaching and learning in the classroom?

RESOURCES AND SUGGESTIONS
FOR FURTHER READING

C. Carr. *On edge: Performance at the end of the twentieth century.* Hanover, NH: University Press of New England, 1993.

Sue-Ellen Case, Philip Brett, & Susan Leigh Foster (Eds.). *Cruising the performative: Interventions into the representation of ethnicity, nationality, and sexuality.* Bloomington, IN: Indiana University Press, 1995.

Sue-Ellen Case. *The domain-matrix: Performing lesbian at the end of print culture.* Bloomington, IN: Indiana University Press, 1996.

Lenora Champagne (Ed.). *Out from under: Texts by women performance artists.* New York: Theater Communications Group, 1990.

Elin Diamond (Ed.). *Performance and cultural politics.* London: Routledge, 1996.

Charles Garoian, *Performing pedagogy: Toward an art of politics.* Albany, NY: SUNY Press, 1999.

Guillermo Gómez-Peña. *Warrior for gringostroika: Essays, performance texts, and poetry.* St. Paul, MN: Graywolf Press, 1993.

José Esteban Muñoz. *Disidentifications: Queers of color and the performance of politics.* Minneapolis, MN: University of Minnesota Press, 1999.

Peggy Phelan, *Unmarked: The politics of performance.* London: Routledge, 1993.

Moira Roth (Ed.). *Rachel Rosenthal.* Baltimore, MD: Johns Hopkins University Press, 1997.

Moira Roth (Ed.). *The amazing decade: Women and performance art in America, 1970–1980.* Los Angeles, CA: Astro Artz, 1983.

Henry M. Sayre. *The object of performance: The American avant-garde since 1970.* Chicago, IL: The University of Chicago Press, 1989.

Catherine Ugwu (Ed.). *Let's get it on: The politics of black performance.* Seattle, WA: Bay Press, 1995.

CHAPTER 10
QUESTIONS AND EXPLORATIONS

1. Within what frameworks does our society value and understand works of art?
2. Within what frameworks do you value and understand works of art?
3. In what ways do you imagine that contemporary artists might deal with the imagination?
4. Describe what you think is meant by the words "the spiritual."
5. Find an example of a work of art that you think falls within the realm of spiritual. Write a brief explanation of the ways in which you see this work as being connected to the spiritual. What types of questions is the artist asking? How does the artist portray the spiritual in the artwork?

Transformation, Invocation, and Magic in Contemporary Art, Education, and Criticism: Reinvesting Art With a Sense of the Sacred

Debra Koppman

In cultures all over the world, religion and art have provided pathways to spirit, providing experiences and insights not easily accessible by other means. While in many cultures

> art and art-like production has been integrally intertwined with either specific religious practices or more generalized beliefs connected with numinous, non-visible, non-rational experiences many would ascribe to a difficult-to-define realm of the sacred, the majority of contemporary Western practitioners of art, criticism, and philosophy appear to be involved in what is perceived as a completely secular activity. (Perlmutter and Koppman, 1999, p. 1)

In spite of this general perception in our own culture of art as secular, "the nature of art and the nature of the spirit remain integrally intertwined in contemporary theory and interpretation" (Perlmutter and Koppman, 1999, p. 145). The issue of the connection between art and the spiritual, which has been a major crux of art throughout history and across cultures, should be of great interest and concern to anyone teaching art. I feel it is crucial that (art) educators be able to acknowledge and articulate this value of the arts. This value will not be measured in test scores, but will filter through the hands and the eyes and the bodies of students throughout their lives in the form of irreplaceable experiences connecting them to themselves, to others, and to the world.

I believe that art and arts education can be the basis, the foundation, the model for learning across the board and throughout life. I am also convinced of the value of integrated school curricula in which the arts play a crucial role, and I believe experientially that art can be invaluable in teaching empathy, sympathy, and respect for all people's cultures and for their lives. At the same time, I have a painful sense that while art is being elevated as an invaluable tool in teaching everything from mathematics to science to empathy to cultural diversity, the meanings of art are being reduced and easily categorized into their social, political, economic, cultural, historical, and other contexts. Despite current trends in art advocacy, many educators at all levels seem to be negating the poetry, the power, and the ineffable that are to be found through the creating and the experiencing of art. A lack of attention to the historical and cross-cultural relationships between art and spirit and the consequent lack of possibilities for their connection in the present is, I believe, directly tied to an overemphasis on linguistically and analytically derived understandings of art.

I hope to suggest ways in which (art) educators might begin to perceive of the arts and of their practice in terms of three spiritually-related concepts of transformation, invocation, and magic (Perlmutter and Koppman, 1999, pp. 89–101). I offer the possibility of using these concepts in combination with phenomenology as a tool for interpretation and evaluation in order to expand a collective vision of contemporary art education.

Many of the terms I use to discuss art and the sacred are laden with layers of implicit meaning and need to be defined. Let me begin by clarifying what I am referring to when I use the word "spirit." While the history of art is certainly filled with images and objects made for specifically religious purposes, to talk of art and spirit in the same breath in a secular context is clearly problematic, especially in the context of most public schooling. I want to talk about art as embodying both the ineffable, and as being possessed of spirit. By tying art to spirit, I want to suggest that art is potentially capable of embodying the ineffable experiences which defy precise description and for which we have no other means of expression. I want to suggest that art has the possibility for investing inanimate objects with an animating principle, for infusing ardor, energy, and life into objects that become alive in our imaginations.

When I refer to transformation together with the concepts of art and spirit, I am drawing on religious and secular notions of human life as a continuous process of growth and change. The idea that art is involved with, the impetus for, or the source of, various levels of transformations of viewer, artist, or materials is seen cross-culturally in both secular and sacred contexts. This may mean that art functions as a transformative agent, as a symbolic bridge between the daily world, the supernatural world, and the material world; it may mean art transforms an otherwise harsh or difficult environment; it may mean that art transforms the viewer who becomes immersed in the work; or it may mean that art simply transforms unformed material or trash into beauty. I believe that artists are essentially agents of transformation, invoking past ideas, power, and spirit, recombining them in the present in magical and mysterious ways.

Artists are a means through which spirit is called and brought forth through contemporary acts of invocation. To quote the native American writer Jamake Highwater,

> The objects of [American] Indians are expressive and not decorative because they are alive, living in our experience of them. When the Indian potter collects clay, she asks the consent of the river-bed and sings its praises for having made something as beautiful as clay. When she fires her pottery, to this day, she still offers songs to the fire so it will not discolor or burst her wares. And finally, when she paints her pottery, she imprints it with the images that will give it life and power—because for an Indian, pottery is something significant, not just a utility but a "being" for which there is as much of a natural order as there is for persons or foxes or trees. (in Maybury-Lewis, 1992, p. 156)

When speaking of magic in the context of art and spirit, I want to suggest the existence of a transcendent quality of mystery, a connection to something indescribable and difficult to grasp, a visionary reality specifically accessible through art, a way of seeing that goes beyond daily life. To again quote Jamake Highwater, (1981) who summarized these ideas most eloquently:

> Artists all over the world have always known that art is fundamentally a way of seeing. Art, like matter-of-fact reality, has a real existence within all of us even though it seems to exist in the imaginal world. Artists are among the very few people in Western civilizations who have been permitted to deal with this visionary reality as something tangible and significant. (p. 13)

Highwater goes on to explain that,

> Art is a way of seeing, and what we see in art helps to define what we understand by the word "reality." We do not all see the same things . . . each society sees reality uniquely. The complex process by which the artist transforms the act of seeing into a vision of the world is one of the consummate mysteries of the arts—one of the reasons that art is inseparable from religion and philosophy for most tribal peoples. This act of envisioning and then engendering a work of art represents an

important and powerful ritual. Making images is one of the central ways by which humankind ritualizes experience and gains personal and tribal access to the ineffable . . . the unspeakable and ultimate substance of reality. (p. 58)

I want to reiterate here my belief that the possibility art offers for experiencing the ambiguity, poetry, and magic of the world is a major value of making and viewing art, and that these experiences are crucial for our psychic well-being as creative individuals and imaginative collaborators in the invention of our cultures. I propose a greater use of phenomenology as both a teaching methodology and as an approach to criticism. Using phenomenology in these ways has the potential to effectively nurture students' imagination and sense of themselves as active and creative beings, while simultaneously functioning as an effective tool for getting past the problem of seeing only what we already believe is present in the world. In the rest of this chapter, I hope to show how the combination of phenomenology and a sense of the sacred might function to expand our vision of art, education, and criticism in art education.

I believe the goals of art education have been and continue to be framed in such a way that teaching cognition of the arts is emphasized to such an extent that one of the main points of the arts, which lie in poetry, is missed or minimized. When I speak here of poetry, I am referring again to the ineffable experiences which are ambiguous, difficult to grasp, hard to describe by any other means outside of the arts. I have heard many art educators at all levels discuss how they teach issues of interpretation to their students, researching artists' biographies, artists' stated intentions, artists' cultural contexts, historians' investigations. The sometimes stated or implied message here is that one must "know" something before one may speak or respond to a work of art. While not dismissing the value that contextual knowledge can bring to relating to art work, I believe the most important things we learn through the arts are experiential rather than intellectual.

The result of focusing on understanding art only through analytical means rather than experiencing the poetry and the stories art has to tell is what Jamake Highwater refers to in his book, *The Language of Vision* (1994), as "a wide-spread cultural illiteracy, a mentality incapable of responding with imagination to painting, dance, architecture, theater, poetry and all other forms of cultural experience" (p. 153). This atrophying of imaginative vision is a serious problem which goes far beyond the issue of art education, for without the power of imagination Highwater believes we are ultimately unable to participate in meaningful ways in our own societies. Highwater (1994) uses the example of Shakespeare to describe the distinction between cognition and poetry. He says about Shakespeare,

He abandoned the kind of prose that merely informs us and created a poetry that changes us. He distinguished once and for all between data that lead to cognizance and visions and myths that lead to discovery. (p. 86)

He goes on to say,

> When ideas become more impassioned than vision, the result, inevitably, is
> ephemeral. Art posing as disposable instruction. *Hamlet* with explanatory foot-
> notes that destroy the unanswerable mysteries of motive and meaning that have
> kept the indecisive Hamlet alive in our minds. When art serves ideas rather than
> venturing beyond them into the realm of metaphor, both the ideas and the art are
> devoured by time. In such idea-bound art the unabated effort is to communicate
> and to captivate . . . We get the point and we get the moral, but what we don't get
> is the story. And it is in the story that the experience of art resides. (p. 262)

I believe that we need, in every aspect of our individual and collective lives, to
learn new ways of being open to stories, visions, experience, and possibilities,
to appreciate that we as humans have the potential for multiple ways of
knowing, ways of learning, ways of being in the world. I believe that art, at its
best, is about expanding these possibilities and our apprehension of them.

I am not suggesting an abandonment of analytical approaches to art, nor
do I wish to negate the importance of contextual meaning. I do want to suggest
that an overemphasis on analysis tends toward diminishing our capacity for
imagination, tends to negate the value of vision itself as an imaginative process.
We are moving beyond the limiting, modernist notion that there are correct
answers that have already been discovered by persons cleverer than ourselves.
The possibility and value of experiential discovery offered through the arts
should not be dismissed when seeking meaning in a work of art.

I recently heard a very well argued talk which focused on getting college
students to be able to give appropriate and internally consistent interpretations of works of art. Using an image by Frida Kahlo, (Mexican, 1910–1954)
one "obvious example of an inappropriate response" was cited in a student's
comment that Kahlo must have been a flapper. I was annoyed by the professor's tidy dismissal of this student's response. I certainly understood that the
identification of Kahlo as a flapper was clearly not historically or contextually
coherent with the facts as we know them about the life of Frida Kahlo. However, I felt that the student's response could have easily been interpreted quite
differently. A flapper is identified as a young woman, especially one, who during the decade following World War I, behaved in a manner free from traditional social or moral restraints. Kahlo herself was not a flapper, but she was a
woman who in many ways behaved in a manner rebellious towards traditional social and moral restraints. By looking at both the details of her biography, as well as the details in her paintings as evidence, I believe we might
identify Kahlo at least as a potential "flapper soul-sister." From this perspective, I believe the student's own vision and sense of the painting could have
been nourished rather than reputed, so that the connections made regarding
Kahlo's sense of independence, her flair, her spirit, her sense of style and presence in a traditionally male-dominated world might have been validated,
even if the historical conclusions were not accurate.

Another issue which comes up in discussions regarding the appropriateness and coherency of interpretations of art revolves around the role of the viewer, and the supposed danger of revealing more about oneself and one's responses than about the art itself. Jean Cocteau told us the artist is a mirror. "When you look at an artist you are likely to find out more about yourself than you will about him or his art" (Cocteau in Highwater, 1994, p. 299). Rather than fearing that as viewers we might miss the point of the art in front of us, I would like to suggest that this potential for self-reflection might be one point, that it might simply be one more invaluable function of art, available to us if we are willing to examine the opportunities art offers us, irrespective of learning about the history, culture, or biographies of artists.

Do we demand that we understand jazz or the blues or Andean flutes or African drumming or gospel song or any other form of music before we listen to it? Can we not have a profound and moving experience with music without first, or ever, knowing anything about it in terms of the musician's biography, intentions, or cultural context? Does our primary response to music necessarily come from understanding the words, which supposedly tell us something of the content of the work? Does one's response to dance come from "knowing" a story, if there is a story to be known? What are the impetuses that get us to join in and sing, which make it imperative that we get up and dance? Do we first want to *understand* a sunset, or a rainbow, or the rising of the full moon?

I have the sense that too often we feel the need to explain the world rather than experience the world. We are, for example, taught very early on the scientific explanations for the stars, the rising and setting of the sun and the moon, and rainbows. In this way we are protected from such foolish visions as imagining the world as flat, as picturing dreams at the end of rainbows, or as living our lives in magic. We are educated as to what is *really* happening. However, to teach scientific explanation as the *only* truth available to us is to teach denial of one's own experience and one's connection to that experience, and is a sad reduction of the world.

In the same way, we seem to need to tell the stories of visual art in linguistic, analytical, concrete terms. By doing this we are making the assumption that few will "get" the point otherwise. Of course, this means that we are negating the uniqueness of visual art itself, assuming that what is there to be told can be better explained or helped along by language, rather than focusing on the fact that the visual arts are essentially non-verbal, and that this is a strength, not a weakness. I have seen very small children respond non-verbally and with sensitivity to music, to dance, to visual art, to the moon, and to rainbows. My sense is that we should be addressing and fostering what seems to be an inborn capacity; at the very least we should not by explicit or implicit example be encouraging its loss.

I believe we need to allow first for the possibility of experience, and to try to limit further information, analysis, and interpretation as a *secondary* activity to follow this initial experience. We know that art is neither created nor experienced in a cultural, historical, political, or social vacuum. However, what makes art particularly potent and important has much to do with its effect on us, with an emotional response that cannot be easily explained through analysis.

In our culture we are trained to value words and analysis over experience and gut feeling. We need to make the effort to allow for the growth of possible spaces for primary experiences, to develop confidence in the truth of our own responses, and our own abilities to make sense of sensual information. If our goals are not framed so explicitly in terms of merely understanding, but towards opening our students to the possibility of immersion in new and unfamiliar experiences we might move them toward greater engagement in a larger world. I believe that phenomenology offers a way to connect with art on a profound level, allowing for the apprehension of each artwork on its own terms, potentially creating the possibility for reforging connections between the sacred and art. What makes this approach potentially profound is that phenomenology allows for the possibility for each person to engage with each work of art *prior* to analysis and interpretation. This encourages and develops each person's ability to observe, to feel, and to experience before they are filled with the facts as they are known. This also encourages each person to question the facts as they are told to them, to begin to make connections for themselves, to develop richer interpretations based on the combination of their own experience and the available data.

We need to help students experience the arts as potentially transformative and to live the possibility of being literally and metaphorically carried away by the song, by the dance, by the vision, by the performance. We need to help them see possible ways that through the arts, through the unexpected and the unknown, through identification, impersonation, and immersion in others' songs, dances, visions, stories, they may be able to find out and imagine who they are.

Many artists live and work in an amorphous, hard-to-describe space between ordinary reality and fanciful vision, changing and playing with language in attempts to embody the ineffable, to speak the unspeakable. What motivates them, in part, is a search for greater understanding of what it means to be human. How do we reclaim the capacity for imaginative vision, and how, as teachers, do we create the possibility for our students to be moved by art in ways which would go beyond simply understanding it, or for using it as a tool toward understanding something else? How do we help our students to have meaningful experiences with art and nurture what seems to not only be a human capacity, but a human necessity to dream?

There is an enormous and complicated literature that surrounds the practice of phenomenology as a philosophical discipline. The practice began with Edmund Husserl, who was originally concerned with investigations in the natural sciences. The problem, whether in the sciences, in the arts, or in the world in general is simply the following: Because we believe we already understand the world, we are in danger of only seeing what we already think and know to be out there, which is terribly limiting, leaves nowhere for the imagination to go, and really nothing to be discovered. Let me explain this with an example from Don Ihde's *Experimental Phenomenology*, (1986) which is kind of a handbook to the practice.

> Imagine two seers, a "cartesian" seer and a "druidic" seer. Both are assigned the task of observing a series of tree-appearances under a set of varying conditions and reporting what the tree "really" is like. The cartesian seer returns with a very accurate description of the tree's color, the shape of its leaves, the texture of its bark and its characteristic overall shape. However, upon questioning him, we find that out of the conditions under which the tree appearances occurred, the cartesian seer chose as *normative* only appearances in the bright sun on a clear day. His clear and distinct tree, characterized as essentially an extended, shaped, colored configuration, is a cartesian tree, which appears best in the light of day, all other conditions being dismissed as less than ideal for observation.
>
> The druidic seer returns with a quite different description. His tree emerges from an overwhelming nearness of presence and is eery, bespeaking its druid or spirit within. It waves and beckons, moans and groans, advances and retreats. Upon interrogation, it turns out that his *normative* conditions were misty nights and windy mornings in the half-light of dawn, when the tree appeared as a vague shape emerging from the fog or a writhing form in the wind. His tree is a druidic tree; a quiet sunny day fails to reveal the inner tree-reality. (pp. 37–38)

From this example, we can see that each viewer's vision is limited by what he already knows to be true. What does not fit his preconceived ideas concerning reality is simply rejected. What practitioners of phenomenology attempt to do is to suspend one's reality beliefs for a period of time in order to have a fuller experience. This temporary suspension of belief must be long enough and complete enough to allow for a new experience, to prevent imposing external information on the experience or the "data," and to prevent from too quickly coming to conclusions. One essentially trains oneself to intensely focus on simply what is presented, in order to attend to only what is in one's perceptual field. This is followed by careful description of that experience, description given in the greatest detail possible before attempting to explain or interpret.

It is true that some interpretations will be more coherent, more believable, "better" than others. Using phenomenology, these can be gauged in terms of internal consistency. Using the practitioner's own descriptions, one can return to this evidence to check the veracity of later claims, thus nurturing confidence and encouraging belief in one's own perceptions. External information, what E. F. Kaelin, in *An Aesthetics for Art Educators* (1989), refers to as "depth counters," which may refer to anything known about the artist or the work which is not available perceptually may of course be included in the process of interpretation, but can also be checked for veracity and coherency against the primary evidence of perceived experience.

We must remember that art is above all about the story, not about the facts. We need to de-emphasize the concept of discovering the correct interpretation of works of art and remember that interpretation is itself an open, creative process of discovery which when most successful will lead to still unimagined insights. Ideally, each viewer would discover something they did not already know; when these insights are shared, we become aware of another manifestation of the richness of art. Obviously the number and content of the interpretations are limited by the physical presence of the work, with more complex, ambiguous, multi-layered pieces offering more space for the imagination to roam. My own approach to writing what is generally, but I think incorrectly, termed "art criticism," is to consider each piece of writing as a story, which has come about and been inspired by the physical presence of a particular piece of work or exhibition. The challenge is to meet each work of art on its own terms, while having and valuing one's own experience of the work. Emphasis must be placed on encouraging each person's ability to imagine, on helping each person find his/her own sense of beauty and coherence, on affirming the value of each person's vision and spirit, on supporting immersion, sensitivity, and openness to art and to life.

The importance of the arts, in terms of life, experience, and specifically education, is that they potentially offer a way we learn about what it means to be human or to belong to a particular cultural group. For the Huichol, an indigenous group living in Mexico, life and art and the sacred are inseparable. Art education is simultaneously spiritual education and is the way the Huichol teach their children what it means to be Huichol. What and by what means do we teach our children about what it means to be either a member of a community, an ethnic or cultural group, or to be an American? What interests me is the possibility for art to be a way of teaching what it means to be human. What does it mean to be possessed of imagination, to have the ability to dream? What would it look like if art were used to encourage the growth and flowering of the imagination from preschool to old age? I have the sense that what education in general does, from the earliest age, is to cut off the imagination, either by neglect, because so much emphasis is placed on what are perceived to be more important academic activities, or by the sense that children get that to spend time imagining, or even drawing, is to be engaged in inappropriate activities.

The experience art offers is essentially both non-verbal and visceral. Access to this non-verbal experience is allusive, ephemeral, and mysterious. It means that we have an alternative to the facts and details with which we fill our daily lives. Access means that we may have experiences outside of the ordinary, may ourselves become extraordinary. Images have the power to elicit extremely strong reactions, giving art a difficult-to-define connection to the magical, the mystical, and the sacred. David Freedberg, in *The Power of Images*

(1989), shows that while contemporary viewers have been educated to repress the significance of their own response to images, disturbing sensations ranging from fear, awe, discomfort, and jubilation are experienced which closely parallel the responses and beliefs about images held by cultures mistakenly named as primitive, within which art is experienced as sacred. In spite of centuries of learned behavior, humans generally respond to images as to living forms. Rational knowledge notwithstanding, through response and belief we attribute lively qualities to inanimate forms. Art offers us multiple visions of the world, creating potentially new versions of reality at every turn. I believe we need to foster belief in the power of the imagination and in the creation of our own realities, and that to do so is a spiritual act.

References

Freedberg, D. (1989). *The power of images.* Chicago, IL: The University of Chicago Press.

Highwater, J. (1981). *The primal mind.* New York: Penguin Books.

Highwater, J. (1994). *The language of vision.* New York: Grove.

Ihde, D. (1986) *Experimental phenomenology.* Albany, NY: State University of New York Press.

Kaelin, E. F. (1989) *An aesthetics for art educators.* New York: Teachers College.

Maybury-Lewis, D. (1992). *Millennium: Tribal wisdom and the modern world.* New York: Viking.

Perlmutter, D., & Koppman, D. (Eds.) (1999). *Reclaiming the spiritual in art: Contemporary cross-cultural perspectives.* Albany, NY: State University of New York Press.

CONCLUSIONS AND FURTHER QUESTIONS

1. What does Koppman argue is missing from current art education theory and practice?
2. How does Koppman connect art and the sacred? What practices inform Koppman's approach to the teaching of art?
3. How does imagination play a role in Koppman's approach? How does experiencing art promote our imaginations?
4. Give a brief explanation of phenomenology as described by Koppman. Discuss the reasons why Koppman thinks phenomenology is an effective tool for teaching art.
5. In the introduction you read about Discipline-Based Art Education (DBAE) as an approach to the teaching of art. How is Koppman's approach to art criticism/interpretation different from a DBAE approach to art criticism? Why is she critical of intellectual/analytical approaches

to understanding art? Are there ways in which these two approaches might compliment each other?

6. How might you see yourself using Koppman's ideas with students? What differences would a phenomenological approach make in how you approach your students?

RESOURCES AND SUGGESTIONS
FOR FURTHER READING

Diane Apostolos-Cappadona (Ed.). *Art, creativity, and the sacred: An anthology in religion and art.* New York: Crossroad, 1984.

Earle J. Coleman. *Creativity and spirituality: Bonds between art and religion.* Albany, NY: State University of New York Press, 1998.

Ellen Dissanayake. *What is art for?* Seattle, WA: University of Washington Press, 1988.

Alden L. Fisher (Ed.). *The essential writings of Merleau-Ponty.* New York: Harcourt, Brace & World, 1969.

Suzi Gablik. *The reenchantment of art.* New York, NY: Thames and Hudson, 1992.

David Ray Griffin (Ed.). *Sacred interconnections: Postmodern spirituality, political economy, and art.* Albany, NY: State University of New York Press, 1990.

Martin Heidegger. *The basic problems of phenomenology.* Trans. by Albert Hofstadter. Bloomington, IN: Indiana University Press, 1988.

Burt C. Hopkins (Ed.). *Husserl in contemporary context: Prospects and projects for phenomenology.* Dordrecht [Netherlands]; Boston: Kluwer Academic,1997.

Edmund Husserl. *Cartesian meditations: An introduction to phenomenology.* Trans. by Dorion Cairns. The Hague: M. Nijhoff, 1977.

Audre Lorde. Poetry is Not A Luxury. In *Sister Outsider: Essays and speeches by Audre Lorde* (pp. 36–39). Trumansburg, NY: Crossing Press, 1984.

Maurice Merleau-Ponty. *The Merleau-Ponty aesthetics reader: Philosophy and painting.* Evanston, IL: Northwestern University Press, 1993.

Henry Pietersma (Ed.). *Merleau-Ponty: Critical essays.* Washington, DC: Lanham, MD: Center for Advanced Research in Phenomenology; University Press of America, 1989.

Section II
Content

Introduction

This section guides teachers in their selection of content for teaching in the elementary classroom. It also prepares teachers by helping them build strategies to uncover content for teaching and incorporate it into an elementary curriculum. Content can be understood as two parts of the same process. The first part pertains to teachers understanding that artworks have multiple meanings and contain potential content for study. The artworks discussed in this section include contemporary art (presented as single works of art, several works by the same artist, and an exhibition of works by different artists), visual culture, religious imagery and objects, civic memorials and historic sites (also understood as built environments), the artwork of students, as well as traditional works of art. The second part builds on the first in applying what the teacher has learned to an elementary classroom—as content for teaching children and/or leading students into their own investigations.

Continuing from the ideas developed in Section I, the authors in this section offer strategies for finding meaningful content that positions art as the basis for learning across the elementary curriculum, derives from contemporary art and visual culture, connects learning to the lives of students and real-life issues, develops critical thinking skills, explores the construction of the multiple identities that students hold, causes us to see the familiar in a new way, and builds school and community relationships. The uncovering of potential content that explores these ideas requires teachers to participate in an investigative process.

Some basic questions addressed by the authors in this section are:

- What kinds of artwork should we study in the elementary classroom and why?
- How does the study of art relate to everyday life? To the lives of our students?
- How do we find meaning in works of art?
- What do teachers need to do to prepare themselves to teach art?
- How can art be integrated into the elementary curriculum?

Sara Wilson McKay and Susana Monteverde introduce a strategy for building an art-centered curriculum in which art serves as a catalyst for learning across the elementary curriculum. Creating a theoretical framework capable of accommodating many artworks, the authors guide teachers through their three-text strategy using the example of a contemporary photography exhibition as a central component of the curriculum. In a three-step process, teachers learn how to build conceptual webs to understand the different contexts that surround the artwork, peel away layers of meaning embedded in the artwork, and find an effective catalyst from the artwork to create an interdisciplinary unit of instruction composed of lesson ideas connected to the artwork.

Carol Jeffers introduces contextualism as an aesthetic theory and a tool to guide elementary teachers dealing with identity construction, social issues, and visual culture as content in their classrooms. Jeffers provides teachers with conceptual tools to understand how and where knowledge is constructed, shape classroom practice, inform artmaking, and interpret meaning. Jeffers shares the collaborative artworks created by her students whose content explores socially relevant issues. Challenging and exposing the limits of a formalist approach to the teaching of art, Jeffers offers contextualism as a theory for teaching issues-based content in the elementary classroom.

Eleanor Weisman and Jay Michael Hanes create a theoretical framework for developing interdisciplinary thematic curricula for the elementary classroom. Using traditional art, contemporary art, and visual culture, Weisman and Hanes offer teachers three different approaches for developing a thematic curriculum—subject-based, art concept-based, and issues-based approaches—and interpret the assumptions inherent in each approach. In their presentation of these approaches, the authors create meaningful units of study based on themes of human experience that require critical thinking about ourselves and the larger world. Supported by a social reconstructionist framework, they also demonstrate how issues can be integrated into any theme, moving it to the level of social action.

Using the idea that the study of visual culture is an integral part of daily living, Don Krug presents a case for studying art in the context of life-centered issues. Krug offers teachers an inquiry-based integrated approach to art through issues of ecology. He exposes the multiple realities that exist with regard to nature and culture, and builds integrated learning around the concept of interdependency through the use of artworks. Krug demonstrates how the in-depth contextual information that surrounds an issue helps us position ourselves in relation to the issue. In addition he discusses the ways in which such contextual information is necessary for understanding issues-based art and its associated meanings within the context of society. It is also necessary for dealing with issues-based content in the classroom, helping us decide what to teach. Krug translates the body of information into elementary ideas usable in a classroom with children.

Shirley Hayes Yokley guides teachers through an in-depth study of one artwork and provides strategies to filter contextual information into content for multiple lessons. Hayes Yokley assists teachers in a thinking-through process to select an artwork, interpret it for meaning, and plan a unit of instruction using an issues-based approach to discipline-based art education. She models her approach through a unit on the painted quilt *Tar Beach* by Faith Ringgold. Hayes Yokley promotes humanistic themes for lessons/units and the selection of contemporary artwork with issues-based content that will help students think critically about their lives and the world that they live in.

Mary Wyrick integrates political issues in the news media with the work of contemporary artists to develop curricula that link to the world outside of the classroom as well as to the lives of students. Wyrick uses the news media as a source for issues and as a point of entry into the classroom. She connects issues to contemporary artworks to explore perceptions of public information for the purpose of developing critical-thinking skills and informed opinions on relevant issues. In her chapter she discusses how teachers learn to identify and research an issue, connect it to artwork, interpret these artworks, develop a theme, and create lessons that will connect to learning in other subjects. Through an issues-based approach to DBAE, Wyrick introduces teachers to the idea that issues and themes in art could connect to issues and themes in other subjects and that art could be central to the elementary curriculum.

Through the media and contemporary art, Dan Nadaner brings issues of the body and self-concept into the elementary classroom as content for teaching. Critical of the constructed images of the body in print and electronic media and the negative influences of these images on children's self-concepts, Nadaner uses the content of contemporary artworks to counter the typical messages of the media and critique them. Nadaner sifts out key points in the approach of contemporary art to the body and applies them to elementary classroom. He offers suggestions for meaningful art content that encourages students to develop positive self-images and positive ways of thinking about people who may be different from them.

Paul Briggs deals with the issue of difference with regard to religious expression and presents a compelling case for the study of religious content in imagery and objects beginning at the elementary level. Briggs supports his position by discussing religious content in contemporary art and art history and provides ways to understand these images as potential content for the classroom. Briggs believes that children, as future artists and future art audiences, need to be prepared for later encounters with art and that art education is inadequate when it lacks references to religious influences and expression. He cites examples of negative public reaction to contemporary art with religious content by those who retain unexamined traditional views of how religious art is supposed to look. Briggs examines how this attitude affects artistic expression, critical public dialogue, the art world, and art education.

Joanne Guilfoil approaches the content of the built environment from a social perspective and includes human experience and everyday life in relation to historic sites and civic memorials for study in the classroom. As examples, she examines the social contexts that surround historic places such as Mount Vernon and Ellis Island in order to understand why they were built and for whom and the social and cultural memories and meanings that they embody. Guilfoil discusses civic memorials through approaches to design, development, and management. She also cites examples of how studying the built environment encourages social action. Guilfoil suggests looking for content at the local level and helps us develop our awareness to see everyday sites in a new way and learn from them.

Mary Stockrocki increases our awareness of the need to include the cultural identity of students as she observes Apache middle-school students on a reservation studying computer animation with their art teacher in a summer program. Stokrocki interprets the content of students' artwork within the everyday frameworks of their lives by including contextual information she has researched about Apache culture. Such contextual information helps develop our understandings of what the students create. Stokrocki also interprets the work and the working process through social contexts related to gender, age, and experience. She shows us how knowing who our students are in the classroom is significant in the teaching and learning process.

CHAPTER 11

QUESTIONS AND EXPLORATIONS

1. Think about the title of this chapter's essay. What meanings come to mind when you hear "context," "subtext," and "schooltext?"
2. What types of contexts do we normally view artworks in?
3. How might the meaning of a work of art be determined by the context in which we viewed it?
4. Using an example of a work of art, describe how its meanings might change as the settings in which we view it change.

Context, Subtext, Schooltext: Building Art-Centered Curricula

Sara Wilson McKay
and Susana Monteverde

Educational approaches to works of art span the spectrum from analyzing them formally for the elements and principles of design contained within them to using the latest digital technology for approximating ways of thinking about works of art (Julian, 1997; Keifer-Boyd, 1996). Some teachers prefer to use Feldman's Model as a step-by-step guide and some describe their approach as issues-based (Milbrandt, 1998; Freedman, 1994). The terrain is often confusing for future elementary school teachers trying to navigate their way within the world of art education.

Working with aspiring preservice elementary teachers whose earliest memories of art usually involve hand turkeys and whose most recent encounters with art involve "art in the dark" art history courses brimming with dates and "expert" interpretations, we found it necessary to rethink our approach to using works of art in the classroom. Unfortunately, preconceptions that art is merely an extra, a filler, or a fun supplement to a curriculum are pervasive with many preservice elementary teachers. The art course they are often required to take as they complete their coursework towards an elementary education certificate is sometimes thought of as little more than an opportunity to gather a handful of "make-and-take" art projects for the classroom.

Our approach to building art-centered curricula seeks to expand preservice teachers' expectations of the functions of art in an elementary classroom. By engaging with challenging contemporary artworks, we seek to challenge traditional thoughts about art and motivate an approach to artworks that goes beyond the usual conception of elementary art education, often epitomized by "cut and paste" projects and holiday art. The effects of such an approach include an increased awareness of art as a catalyst in the classroom and recognition of the integral role that art may play in knowledge construction.

Three Texts

We advocate and teach an approach to curriculum building based on the development of three texts: *context, subtext,* and *schooltext.* Briefly, we consider context to be an investigation of all facets surrounding a work of art and subtext to be the multiple layers of meaning embedded within works of art. The schooltext is the interdisciplinary unit of instruction stemming from a catalyst generated by the works of art. Each of these texts builds upon the previous, constructing a solid foundation for the resulting curriculum. We have practiced this approach to works of art in the university classroom and have honed its development by implementing it in the museum setting.

We contend that this three-text approach extends many ideas already prevalent in art education today and is, therefore, an important strategy to consider for several reasons. First, the development of these texts involves webbing and connections similar to the inclusive museum approaches advocated by Hazelroth and Moore (1998). Also, our approach to building the three texts emphasizes fluidity and non-linearity, much like the webbing advocated by Karen Keifer-Boyd (1996). Further, the openness fostered throughout the development of the three texts is an extension of these ideas since preservice teachers are encouraged and equipped philosophically to move away from fixity and concreteness toward an approach to curriculum-building predicated on non-linear investigative webs and constant creative inquiry.

Second, the development of the three texts entails active participation and imaginative selection by teachers. The three-text strategy solidifies the connection of context-building to schooltext-development through the exploration of meaningful subtexts. Similarly, discipline-based art education encourages the development of a contextual background for works of art addressed in the curriculum (Wilson, 1997). However, far too often, contextual work as an end unto itself can be superficial and result in weak curricular connections. In contrast, the three-text approach allows room for, and in fact requires, teacher creativity based on contextual information within curriculum development. The second component of our approach, the exploration of subtexts based on the meaningful incorporation of contextual information, demands that teachers be open and creative in how they develop schooltexts. Thus, the three-text process aids in solidifying the connections between contextual work and cohesive meaningful schooltexts.

Third, because of these concrete connections from contexts to curriculum development, we feel that the three-text approach is useful for engaging with all art. It is especially helpful in addressing contemporary works of art since much of contemporary art poses challenging questions that are based on current social and political situations. This approach advocates building the texts in ways that seek consideration of diverse points of view. Take for example "Dread" Scott Tyler's *What is the Proper Way to Display a U.S. Flag?* (1989), an installation work by a graduate student at the Art Institute of Chicago. The controversial installation was composed of several items including two photographs, one of South Koreans burning the American flag and one of flag-draped coffins. A ledger and pen were affixed on the wall, and the American flag lay on the floor directly on the space in which one might stand to write in the ledger. In our discussion of this installation, we explored the diverse contexts within which this work of art existed. Students discussed patriotism and sacrilege, freedom of speech and Supreme Court rulings, the Korean War and Taiwanese manufacturing. They considered the artist's role in the community, as well as the role of the audience in viewing and participating in the artwork. When the students looked up, they discovered a chalkboard full of interconnecting ideas. Though the installation elicited an emotional first response, the development of the three texts surrounding this piece of art resulted in engagement with the work of art on a deep level, yielding thought-provoking, interdisciplinary lesson possibilities. In this case, the development of the three texts facilitated the concrete consideration of diverse points of view, effectively incorporating art in all its complexity and richness into the elementary classroom.

In the next section, we build three texts around contemporary works of art in order to exemplify the process we advocate. The following texts represent one group of students' way of addressing a particular exhibition employing our strategy. Other groups looking at the same works of art developed very different texts. It is precisely within this aspect of openness that the strength of this pedagogical strategy lies. Consider the following example of the three texts and determine for yourself how it might be useful to you.

Case Study

The following case study was built around an exhibition entitled *Hospice: A Photographic Inquiry*, on view at Blaffer Gallery, the Art Museum of the University of Houston, during the Fall semester of 1999. The exhibition was organized by the Corcoran Gallery of Art in Washington, DC that commissioned five vastly different photographers to explore the concept of hospice care. The photographers who participated in the show were Nan Goldin, Jack Radcliffe, Kathy Vargas, Jim Goldberg, and Sally Mann, each of whom addressed a different aspect of hospice that was relevant to his/her own work. Kathy Vargas created posthumous photo collage shrines for hospice patients and their caregivers. Sally Mann produced a series of landscapes based on what hospice patients saw from their windows or the places they hoped to visit. Jim Goldberg chronicled the death of his own father, and Nan Goldin colorfully captured patients' relationships to their environments and their families. Jack Radcliffe's black and white photographs were the most documentary and yet, he inserted his own self-doubt and concerns about the right to represent people in their most vulnerable states as they approached death. The intimate relationships the artists developed with their subjects were laden with questions and filled with trust. This exhibition did not simply represent the hospice experience from a single photographic angle or tritely include specialty lenses for effect. Rather, this exhibition framed photography as open-ended, not definitive. It positioned vision as a question, not as a testimony, inviting diverse views on the end of life beyond the five perspectives suggested by the photographers.

In the sections that follow, we have outlined the way one group of students engaged with this exhibition, especially in terms of developing the three texts we advocate. We should mention, however, that this was a difficult exhibition in many ways—difficult to view, difficult to discuss, and difficult to imagine, initially, bringing into a classroom setting. Because of the profoundly personal nature of each of our views regarding the end of life, exploring this show with students prompted, in all of us, a recognition of our own positions towards these issues, as well as a tremendous respect and sense of empathy for others. Through our work with this challenging exhibition, we became more fervent believers in the open-ended development of the three texts, as well as the invaluable role that challenging artwork can play in the elementary classroom. It is our hope that the following account of our experience, organized through what we consider "big questions," will lead you to similar revelatory conclusions.

Building Contexts: What Surrounds this Work of Art?

When the class first met in the museum, we began with a simple introduction to the concept of hospice care, a loving and humane approach to caring for the dying. Additionally, we discussed the title of the exhibition, particularly its emphasis on inquiry and how that connects with photography. From our brief exchange, we asked: *What do you expect to see?* Some students answered by drawing on their personal experiences with hospice or extended hospital care while others drew from their knowledge of photography. At this point we asked: *What else do we need to know?* leading us to the concrete building of our first text.

As we build our three texts, we conceptualize "context" in a plural sense and thus seek out multiple categories of contexts provoking us to be thorough in our thinking. Additionally, we pose questions that are directed towards the time period during which the artwork was produced. Keeping these two guidelines in mind, we consider the following contexts:[1]

- *Artistic/Aesthetic Context:* What art, artists, styles, movements, "-isms," and ideas are contemporaneous with and/or relevant to the primary works of art?
- *Intellectual/Philosophical Context:* How is art defined at the time the artwork was produced? What other major theories or ideas are prominent at the time the artwork was created?
- *Social/Political Context:* What are the social conditions and issues of the time? Who are the prominent political leaders? How is the political situation described?
- *Beliefs/Religious/Spiritual Context:* What are the beliefs about deities related to the artwork? What are the prevalent beliefs, rituals, or customs of the culture?
- *Scientific/Technological Context:* What are scientists exploring? What are the technological advances of the time?

In exploring these contexts, we draw out specific ideas from students' personal experiences, readings, and research on the genre and topic, as well as specific artists involved. In this particular case, students were given something to read or skim—perhaps an article about one of the photographers, a catalogue excerpt, a hospice brochure, an interview with a hospice worker, a hospice fact sheet—clues to the contexts surrounding this exhibition. Then, as a group, we built a contextual web. Students talked about AIDS issues, aging, health, and pain management. They shared their views on end of life choices and what it means to die with dignity. They discussed photographs as memo-

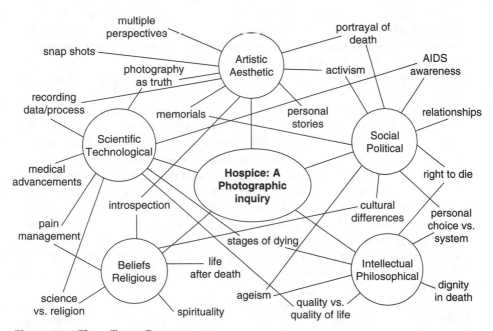

Figure 11.1 Three Texts: Context

rials, tributes, documents, snapshots, and personal histories. By building this kind of a web, we emphasized the relevance of the information surrounding the artwork and, most importantly, we were not limited to biographical information about the artist, which, although at times helpful, is not the only information that is of importance.

Building Subtexts: What is being Said Without being Said?

After building this web of contexts, we moved on to viewing the exhibition. We encouraged the students to view the exhibition in pairs to cultivate what we call dialogic looking—looking together, talking, and being aware of the dialogue that ensues. In paying attention to *What do you see?*, partners exercised dialogic looking both externally and internally. External dialogue, similar to that advocated by art critic Terry Barrett (1991), encouraged students to share their personal perceptions with their partner and later with the whole group. In dialogic looking, students focused on the works, but explored their interpretations, reactions, and understandings of the works of art together. This informal dialogue seemed to diminish students' insecurities about their ability to comment on works of art, in turn increasing their level of engagement with the exhibition.

Secondly, dialogic looking also entails an internal component, one that continues long after an encounter with an artwork. In the gallery, we encouraged students to be aware of the questions they asked themselves about the artworks while they looked. Keeping track of the questions and the resulting internal dialogue contributes to the formation of rich and personal interpretations (Bakhtin, 1981). We found that these same questions were essential to discussing the works as we began to build a subtext web with the class as a whole.

However, the most important element of dialogic looking is the crucial role played by the sharing of personal experiences among viewers. External dialogue entails an outward connection of ideas among students, ideas that are necessarily situated in different points of view. Each student's personal experience and consequential internal dialogue creates a particular perspective from which each student looks. The exchange of such perspectives creates a multifaceted looking experience that is greater than any individualized perspective on its own—in short, "I see more because I now see what you see, too." Dialogic looking values these differing perspectives and holds them up as richer ways of engaging with works of art over other methods that might involve a group leader, such as a teacher or a museum docent, telling students what and how to see.

In order to build our second text about subtexts, after the students looked at the exhibition we asked the question, *What is being said here without being said?* Important to note here is the difference between a subtext and a

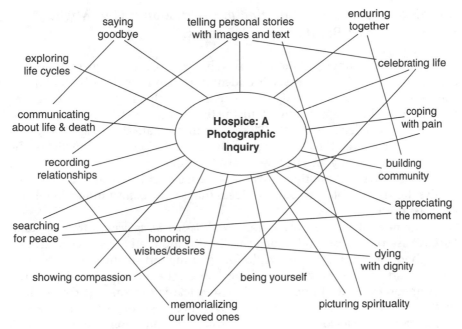

Figure 11.2 Three Texts: Subtext

theme. A theme is more generalized and often somewhat neutrally perceived. For example, the *Hospice* exhibition is about Death and Dying (the theme), but *what else is it about?* For us, developing the subtexts requires careful attention to the multiple layers of meaning that lay underneath (in support of) the overt theme. We think of subtexts as a fusion of the artist's worldview, evidenced in the contexts, and the viewer's informal knowledge, drawn from personal experience.

Subtexts generally go unnamed but, through dialogic looking, they are seen and expressed. Sometimes students call out general ideas that they think the artwork is about; we then work together to state what else is being said in a phrase. For example, some students identified subtexts like relationships, the life cycle, and tributes in the *Hospice* exhibition. We asked students to restate the subtext considering what the art says about these specific ideas. So when asked to restate the subtext about tribute, the student suggested, "differing ways of paying tribute." This phrase better defines a possible subtext because it takes a position on the idea. We have found through experience that often these subtexts are best worded as a verb phrase, for example, recording relationships, building community, and exploring the life cycle. These phrases activate the subtexts and give them direction so that they better express the results of dialogic looking.

Building Schooltexts: What kind of Instructional Unit Might this Work of Art Build in the Classroom?

During the development of the subtext web, keeping track of questions generates fruitful schooltext catalysts. We identify possible catalysts by looking at the web of subtexts generated and discussing which subtext could best support an interdisciplinary unit of instruction, rather than just one or two lessons. Our challenge is choosing a catalyst that is narrow enough to connect to the artwork, yet broad enough to be interdisciplinary. Sometimes the process of identifying an effective catalyst requires combining or rephrasing subtexts in ways that multiple possibilities emerge. Additionally, creating the catalyst from the subtext web makes ideas that seem abstract more tenable for the classroom.

The next phase involves asking, *What lesson ideas develop from the catalyst?* We ask this question thinking specifically about all the subjects elementary school teachers are responsible for teaching: art, math, music, science, language arts and reading, social studies, physical education, health, etc. The most important factor in building the schooltext is showing the connections of the lesson ideas to the artwork(s). We encourage preservice teachers to highlight how the lesson idea develops from the connection to the artwork. A weakness of some art-centered curricula lies in the disconnection of the lesson from *both* the artwork and the catalyst. A good way to identify strong lesson ideas on the schooltext web is to take note of those lessons that connect between more than one subject area and maintain a strong connection to the catalyst.

For example, in Figure 11.2, several subtexts address similar ideas as shown by the lines connecting them. These linked ideas for this exhibition became the primary ideas to consider as catalysts for the schooltext because of their apparent versatility and breadth. The students first explored the idea of "memorializing loved ones" but found that they could address similar issues in more positive ways by selecting "celebrating life" as the catalyst for the development of the schooltext (see Figure 11.3). Upon further reflection while writing this chapter, we noted another rich possibility for a fruitful combination of two subtexts to yield "celebrating life through images and text." This further evolution of a schooltext catalyst embodies the strength inherent in web-building for the three texts.

From the schooltext web above, consider the following lesson objectives that are just a few of the many ideas that can be developed into lessons:

Art objective: After looking at Nan Goldin's photographs and comparing them to 17th century *vanitas*[2] paintings, the students will be able to construct and photograph a three-dimensional *vanitas* using at least three objects from home that are symbolic of time passing in their lives.

Language arts objective: After looking at Sally Mann's landscapes and discussing Katherine Paterson's novel *Bridge to Terabithia,* the students will be

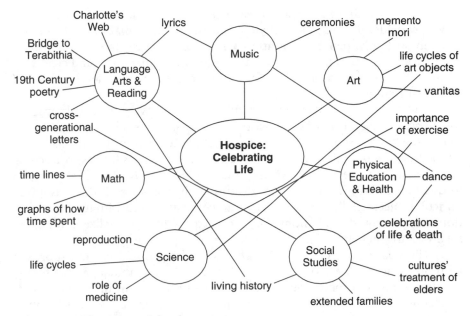

Figure 11.3 Three Texts: Schooltext

able to write a descriptive essay about an imagined place where they would feel most alive.

Social studies objective: After looking at Kathy Vargas's shrines and tracing her process to Mexico's celebration of *Dia de los Muertos* (Day of the Dead), the students will be able to research and present oral reports on a specific culture's rituals of life and death.

Math objective: After discussing how these photographs reflect celebrations of life, the students will be able to list the activities during which they feel most alive, graph the percentage of time they spend doing them, and write short paragraphs interpreting the data on the graph.

Music objective: After reading the stories accompanying the photographs and highlighting phrases that celebrate life, the students will be able to identify lyrics in the music they listen to that celebrates life and then write additional stylistically similar verses to the song.

Conclusion

In this chapter, we have discussed and exemplified the building of three texts—context, subtext, and schooltext—in order to create unique art-centered curricula. We advocate this approach because it inspires connections in both teachers and students that move learning away from an idea of a fixed body of knowledge with a fixed way to teach it. This approach is also a concrete way to consider diverse points of view and the richness that plurality entails. Most importantly, perhaps, this approach values teachers and their ability to build creative units of instruction, drawing on their experiences and creativity, while still providing a guideline for thinking through the development of such a curriculum.

Our pre-service teachers who use this approach have provided glimpses of its impact through their reflective writings in class. One student wrote, "This is one of the hardest subjects to explore and yet the discussions in class definitely opened up the options and allowed me to see some possibilities in teaching this subject." Another student wrote, "This exhibition moved my heart. I began to question myself, 'What role does death play in our society?' Death is a very difficult subject to talk about and yet we all come in contact with it. This exhibition truly presents death in front of us. Now, I am starting to realize how powerful art is. Art can help explain difficult things in a special way."[3]

The goal of our collaborative efforts in using this three-text approach with preservice teachers in the museum is focused on a mutual passion for expanding students' expectations about the possibilities of art in the classroom. By delineating an approach that is creative, not formulaic, we teach future teachers a holistic way to successfully build art-centered curricula, thereby interrupting the perpetuation of limited ideas about the roles of art in education and in society.

Endnotes

1. The categories and questions that we use to spur on our thinking are flexible and may be replaced or refashioned with others you deem more appropriate. Other categories might include cultural context, linguistic context, geographic context, etc.
2. Latin for vanity, *vanitas* refers to a type of still life consisting of a collection of objects that symbolize the brevity of human life and the transience of earthly pleasures and achievements. Such paintings were particularly popular in the sixteenth and seventeenth centuries, especially in the Netherlands.
3. A special thanks to Elizabeth Hiserodt and Hsaio-Wei Peng for sharing their insights for the benefit of others.

References

Bakhtin, M. M. (1981). *The dialogic imagination: Four essays.* Emerson, C., & Holquiest, M. (Trans.). Austin, TX: University of Texas Press.

Barrett, T. (1991). Criticizing art with others. In Blandy, D., & Congdon, K. G. *Pluralistic approaches to art criticism.* Bowling Green, OH: Bowling Green State University Popular Press.

Freedman, K. (1994). Interpreting gender and the visual culture in art classrooms. *Studies in Art Education, 35* (3), 157–170.

Hazelroth, S., & Moore, J.G. (1998). Spinning the web: Creating a structure of collaboration between schools and museums. *Art Education, 51* (2), 20–24.

Julian, J. (1997). In a postmodern backpack: Basics for the art teacher on-line. *Art Education, 50* (3), 23–24, 41–42.

Keifer-Boyd, K. T. (1996). Interfacing hypermedia and the internet with critical inquiry in the arts: Preservice training. *Art Education, 49* (6), 33–41.

Milbrandt, M. K. (1998). Postmodernism in art education: Content for life. *Art Education, 51* (6), 47–53.

Wilson, B. (1997). *The quiet evolution: Changing the face of arts education.* Los Angeles, CA: The Getty Education Institute for the Arts.

CONCLUSIONS AND FURTHER QUESTIONS

1. What do the authors mean by the terms "context," "subtext," and "schooltext?" What relationships exist between these three terms?

2. What is the purpose of building contexts? In building contexts, what sources do we draw from? What do we do with the information?

3. What is dialogic looking? What is its purpose with relation to subtexts? What are the external and internal components of dialogic looking? Why are these components valuable?

4. How do Wilson McKay and Monteverde define the difference between a subtext and a theme? How do the authors determine which subtexts could support an interdisciplinary unit of instruction?

5. How do Wilson McKay and Monteverde move from subtext to schooltext?

6. Describe the ways that the students used the artworks in the exhibit. Why was it important that the photographs in the exhibit did not depict similar views? How might you see yourself using a similar grouping of artworks?

RESOURCES AND SUGGESTIONS
FOR FURTHER READING

Carol Becker. *Zones of contention: Essays on art, institutions, gender, and anxiety.* Albany, NY: State University of New York Press, 1996.

Carol Becker. *Different voices: A social, cultural, and historical framework for change in the American art museum.* New York, NY: Association of Art Museum Directors, 1992.

Susan A. Crane (Ed.). *Museums and memory*. Stanford, CA: Stanford University Press, 2000.

Douglas Crimp, *On the museum's ruins*. Cambridge, MA: The MIT Press, 1993.

Carol Duncan. *Civilizing rituals: Inside public art museums*. New York: Routledge, 1995.

George E. Hein. *Learning in the museum*. New York: Routledge, 1998.

Ellen Cochran Hirzy, (Ed.). *True needs, true partners: Museums and schools transforming education*. Washington, DC: Institute of Museum Services, 1996.

Eilean Hooper-Greenhill. *Museums and the shaping of knowledge*. Leicester, UK: University of Leicester Press, 1992.

Rita L. Irwin & Anna M. Kindler (Eds.). *Beyond the school: Community and institutional partnerships in art education*. Reston, VA: National Art Education Association, 1999.

Ivan Karp, Christine Mullen Kreamer, & Steven D. Lavine (Eds.). *Museums and communities: The politics of public culture*. Washington, DC: Smithsonian Institution Press, 1992.

Suzanne Lacy. *Mapping the terrain: New genre public art*. Seattle, WA: Bay Press, 1995.

Lisa Roberts. *From knowledge to narrative: Educators and the changing museum*. Washington, DC: Smithsonian Institution Press, 1997.

Alan Wallach. *Exhibiting contradiction: Essays on the art museum in the United States*. Amherst, MA: University of Massachusetts Press, 1998.

Stephen E. Weil. *A cabinet of curiosities: Inquiries into museums and their prospects*. Washington, DC: Smithsonian Institution Press, 1995.

CHAPTER 12
QUESTIONS AND EXPLORATIONS

1. How do we come to know things?
2. What are some examples of public knowledge, that is, knowledge that we all share?
3. What are some examples of individual knowledge, that is, knowledge that is private?
4. How do these spheres of knowledge intersect and interact with each other?
5. What determines which sphere of knowledge our various knowledges fall into?
6. What type of knowledge is typically transmitted in the school classroom?
7. Are other types of knowledge transmitted in other school locations? What might some of these be?
8. How do we effect change in public and private knowledge?

Tools for Exploring Social Issues and Visual Culture

Carol S. Jeffers

For generations, pre- and in-service teachers have thoughtfully explored the essential question, what does it means to be a teacher? Or more specifically here, what does it mean to be a teacher *of art and visual culture?* Today's pre- and in-service teachers still explore these questions, but in the context of a dynamic postmodern society that forcefully influences the ways in which they can respond. This means, among other things, that contemporary teachers must construct their own professional identities *in relation to others* and in the midst of a complex pluralistic, visual, and often violent society. If they are to understand themselves, the notion of "otherness," and the complex nature of social issues and visual culture, then these teachers must dig into and build upon the layers of meaning that exist in everyday life. According to Mirzoeff (1998b), everyday life is the "key terrain" for visual culture (p. 125). To explore visual culture is to come to grips with society's dependence upon "picturing" everyday life or visualizing things that are not in themselves visual.

It is to address society's priority on "rendering experience in visual form" (Mirzoeff, 1998a, p. 6).

What is visual culture and how does it represent our society? What are the signs, symbols, and metaphors of visual culture that both shape and reflect our society? How are these constructed and what do they mean? How do preservice teachers "read" these constructions? How are their future students likely to read them? These questions, like those above, are open-ended and provocative, and must be thoughtfully explored. Indeed, student and teacher explorations of these questions—of the layers of meaning in visual culture—can become the *focus and purpose of postmodern teaching and learning in the studio classroom.* In this chapter, I suggest a range of conceptual tools that teachers and students of art can use for digging into and building upon cultural meanings. In turn these tools and the insights they yield are used in constructing knowledge. Among the tools in this "tool kit" are powerful concepts acquired from philosophy and aesthetic theory. I also discuss how some groups of ethnically diverse preservice teachers enrolled in art methods courses have used these conceptual insights to interpret and construct meanings in and knowledge about the vibrant cultures of Los Angeles.

Philosophical Tools

Philosophy, in general, offers many tools to those preservice teachers who seek answers to important questions about the meaning of their existence or experience and the place of art and culture in the world. (See, for example, the writings of Maxine Greene, including *Releasing the Imagination: Essays on Education, the Arts, and Social Change,* 1995; *Dialectic of Freedom,* 1988; *Landscapes of Learning,* 1978. Also, see writings about Maxine Greene in *The Passionate Mind of Maxine Greene: "I am . . . Not Yet;"* William Pinar, Ed., 1998.) Questioning how, as well as *where,* meaning and knowledge are constructed also is essential for preservice teachers who strive to understand how art teaching and learning occur. In particular, tools that enable them to delve into questions about how they and their future students come to know the world—actively construct knowledge about it—are found in the branch of philosophy devoted to the study of knowledge construction, also known as *constructivist epistemology.* In exploring such epistemological questions, preservice teachers may want to ask, for example: Is knowledge of self, others, art, visual culture, and society constructed by individuals, i.e., in individual minds? Is such knowledge constructed in and by public bodies of subject matter in the domain of art and the relatively new interdisciplinary field of visual culture? What is the role of society in constructing this public knowledge?—In constructing individual knowledge? Does knowledge construction involve some combination of the individual mind and the "public mind" of society?

From teacher to teacher and student to student, answers to these questions will vary widely. Chances are, they will fall at various points along some continuum of possible responses. For instance, the educational philosopher, D. C. Phillips (1995), describes two different continua, or dimensions, that preservice teachers may find useful as tools for situating, as well as relating their respective epistemological positions. One dimension is labeled "individual psychology versus public disciplines" (p. 7). Interest in how the individual learner constructs meaning and knowledge "within his or her own cognitive apparatus" is concentrated at one end of this continuum (p. 7). At the other end, the interest is in general human knowledge and in particular domain-specific bodies of knowledge built up across time. To locate themselves along this continuum, preservice teachers must clarify their interests in understanding "how individuals build up bodies of knowledge and how human communities have constructed public bodies of knowledge known as the various disciplines [including art]" (p. 7).

The other continuum is based on the assumption that knowledge construction is an *active process*. At one end of this continuum, the act of constructing knowledge is described as an individual cognitive process. Interests in genetics, physiology, memory, language, creativity, and other internal factors influencing development are concentrated here. At the continuum's other end, social and political processes are understood as those that actively construct knowledge (Phillips, p. 9). Here, knowledge construction is considered a social, communal activity that is subject to the rules, methods, and procedures agreed upon by particular cultural groups. Because social processes construct the rules, power relations and the pertinent interests of the group influence them. To situate themselves along this continuum, then, preservice teachers must clarify their positions on knowledge construction as an individual process, as a social/political process, or some combination of both.

Theoretical Tools

Whereas aesthetics (broadly defined) is the study of concepts, issues, and practices related to art, an aesthetic theory is a set of beliefs, facts, and principles that is offered to explain the phenomenon of art and related concepts, issues, and practices. Either explicitly or implicitly, aesthetic theories and their underlying epistemological positions inform art teaching, learning, and curriculum planning. In the hands of a skillful teacher of art, an aesthetic theory can be used consciously and effectively as a tool to inform classroom practices. Contextualism is an aesthetic theory—and a powerful tool—which is available to teachers who wish to guide their students' artistic explorations of identity construction, social issues, and visual culture. Appropriately, this theory tends to envision knowledge construction as a social/political process. As the name suggests, contextualism emphasizes *context* and holds that the meaning and worth of a work of art or other aspect of visual culture "can only be determined in the context in which it was made and used" (Anderson and McRorie, 1997). In this view, the meaning of a work does not reside within its form, but rather, is *constructed* in the context of its cultural, historical, social, and political *functions*. The viewer's (or group of viewers') task, then, is to construct meaning about the work in these contexts—which themselves have constructed meanings. Emphasizing the functional, rather than the aesthetic value of art and visual culture, contextualism involves *communication* (rather than expression) and socially-relevant subject matter. Thus, artists who subscribe to a contextualist aesthetic theory are interested in communicating with viewers, often in direct and active ways, about issues related to, for example, social injustice and disparate conditions; changing social mores, roles, relations, and immigration patterns; or the meaning of social responsibility.

Practical Tools for Shaping Contextualist Art Programs

According to Anderson and McRorie (1997), a contextualist art program focuses on "collaborative experiences and social issues" (p. 13). In such a program, teachers and students might *jointly* explore social issues and visual culture using questions such as: What is art *for?* What story does it tell? What does it mean? What does it say about the person or persons who made it and used it? What does it say about us? (Anderson, 1995). Asking these questions within a contextualist classroom, teachers and students can break free of traditional Western hierarchies that categorize and rank various artforms and aspects of visual culture. Categories, such as ethnic art or non-Western art, folk art, crafts, advertising art, graphic design, popular culture, and high art or *haute culture*, are not meaningful, nor is a rank ordering among them. In context, teachers and students can construct meanings about a broad range of cultural or visual artforms. They can be open to exploring the possibilities of, say, an Inuit aesthetic, a black or a Latino aesthetic, a Madison Avenue or a Las Vegas aesthetic, *in terms of its functional or communicative values*. This means, for example, that preservice teachers of Southern California might ask what does a Las Vegas aesthetic mean to casino owners, employees, performers, and visitors who create the culture of The Strip? What does this aesthetic mean to Southern Californians who visit The Strip every other weekend?

In the contextualist classroom, students and teachers also resist judging the worth of these artforms and aspects of visual culture in terms of traditional Western ideals of beauty and taste; that is, in terms of the "standard Western aesthetic," whose characteristics, according to Hart (1991), are "generally taken by art historians to define aesthetics" (p. 147). So defined, aesthetics can be considered only as that branch of Western philosophy devoted to the study of beauty and taste. On the other hand, contextualist students and teachers stand up to the authority and Western traditions of art history and critically examine the characteristics typifying the standard Western aesthetic. This means they must challenge notions that: (1) art is created by individuals, and thus, vests an authority in the *individual* art-maker; (2) each work is created as a unique expression and thus, is valued for its *originality*; (3) art is enduring, *permanent*, and thus, has institutional value; and (4) art is based on *form*, rather than on issues—that is, understood in terms of its form, or *formal elements* (line, shape, color, texture, space) and the compositional principles governing their arrangement (e.g., rhythm, symmetry, balance).

By challenging these four characteristics, students and teachers also are questioning the utility of formalism, the long-dominant aesthetic theory that has tended to inform art teaching, learning, and curriculum planning. As the name suggests, formalism views form as paramount. In this theory, form also is self-referential and expressive. Through form, beauty and pleasure are universally expressed to all who respond. The viewer's (or student's) task is to appreciate the meanings and intrinsic beauty that reside within these aesthetic forms. In short, formalism values art for art's sake, not for its functional and communicative value. It is not a tool to be used primarily or exclusively by teachers and students of art who strive to dig into and build upon layers of meaning in contemporary social issues and visual culture.

Classroom organization and art-making activities in a contextualist program are markedly different from those in the formalist program, which, according to Anderson and McRorie (1997), emphasizes "individual creativity, skills development, and compositional excellence" (p. 13). Students in a formalist classroom, for example, work individually to complete assigned projects, such as color wheels, value scales, self-portraits, still-life, landscape, and two-point perspective paintings. In a contextualist classroom, however, students often work together in groups to brainstorm ideas, research the issues, gather materials, props, or equipment, and install assemblages, create murals, or do performance pieces. Student groups may decide to integrate reproductions of existing artwork, or photographs, advertisements, posters, cartoons, computer graphics, and other print materials. They also may project existing slide images or present existing video footage as part of the group's piece. Following in-class exhibitions and documentation of these otherwise ephemeral pieces, the student groups de-install and completely disassemble them. Whereas contextualist activities challenge notions that art is individually produced, that it is original, permanent, and form-based, formalist activities reinforce them.

Exploring Socially-Relevant Subject Matter: An Example

Preservice teachers living in contemporary society are confronted by a host of social issues on a daily basis. Questions about how to respond to school shootings, gun ownership, gang violence, and child abuse are difficult to leave outside the classroom door. Such national issues are pressing, encompassing, and are particularly important to these university students preparing to teach in elementary classrooms. If they were to enter a contextualist classroom, however, preservice teachers taking their art methods course would focus on these and other local issues and interpret their meaning and construct knowledge about them through various art activities. In practice, what is a contextualist classroom really like? What are some art activities through which preservice teachers construct meanings and knowledge about social issues and visual culture?

One such classroom has been established in Los Angeles. It is a forum for ethnically diverse preservice elementary teachers, who are majoring in child development and have extremely limited backgrounds in art. While taking the required art methods course, these preservice teachers explore what it means to live and eventually teach in L.A.—a huge, congested multicultural city, often characterized as the capital of the Third World. Many of these preservice teachers are first- or second-generation Americans, bilingual, and striving to construct their bicultural identities—even as recent voter initiatives have outlawed bilingual education programs and denied state services and rights to undocumented immigrants. Other prospective teachers are concerned about the ever-widening gap between the very wealthy of Beverly Hills and Malibu and the very poor of South Central and East L.A. They also have questions about the meaning of home and homelessness and find it ironic that some of the homeless have made a home for themselves under the famed Santa Monica Pier (featured as one triumphant destination of Forrest Gump's cross-country trek in the movie of the same name).

Still other preservice teachers work at deconstructing the notorious car culture, popular culture, and the cults of health, fitness, and plastic surgery. Sitting in traffic on the freeways, they question their own roles in a consumer-driven, media-dominated city rightfully known as the entertainment capital of the world. They worry about drive-by shootings and other activities of the Bloods, Crypts, and the 18th Street Gang. They wonder about an over-dependence on technology, which has broken its promise of keeping them in touch, and is only valued for its own sake. In particular, the women are frustrated by an over-emphasis on the packaging and marketing of the Hollywood look worn by the beautiful people.

With such issues dominating their thoughts and framing their discussions, these preservice teachers formed groups of five or six members. Each group kept a journal or log in which members documented and reflected on their five-week-long process of translating a particular social issue into a compelling piece of visual art. The piece was to communicate a provocative or powerful message about the social issue that they had chosen to explore. Gathered around the classroom worktables, each group began this process by discussing and deliberating on socially—and personally—relevant issues they brought to the table. They worked at choosing an issue, refining it, honing an edge, and understanding the point they were to put on it. This conceptual planning phase, which was intense and arduous, required collaborative discipline, vision, and time. Growing impatient, some group members were eager to start working with materials before the brainstorming and research processes were complete. They soon realized that it was vital to the group vision to first understand *why* particular materials and equipment were needed, not just where to find them or how to use them.

The groups continued to log their progress, even as they moved into libraries, onto the Internet, and visited color-copy centers, hardware and discount supply stores. Soon, large cardboard boxes, felt, yarn, plaster, coat hangers, stacks of magazines, *papier mâché*, glue guns, a mannequin, and a computer appeared on the scene. The groups used the contextualist classroom as a clearinghouse, command center, storage facility, work site, assembly plant, and finally, as a gallery. In this "classroom of postmodern art," or the "COPA" Gallery, the course instructor and other viewers sat down with the artist groups to interpret the meaning of the pieces and give each a title. The following is a description of some of the pieces and their interpretations that resulted from the contextualist process.

Las Fronteras

Created by a group of Mexican-American preservice teachers, this table-top assemblage explored the issue of immigration, symbolically using borders, or *las fronteras*, in Spanish. On a map of Southern California, the group erected a small fence on the U.S.-Mexico border. Moving northward from Tijuana toward San Diego and on to Los Angeles, the viewer's eye, like the Latino émigré, encountered a series of parallel fences, each one higher than the last. This simple presentation carried a powerful message that geopolitical borders are not the only ones that must be crossed, nor are they the most difficult for those emigrating from their home countries. Rather, it is the cultural, sociopolitical, and economic barriers that are much more difficult for new arrivals to hurdle. Many immigrants, who evade being caught illegally crossing a physical border, later find themselves caught between cultural borders in a kind of no man's land. In the minds of many immigrants, both legal and illegal, this piece effectively raised questions about how (or whether) to assimilate into mainstream American society, preserve cultural heritage, and develop a bicultural identity.

The Face of Poverty

This piece, a large, two-dimensional collage, developed out of the group's focus on poverty and its persistence, despite the current economic boom. Group members were struck by Manet's large, haunting painting, *The Ragpicker*, that they had seen at the Norton Simon Museum of Art in nearby Pasadena. Painted in Paris in 1869, this work made them realize that poverty is found everywhere and has persisted for a very long time. In the painted image of an old, raggedy, and very familiar-looking man, the group could recognize the homeless men living in Pasadena's Central Park, who pick up cans, rather than rags. For this group of preservice teachers, Manet captured the essence of this human condition in both a literal and metaphorical way. As a metaphor, the painting is a poignant answer to the question of what it means to be human; it is a reminder that every human being could be subject to this socio-economic condition.

To present their message, members of the group decided to use the Manet painting itself. Copying and enlarging a color reproduction of the work, the group then removed the face. In its place, they inserted a mirror. Then they mounted it, together with scores of black, brown, yellow, and white faces, some that were young, some old, some male, some female, but all the same size, and all capable of fitting into the space now occupied by the mirror. Finally, the group invited the other members of the class to view the piece and themselves in it. As they reminded their peers, "it could happen to you."

Who's the Victim?

The recent rash of shootings in schools, on the freeways, and in the nearby North Valley Jewish Community Center prompted a group of preservice teachers to think about gun violence in terms of its social consequences. In a recent shooting, both the shooter and his victim were killed. Both were needlessly lost, the group observed. What did such losses mean to society? Acknowledging that society at large is victimized twice by such violent acts, the group examined the lives of the shooters, as described by the news media in various accounts. They concluded that most shooters were disenfranchised and disempowered, social outcasts. Does society have a responsibility to even its most desperate and unsavory members? Who *is* the victim?

Using these questions as a message and the latter as a title, the group began work on an installation piece. Members created a large, stunningly realistic 9mm semiautomatic pistol out of cardboard. From its barrel, the gun sprayed headlines taken from recent news reports. The gun was suspended from the ceiling so that it could swing and take aim at either of two large red and white targets. On one target, the images of innocent victims of local and national shootings were placed. The other bullseye presented images of the shooters. Even as the piece was being installed, the group added two identical photos, one on each target. These images were of the latest shooting that had occurred just days earlier. In a terribly desperate act, a paroled felon, fearing his third strike, (in a state with a tough three strikes law) had shot himself after a long, televised police chase from Riverside to San Diego. In a literal sense, he was both the victim and the shooter and embodied the group's message: who is the victim?

Patchwork Violence

This group's installation grew out of a deep concern about the unwholesome and pervasive influence of violent toys, cartoons, computer games, television, and movies on children. Most of the group members were parents, who found themselves having to do quite a bit of soul-searching. They had begun their discussions by vilifying and blaming "the media" for intruding, for desensitizing children and devaluing the sanctity of human life. Through continued discussions, these parents were forced to admit they had purchased toy guns and other weapons, Power Rangers, GI Joe and other action figures, Mortal Combat and other violent computer games in an effort to fulfill their children's wishes. The group found it terribly ironic that parents, like themselves, were undercutting their own efforts to provide a safe, secure, and loving environment for their children. They were not protecting their children from violence in the media, but in fact, providing it to them. Rather than bash the media, then, the group decided to draw attention to this irony.

The group created a child's bedroom. Indeed, these preservice teachers succeeded in building an environment, which at first glance, looked cozy and convincing. It was one in which a child would feel snug and safe. The group created a quilt to put on the child's bed and completed this cuddly look with a teddy bear. However, the quilt was stitched together using 9 inch squares of violent images collected from coloring books, games, CD covers, and toy advertisements. Beside the bed and its disquieting comforter, the group placed a nightstand, consisting of a box covered with GI Joe wrapping paper. (The group had thought about putting GI Joe sheets on the bed). An open box of Crayolas and several loose crayons were placed on the nightstand, together with the violent coloring book turned to a half-colored page. During the exhibition, this stunning piece gave everyone pause to stop and take a much closer look at violence and how it creeps into a child's world.

Living in the Car

Feeling like they were "living" in their cars, preservice teachers in this group wanted to take on the Los Angeles car culture as an issue having social implications. They talked about having to commute long distances throughout the L.A. Basin to get to work or school. During their commutes, preservice teachers admitted they ate all kinds of meals, studied for tests, and fed babies or pets—in addition to playing CDs, using the phone, putting on makeup, and listening to the radio (in the largest radio market in the world). They laughed at themselves for making lunches while driving their children to school, or wrapping gifts while taking kids to birthday parties. The group grew more serious as the preservice teachers realized their cars had replaced their homes. The terrible irony was that they had moved to distant areas so they could afford to buy dream homes they were never going to enjoy or spend any time in. Inhabited only at night, their lovely neighborhoods were abandoned ghost towns during the day. They began to question the meaning of "home" as a construct involving personal privacy, security, and family stability. What if home, as deconstructed, really meant having the illusion of stability and security in a place with a fixed address? Perhaps "home" meant achieving a certain status in a consumer society. Was it possible to reconstruct the notion of home as a private car, a mobile environment in which many daily and even special moments are shared with family members?

The group created a large dashboard with a map of Los Angeles County as the windshield. Viewers of the piece felt as if they were in the front seat. As if on the floor of this front seat were two rubber mats, partially covered with McDonald's trash, empty water bottles and soda cans, a spiral notebook, some pens, CDs, a toothbrush, a pair of shorts, a tennis shoe, and a bottle of sunscreen. All of these items—the evidence of real life unpacked—were retrieved from the group members' own cars. The viewer, as a driver in the piece, apparently had no particular or fixed destination; the whole of Los Angeles County was available. Interestingly, this driver could not see the road ahead. Rather, he or she could see only his or her own image in the large rear view mirror. In this reflection, the viewer was forced to confront him/herself and his/her role in redefining home, sweet home.

Prisoner of Technology

Preservice teachers in this group did not know what to make of technology and its social consequences. On the one hand, they admitted to feeling a need to carry pagers and cell phones in their backpacks and to spend time on line, ostensibly, so they could stay in touch with the rest of the global village. On the other hand, they had to admit they did not feel connected, despite their being wired. Instead, they sometimes were interrupted and felt embarrassed when their pagers and cell phones went off during class or other equally inconvenient times. Nevertheless, they did not turn off these devices for fear of missing important, if unpredictable (and uncontrollable) calls. They also felt guilty for wasting precious time playing seductive computer games and surfing the net when they could be spending this time face-to-face with some of the very same people they were trying to stay in touch with via cell phone. However, despite feeling embarrassed, frustrated, or controlled by technology, even trapped and isolated by it, these preservice teachers did not want to give it up.

Keenly aware of this paradoxical situation, they created a piece to illuminate the idea that technology is a prison. Its bars may be used intentionally to keep out the distractions, nuisances, and people of the real world, while simultaneously trapping and isolating the user inside a narrow virtual world. The members of this group built a small jail cell using long, black dowels. Inside the jail, they placed a computer keyboard and monitor on a small office table. As if it had just been pushed back from the table, a secretarial chair was sitting in the jail cell. Dirty coffee mugs, empty soda cans, candy wrappers, and some Twinkies were strewn about on the table and floor, along with various CDs and a flannel shirt. As the rest of the preservice teachers gathered outside the bars looking in, they contemplated: Was this phantom user happily connected to the virtual world, or cut off from the real world? Was this user trapped and powerless to escape technology? What are the costs to the user's health and social relationships? Who is this user?

Concluding Remarks

These several examples illustrate some of the ways in which particular groups of preservice teachers constructed cultural meanings and knowledge about themselves and society within a contextualist art classroom. Moreover, and perhaps more importantly, these examples reveal that these preservice teachers were able to use philosophical and theoretical tools to construct the conceptual frameworks within which they translated provocative issues into equally provocative pieces of visual art. Through collaborative art activities, these cohesive groups of preservice teachers were actively involved in a social process of constructing knowledge that also allowed for individual cognition and personal meaning. In addition, such activities enabled the preservice teachers to address questions about how and where art, social, and political knowledge is constructed and what it means to be a teacher of visual art and culture.

While these epistemological and artistic activities are situated in a particular (Los Angeles) context, they can occur in any classroom in which explorations of identity, social issues, and visual culture become the focus and purpose of the curriculum. Even with such a focus, other groups, of course, will explore in different ways and construct different meanings. The hope is that these teachers, as well as many others like them, will explore such complex issues with their future students in their own contextualist classrooms. When they do, they and their students will empower themselves to make sense of the complex, postmodern society and their places within it.

References

Anderson, T. (1995). Toward a cross-cultural approach to art criticism. *Studies in art education, 36*(4), 198–209.

Anderson, T., & McRorie, S. (1997). A role for aesthetics in centering the K–12 art curriculum. *Art education, 50* (23), 6–14.

Greene, M. (1978). *Landscapes of learning.* New York: Teachers College Press.

Greene, M. (1988). *Dialectic of freedom.* New York: Teachers College Press.

Greene, M. (1995). *Releasing the imagination: Essays on education, the arts, and social change.* San Francisco, CA: Jossey-Bass.

Hart, L. (1991). Aesthetic pluralism and a multicultural art education. *Studies in art education, 32*(3), 145–159.

Mirzoeff, N. (1998a). Introductions/provocations. In N. Mirzoeff, (Ed.). *The visual culture reader.* New York: Routledge, pp. 2–13.

Mirzoeff, N. (1998b). Introduction to part two: Visual culture and everyday life. In N. Mirzoeff, (Ed.). *The visual culture reader.* New York: Routledge, pp. 124–129.

Phillips, D. C. (1995). The good, the bad, and the ugly: The many faces of constructivism. *Educational researcher,* 5–12.

Pinar, W. (Ed.). (1998). *The passionate mind of Maxine Greene: 'I am . . . not yet.'* London: Falmer Press.

CONCLUSIONS AND FURTHER QUESTIONS

1. In a contextualist classroom, how do individual and group contexts intersect? How does this intersection affect the production of knowledge?

2. What tools does Jeffers offer teachers for art making and the construction of meaning and knowledge? In what ways can you imagine yourself using these tools?

3. Jeffers describes the different ways that knowledge is constructed in the two continua developed by D.C. Phillips. Where would you place yourself on these continua? What would cause your location to change?

4. Jeffers describes the context of her classroom, the students within it, the larger community in which her students live, and the issues they face. Who will be present in your classroom and what contexts do they live in? What issues will your students be dealing with?

5. If you were to adopt this approach to teaching, what are some of the issues that you would choose to address? How would creating a work of art about this issue change the private knowledge that you hold? How would creating a work of art about this issue change the public knowledge that you hold?

RESOURCES AND SUGGESTIONS
FOR FURTHER READING

Stephen J. Ball (Ed.). *Foucault and education: Disciplines and knowledge.* London; New York: Routledge, 1990.

Carol Becker. *Zones of contention: Essays on art, institutions, gender, and anxiety.* Albany, NY: State University of New York Press, 1996.

Norman Bryson, Michael Ann Holly, & Keith Moxey (Eds.). *Visual culture: Images and interpretations.* Hanover, NH: University Press of New England, 1994.

John Caputo & Mark Yount (Eds.). *Foucault and the critique of institutions.* University Park, PA: Pennsylvania State University Press, 1993.

Jessica Evans & Stuart Hall (Eds.). *Visual culture: The reader.* London: Sage in association with the Open University, 1999.

Chris Jenks (Ed.). *Visual culture.* London; New York: Routledge, 1995.

Suzanne Lacy (Ed.). *Mapping the terrain: New genre public art.* Seattle, WA: Bay Press, 1995.

Suzanne Lacy. *The Roof is on Fire.* A performance with Chris Johnson and Annice Jacoby. Oakland, CA, 1994.

Nicholas Mirzoeff. *An introduction to visual culture.* London; New York: Routledge, 1999.

Thomas S. Popkewitz & Marie Brennan (Eds.). *Foucault's challenge: Discourse, knowledge, and power in education.* New York: Teachers College Press, 1998.

John A. Walker & Sarah Chaplin. *Visual culture: An introduction.* Manchester, UK: Manchester University Press, 1997.

CHAPTER 13
QUESTIONS AND EXPLORATIONS

1. What do you think is meant by the phrase "cultural worker?" What is the responsibility of the teacher as a cultural worker?
2. What is meant by the term "democracy?" In what ways can schooling and curriculum work towards democracy? Would you describe your education as democratic? Would you describe your ideal classroom as democratic?
3. Have you ever taught a thematic curriculum? If so, describe the characteristics of this type of curriculum.
4. What do you understand the relationships between issues and themes to be?
5. What responsibilities do teachers and schools have as shapers of cultural, social, and political understandings?

Thematic Curriculum and Social Reconstruction

Eleanor Weisman
and Jay Michael Hanes

As we move into the twenty-first century, we continue to see educational reform and witness change in public schools. One response to such change is the establishment of standards. Another response is the improvement of teaching practices.

In meeting both responses, many public school teachers are exploring the use of thematic curriculum. Additionally, there are art educators (Freedman, 1994a &1994b; May, 1994; Hicks, 1994; Stuhr, 1994; Blandy, 1994) who are calling for more meaningful and relevant curricula. Theirs is a social reconstructionist agenda that validates our responsibilities for ourselves, community, feminism, multiculturalism, disability rights, and environmentalism. We are encouraged by social reconstructionism in education, for within such a context the curriculum can affirm the values of a democracy that includes social action towards an equitable distribution of power and a responsible use of resources worldwide.

In our work at the University of Maine teaching art methods both to elementary education majors and art education majors, as well as providing professional development to inservice teachers, we have observed the effectiveness of thematic curriculum integrated with art and cultural studies. Elementary education majors frequently enter our classroom with exposure to thematic curriculum construction from their other methods courses. We are encouraged when they leave the art methods course with an awareness that visual culture can infuse a theme with a sense of purpose or meaning. On the other hand, art education majors have little experience with thematic units. They find the thematic structure helpful for organizing and enriching the art content and skills they want to teach. In both cases, and with inservice teachers, we find that curriculum design based on themes of human experience and infused with visual culture helps teachers meet state standards, while remaining true to the ideas of social reconstruction.

In this chapter we discuss several aspects of thematic curriculum and how visual culture furthers its development. We cover a brief overview of thematic design, describe types of themes we have observed, analyze thematic approaches in terms of perspective, and provide suggestions for elementary teachers and art specialists working with thematic curriculum.

Thematic Curriculum

Michael Parsons (1998) writes about the importance of having a purpose for learning. According to Parsons,

> Purposes lead us to find, organize, remember and use information, and information helps us to reach or modify our purposes. Purposes lend meaning and information provides accuracy. They are mutually dependent and both necessary. (p. 104)

The teacher must determine how to connect ideas and concepts from different areas of study in the construction of curriculum that has a purpose.

Perhaps art education can provide an important link in the construction of purposeful curriculum. J. Ulbricht (1998) provides a historical overview of the integration of art into the school curriculum. He discusses the trends in education that attempt to make connections between disciplines. He states,

> Interdisciplinary art instruction should be organized around important themes. A theme is a large idea that integrates concepts from different disciplines. Themes give form to isolated facts, serve to integrate discrete bits of knowledge, and develop frameworks that enable meaningful and purposeful learning. (p. 16)

We conclude that meaningful curricula can be created based on themes of human experience, especially as expressed through art or visual culture. Then, we might ask, if themes provide a reason for study, as both Parsons and Ulbricht suggest, and art is a part of interdisciplinary thematic curriculum, how does a teacher design a thematic unit?

James Beane (1995) suggests that curricular themes be designed around "(1) self—or personal concerns and (2) issues and problems posed by the larger world" (p. 616). These are similar to the questions and problems that humans tend to explore through artistic expression. By viewing a topic or subject through Beane's framework of the self and the larger world, teachers can turn to visual culture for examples of different perspectives on a theme. In this regard art, or more broadly visual culture, can be a tool for creating a unit of study based on a theme of human experience.

Through the classroom examination of the self and of the larger world as expressed in visual culture, issues that are relevant to the local community or even nationally or globally important will undoubtedly arise. Critical thinking becomes integral to the study of a theme of human experience. Mary-Michael Billings (1995) presents a different analysis. She makes a distinction between thematic and issue-oriented approaches to curriculum construction. For her, the difference lies in the initial selection of topics for study. Unlike Beane, she defines the thematic approach as the presentation of a subject that has been expressed with visual imagery. Billings describes an issue-oriented approach as the presentation of a matter of general concern with the goal of students making a visual statement on the issue.

We see other complexities arising in the design of thematic curriculum. In this chapter, we further analyze approaches to thematic curriculum, pointing out both their similarities and differences. We also discuss the use of artistic expression, formalist art concepts, the study of aesthetics and cultural values, as well as the reconstructive social criticism and action possibilities in any thematic unit.

Approaches to Thematic Curriculum Design

In our work, we have observed three types or approaches to the design of thematic curriculum. We describe them as: academic topic or subject based; design topic or art concept based; and social issue based for critical thinking. Each includes or incorporates looking at visual culture and producing creative expressions with visual media. In the following paragraphs we will briefly describe an example of each type and interpret the assumptions inherent in each. Our categories are perhaps a continuation of Billings's work. However, it is in the examination of assumptions where we find Beane's framework most useful. It is important to look at the theme's relationship to both the self and the larger world.

Subject Based—"Life by the Sea"

The most common approach to thematic curriculum for elementary education majors and practicing classroom teachers that we have seen is subject based. In fact, some school systems choose a subject for a school wide theme. These are often based on a social studies subject, such as a specific nation, or a science subject, such as the sea. Because we are based in Maine where the Atlantic Ocean is an important geographic and economic influence, we have developed "Life by the Sea" as an example of a subject-based thematic unit for use with our higher education students.

When presented purely as a scientific topic the sea as a theme diminishes the human experience. Therefore, it is necessary to look to a variety of cultural objects, be they paintings, poems or propaganda, to provide witness to the human experience. Finding examples of art works based on the sea is an easy task. Local Maine artists abound who have been inspired by Maine's rocky coast. We draw on the more historical works of the well-known artist, Winslow Homer (1836–1901), who spent his later years living and painting in Maine. His seascapes of the coast and rocky cliffs evoke a feeling of the power and grandeur of the sea. A response to these images might be to have students create their own interpretations of the movement of waves and tides.

Studying Homer's images that include human subjects can generate a description of the historic content of life in the late 1800s, one that describes a culture of people dependent on the fishing industry. For example, a letter-writing exercise from the perspective of a figure in *Waiting for Dad* offers students metaphoric interpretations of the painting that touch on the emotional depth of human experience. Similarly, writing dialogue for Homer's *Eight Bells* provides an understanding of life at sea with technology from a pre-electronic era. These types of writing exercises provide opportunities for discussing art, aesthetics and criticism, and for discovering cultural and historical meaning.

Although it can be important to start with and even concentrate on paintings to which students have some point of reference (in this case images of the coast of Maine), to us the unit seems incomplete without at least one example for comparison. We suggest that using various examples for comparison strengthens a theme and provides multiple perspectives for interpretation. In this case, there are many cultural groups and geographical locations that could be chosen. Examples could be taken from Northwest Coast American Indians or from many island peoples. We chose an example from Japan, another area dependent economically on the sea. Students are asked to write haiku, a well-known Japanese poetic form, to describe the image. Discussions on differences in cultural aesthetics then ensue.

In summary, a thematic unit based on an academic topic is enriched when visual culture examples are examined. An elementary classroom teacher also would, of course, provide instruction on the appropriate science information. However, students can learn more about the significance of the ocean on the lives of humans through the inclusion of visual art discussions and exercises. In a similar manner, thematic units can be designed around art concepts.

Art Concept Based—"Finding Balance"

Art history movements, styles of art, and the elements and principles of design can all provide content for thematic units. For a comparative example, we chose to work with the design principle of balance and turn it into a theme of human experience. To do so, we ask several questions about how artists use balance to express meaning and how cultures express their values through compositional balance. The unit is titled "Finding Balance" and begins with students writing about their own lives and what elements they feel they must balance, whether it is school, work, family, or internal struggles.

For this theme, we looked for images that obviously exhibit radial, symmetrical, or asymmetrical balance and artworks in which the compositional balance correlates directly with the meaning of the work. We soon found that the theme itself provided us with a foundation for cultural and historical analysis and comparison. From thirteenth-century Gothic rose windows and Buddhist mandalas that predate Christianity, we took examples of radial balance that implied the central importance of divine spirit. Jan Van Eyck's *Arnolfini Wedding* (1434) suddenly connected in meaning to the T'ai Chi symbol for yin-yang. Both represent metaphors for female-male energy systems. By examining the asymmetrically balanced compositions of the nineteenth-century French Impressionists, we saw the influence of Japanese woodcuts that were used as packing material for the imported porcelain products at that time.

Finally, we recognized a similarity in Joseph Albers's *Homage to the Square* (1958) to the design of a nineteenth-century Apache shield with medicine wheel motif. Albers's work celebrates the conceptual fascination with the structure of a square using theoretical relationships of space and color. The medicine wheel represents one's place in the universe spiritually, physically, emotionally, and intellectually. Both of these images used abstract geometrical forms to convey their culturally and historically different messages.

For a creative expression activity to culminate this unit, we asked students to design their own compositions of how they find balance, using symbols to represent the various aspects of their life. This led to further discussion of cultural aesthetics when we found most of our students chose to represent a balanced life through a symmetrical design. In this theme based on the art concept of compositional balance, we applied the concept both to students' lives and to cultural aesthetics and values as evidenced in the above examples.

Social Issue Based— "Images of Patriotism"

To motivate critical thinking on patriotism, we developed a thematic unit based on a variety of images representing the United States flag. In "Images of Patriotism" two major issues arise: the experience of people of color in this country and the metaphoric use of the colors red, white, and blue in advertising. The resulting discussions and reflective writings reveal that many students appreciate having their eyes opened to exploitative uses of the flag image while others do not.

Usually no one objects to historic examples of the flag or to quilts using the flag motif. A few eyes are raised when we show a candid shot of a young man at a Fourth of July parade wearing a flag shirt and holding a red, white, and blue Pepsi™ can. However, many students actually are offended by Faith Ringgold's painting *The Flag is Bleeding* (1967) or "Dread" Scott Tyler's installation *What Is The Proper Way To Display A U.S. Flag?* (1989). The red stripes of Ringgold's flag drips like blood and is superimposed with three figures: an African-American man holding a knife, a white woman, and a white man. In the presentation of Tyler's work, one must stand on a flag in order to read a displayed text. It seems that students are offended by both the idea that people of color are discriminated against in this country and that the flag, as a sacred symbol of the U.S., is being altered or stepped upon.

Another controversial image that is probably found throughout the U.S. is a photo of the U.S. flag motif to attract attention to car dealerships, even those makes manufactured in other countries. The image that seemed to be less offensive to our students and yet influenced their awareness of others was one of several frames in Alfredo Jaar's Times Square Spectracolor Board, *A Logo For America* (1984). Like the others in the set, this image redefines the word "America" by overlaying "this is not America's Flag" on top of the stars and stripes. Native Chilean Jaar is commenting on the use of the word "America" to refer to the U.S. while excluding the many countries in North, South, and Central America. It seems as if the collection of images inspires discussion that each one alone could not have created.

Besides reflective writing and class discussions, this thematic unit includes a design assignment based on the metaphoric use of the three colors red, white, and blue. The expressive activity gives students an opportunity to ponder their interpretations of challenging images and to ruminate on their own consumer choices. The theme becomes a challenge to the individual to change perceptions and thus bring about social change. Increased awareness of the perspectives of people of color could lead to less discriminatory relationships on a local level. Further, critical thinking about advertising could lead toward conscious consumerism.

Analysis of Approaches: Pushing Limits in Designing Thematic Curriculum

Social change, or social action, begins with critical thinking. In our work with students, elementary education, and art education majors alike, we have observed a variety of comfort levels with classroom content that challenges by questioning assumptions and suggesting change. These comfort levels are evident not only in discussion, but also in the approaches taken by students as they write their own thematic curriculum. Approaches to theme development result in content that ranges from the safe, maintaining the social status quo and the inequities inherent in this, to challenging material that urges reconstructing social values and lifestyles. This is true of the three examples of thematic units that we present as well.

The subject-based theme, "Life by the Sea," is the safest one. It is mostly descriptive and presents a historical, almost mono-perspective view of living by the ocean and making a living from it. The theme could be expanded to stylistically analyze Homer's paintings for more metaphorical interpretations of the power of the sea and the rocky coastline. In this manner the unit would become more concept based. However, there also are issues imbedded in this theme that challenge the fishing industry. Although pollution of the planet's oceans is all too well-known, how many Mainers will discuss the effects of corporate depletion of fish supply and the tonnage of salmon wastes caused by fish farms? Only a teacher and students who are concerned with thinking critically about their lifestyle choices and their local environment will take this theme to the level of social action. Student research could inform debates representing the many perspectives on the issues. Students also could create posters discussing the endangered status of the salmon and the condition of the coastal waters. Illustrated books on the topic could be sent to legislators and government officials.

As a concept-based theme, "Finding Balance" does present more than one perspective and is more interpretive in nature. It does present the dominant values of Western aesthetics and alternatives from other cultures, but it too needs a push to take it to the level of social change. One example of the theme that students can discuss concerns the fact that many people are distanced from their sources of food. Students could also question the idea of balance that is presented in an artificially designed food pyramid that does not consider locally grown food and climatic dietary needs. The distribution of wealth is another area that is certainly out of balance and deserves questioning. There are very few social issues that do not fit into the question of balance; a teacher and students together can determine what issue is most crucial to their particular community.

Our thematic unit on "Images of Patriotism" is based on several social issues as expressed by a variety of artists and in visual culture. However, it too can be developed further. Historical subject matter could be studied at any time period of a country's development. At the art-concept level, the design element of color and its symbolic use can be addressed. Furthermore, the social issues could be brought to the level of social action. In general, once an issue has been identified and explored from many perspectives, the remaining step is to artistically design social action. This can be accomplished by students designing posters, writing articulate statements and illustrations, composing poetry, dramas, or street theatre; creating metaphoric movement or dances; and, publicly presenting any of these.

Conclusions

From educator David Trend (1992) we define both teachers and artists as cultural workers. Thus both are responsible for defining their attitudes towards the status quo and the improvement of social and environmental conditions. It is important for teachers at all levels to reflect upon the values and influences upheld and produced in the mono-culture of the U.S. At this time in history, when wealthy corporations may be determining worldwide government agendas, it is imperative that our students look beyond a limited acceptance of existing inequities and work toward democracy. Exploring and pursuing themes of human experience as curricular units is a strategy for thinking critically about ourselves and our interactions with other cultures, other species, and our local and collective environment.

As elementary preservice and inservice teachers become more aware of the potential of visual culture as a resource for exploring themes of human experience, it becomes more important to integrate art specialists as thematic consultants. Teachers are networking and collaborating to share their expertise and to create holistic learning experiences for students and each other. As we work together, we must acknowledge our social and political assumptions that are imbedded in our choice of curricular content and our pedagogical approaches.

Whether a thematic unit is based on a subject, an art concept, or a social issue, it can be approached in a manner that encourages self-growth, a better understanding of those who are different, and social action, all steps toward social reconstruction. Students can be empowered by classroom experiences. Creative expression can effectively communicate knowledge. Collaborative art works can create and enhance a sense of community. We must acknowledge that merely recycling past knowledge is not a solution; our children face crucial issues in their future. To expand on the metaphor, recycling plastic bottles will not solve the rapid depletion of petroleum supplies on which many people are dependent. We must guide our students in discovering and stating what is important to them, and encourage them to take action.

References

Beane, J. A. (1995). Curriculum integration and the disciplines of knowledge. *Phi Delta Kappan, 76*(8), 616–629.

Billings, M. M. (1995). Issues vs. themes: Two approaches to a multicultural art curriculum. *Art Education, 48*(1), 21–56.

Blandy, D. (1994). Assuming the responsibility: Disability rights and the preparation of art educators. *Studies in Art Education, 35*(3), 179–187.

Freedman, K. (1994a). About this issue: The social reconstruction of art education. *Studies in Art Education, 35*(3), 131–134.

Freedman, K. (1994b). Interpreting gender and visual culture in art classrooms. *Studies in Art Education, 35*(3), 157–170.

Hicks, L. E. (1994). Social reconstruction and community. *Studies in Art Education, 35*(3), 149–156.

May, W. T. (1994). The tie that binds: Reconstructing ourselves in institutional contexts. *Studies in Art Education, 35*(3), 135–148.

Parsons, M. (1998). Integrated curriculum and our paradigm of cognition in the arts. *Studies in Art Education, 39*(2), 103–116.

Stuhr, P. L. (1994). Multicultural art education and social reconstruction. *Studies in Art Education, 35*(3), 171–178.

Trend, D. (1992). *Cultural pedagogy: Art/education/politics*, New York, NY: Bergin & Garvey.

Ulbricht, J. (1998). Interdisciplinary art education reconsidered. *Art Education, 51*(4), 13–17.

CONCLUSIONS AND FURTHER QUESTIONS

1. What do teachers need to know and what kinds of skills are required to follow a thematic approach to the teaching of art?

2. Weisman and Hanes provide examples of three types of thematic curriculum. Describe each of these approaches and discuss ways that they are similar and different.

3. What do the authors mean when they say, "we must acknowledge our social and political assumptions that are embedded in our choice of curricular content and our pedagogical approaches?" In what ways have your understandings and assumptions played a part in curricular choices you have made?

4. How does the study of art through a thematic approach add to interdisciplinary learning in an elementary curriculum?

5. Describe the intersections, similarities, and differences between an issues-based and a thematic curriculum.

6. Weisman and Hanes advocate a social reconstruction approach to art education and curriculum development. Describe what this approach is and discuss ways in which it can help us make connections to the lives of our students and raise contemporary issues in the elementary classroom.

7. How are Weisman and Hanes able to shift a subject-based thematic curriculum to one that is issues-based? How do the authors attempt to create social change through the units they develop? What strategies do they use to make the units more critical?

RESOURCES AND SUGGESTIONS
FOR FURTHER READING

Paula Allman. *Revolutionary social transformation: democratic hopes, political possibilities and critical education.* Westport, NY: Bergin & Garvey, 1999.

Carol Becker (Ed.). *The subversive imagination: Artists, society, and social responsibility.* New York: Routledge, 1994.

Kathleen Casey. *I answer with my life: life histories of women teachers working for social change.* New York: Routledge, 1993.

Trevor J. Fairbrother. *In and out of place: Contemporary art and the American social landscape.* Boston, MA: Museum of Fine Arts, 1993.

Nina Felshin (Ed.). *But is it art? The spirit of art as activism.* Seattle, WA: Bay Press, 1994.

Maxine Greene. *Releasing the imagination: Essays on education, the arts, and social change.* San Francisco: Jossey-Bass Publishers, 1995.

Janice Jipson. *Repositioning feminism and education: Perspectives on educating for social change.* Westport, NY: Bergin & Garvey, 1995.

Roy Lowe. *Schooling and social change, 1964–1990.* London; New York: Routledge, 1997.

Noel F. McGinn & Erwin H. Epstein (Eds.). *Comparative perspectives on the role of education in democratization.* Frankfurt am Main, Germany; New York: Peter Lang, 1999.

Gladys R. Capella Noya, Kathryn Geismar, & Guitele Nicoleau (Eds.). *Shifting histories: Transforming schools for social change.* Cambridge, MA: Harvard Educational Review, 1995.

Thomas S. Popkewitz & Lynn Fendler (Eds.). *Critical theories in education: Changing terrains of knowledge and politics.* New York: Routledge, 1999.

Seymour B. Sarason. *Barometers of change: Individual, educational, and social transformation.* San Francisco, CA: Jossey-Bass Publishers, 1996.

Ira Shor. *Empowering education: Critical teaching for social change.* Chicago, IL: University of Chicago Press, 1992.

Patricia L. Stuhr. Social reconstructionist multicultural art curriculum design: Using the powwow as an example. In Ronald W. Neperud (Ed.). *Context, content, and community in art education: Beyond postmodernism* (pp. 193–221). New York: Teachers College Press, 1995.

Catherine E. Walsh (Ed.). *Education reform and social change: Multicultural voices, struggles, and visions.* Mahwah, NJ: L. Erlbaum Associates, 1996.

1. What images and ideas do you associate with the word "ecology?" With the word "environment?" What differing meanings do these two terms suggest?
2. Would you describe yourself as being involved in any sort of ecological and/or environmental activities? If so, describe your involvement. What effects has this had on the ways that you think about the environment? If you are not, describe your reasons for not choosing to be involved.

Teaching Art in the Contexts of Everyday Life

Don H. Krug

"In my dream, the angel shrugged and said, If we fail this time, it will be a failure of imagination and then she placed the world gently in the palm of my hand."

(Brian Andreas, 1994, Still Mostly True)

Visual culture can be understood in relationship to the meanings and values of people's daily ways of living. Lucinda Furlong (1994) suggests that "how we experience the landscape is shaped not only by factors such as class, gender, race, age, and politics, but by the cultural forms employed to represent it" (in Krug, 1997). The earth is an ecological community rich in biological, social, and cultural diversity. Human existence is one of the greatest contributors to the destruction of our fragile environment. Christo's (b.1935) *Earth Wrap* is one example of an artwork that depicts the dynamic tensions among human use of the earth and the industrial degradation that most often accompanies this use and human responsibility to act as stewards of the natural environment on a day-to-day basis. His artwork vividly warns us that the earth is not a package that can be exchanged for a new globe at the local outlet store.

Figure 14.1 Christo, *Earth Wrap.* (Magazine cover from Time/Life Syndication)

The arts have often served political, institutional, expressive, sacred, and/or utilitarian roles simultaneously in society. Before the nineteenth century, Gowans (1971) suggests that most art was neither *fine* nor *popular*, but connected to lived experiences. Connecting art and life-centered issues is not new in art education. Culture is interdependent with nature and the arts represent some of the most telling and extraordinary examples of everyday life.

In this chapter, I discuss an approach to curriculum integration that facilitates inquiry about art in the contexts of life-centered issues. I discuss these ideas[1] using the concept of interdependency. Examples are provided from an Art & Ecology[2] web site published on ArtsEdNet.[3] Emphasis is given to understanding the generalization of interdependency in relationship to the dynamic interplay of certain social, historical, and cultural issues and interests: philosophy—dominion, stewardship, and union, (Stankiewicz and Krug, 1997), perspectives—environmental design, ecological design, social ecology, ecological restoration, and the selection of teaching concepts—location, time, material, and change, (Krug, 1997). In conclusion, I discuss how educational experiences based on an integrated approach to studying about everyday life-centered issues can enable students to understand the ways in which many different realities are constructed from diverse cultural perspectives.

Figure 14.2 Bea Zuehlke is a community artist. In this photo she demonstrates to elementary students how to comb and card wool (rabbit hair) and spin it into yarn. (1988 Photograph © Don Krug)

Identifying Life-Centered Issues

During my undergraduate education, I can still recall standing in front of a large abstract expressionist painting waiting to have an "aesthetic experience." The work didn't seem to move me in a way that allowed me to transcend my immediate experience. I searched for inherent meaning in the work but instead found my everyday encounters and situations to be extremely important to understanding the symbolism and metaphors that the artist used. I was unable to use a systematic approach to describing, interpreting, analyzing, and evaluating the art. Instead, I made random and systemic connections almost simultaneously, piecing together a story out of personal, historical, and social contexts. I was confused by any attempt to distance myself from the work in order to see it anew. My personal biases were evident, and rather than trying to hide them, it seemed more important to bring these issues to the surface so that I could examine them in light of their social, historical, and cultural formation. Even though I enjoyed the artwork immensely, I was uncertain of how I was to critique the work using an "educational model of art criticism." Imagine my disappointment when I realized the work did not move me in any of the ways that I had been reading about in the art-education course literature.

Later, I was hired to teach art in grades K–5 and coordinate an aesthetic enrichment program called "Learn by Looking" in a small Midwest community. This federally funded consortium of three rural school districts purchased several hundred, art reproductions. I coordinated adult volunteers to instruct elementary students about artists and artwork at the school where I taught. At first, I struggled with the selection of artwork. Which artists were most significant for the students to learn about? Should I choose work around themes based on art history and art criticism instruction I had received at the university? Why would young K–5 grade students in a rural community find the work meaningful and relevant to their lives? In the end, this last question carried the most value for me as an art teacher. I quickly learned that students also had a hard time appreciating a laminated reproduction of a Mark Rothko (1903–1970) abstract painting. However, these same students participated with delight when their grandmother came to school to share how rabbit wool could be spun into yarn and dyed different colors using flower petals or vegetable scraps from a garden. Based on these experiences and classroom practices, I became interested in curriculum integration and life-centered issues. I began to realize that the arts should not be viewed as separate from other disciplines, and that the study of visual culture is an integral part of daily living.

Currently, I teach curriculum classes for undergraduate and graduate certification students at the Ohio State University. Students ask some of the same kinds of questions about knowledge selection and organization that I asked when getting started. One goal of the Ohio Department of Education calls for teaching with flexible educational programming in art education that is responsive to local and global concerns (Ohio Comprehensive Arts Education, 1996). I believe teachers should ask what is important to teach and why it is significant. Ideas can be connected to a diverse range of subject matter in art education and across other fields of study. Learning about ideas can invite questions from students about their sense of place in the world. What forms of inquiry are needed in order for students to investigate everyday issues within their own communities nationally and globally? Life-centered approaches encourage inquiry as a means for understanding ideas as part of life-long learning. In this way, learning is part of continuous processes of critically investigating and generating knowledge and not acquiring content as an end in itself (Perkins and Blythe, 1994; Perrone, 1994). Life-centered issues encompass a broad range of subjects and reflect interpretations of people's social interests and differences.

Interpreting Life-Centered Issues about Interdependency

Interdependency is a concept about the relations of nature and culture. In ancient times, spiritual leaders mediated among people and the world of plants and animals. Cultures from around the world have interpreted ideas of earth, ecology, and environment through artifacts and practices in different ways. For example, tribal shamans of indigenous peoples have long represented the power, energy, and spirits of place as both male and female deities. In ancient Egypt, the world's vegetation was believed to have sprouted from the Earth father's back. The Algonquin people regarded the Earth as their mother. Similarly, creation myths of the Hopi tell of Tiowa or Spider Grandmother who in the beginning gave structure and form to the earth. Concepts of earth, ecology, and environment are also represented through objects and ritual practices in contemporary societies. "Shimenewa," ceremonial straw rope, is used to mark the spiritual power of place in Japan. In the Amazon region, shaman Pablo Amaringo (b. 1943) creates paintings of animals, plants, spirits, and mythological beings as a way to help preserve this bioregion's ecosystem. Spiritual, social, and physical connections are also simultaneously referred to in the sandpaintings of Navajo healing ceremonies. Stones, plants, and sacred objects are often placed inside the painting to represent the interconnectedness of the physical, social, and spiritual needs of people and the earth's greater life forces.

In the United States, the study of interdependency emerged in the 1960s as a response to growing concern about environmental issues that plague the earth. Though the Clean Air Act was passed in 1955 and the Wilderness Preservation Act was passed in 1964, the government did not act on behalf of the environment in a significant way until the 1970s, following the first Earth

Figure 14.3 Robert Rauschenberg. *Earth Day*, 1970. (©Robert Rauchenberg and Gemini G.E.L./Licensed by VAGA, New York, NY. Museum number M.80.241.6. Title/Date: Earth day, 1970. Artist: Robert Rauchenberg. Credit: Los Angeles County Museum of Art, Gift of the Sidney and Diana Avery Trust. Copyright notice Photograph © 2000 Museum Associates/LACMA.)

Day, on April 22, 1970. This event, initiated by Wisconsin senator Gaylord Nelson, was observed in thousands of rallies, demonstrations, and clean-up initiatives around the country. Earth Day motivated a larger public to get involved in environmental affairs and established environmentalism as a worldwide movement. Following the event, membership in environmental organizations swelled to unprecedented levels, and politicians suddenly scurried to respond to voters' concerns.

In the 1950s, artist Robert Rauschenberg (b.1925) experimented with using new media that included everyday objects and materials in his work. "Earth Paintings" were indoor wall hangings composed of soil and grass. His "combines" extended the conception of painting as a flat two-dimensional space off the wall into the three dimensional space of the viewers. "Mud-Muse" (1968–1971) was an installation created in collaboration with engineers at Teledyne Inc. that re-circulated ordinary soil through a system of mechanical apparatuses. It drew attention to the taken-for-granted perception and use of natural "resources" in industrial societies. In the 1960s he featured the interdisciplinarity of his ideas in collage-like montages. *Earth Day* (1970) was a poster in a montage style commissioned by the American Environment Foundation and commemorates the first Earth Day. These early forms of environmental art explored ideas of the artist's relationship to society and society's interconnectedness with nature.

A number of federal laws were passed, beginning with the National Environmental Policy Act, the Occupational Safety and Health Act, and the Solid Waste Disposal Act in 1970 and the Endangered Species Act in 1973. President Richard Nixon also created the Environmental Protection Agency (EPA) in 1970 to enforce the new laws. Environmentalism suffered a serious setback in the 1980s, when the federal government became more responsive to the demands of industry, development, ranching, mining, and logging. The budget of the EPA was slashed during this period and programs to develop alternative energy sources, such as solar and wind power, were discontinued. In the 1990s, ecologists mediated relationships between humans and the environment by reintroducing native plants and animals into sites to help reclaim and sustain biodiversity. Ecology is a biological science in which the relationships of living organisms with each other and with their environment are studied. Ecology and the environment are often mistakenly used interchangeably. Ecology is a concern for the maintenance of the integrity of natural systems, including homeostasis and diversity. A broad definition of environment simply is the objects and conditions surrounding someone. Wetlands and forests are two types of ecological systems or habitats vanishing around the world that ecologists are concerned about and that contemporary ecological artists are recreating on city streets, parks, and nature preserves.

Most ecological artworks are conceived as sanctuaries within which human beings can experience nature's beauty along with the natural abundance of ecological systems. Changes in the ways that people look at the relationships between nature and culture from ancient times to the present continue to evolve. People are beginning to understand that "the planet" includes their own backyards.

From a more contemporary and philosophical position, educators have generally identified three views that characterize approaches to interdependency: *dominion*—human control of nature, *stewardship*—human care of nature, and *union*—humans as part of nature. (Heimlich, 1992). It is important for elementary teachers to understand their own view of the interdependency of the environment and culture in order to understand and teach about contemporary ecological art.

Dominion is a view that humans should dominate nature. In art education, examples of this approach were prevalent in textbooks of the late 19th century that instructed students to re-imagine and re-design nature in unique ways through their art. Today, this anthropocentric view of controlling the natural environment is still prevalent in some environmental art projects that attempt to reshape natural spaces for the sake of urban renewal or public art that is premised strictly on order, beauty, and a purely formal aesthetic purpose.

Another view of interdependency has used scientific observation of nature as a means to affirm beliefs about caring for the natural world. Science and the arts have been combined and introduced to schoolchildren through nature study and outdoor education programs. Nature study is a form of stewardship that is concerned with both the aesthetic attributes of landscape design and a bioregions natural order. Much of the urban improvement of the early 20th century combined dominion with stewardship.

Union is an orientation that values ecologically sustainable development. It is an approach to understanding interdependency arrived at by locating and not privileging humans within complex ecosystems of nature. Views of art and ecology premised on this perspective strive to understand the relationships of all living organisms within particular places through art. In art education, teachers are beginning to work for more inclusive approaches to integrated curricula that examine environmental issues through the study of various forms of visual culture.

Some contemporary ecological artists believe that what matters most are concerns about union or ecological sustainability. Educators and artists working toward ecological sustainability have as their task the responsibility of "finding alternatives to the practices that got us into the trouble in the first place; it is necessary to rethink agriculture, shelter, energy use, urban design, transportation, economics, community patterns, resource use, forestry, the importance of wilderness, and our central values" (Orr, 1992, p. 22).

One example of ecological sustainability through art is Mel Chin's (b.1957) *Revival Field* (1990–present) in St. Paul, Minnesota. Chin worked with Rufus L. Chaney, a Senior Research Scientist at the U.S. Department of Agriculture, to develop plans for the *green remediation* of toxic waste from the Pig's Eye landfill. Chaney developed a *hyperaccumulator* plant for extracting toxic substances from the soil through the plant's vascular system. The goal of the artist was to eventually restore the area for plants, animals, and humans. In this way art, aesthetics, ecology, and culture become inseparable. Methods commonly employed to initiate ecological sustainability include artistic actions, rituals, performances, and process dramas. It is important to understand, however, that ecological sustainability has many meanings. Van der Ryn and Cowan (1996) point out,

> Sustainability is not a single movement or approach. It is as varied as the communities and interests currently grappling with the issues it raises. The shape that it will take is being contested now, and the stakes are high. On the one hand, sustainability is the province of global policy-makers and environmental experts flying at thirty-five thousand feet from conference to conference. On the other hand, sustainability is also the domain of grassroots environmental and social groups, indigenous peoples preserving traditional practices, and people committed to changing their own communities. (p. 4)

Most contemporary ecological artists are keenly attuned to the fluctuating interconnectedness of art, aesthetics, ecology, and culture. Artists are working collaboratively with members of communities to use their creative energies to solve real life-centered problems that affect the interdependency of nature and culture. Below, I will discuss a few ideas and issues that can be studied about interdependency through an integrated curricular approach in elementary education.

Ecological Art Perspectives

I have struggled over how to present these typologies without suggesting that ideas and issues can fit neatly into any one type of category. Ecological ideas and issues involve differences in people's perspectives of human and environmental conditions. Such issues are deeply connected to past and existing social and cultural contexts. Raymond Williams (1961) used dominant, residual, and emergent points of view as a way to understand how issues affect what we experience, how changing perspectives influence the formation of diverse life styles, and how contexts contribute to our personal perspectives. Many issues addressed by ecological artists are connected to specific community concerns and environmental conditions associated with location, time, material, and change. For the purpose of studying about interdependency, a stream metaphor can be useful for students to understand how perspectives on ecological issues are very dynamic.

Perspectives change like a streams' many currents with different dimensions and directions. Typically in a society, one particular perspective is the strongest current or most dominant point of view. From the many perspectives that different people hold, no one current (perspective) ever quite dries up and its residual effect occasionally reappears. When the weather or conditions are suitable, a weaker or less powerful point of view might emerge and assume more force and prominence only to decline when conditions particularly conducive to its newfound strength no longer prevail. Ecological artists interpret ideas of interdependency differently through their art. Andy Goldsworthy (1990) states, "When I touch a rock, I am touching and working the space around it. It is not independent of its surroundings and the way it sits tells how it came to be there." Art is a way to inquire critically about relationships and interactions of all life forms within their ecosystem. Artists such as Mel Chin, Viet Ngo, Alan Sonfist, and Nancy Holt (b.1938) introduce new plant life into toxic areas to help heal and sustain the interaction of land and life forms. They ask viewers of their art to reinterpret people's relationships to the land.

Four ecological art perspectives—*environmental design, ecological design, social restoration,* and *ecological restoration*—encompass a wide range of interpretations of contemporary ecological art based on the philosophical positions of dominion, stewardship, and union discussed earlier. Dominion is a philosophical position held by some artists working with nature as a resource for particular aesthetic endeavors. Artists with an orientation to *environmental design* have been interested in designing the environment. However, in the 1980s and 1990s, artists, architects, designers, and civil engineers have explored ways to link art, aesthetics, ecology, and culture.

Artists who address local ecological issues through their artwork might hold views associated with dominion and stewardship simultaneously. Artists who work in the area of *ecological design* are concerned with how the art they create is contingent on direct experiences and interactions with a particular place where the art is created. An ecological view of design considers the artwork within larger contexts of how people, plants, and animals are interconnected with each other, the site, and/or the earth.

An ecological ethic where humans live in relationship to larger communities of life has catalyzed some artists to create socially responsible artworks. Artists who explore *social ecology* critically examine everyday life experiences for bringing about positive ecological change. These artists strive to mediate ideas of union and stewardship by questioning the ecological impact of the built environment and social unrest. Guillermo Gómez-Peña (b.1955) writes, "Real life is calling. I can no longer ignore the clamor of disaster— economic, spiritual, environmental, political disaster—in the world in which I move" (in Krug, 1997). These artists scrutinize relations of power that produce community tensions about ecological issues. They encourage viewers to question individual and collective assumptions, beliefs, and practices and take action to bring about positive and healthy conditions of social change.

Ecological restoration projects usually involve long-term commitments that help reclaim and restore ecological systems. These artists typically hold a philosophical position of union. Ecological restoration artists attempt to alert viewers to environmental issues and problems through shock, humor, and educational documentation. They seek to educate the public to the systemic character of bioregions through the use of ritual, performance, and process drama. Some ecological artists engage people directly in environmental activities or actions by confronting environmentally unhealthy practices with social, ethical, and moral ecological concerns.

Location, Time, Material, and Change

At this point, let us now turn to a more practical look at how these philosophies and perspectives can be taught at an elementary level through the identification of four concepts of interdependency: *location, time, material*, and *change*. It is relatively easy to select an artist of renowned reputation or artwork based on resource availability or pre-made unit information about the environment. However, if we are asking students to understand the associated meanings of art within the contextual conditions of society, then it is necessary to do inquiry about the way these issues emerge, become dominant, and have residual effects on the formation of their self and social points of view. I believe that for students at an elementary grade level many of the ideas and issues discussed above are too complex, as stated, to ask young children to remember and apply to their day to day lives. A more approachable way for young children to understand these issues is through the following four concepts—*location, time, material*, and *change*—which are also frequently addressed by ecological artists. These concepts derive from the positions and perspectives above and can provide a more accessible way for teachers of elementary students to explore the many different meanings of interdependency. Teachers and students can also use these concepts to help examine ideas expressed through artworks across diverse subject areas such as reading, science, music, social studies, and to make connections with everyday life-centered issues.

Location

The concept of location has been defined in many distinct ways with subtle distinctions such as, *bioregion, space, locale*, and *place*. To talk about this with students we might explore a bioregion such as an old growth forest that was once populated by spotted owls. The plight of the spotted owl, now an endangered species, is particularly significant because it is also an indicator species. Its disappearance is a sign of forest depletion. *Bioregions* are geographic areas of land defined by physical factors such as soil, water, and climate and the associated biotic systems of living organisms within a region. Location has also been defined by geographic *spaces* and topological features. Landscape paintings

Figure 14.4 Andy Goldsworthy, *Red Sand from Stone*, July 1991. Performance Mount Victor Station, South Australia.

represent this view of location. Culture and experience strongly influence how people interpret aspects of the physical landscape. In addition location has been defined by cultural boundaries—as the *locale* where culture is lived (Lippard, 1997). Artists such as Robert Glenn Ketchum (b.1947), Neil Jenny (b.1945), and Susan Middleton and David Liitschwager (b.1961), have addressed these issues about locations through their art.

In recent years, ecological artists have conceived of *place* as the union among the physical, spiritual, historical, and social diversity of a particular geographic region. This concept of place includes how people understand themselves within the contexts of particular locations. Marlene Creates writes, "The land is important to me, but even more important is the idea that it becomes a place because someone has been there" (in Lippard, 1997, p. 32). Art critic, Lucy Lippard (1997) states, "The lure of the local is embedded in land, history, and culture and the possibilities they hold for place-specific, place-responsible public art and photography that share the goals of a 'humanistic geography, to recover the geographical imagination . . . and to introduce moral discourse.'" (p. 14).

Time

Another dimension to making art is the temporal aspect of lived experiences. Throughout history, cultures have developed systems to measure time and used them to predict natural cycles of day and night, passing seasons, and other natural phenomena. Ecological artists frequently deal with the relationship between time and nature. For example, in the early 1970s Nancy Holt highlighted aspects of time in *Sun Tunnels*. She positioned concrete pipes to catch the rising and setting sun for about ten days during the winter and summer solstices.

Western historians generally view time to be a simple, linear, chronological sequence of social events. However, there are cultural groups from around the world who view time differently, for example, as a circle based on folklore about creation myths or recurring cycles of seasonal change. Recent Western scientific theory presents more fluid and unexpected definitions of time. Systems of measure like time can both limit and clarify our understanding of the complex relationships operating in integrated ecosystems.

Materials

When making art, the use of materials is not immaterial. Contemporary ecological artists select material based on conceptual, cultural, and systemic circumstances of their particular project. Mel Chin used hyperaccumulator plants in *Revival Field* (1990-present), Viet Ngo used Lemnaceae or the lemna plant in his water cleansing and reclamation projects; and Ann Hamilton (b.1956) used one human being and 750,000 pennies, three sheep, straw, a tooth grinder, honey, a chair, and a felt hat to create her multisensory installation *Privations and Excesses*. Materials are carefully selected and usually carry both literal and metaphoric meanings. A careful exploration of the potential meanings of materials used in various artworks will help students and teachers better understand contemporary ecological art.

Change

Change is an inherent certainty in life and affects all dimensions of existence. Involvement in art provides a means of gaining insights into changes in one's life and how subtle and profound forms of transformation expressed through

Figure 14.5 Mel Chin, *Revival Field*, 1990-present, view during early July 1991. Land-fill, chainlink fence, six plant varieties, perennial and annual seeds, and seedlings, 60 square feet. Pig's Eye landfill, St. Paul, Minnesota.

art can convey ideas, expressions, and reactions to local community environments. Art can be an impetus for affirmation and positive socio-ecological change. These beliefs guide the work of many ecological artists.

For example, in 1992, Barbara Westfall (b.1958) worked with the University of Wisconsin Arboretum system to raise public awareness about seasonal changes that influence the maintenance of prairie landscape across the Midwest. Time was another concept that Westfall explored as she collaborated with Arboretum personnel. Each year the University staff girdle young aspen that begin to intrude into the open prairie grasses and foliage. The girdling process is used by the staff to kill the aspen. It is believed that the girdling process replicates the natural cycles of woodland growth and decay.

In Westfall's project titled, *Daylighting the Woods*, she spent a year highlighting the act of girdling young aspen and burning open prairie. She stripped the trees' bark in sections approximately five feet from the ground and sanded their surfaces over a period of six months. Natural oils were used to draw attention to the human manipulation of stripping bark from the aspens to slowly kill the young trees. Later, controlled burning was used to stimulate new growth. Photographs were taken to document her working processes over the year and the photographs were exhibited during a performance designed to

Figure 14.6 Barbara Westfall, *Daylighting the Woods*, 1993. University of Wisconsin-Madison Arboretum. Girdled Aspen, Madison, Wisconsin.

educate visitors at the arboretum about the effects of human intervention within natural ecological systems.

Conclusion

In this chapter I have discussed an approach to curriculum integration that facilitates inquiry about art in the contexts of life-centered issues. I provided a range of ideas associated with the conceptual generalization of interdependency. I analyzed this generalization by clustering three typologies of social interests: philosophy (dominion, stewardship, and union), perspectives (environmental design, ecological design, social ecology, ecological restoration), teaching concepts (location, time, material, and change). I believe elementary students can begin to understand how many different realities are constructed from diverse cultural perspectives. However, for this to occur, students will need to be actively involved in their own learning, conduct collaborative inquiry, be allowed time to reflect, disagree, agree, and negotiate how they understand different interpretations about art and ecology. This includes asking questions and solving problems based on everyday encounters and events.

Of course, there are many ways that teachers can conceptualize curriculum. Certainly, curriculum development is influenced by a broad range of educational policies associated with community and educational curriculum standards, reform movements, and assessment structures. As we enter the twenty-first century, however, curricula based on projects, techniques, over-simplified metaphors, and pre-made units continue to "de-skill" (Apple and Christian-Smith, 1991) teachers and students. Curriculum activities should help to generate new knowledge about everyday life-centered issues. I believe curriculum represents living processes of classroom cultures that change over time and reflect a teacher's philosophical position and perspective (Dewey, 1938; Grauer, 1998). Ideas selected for study need to reflect the contextual meanings and values associated with our ability to hold multiple interpretations of an idea simultaneously. Dewey (1938) wrote that the value of educational experiences can be understood within the active interaction and continuity of knowledge in society and within classroom cultures. Educational experiences can be developed around personal and social knowledge across many different subject areas. It is for this reason that I advocate using an integrated curricular approach based on broad generalizations and life-centered issues.

Endnotes

1. Curriculum metaphors represent the "value placed" on educational ideas for organizing knowledge. *Idea, notion, thought,* and *conception* are forms of language used to distinguish among denotative, connotative, intertextual, and intercultural forms of communication. *Idea* generally refers to cognitive activity of any degree of seriousness or triviality. However, an *idea* is commonly used for representing processes considered more important or elaborate than say a notion, thought, or concept.
2. Ecology is derived from the Greek word *"oikos"* meaning house. Metaphorically it can be understood to connote one's home or earth's house.
3. ArtsEdNet is both a set of resources for teachers and an on-line exhibition of contemporary art. The Art & Ecology web site investigates artistic orientations, artworks, and community and/or global issues along with historic, critical, and aesthetic dimensions of art education, ecology, and interdisciplinary approaches to developing comprehensive curricula. The Art & Ecology site can be accessed using the following URL: Krug, D. (1997). Art & ecology: Interdisciplinary approaches to curriculum, In ArtsEdNet, [On-line]. Available: http://www.artsednet.getty.edu/ArtsEdNet/Resources/Ecology/index.html.

References

Apple, M., & Christian-Smith, L. (1991). *The politics of the textbook.* New York: Routledge.

Dewey, J. (1938). *Experience and education.* New York: Macmillan.

Furlong, L. (1994). In Krug, D. (1997) q.v.

Goldsworthy, A. (1990). *Andy Goldsworthy: A collaboration with nature.* New York: Harry N. Abrams, Inc.

Gómez-Peña, G. In Krug, D. (1997) q.v.

Gowans, A. (1971). *The unchanging arts: New forms for the traditional functions of art in society.* New York: J. B. Lippincott.

Grauer, K. (1998). Beliefs of preservice teachers toward art education, *Studies in Art Education, 39*(4). pp. 350–370.

Heimlich, J. (1992). *Promoting a concern for the environment.* [Microform]. The Ohio State University Library System.

Krug, D. (1997). Art & ecology: Interdisciplinary approaches to curriculum, In *ArtsEdNet.* [On-line]. Available: http://www.artsednet.getty.edu/ArtsEdNet/Resources/Ecology/index.html.

Lippard, L. (1997). *The lure of the local: Senses of place in a multicultural society.* New York: The New York Press.

Ohio Department of Education. (1996). *Ohio comprehensive arts education.*

Orr, D. (1992). *Ecological literacy: Education and the transition to a postmodern world.* Albany, NY: State University of New York Press.

Perkins, D., & Blythe, T. (1994). Putting understanding up front. *Educational Leadership, 51* (5), 4.

Perrone, V. (1994). How to engage students in learning. *Educational leadership, 51*(5), 11–13.

Stankiewicz, M. A., & Krug, D. (1997) Editorial: Art & Ecology (Special Theme Issue). *Art education, 50*(6) 4–5.

Van der Ryn, S., & Cowan, S. (1996). *Ecological design.* Washington, DC: Island Press.

Williams, R. (1961). *The long revolution: An analysis of the democratic, industrial, and cultural changes transforming our society.* New York: Columbia University Press.

CONCLUSIONS AND FURTHER QUESTIONS

1. Krug works within a framework that he calls "the contexts of everyday life." Explain this concept and describe why the idea of everyday life is important to teachers and students.

2. Krug suggests that it is important for elementary teachers "to understand their own view of the interdependency of the environment and culture in order to understand and teach about contemporary ecological art." Describe your views about this interdependency. How did your views change through reading this chapter?

3. List three positions that characterize philosophical approaches to interdependency. Think of three examples from your own community that reflect each of the three views of interdependency with the environment.

4. List four ecological art perspectives discussed by Krug. How are they different? What kinds of art fit within each of these categories? How are these perspective related to each other?
5. What is ecological sustainability? Give an example of it in art.
6. What life-centered issues are you aware of in relation to the earth and ecology? How could you learn more about these types of issues? What can we do as teachers in our classrooms to incorporate these issues? Why should we include life-centered issues as a part of the curriculum?

RESOURCES AND SUGGESTIONS
FOR FURTHER READING

Carol Becker. *Zones of contention: Essays on art, institutions, gender, and anxiety.* Albany, NY: State University of New York Press, 1996.

Arnold Berleant. *The aesthetics of environment.* Philadelphia, PA: Temple University Press, 1992.

Arnold Berleant. *Living in the landscape: Toward an aesthetics of environment.* Lawrence, KS: University Press of Kansas, 1997.

Michel de Certeau. *The practice of everyday life.* Steven Rendall (Trans.). Berkeley, CA: University of California Press, 1984.

Clearing and *Green Teacher* magazines offer teachers a variety of K–12 environmental education resources, many of which are written by teachers. (*www.teleport.com/~clearing* and *www.web.net/~greentea*)

Peter Davis. *Ecomuseums: A sense of place.* Leicester, UK: Leicester University Press, 1999.

Green Brick Road (GBR) is a non-profit organization offering resources and information for students and teachers of global and environmental education (*www.gbr.org*)

Nicola Hodges. *Art and the natural environment.* London: Academy Group Ltd., 1994.

Jeffrey Kastner (Ed.). *Land and environmental art.* London: Phaidon, 1998.

Suzanne Lacy (Ed.). *Mapping the terrain: New genre public art.* Seattle, WA: Bay Press, 1995.

Barbara C. Matilsky. *Fragile ecologies: Contemporary artists' interpretations and solutions.* New York: Rizzoli, 1992.

Carolyn Merchant. *Earthcare: Women and the environment.* New York: Routledge, 1996.

Carolyn Merchant. *Radical ecology: The search for a livable world.* New York: Routledge, 1992.

Barney Nelson. *The wild and the domestic: animal representation, ecocriticism, and western American literature.* Reno, NV: University of Nevada Press, 2000.

Project Learning Tree is a K–12 environmental education program that is administered by the American Forest Foundation and the Council for Environmental Education. (*www.plt.org*)

Alan Sonfist (Ed.). *Art in the land: A critical anthology of environmental art.* New York: Dutton, 1983.

Erika Suderburg (Ed.). *Space, site, intervention: Situating installation art.* Minneapolis, MN: University of Minnesota Press, 2000.

Karen J. Warren (Ed.). *Ecological feminist philosophies.* Bloomington, IN: Indiana University Press, 1996.

Michael E. Zimmerman. *Contesting earth's future: Radical ecology and postmodernity.* Berkeley, CA: University of California Press, 1994.

1. Hayes Yokley's chapter title introduces the idea of an artwork speaking. What meanings does this use of the word "speak" suggest to you?

2. If you were asked to choose an artwork for elementary students to study what criteria would you use to make your decision? What aspects of the artwork do you think are the most important when choosing works for the elementary classroom?

3. Select an artwork that you are familiar with. What do you know about the work of art and the artist who created it? What do you know about the work of art that you could share with others/children?

4. What can a teacher learn from a work of art? What can elementary students learn from a work of art? Why is it important for teachers to research a work of art? How can we discover meaning in a work of art? What kinds of information are necessary to help us understand a work of art?

If an Artwork Could Speak, What Would It Say? Focusing on Issues for Elementary Art Education

Shirley Hayes Yokley

As a teacher, if you could choose the most important work of art for your students to study this year, what would it be? Would it be a famous work from the Renaissance such as Leonardo da Vinci's *Mona Lisa*, (c. 1503–05) a Post-impressionist work such as Vincent van Gogh's *Starry Night*, (c. 1889) or perhaps an abstract sculpture such as *Royal Tide*, (c. 1961) by Louise Nevelson? While all these works are noble choices in their own right, are they the best selections for in-depth study by students who live after the year 2000? How might these works help elementary students to think critically about today's lives, events, ideas, emotions, or values? Simply the fact that a work of art is famous or considered important in the artworld may or may not qualify the work as the best choice for in-depth study in today's classrooms. Before making choices for the elementary classroom, teachers need to consider the appropriateness of a work of art to a particular community or audience. The stories that the art tells should suit the needs of student growth and experience. Choices must contribute in a positive way to how students think and sort out life in a complex world.

Teachers can challenge students with artworks that speak about issues in ways that elicit dialogue and create active interest in multiple versions of worlds (Goodman, 1978)—past, present and future, imaginary and real, immediate and beyond. During the elementary years, children begin to think about and deal with issues that affect their lives. Our responsibility as teachers, from my perspective, is to provide students with a variety of opportunities for developing insightful and reflective thinking about how personal worlds may be implicated in broader worlds (Goodman, 1978). Through responding to and making art, students take a closer look at the realities of the everyday, dig into questions of identity, project into the future, and work out right and wrong, good and evil (Krietler and Krietler, 1972). Teachers willing to journey with students into the worlds of contemporary art have the opportunity to touch students' lives in ways that educate about life and its realities. In the following sections, I make suggestions for planning issues-based lessons that help teachers think through what they want to do, how they need to do it, and why these ideas and issues are important for students to learn about and understand.

Thinking through the Planning Process

Teaching art is a highly complex endeavor, and, if it is to be done well, requires research into the content of art accompanied by methodological finesse (Yokley, 1997, 1999). That finesse comes through learning and adapting methods and strategies to art content and understanding how the mind works and manifests itself in the institutional setting of the classroom. Many resources are available to help teachers learn a variety of these processes (e.g., Caine and Caine, 1994, 1997; Kindsvatter, Wilen, and Ishler, 1988). As teachers build a repertoire of methods and strategies and develop an attitude of experimentation, they find their teaching more effective.

Recent cognitive research indicated that students learn depth of thinking processes through active involvement (Roland, 1992). Teachers need to provide time for students to explore a subject in depth in order to build better knowledge structures that can be used to interpret new experiences, to solve new problems, to think, and to reason—all facets of independent learning (Roland, 1992; Resnick and Klopfer, 1989). Roland (1992) proposed that art curricula be organized around conceptual clusters that involve students in the key ideas, problems, questions, and values that illuminate art as a field of inquiry. A comprehensive, holistic, open-ended approach (Wilson, 1997) to art teaching can satisfy these objectives. As comprehensive approaches to art education are more widely understood, teachers forego the fragmentation that often exists among the disciplines of art—art production, art history, art criticism, aesthetics—and integrate those disciplines within the historical/cultural contexts that surround one artwork. Wilson (1997) reminded us that "the art disciplines are the means through which the meaning of works of art many be understood" (p. 213). As works of art are insightfully created, studied, interpreted, and evaluated, we learn that different works have different meanings and thus educate differently (Wilson, 1997). Opportunities to examine those differences through exploring the various layers of meaning can enhance inquiry skills as well as enhance life skills.

Teachers can learn to plan encounters with works of art that raise questions about society and the human condition: What is fairness? Why do we suffer loss? What does equality mean? What are human rights? Who is a friend? When is science also art? As Dewey (1916) noted, for content to become important to children, there must be a question of concern (as cited in Roland, 1992). Student concerns are often embedded in social, political, or economic issues that arise from the historical/cultural contexts surrounding their lives. When teachers select content related to students' personal concerns or concerns attuned to the personal, the more meaningful the content and the more actively involved students become.

For children to be able to assimilate meaningful content and develop critical and creative thinking skills, they need frequent opportunities to build these skills in dialogue and debate. The most benefits, according to Eisner (1983), come when students are able to: (1) relate the topic to their own knowledge and beliefs; (2) rethink their initial ideas and assumptions in light of possible contradictions; (3) explore alternative views and explanations for the same situation; and (4) refute views expressed in class (including their own) by means of available evidence (as cited in Roland, 1992). Roland (1992) placed confidence in Kuhn's (1986) notion that, "It is through such planned encounters, that ordinary thinking becomes critical thinking" (p. 33). Roland (1992) pointed out that students need to reflect on how they arrive at their conclusions, decisions, and solutions through processes of metathinking, or reflective thinking about their own thinking and how they go about doing it (see Caine and Caine, 1994). Ultimately, one goal is to teach content and thinking skills as complementary rather than oppositional (Roland, 1992). Choices of artworks for issues-based study become extremely important in this regard, leading us to ask what choices teachers should make to insure meaningful encounters with artworks?

- Choose meaningful, issues-based works of contemporary art that fit the particular community.
- Choose works of art that fit students' needs, interests, concerns, and development.

- Choose works that challenge and expand established and unquestioned views of the world.
- Optimally, choose works that show how contemporary works of art bridge the history of ideas to art of the past.
- Choose works that generate an interdisciplinary unit/lesson theme that relates to a key idea in the work.
- Choose works that present a variety of points of view about the human condition.
- Choose works that evoke personal passion and interest for the teacher.

In making wise choices of artworks for study in the classroom, teachers are ready for the next steps in the planning process.

Through art and the vision and ideas of many artists, we are fortunate enough to be able to develop our own visions of the world as we read the depth of thought and content embedded in works of art. Without art, we are denied access to that knowing. Our job as teachers is to help children to uncover that depth at their level, learn how it affects them, and respond visually and critically.

Teachers structure the richness of these encounters with systematic planning. What thinking must a teacher do in order to plan a successful in-depth issues-based lesson?

- Thoroughly research a work of art for in-depth understanding of its layers of meaning and context in order to be able to ask open-ended questions that enable a depth of exploration and discovery.
- Relish the discovery of the layers of meaning or "aboutness" (see Barrett, 2000) of an artwork by learning to critically read the signs and symbols (iconography or denotation) in works of art that allow the artwork to "speak."
- Help students discover (connote) the layers of meaning in the artwork, termed "reading" the work.
- Develop broad-based, divergent questions along with probing, follow-up, or "feeder" questions to elicit meaningful dialogue.
- Help students bridge or connect the meanings in the work to personal life experiences through artmaking (this includes what the student knows beyond actual life experiences).
- Encourage dialogue about ideas for student artwork during large or small group brainstorming sessions.
- Integrate writing about art as a regular part of creative and critical thinking about art.

As teachers learn how to understand the richness of content in works of art they can make better use of the educative possibilities of art. As teachers develop a repertoire of strategies, methods, and approaches that enable versatility, they learn how to activate discovery learning for students. In helping bridge or connect ideas from artworks to students's understanding of life through dialogue, writing, artmaking, and reflective thinking, teachers come to realize how important a study of art is to the general education of children.

How Can Art "Speak" to Issues?

Often, contemporary works of art speak in ways that address questions and issues of concern in today's society. Why is James Luna's performance of *Artifact Piece*, (c. 1987) so intriguing? Why do Amelia Mesa Baines's altars such as *Delores del Rio VI*, (c. 1990) elicit reverence? Why are Mel Chin's environmental works such as *Revival Field*, (c. 1991) so compelling? (see Weintraub, Danto, and McEvilley, 1996; Cahan and Kocur, 1996). These artworks elicit points of view that often remain invisible and that can be missing from mainstream education.

In his work, Luna became the art, the native American artifact, as he displayed himself on a table in a museum setting. As people walked by, they questioned why he chose to present himself in such a way. His intention was to unsettle stereotypical perceptions of Native Americans. Mesa-Baines created church-like altars based upon those found in the homes of many devout Latino peoples. Her objective was to validate the lives and beliefs of Chicano/a peoples. The tribute to Delores del Rio called our attention to the struggle and success of a movie star who broke racial barriers. Chin sought an aesthetic through which to revitalize the environment by merging science and art. In *Revival Field*, he constructed a chain-link fence configuration at a toxic waste site. Inside grew plants that were able to absorb toxic waste and renew the environment. By problematizing or opening to question different points of view about issues, including definitions of art, these artists created spaces for dialogue and debate on important issues concerning race, gender, and environment.

An issue may be defined as any idea that opens a matter to discussion, controversy, debate, or dispute. Issues occur within particular contexts such as political, social, economic, ecological, biological, technological, philosophical, aesthetic, or psychological. Issues run the gamut from the general to particular. Generalities that deal with the human condition may include issues that form around culture, ethnicity, race, class, gender, environment, relationships, ability, age, or health. Particularities may include stereotypes, racial barriers, toxic waste, drug abuse, AIDS, suppression of immigrants, single parenting, the social construction of knowledge, equality of education, gang violence, sweat shops, reproducing bias and prejudice, war, homelessness, social construction of the ideal of beauty, social promotion in education, influences of material culture, or the cumulative effect of mass media on personal and national identity. As issues are found in the contexts that surround works of art, they integrate well with the contexts for subjects such as health, science, safety, current events, social studies, literature, or history at the elementary level.

Works of art that address issues offer opportunities for dialogue and debate about important concerns in the daily lives of the world's diverse peoples, including the world's children. Through questions raised and conversation elicited by the artwork, people can come to better understand each other's differences and expand notions of self.

Elementary teachers may find time to add only one work of art to their curriculum each year; but, the study of one rich work can bring tremendous educative possibilities for students. Using journals and other library resources, teachers can locate information about a contemporary work of art, its critical, historical, social, and political contexts, the artist, the artist's body of work, and any related works, including works from popular culture as well as works from the past and other cultures (see Sobol, 2000).

By forming a continually expanding list of artworks by contemporary artists who deal with present-day issues, teachers can choose works that may be more important, meaningful, or understandable given a particular audience, place, and time. Works of art can help students realize that other people in the world may share the same quandaries or excitement about life. Works of art can cause students to question and hope for improvements in personal and world conditions. Students also develop a respect for the multitude of ways that artists create artworks that speak to us. They learn to expand that dialogue and reflect on the depth of those inferences, ideas, feelings, and possibilities that artworks elicit in each individual. In this way, students also gain a healthy respect for the thinking processes necessary for making thoughtful, meaningful works of art. Teachers prepare themselves in dialogue with the artwork and the study of its contexts to elicit dialogue among students. In the following sections, the reader is invited to look at some possibilities for a critical, in-depth reading of one work of art.

Finding Out about the Context of Faith Ringgold's *Tar Beach*

A good choice of artwork for instruction at any level of elementary classroom is Faith Ringgold's *Tar Beach,* (c. 1988) with its focus on issues of gender, race, and class (Figure 15.1). This reading deals with the first of her two paintings with the same title, the text of which became a children's book (Ringgold, 1996/1991) of the same name. In this artwork Ringgold, explores the issues of hope and oppression.

To begin the exploration, take an imaginary walk into the work. What do you see, taste, smell, hear, or touch (Geahigan, 1999)? Explore and write about the work for its impressions, illusions, emotional impact, abstractions, imaginative possibilities, reminders, sensory and perceptual appeal, and/or intuitive responses. Then, dig into the work using contextual information to

Figure 15.1 Faith Ringgold, *Tar Beach*, 1988.

gain deeper insights in preparation for semiotically reading (see Blonsky, 1985) the signs (likened to symbols) and sign meanings (likened to metaphors) that help us to make meaning in response to the artwork.

In researching the historical/cultural context of this painted quilt, biographical information about the artist revealed that Faith Ringgold was born in Harlem, New York in 1930 (Witzling, 1991). Early in the twentieth century, Harlem was a cultural center for African-Americans. In the 1920s, the arts of this community began to flourish with the influx of people moving to cities after World War I. New York City became a center for intellectual and artistic growth. American culture was affected most positively by these advancements. African-American artists, political leaders, and scholars such as W. E. B. DuBois, Mary McLeod Bethune, Arna Bontemps, Langston Hughes, Billie Holiday, Paul Robeson, Aaron Douglas, Marcus Garvey, and Charles W. Chesnutt are but a few whose contributions are well known (Witzling, 1991; Flomenhaft, 1990). In addition, the Harlem Theater, the Universal Negro Improvement Association, and, of course, jazz impacted the world in ways that changed and enriched life and the arts. That rich and progressive period was known as the Harlem Renaissance.

Despite the flourishing of the Harlem Renaissance and the fact that the Roaring Twenties brought personal liberty for many whites in the United States, African-Americans remained bound by repressive laws and could not vote or join unions (Ringgold as cited in Witzling, 1991). Proclaimed "free" for over half a century, African-Americans found that equality was far from being achieved. A "separate but equal" socio-political policy permeated education and life in the United States (Kozol, 1991). Many scholars felt that the civil rights movement of the 1960s would have taken place much earlier had it not been for the Great Depression. As a child Ringgold observed conditions in Harlem during this time of worldwide economic suffering. Ringgold understood the shattered dreams of the civil rights struggles that many African-Americans experienced following the Harlem Renaissance. Her art reflects those struggles and disappointments.

Ringgold taught art in New York City public schools for eighteen years. In the 1950s, she began seriously working as a painter. In her early work she explored traditional Western fine-art painting techniques on canvas. Yet, she longed to express her heritage as an African-American woman, and started working with soft-sculpture, performance art, and with painting on quilts (Witzling, 1991). The thematic complexity of Ringgold's body of work changed to incorporate the dilemmas involved in the hope for transformation, change, and the flight to freedom from oppression.

In her work, Ringgold questioned biased definitions of women, especially those of women of color. As a political activist she was an avid supporter of African-American rights, and helped found "Where We At," an organization of black artists (Witzling, 1991). In 1988, based on these issues of race, class, and gender, she began the *Women on the Bridge Series* of which *Tar Beach*, c. 1988, is the signature piece. As a result of her childhood experiences with a family rich in storytelling, the visual format of many of her works reflected her need to tell stories with pictures, symbols, and words. The narratives that accompany her works provide opportunity for multiple responses so that the artwork functions on many levels with signs and sign meanings that lead the viewer to examine the richness and depth of those layers of meaning. The viewer finds that Ringgold's works reflect American culture. While the artworks tell her personal story, they poignantly speak about the African-American experience in this country.

Reading Sign Meaning into the Work

Artworks are able to "speak" because the visual images become signs that can be read for meaning. Each color, line direction, action, setting, subject, and mood become symbols and signs for reading. *Tar Beach*[1] is based on Faith Ringgold's childhood memories and her ideas about issues that affected women and African-Americans in the United States. While her early works were highly charged political indictments of racial and gender inequalities, the painting *Tar Beach* suggested possibilities for change. The work used flying as a metaphor for freedom (DeVuono, 1989) that suggested conquering the unconquerable. The themes of freedom, liberation, or transformation reflected the struggles of many people to make the best of life despite adverse conditions. The narrative, dreamed and told by Cassie Louise Lightfoot, an eight-year-old black girl (a sign to be read for meaning), began with the text written directly on the painted story-quilt with a permanent fine-point marker, "I will always remember when the stars fell down around me and lifted me up above the George Washington Bridge" (Ringgold, c. 1988, as cited in Witzling, 1991, p. 363). Ringgold juxtaposed the George Washington Bridge, the most dominant structure in the city, with the stereotypical and historical "femaleness" of the quilt that she used as a vehicle for telling women's stories (Flomenhaft, 1990). Ringgold commented:

> In the *Women on the Bridge Series*, I painted about women's courage; comparing women with something as monumental as a bridge. It's always constructed by men who get up there and die making it; and I wanted to pit women against that. I had no idea that they would be flying. That happened later. As I drew my pictures, and got them together, I realized the women could not be grounded. I wrote down some things to remember that the bridge idea was significant to me and it would be about women's courage, women doing great, creative, exciting things, which I parallel with the painting of a bridge, and being able to be visible about it, because a bridge is visible all over the city. The story has to come together a lot before I know what the painting's going to be, because I want the story to speak to the painting, and the painting to speak to the story. (Flomenhaft, 1990, p. 11–12)

Vision comes with insight into important ideas. Cassie began to fulfill Ringgold's vision of a black female doing heroic, creative things, for Cassie emancipated her father through the symbol of being free to fly wherever she wants (Witzling, 1991). Cassie broke the bondage of the patriarchal white society that dominated African Americans and Native Americans in the gesture of claiming the George Washington Bridge. That claiming, in narrative and in flight, is a sign.

Cassie's father, "they called him the Cat," helped build the bridge, but he was not permitted to join the union because of the Jim Crow laws that excluded non-whites by requiring that men could only join the union if their fathers or grandfathers were members. As a result, jobs were insecure and wages for non-union members were lower. When Ringgold painted this work in 1988, discrimination and injustice were resurfacing in United States society as Kozol (1991) documented. The repeal of civil rights legislation and the acceptance of open political oppression hindered equality both politically and socially (Kozol, 1991). The crossing-over or the "bridge" that political and even judicial progress promised appeared usurped by the dominant power structures (Kozol, 1991). Ringgold's painted setting of the 1930s and time of completion of the work in 1988 become signs for reading the work in terms of questioning how conditions have improved.

Ringgold helped the audience to see the injustice in the fact that African-Americans and Native Americans aided in building the bridges that enabled those who could afford automobiles, especially in New York, the freedom to come and go, and to provide access to business ventures in Harlem. With this sign, she pointed out inequalities inherent in the freedoms that some people enjoy and take for granted in society that others have yet to enjoy. Yet, Cassie understood that the bridge might be an important connection from her world to other worlds—a bridge to emancipation. She soared above the bridge that links the world of her community to a different world sprinkled with hopes and dreams of a better tomorrow.

That better tomorrow was expressed in a different way in Jacob Lawrence's *Daybreak: A Time of Rest*, (c. 1967). The fugitive slave family in this painting (Figure 15.2) sought escape by way of the Underground Railroad under the watchful guidance of Harriet Tubman. Tubman's role was as guide and protector. Teacher materials from the National Gallery, Washington, DC, explain that Lawrence's ideas and feelings expressed the loss of a nation of people, the potential for alienation and loneliness within a modern society, and the need to protect the family as the nucleus of the human race. These two works share similar themes, enrich each other's meaning, and involve the viewer in their varied interpretations of these flights to freedom.

Many of Ringgold's narratives were influenced by African dilemma tales (Witzling, 1991) combined with her own personal stories. Dilemma tales do not have the happy endings typically found in Western popular culture. The irony and sometimes uneasiness of endings in these dilemma tales seem more attuned to the precariousness of life with all its maladies, as problems

Figure 15.2 Jacob Lawrence, *Daybreak: A Time of Rest*, 1967. (Tempera on hardboard, 30 x 24 inches, National Gallery of Art)

are posed but inconclusively resolved (Witzling, 1991). Ringgold used these tales to entice the viewer into deeper contemplation of her works. The contextual research on African dilemma tales offers us yet another sign by which the work can be read (see Sunwolf, 1999).

Cassie soared above the star-sprinkled lights of the city with a freedom that speaks to those who can permit those vicarious dreams a pathway to reality. "(A)nyone can fly. All you need is somewhere to go that you can't get to any other way. The next thing you know, you're flying among the stars" (Ringgold, c. 1988, as cited in Witzling, 1991, p. 364). She had no use for the wax wings of Icarus to enable flight. As she empowered herself, like Harriet Tubman, she engendered hope for survival, hope for an end to oppression, and hope for change for a more democratic and egalitarian society.

In addition, Ringgold questioned the viewer's role in historical memory. Using a skewed perspective and cropped edges of the rooftop of a "tar beach" (other signs), Ringgold caused the viewer to examine his or her relationship to the entire issue of oppression by visually dumping the contents of the rooftop into the lap of the viewer. By creating potential proximity, the viewer is implicated in that history. Further investigations into the historical-cultural context raised other questions: For whom is this work made? Who has the power? Who is responsible? Though the work may "rub against the grain" of a dominant white culture, the messages are those through which all of us, including elementary-aged students, learn to question our biases and prejudices and their origins. *Tar Beach* reflected Ringgold's historical memory of gender, race, and class inequalities that continue to exist in contemporary society. One problem for students is to determine how those conditions continue to exist and to develop projects of possibility wherein their own artworks "speak" to those issues. Ringgold, in a visionary way, used art to educate about issues in ways that take her classroom to the world. All teachers have that same opportunity.

Endnote

1. Ringgold also writes children's books with an integrated approach to teaching. She has a children's book (see References) and two paintings titled *Tar Beach*. This reading deals with the first of these two paintings, c. 1988. The story told by Cassie may be found in Witzling, (1991).

References

Barrett, T. (2000). *Criticizing art: Understanding the contemporary.* Mountain View, CA: Mayfield.

Blonsky, M. (1985). *On signs.* Baltimore, MD: The Johns Hopkins University Press.

Cahan, S. & Kocur, Z. (1996). *Contemporary art and multicultural education.* New York, NY: New Museum of Contemporary Art.

Caine, R. & Caine, G. (1994). *Making connections: Teaching and the human brain.* Menlo Park, CA: Addison-Wesley.

Caine, R. & Caine, G. (1997). *Unleashing the power of perceptual change: The potential of brain-based teaching.* Alexandria, VA: Association for Supervision and Curriculum Development.

DeVuono, F. (1989, February). Faith Ringgold. *New Art Examiner, 16,* 55.

Dewey, J. (1916). *Democracy and education.* New York: Macmillan.

Eisner, E. (1983). The kind of schools we need. *Educational Leadership, 41*(2), 48–55.

Flomenhaft, E. (1990). *Faith Ringgold: A twenty-five year survey.* [Exhibition Catalogue]. Long Island, NY: The Fine Arts Museum of Long Island.

Geahigan, G. (1999). Teaching preservice art education majors: The world of the work. *Art Education, 52*(5), 12–17.

Goodman, N. (1978). *Ways of worldmaking.* Indianapolis, IN: Hackett.

Kindsvatter, R., Wilen, W., & Ishler, M. (1988). *The dynamics of effective teaching.* White Plains, NY: Longman.

Kozol, J. (1991). *Savage inequalities: Children in America's schools.* New York, NY: Crown Publishing.

Krietler, H. & Krietler, S. (1972). *Psychology of the arts.* Durham, NC: Duke University Press.

Kuhn, D. (1986). Education for thinking. *Teachers College Record, 87*(4), 495–512.

Resnick, L. & Klopfer, L. (1989). *Toward the thinking curriculum: Current cognitive research.* Alexandria, VA: Association for Supervision and Curriculum Development.

Ringgold, F. (1996). *Tar beach.* New York, NY: Random House Value Publishing, Inc. (Original work published 1991)

Roland, C. (1992). Improving student thinking through elementary art instruction. In A. Johnson (Ed.), *Art education: Elementary* (pp. 13–42). Reston, VA: National Art Education Association.

Sobol, R. (2000). Studying art history through the multicultural education looking-glass. *Art Education, 53*(3), 12–17.

Sunwolf. (1999). The pedagogical and persuasive effects of Native American lesson stories, Sufi wisdom tales, and African dilemma tales. *Howard Journal of Communications, 10*(1), 47–71.

Weintraub, L., Danto, A., & McEvilley, T. (1996). *Art on the edge and over: Searching for art's meaning in contemporary society 1970s–1990s.* Litchfield, CT: Art Insights, Inc.

Wilson, B. (1997). *The quiet evolution: Changing the face of art education.* Los Angeles, CA: J. Paul Getty Trust Publications.

Witzling, M. (1991). *Voicing our visions: Writings by women artists.* New York, NY: Universe.

Yokley, S. H. (1997). *Art, art education, and critical pedagogy: Case studies of elementary education preservice teachers* (Doctoral dissertation, The Pennsylvania State University, 1997). Dissertation Abstracts International, 58–07, A2499.

Yokley, S. H. (1999). Embracing a critical pedagogy in art education. *Art Education, 52*(5), 18–23.

CONCLUSIONS AND FURTHER QUESTIONS

1. Before reading this chapter you were asked to discuss what makes a work of art "important" for study in an elementary classroom. What factors and ideas does Hayes Yokley suggest that teachers consider when choosing a work of art for study? How do these ideas compare to the reasons that you had for choosing a work of art for the elementary classroom?

2. What do students gain by exploring a subject in-depth? How does Hayes Yokley propose that elementary teachers approach an in-depth study of art in the classroom?

3. What kinds of activities promote critical thinking skills? Why are critical thinking skills necessary for elementary students?

4. According to Hayes Yokley, what is an issue? Why does she think that elementary teachers should consider studying works of art that address issues?

5. How should our choice of artwork relate to the children in our classroom? How does choosing an artwork relate to the teacher?

6. What are the teacher's responsibilities in teaching a lesson?

7. What form of storytelling does Faith Ringgold use? How does Ringgold's use of narrative function? What is the relationship between narrative and identity construction? How might you use narrative with students? What types of narratives might our students construct?

RESOURCES AND SUGGESTIONS
FOR FURTHER READING

Stephen J. Ball (Ed.). *Foucault and education: Disciplines and knowledge.* London; New York: Routledge, 1990.

Mary Beattie. *Constructing professional knowledge in teaching: A narrative of change and development.* Toronto; New York: Ontario Institute for Studies in Education; Teachers College Press, 1995.

Carol Becker. *Zones of contention: Essays on art, institutions, gender, and anxiety.* Albany, NY: State University of New York Press, 1996.

Diane DuBose Brunner. *Inquiry and reflection: Framing narrative practice in education.* Albany, NY: State University of New York Press, 1994.

Thomas S. Popkewitz and Marie Brennan (Eds.). *Foucault's challenge: Discourse, knowledge, and power in education.* New York: Teachers College Press, 1998.

David H. Richter (Ed.). *Narrative/theory.* White Plains, NY: Longman, 1996.

Faith Ringgold. *If a bus could talk: The story of Rosa Parks.* New York: Simon & Schuster Books for Young Readers, 1999. (Children's book)

Faith Ringgold paints Crown Heights. Chappaqua, NY: L & S Video, Inc., 1995. (28 minute videocassette).

Faith Ringgold. *Aunt Harriet's underground railroad in the sky.* New York: Crown, 1995. (Children's book)

Joy S. Ritchie and David E. Wilson. *Teacher narrative as critical inquiry: Rewriting the script.* New York: Teachers College Press, 2000.

Robyn Montana Turner. *Faith Ringgold.* Boston, MA: Little, Brown, 1993. (Children's book)

Kathleen Weiler and Sue Middleton (Eds.). *Telling women's lives: Narrative inquiries in the history of women's education.* Philadelphia, PA: Open University Press, 1999.

Carol Witherell & Nel Noddings (Eds.). *Stories lives tell: Narrative and dialogue in education.* New York: Teachers College Press, 1991.

CHAPTER 16

QUESTIONS AND EXPLORATIONS

1. How would you define an issue? How would you define a theme?
2. What differences and similarities do issues and themes have?
3. Think back to your elementary education. Were you ever taught through a curriculum that was based upon issues? What might be the advantages of teaching in this way?
4. What are the connections between teaching and the political?
5. Watch the news on television or read a news article from a newspaper or magazine. How are the issues that are a part of the story presented? What rhetorical strategies are used in presenting the news? In what ways is the news political? How is the presentation of the news related to the idea of the construction of knowledge?

Art for Issues' Sake: A Framework for the Selection of Art Content for the Elementary Classroom

Mary Wyrick

Dialectics in News and Art

For the past eight years, I have been integrating political issues from the news media with art education in teacher preparation. The study of current news sources provides a starting point for the debate and discussion of socially relevant issues in the classroom. Such discussion shows that the classroom is not an isolated site, but is part of a local and global community. Using news media and the issues represented therein as a source for classroom discussion and learning helps us look outside of the classroom to the changing world and take an active role in the development of curriculum that is sensitive to social change. The study of the social and political contexts of art production is also in keeping with current national standards that call for understanding the visual arts in relation to history and cultures.

Studying artists' responses to news media and synthesizing them into written and visual forms can challenge students to interact with both art and news media. Many contemporary artists respond to systematic discrimination and social inequities by synthesizing news media into their work. News media are being appropriated, critiqued, and accessed by artists to include disenfranchised groups such as people with AIDS, women, and minorities. An important dimension of the study of news media in the classroom is the potential for an active and interactive role of the viewer in using news media. The student's role as member of an audience in which a debate develops and influences the character of the news is an empowering concept. In *Television Myth and the American Mind*, Himmelstein (1984) says, "a public issue is one about which there already exists some division of opinion" (p. 258). He writes that news is defined by its effect on the audience in the community and he further defines news as "the provision of significant facts relevant to the formation of an opinion, or to the change of an attitude on some current public issue of importance to a community of persons" (p. 258). This definition requires an informed audience willing to participate in a dialectic. Children need to be taught to develop informed opinions and to interact critically with news media. Even those who are motivated to consume news media need to be prodded out of a passive reading of what they consider "facts" to an active forming of opinions on relevant and important issues.

Components of "Art Education 003: Art in Elementary Education"

I first used issues in the news media as a source for art teaching in "Art Education 003," elementary teacher preparation classes in art that I taught as a graduate student in 1991 at the Pennsylvania State University. Most of the students in the class were female elementary education majors who had practicum experience in the classroom but had not yet completed the student teaching experience. Students wrote that they had no art experience, and that they typically had not visited a museum of any kind since they were children. Some were overextended, on the first day of class, to recall the name of one artist. My approach to teaching this group placed an emphasis on how to integrate research, reflective writing, and curriculum development with study of art. The course culminated in the preservice teacher's design of a unit plan, lesson plan, a visual art work (such as that shown in Figure 16.1), and presentation to the class based on art and centered around a studio art lesson.

The syllabus for the course, written by Dr. Marjorie Wilson and Dr. Elizabeth Garber, outlined a mission that was in keeping with a discipline-based approach to teaching of art that combined aesthetics, art criticism, and art history with studio art. A major goal was to foster an understanding through the visual arts of the world and self that can be applied to teaching children in various settings and subjects. In writing about contemporary artworks that dealt with information as presented through the news media, preservice

Figure 16.1 An Elementary Education major did this watercolor as a teacher exemplar addressing the issue of AIDS/HIV.

teachers connected the content of the artworks with their own perceptions about current public information. Through the use of print and broadcast news media, students in Art Ed 003 used issues close to their own experiences. I gave a series of writing assignments, "Research Logs," that I list in the Appendix, to explore preservice teachers' perceptions of issues and representations in news media.

An important goal in teaching the course was to introduce the concept of making artists and artworks central to the curriculum. To utilize artworks in the general elementary classroom, I ventured to lay the groundwork for a structure for selecting artworks that can be used to develop interdisciplinary instructional materials. Elementary education majors generally cannot rely on art historical knowledge or on knowledge of contemporary art, since they are not required to take coursework in either area at most colleges and universities. A one semester teaching-methods course cannot provide an adequate historical survey of "important works," even if we could agree on an approach to teaching art that reduces all art knowledge to one canon or one critical perspective. At the same time, preservice teachers need some kind of knowledge base to help them teach art and to integrate art teaching with the teaching of other subjects.

An astute student in my spring 1992 class wrote that one can easily find art historical information about artists in the canon but that one needs art education to see the educative potential in alternative and contemporary artistic practices. News media and contemporary art increasingly operate within the realm of popular and visual culture that is available to us, and both provide varied insights about our world. Many preservice teachers embrace media culture as a valid source of information, but they need instruction to consider artists as contemporaries who are critically interacting with popular culture. Many regard artists as great masters of bygone eras that have little relation to what goes on in an elementary classroom.

I opened the class with a simple assignment that they search through news periodical sources to find issues that might be incorporated into the elementary classroom. We defined "current periodicals" as recent newspapers or newsmagazines and "issues" as points of political debate or controversy. Students during the 1991–92 school year at Penn State were drawn to issues that involved: multicultural education, race relations, social class relations, the Middle East, the Persian Gulf, media violence, gun control, crime, capital punishment, homelessness, gender relations, reproductive rights, the environment, animal rights, nuclear power, health care, substance abuse, censorship, the AIDS epidemic, teen pregnancy, the breakdown of communism, and political protest. Many of these issues are still relevant.

In a class discussion, we grouped issues under themes and categories. Overarching and unifying categories were the self/social self, education, representation, new technologies, and oppression/power. Beginning with current events allowed students to shift emphases each semester in response to changing concerns. During a class discussion, the students' task was to find an issue or a theme and then to find several artists who explored the theme or issue in their works. Three major issues related to current events surfaced: race relations, feminism, and AIDS/HIV. In the following analyses, I focus on students in two classes of "Visual Arts in the Elementary School" during the spring 1992 semester. These specific issues provided sources for finding general themes that transferred to studying artworks. After having found an issue in a news source, preservice students' second assignment was to analyze the issues.

Research Logs: Writing as Pedagogy

Using weekly Research Logs, preservice teachers applied critical perspectives and learned about various issues through their writing. Many educators incorporate journal/diary writing into their curricula to teach writing and to have students record their reflections and develop their ideas in other areas. Cooper (1991) concluded that students need to find a personal voice before dialogue can take place with the larger culture, and that journal writing develops that voice. Pagano (1991) successfully used research journals in a seminar on curriculum and teaching in the humanities and with student teachers. Stout (1992) discussed using response journals in high school art teaching to develop critical thinking skills. In my class, I referred to Berger's (1991) handbook *Media Research Techniques* to introduce the Research Log. In the Research Log, students regularly recorded "thoughts and speculations" as they worked on research problems (p. 15).

As I taught the course, I proceeded each week to collect a one page Log entry on a given question or "research problem." Most of the questions (see Appendix) were directed toward the interpretative and critical writing about artists for final lesson presentations to the class. The questions that I asked were also designed to make students "critical" as defined by making judgments about the merit and quality of arguments offered to support claims and premises. The logs were designed to help preservice teachers make informed interpretations about complex artworks in order to incorporate issues-based artworks into their planning. Log entries #2, #5, #8, #9, #11, and #13 were designed to help the preservice teacher learn to arrive at an informed interpretation and to direct students to recreate this same process. The Research Log writing helped these preservice teachers develop a questioning strategy to help their students, through group discussion, to arrive at a good interpretation of a work of art. The questioning strategy, developed in the lesson plan, does more than poll students for gut reactions and opinions; it probes for plausible conclusions. The Research Log questions were thus used to refine lesson plans with components in interpretation and criticism. Log entries #3, #6, and #12 directly focus upon teacher development and evaluation of teaching materials, methods, and presentation. In some of the following examples, preservice teachers used writing to develop and critique their philosophies and methods of teaching.

Targeting News Issues and Selecting Artists

Research Log question 1 reads: Respond to the issue in your periodical source. Discuss how and why you would use it in the classroom. In response to this question one student chose a news article about animal testing from PETA News, a publication of an animal rights organization. She identified the pro-animal rights stance of the journal and strongly agreed that animal testing is generally unethical. She was critical of the graphic photographs accompanying the articles in the journal and indicated her hesitance about using these in the elementary classroom. She believed that a role of the teacher is to inform students about alternative news sources that focus on issues such as animal testing. She acknowledged that mainstream news sources and media advertising might not present the whole picture and that the teacher should provide such alternative sources as PETA News. She dealt with the general theme of oppression in a way that she believed the elementary students could understand through the issue of animal rights and discussed the implications of using particular graphic images even though it might be justified within the context of activism for animal rights. As a major artist addressing this issue, she used Sue Coe.[1]

Another student identified, in response to this question, the issue of the quincentennial anniversary of Columbus as one related to oppression and thus important to use in the general classroom. She presented both sides of the debate—the standpoint of indigenous peoples who view this as a celebration of domination and the celebrants who wish to honor the tradition of

Figure 16.2 In a charcoal drawing, an elementary education major addresses the issue of sexual harrassment against women.

Columbus Day. Interested in multiculturalism, she showed awareness of the theme of oppression, focusing on a particular issue involving colonialism and Latin American cultures and using those themes to develop a lesson using the artist Juan Sanchez.

Several students followed consistent themes related to women's issues throughout the semester. In Figure 16.2, a charcoal drawing by one of the students uses sexual harrassment and date rape as a theme. Another student acknowledged her own mixed feelings toward an article on rape trials, "Are You a Bad Girl?" She recounted information in the article regarding how past histories of rape victims are entered into rape trials as evidence. She was critical of this article by her remark, "I feel when a woman is tried for rape today the press and media paint a picture for the public, whether it is right or wrong, and the public listens." She also concluded, "Women in our country today definitely should not have to be classified as a 'bad girl' for coming forth in a courtroom admitting she was raped." She recognized how the media could produce a false consciousness that enables the public to blame the victim in rape trials and then went further to question the ethics of the media and judicial systems. She noted that feminist artists effectively show how news media operate between social reality and ambiguous, stereotypical, or damaging representations of women. She used the artists Adrian Piper and Barbara Kruger to complete a teacher exemplar (see Figure 16.3.)

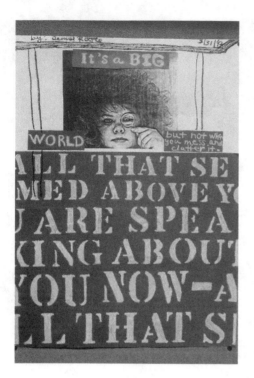

Figure 16.3 Using mixed media, this elementary education major created an exemplar for a unit on women's issues based on *It's A Small World, But Not If You Have To Clean It* by artist Barbara Kruger.

Another student developed the theme of feminism and women's rights throughout the semester. She identified the issue through a local student newspaper article (that also appeared in national news sources) about the removal of a painting, Goya's *La Maja Desnuda* from a classroom on a Penn State branch campus. She decided that she would not discuss this with children, but speculated that the removal signified a general contemporary insecurity about women's sexuality. She formed a "Women in Society" group and asked for suggestions of artists dealing with the issue of "rape." Her lesson presentation included slides of her own performances based on work by Faith Wilding in Judy Chicago's feminist art workshop. These were done as sample artworks for the class. The studio assignment that she created was to design a paper quilt square about women's issues that would be combined into a class quilt. She presented women's issues in a form appropriate for third through fifth graders through her selection of news articles, lesson planning, and performance art.

Summary of Elementary Education Major Responses

By the end of the semester, all but one of the students in Art Ed 003 could identify an issue as a point of debate and describe opposing viewpoints about the issue. Most could argue those points and support their arguments by citing examples. Most viewed the news as a transparent reflection of truth achieved through transmission of objective information and believed that a neutral, unbiased news presentation was commendable. These elementary education preservice teachers believed that the news media could be used as source for study in the elementary classroom in several instrumental ways. One wrote that students could model the rhetorical techniques of news writers to write persuasively. Another encouraged the use of alternative advocacy publications for information. Although many acknowledged that the news media could create a kind of false consciousness, most viewed the news media as reliable sources of public information. Few looked to larger political and economic structures that shape the news, although they often took this perspective in the criticism and interpretation of artworks. Using current social and political issues as a starting point helped students understand themes in art that could be connected to themes in other subjects.

Preservice Art Educators

I have continued to emphasize social and political issues in news media as a source for art teaching in methods classes in art education at Buffalo State from 1992–2000. Students in these classes are undergraduate art education majors or teacher-certification students who already have undergraduate degrees. They have not completed the student teaching experience required for certification and have a prerequisite Grade Point Average of 3.0. Their first practicum experience in the classroom is in a Pre–K to third-grade school in my introductory teaching methods class.

Unlike the elementary education majors, these students have art experience, some of it extensive work as visual artists, graphic designers, museum staff people, and in other related arts fields. I continue to focus on teaching aesthetics, art criticism, and art history with studio art appropriate to children. These art education majors are required to develop a unit plan of ten lessons around a theme. In writing art interpretation and criticism for a research paper on their unit art works, and in making art exemplars, they develop a rationale for using the theme. While they are not required to use social and political issues as themes, they are required to write about social and cultural phenomena surrounding the making of the artworks in their research paper.

As with elementary education majors, one goal of the writing assignments that are given early in the semester is to push students to find alternative forms of art making and teaching relevant to contemporary concerns. To do this, they need to develop some critical perspectives that enable them to move beyond a traditional conception of art as a continuation of Eurocentric tradition. I also provide the students with some resources that address teaching and writing contextual criticism (Chanda and Daniel, 2000; Fehr, 1994; Wasson, Stuhr, and Petrovich-Mwaniki, 1990; Wolcott, 1996; Wolff and Geahigan, 1997). Studying various kinds of contextual criticism can change a common perception from seeing art as a commodity to understanding art as a form of cultural production with embedded social and ideological dimensions. Class writing assignments using several of the Research Log questions (see Appendix) and discussions are designed to help students identify political issues reflected in artworks.

An exemplary lesson, "Caring for the Earth and its Animals," presented to kindergarten children by Laura King and Jennifer Russo, used environmental issues as a theme. Ms. King and Ms. Russo wrote that their major goals were for students to learn about keeping the environment clean as a responsibility to the earth and its animals. After mounting a large relief painting of the earth (see Figure 16.4) Ms. King disappeared, while Ms. Russo discussed how students could live harmoniously with animals, think globally, and think of ways to keep our environment clean.

Ms. Russo also showed some art works with animals as a theme and discussed "what the art is saying" about each animal and its habitat. Ms. King emerged as a "sick squirrel" (see Figure 16.5) in a costume with furry paws, ears, whiskers and long, long tail ensnared by garbage. To the fascinated kindergarten and first graders, the squirrel lamented the trash and pollution in a neighborhood park. The children came up to rid the squirrel of the trash, and the squirrel gradually recovered. While Ms. Russo talked about how to draw animals, the squirrel disappeared and was replaced by Ms. King, who assisted in pointing out attributes of specific animals, their movements, char-

Figure 16.4 Jennifer Russo discusses the final group project with first graders. After drawing animals, children attached them to a paper and tempera globe and discussed how animals and children can live together.

acters, and habitats. After drawing and cutting out their animals, the children came up and attached them to the earth. Each child told the class something about their animals. The class closed with a conversation about how humans and animals live together on the planet and how humans have to take steps to keep our environment clean.

Conceptual Predispositions

Many elementary teachers give a "draw an animal" assignment of some kind, but many would balk at making it an experience with environmental issues. While most preservice teachers I have taught are open to thematic teaching based on political issues, there are some objections that I commonly hear from teachers who have a predisposition toward traditional art teaching. Traditional teaching leans toward conserving existing systems and transmitting knowledge in a seemingly neutral, non-political way. To apply various critical strategies to evaluate political issues requires critical thinking that is sometimes conflated with overthrowing authority and encouraging unruly behavior. Traditional educators tend to be conservative, believing that the existing system is successful as it is. Many have a positivist approach to education and think that knowledge can only be discovered in an objective and disinterested way through scientific

Figure 16.5 Laura King and Jennifer Russo begin their lesson on environmental issues for K–first-grade children with a performance. After discussion of how trash affects animals, children come to the aid of a "sick squirrel" by removing trash from her long tail.

methods. A commonsense worldview is that reality is fixed and that news, art, and other knowledge-producing systems present a transparent reflection of this reality. This world view leads to a conception of knowledge as accumulated data objectively passed on to their students using handouts acquired in teaching-methods classes or inservice workshops. The accumulated knowledge in art education is subsequently often limited to perspective drawing on one hand, and elements and principles of design on the other.

Many say there are not enough artists available whose works are appropriate to teaching at the elementary level in order to go beyond traditional teaching. My answer to these objections is not necessarily to use art works based on potentially political themes as providing an alternative canon of "true" information. More development is needed in the criticism and aesthetics components in teacher-education programs to cultivate an understanding that art teaching is more complex than the formal appreciation of artworks or the execution of marketable products. Using social and political content as a springboard for studio art does not preclude teaching craft and skillful composition. A focus on social issues creates an attitude that art, whatever it looks like, is never politically neutral.

Such an attitude can lead students to an acceptance of their own worlds as socially constructed and thus changeable. They can learn how artists, critics, and journalists make meanings and offer plausible alternative worldviews. Instead of passively receiving teacher training, preservice teachers can become active, thinking participants in developing a knowledge base of relevant themes and issues at the core of art and other subjects. Teachers and students should begin to sort out written, broadcast, and visual representations of contemporary social realities and relate them to their own lived experience. By studying and modeling selected contemporary artists, preservice teachers can learn diverse modes and strategies for socially responsible critique. They can develop ways to apply those strategies to teaching in elementary schools that lay the groundwork for equitable race, ethnic, gender, and class relations in a democratic society.

Endnote

1. I tell students that I generally consider artists living from the fifties on as contemporary, since that is my own lifetime.

References

Berger, A. A. (1991). *Media research techniques*. Newbury Park, CA: Sage Publications.

Chanda, J., & Daniel, V. (2000). ReCognizing works of art: The essences of contextual understanding. *Art Education, 53*(2), 6–11.

Cooper, J. E. (1991). Telling our own stories: The reading and writing of journals and diaries. In C. Witherall & N. Noddings, (Eds.), *Stories lives tell: Narrative and dialogue in education.* New York: Teacher's College Press.

Fehr, D. (1994). From theory to practice: Applying the historical context model of art criticism. *Art Education, 47*(5), 52–58.

Himmelstein, H. (1984). *Television myth and the American mind.* New York: Praeger.

McFee, J. K. (1995). Change and the cultural dimensions of art education. In R. Neperud, (Ed.), *Context, content, and community in art education: Beyond postmodernism.* New York: Teacher's College Press.

Pagano, J. (1991). Moral fictions: The dilemma of theory and practice. In C. Witherall, & N. Noddings, (Eds.), *Stories lives tell: Narrative and dialogue in education.* New York: Teacher's College Press.

Stout, C. (1992). Soft writing, hard thinking: The journal in a visual arts context. Paper presented at the National Art Education Conference, Phoenix, Arizona.

Wasson, R., Stuhr, P., & Petrovich-Mwaniki, L. (1990). Teaching art in the multicultural classroom: Six position statements. *Studies in Art Education, 31*(4), 234–246.

Wolcott, A. (1996). Is what you see what you get? A postmodern approach to understanding works of art. *Studies in Art Education, 37*(2), 69–79.

Wolff, T. & Geahigan, G. (1997). *Art criticism and education.* Chicago, IL: University of Illinois Press.

Appendix: Research Log Questions

1. Respond to the issue in your periodical source. Discuss how and why you would use it in the classroom.

2. When distinctions are made between fine arts and "other" arts, who might benefit, and who might suffer? How?

3. To what extent do we transmit our personal values to students? To what extent do we teach them strategies for argument/debate and/or code of ethics?

4. A child asks you (the teacher) "Is God a man?" You teach in a public school. How do you respond? Support your answer.

5. Discuss how specific artworks of your chosen artist reflect the artist and the culture in which they were made.

6. Discuss how the artwork(s) you have chosen for your lesson are a source of ideas for various subjects and activities in the classroom.

7. Write a critical response to "Change and the cultural dimensions of art education" by June King McFee (1995).

8. Find a good interpretation of an artwork by your artist and discuss why it is a good interpretation.

9. Write your interpretation of the lesson artwork(s) you have selected. Support your interpretation with visual information in the work as well as your research about the artist.

10. Write a letter from your artist to your students.

11. How does your artwork reflect your culture? What socio-political issue might you relate to your work?

12. Choose your favorite student lesson presentation and evaluate it.

13. What ideologies/beliefs/philosophies/"ulterior motives" do the artists we have studied in this class have? How do you know?

14. Watch a news broadcast or read a news report that you can use in your classroom. What ideologies/beliefs/philosophies/"ulterior motives" does the newsperson have? How do you know?

15. Write an interpretation of the artwork (teacher exemplar) that you made.

CONCLUSIONS AND FURTHER QUESTIONS

1. What approach to art education does Wyrick use?

2. What is the definition of an issue that Wyrick is using? Describe the sources and the methods that Wyrick uses to generate social and political issues for use in the classroom. What connections does she make between issues and the works of contemporary artists?

3. What is the news? What is the potential in using news media in the elementary classroom?

4. What are the differences between thematic teaching that is based on social and political issues and traditional art teaching?

5. How did Wyrick use the Research Log in the classes that she describes? Have you ever kept a journal? In what ways might you and your students find such writing useful?

6. Find a news source that presents you with an issue that fits Wyrick's definition and that you think is important. Based on what you have read in this chapter, how might you make this issue the basis of a unit of study for the elementary classroom? How might you develop interdisciplinary approaches based on this issue?

RESOURCES AND SUGGESTIONS
FOR FURTHER READING

Stephen J. Ball (Ed.). *Foucault and education: Disciplines and knowledge.* London; New York: Routledge, 1990.

Mary Beattie. *Constructing professional knowledge in teaching: A narrative of change and development.* Toronto; New York: Ontario Institute for Studies in Education; Teachers College Press, 1995.

Carol Becker. *Zones of contention: Essays on art, institutions, gender, and anxiety.* Albany, NY: State University of New York Press, 1996.

Diane DuBose Brunner. *Inquiry and reflection: Framing narrative practice in education.* Albany, NY: State University of New York Press, 1994.

John Caputo & Mark Yount (Eds.). *Foucault and the critique of institutions.* University Park, PA: Pennsylvania State University Press, 1993.

Jessica Evans & Stuart Hall (Eds.). *Visual culture: The reader.* London: Sage, in association with the Open University, 1999.

Nina Felshin (Ed.). *But is it art? The spirit of art as activism.* Seattle, WA: Bay Press, 1994.

Mary Renck Jalongo, Joan P. Isenberg, with Gloria Gerbracht. *Teachers' stories: From personal narrative to professional insight.* San Francisco, CA: Jossey-Bass, 1995.

Suzanne Lacy (Ed.). *Mapping the terrain: New genre public art.* Seattle, WA: Bay Press, 1995.

Barbara C. Matilsky. *Fragile ecologies: Contemporary artists' interpretations and solutions.* New York: Rizzoli, 1992.

Nicholas Mirzoeff. *An introduction to visual culture.* London; New York: Routledge, 1999.

Thomas S. Popkewitz & Marie Brennan (Eds.). *Foucault's challenge: Discourse, knowledge, and power in education.* New York: Teachers College Press, 1998.

Joy S. Ritchie & David E. Wilson. *Teacher narrative as critical inquiry: Rewriting the script.* New York: Teachers College Press, 2000.

1. In what ways have you come to know and understand your body? How have you learned to see and value your body? What is the relationship between your body and your identity?

2. How is the body generally treated within a school setting? What subject areas teach about the body? Why? What are your memories of learning about your body in school?

3. Find several media representations of female and male bodies. What types of images did you find? Are the bodies active or passive? What range of body types are represented in the images that you found? What bodies are not represented in these images? What kinds of gender expectations and stereotypes are shown in these images?

4. How might the images that you found affect elementary students? In what ways can teachers critically discuss representations and learning about the body?

Issues of the Body in Contemporary Art

Dan Nadaner

Concepts of the Body

The body: so everyday, so common, so personal, so biological. Or is it? The body as we know it keeps changing through the ways we know it. We get many of our ideas about the body through images in the print and electronic media. The body is everywhere in the image-world of the media. Magazines, television, and the web promote images of the body at an unprecedented rate. Hair styles, makeup, clothing, muscles, body-piercing, nutrients that are consumed, air that is inhaled, liquids that are drunk, tattoos, sex, fatness, thinness, and gender-defining imagery are everywhere. Many theorists and artists (Benjamin, 1968; Berger, 1977; Sontag, 1978; Barthes, 1981; Nadaner, 1985; Rorimer, 1989; Linker, 1990) have argued that the image-world is inseparable from the world. They suggest that the nature of reality is defined more by the images and words of the media than by the once-presumed "natural" reality of plants and trees and oceans and birds.

One simple conclusion of much of art theory is that we are controlled by the images around us. We live the lives that we see on TV and in magazines. This conclusion runs counter to the notion that our lives are richer because we have so much more "information," more information about health, about fitness, about science and technology, about cultural events.

How can images control our ideas of the body when so much "good information" is available? Consider fitness as an example of a body-related topic. Coaches today know how to help their athletes swim and run faster, lift more weights, and make greater gains in strength, flexibility, and aerobic endurance than ever before. So it would seem that the good information about fitness leads to good results. But the situation is more complex. Girls (and boys) seeing the ideal of thinness on every magazine cover diet obsessively, and boys (and girls) seeing the ideal of a buff, muscular body lift weights obsessively. Balance is sacrificed for obsession based on images, and sometimes serious health problems occur. So the power of the image-world deserves a critical look.

The Body and the Media

Children today grow up less in the forest of leaves and flowers described by the Boy Scout manual of the 1950s, and more in the forest of signs (Gudis, 1989) coming to them from all directions in the media. A *sign* is anything—a word, a picture, a gesture—that represents something else. Children must make their way through the forest of signs in one way or another. They must (must, in the sense that everyone eventually does) form ideas about their coolness or uncoolness, strength or weakness, gender identity, and sexual attractiveness within a context of images and ideas coming to them from a huge mass of signs in the media.

What difference does it make that children and adolescents must find their way to their own self-concept and own body image within the context of video and zine-scene and cyber-reality? The strong effects of media constructs on self-concept and body image seem irrefutable. Many examples of effects could be mentioned, but one suffices: anorexia. No esoteric research or article from the Harvard Medical Journal is needed for substantiation: this potentially terminal disease is documented in supermarket tabloids and in fashion magazines on every rack. Some fashion magazines run articles alerting readers to the dangers of this terrifying disease, but the covers still overwhelmingly promote a culture of thinness and fat elimination. Adolescent girls read labels to discover which foods have no fat at all, not understanding that at least 10% nutrient fat is necessary for survival, and 20% is recommended. They don't understand because the media culture does not promote the healthy approach.

The media is part of what is on children's minds. In recognizing the preva-
lence and power of media imagery, contemporary art makes a connection to the
society of which it (art) is a part, and of which children are a part. Although
many of my students in beginning college classes initially perceive contemporary art to be esoteric and weird, a brief introduction to some specific contemporary art works and the rationale for them usually changes this perception
dramatically. Much of the most important contemporary art is not more esoteric than the art of the past, but more direct. Subtlety is sometimes abandoned
because the issues being addressed (such as anorexia) demand clear and powerful communication. While the popular image still exists that art is as ephemeral
as the emperor's new clothes (as in the play *Art*, where three friends debate the
value of a blank white canvas), contemporary art is not often so weightless.
Contemporary art is often about as airy as a bag of cement.

The Body in Contemporary Art

Many contemporary artists are contributing innovative and thought-provoking
statements on the body and the media. Three artists who take a very direct approach to issues of self-concept are Barbara Kruger, Cindy Sherman, and
Lorna Simpson. All of these artists are working today, all are very well recognized in the art world, and all are deeply concerned with the self-concepts
that people form within the context of media imagery.

If you wanted to see where contemporary art was at in the fall of 1999,
you could not have done better than to go to Los Angeles to see the Barbara
Kruger retrospective at the Geffen, one of two sites of the Museum of Contemporary Art. In a city that features blockbuster experiences, at Universal Studios, at Disneyland, on the streets of Venice, this show was equally
impressive, in sight, in sound, in kinesthetics. But impressive with a difference. Rather than perpetuate a culture of media bombardment, it mimics that
culture so as to arrest it (Linker, 1990, p. 29) for the purpose of questioning.
Rather than accept typical messages, especially messages about the body, it
counters with critique.

Barbara Kruger (b. 1945) began her career as the art director for *Mademoiselle* magazine (Linker, 1990, p. 14). She learned first hand how images of
beauty and attractiveness are constructed, especially for adolescent girls. She
learned how images are constructed that signify being cool, hip, with it, at-
tractive.

Over a period of years in the 1980s Kruger developed a way of making a
statement that combined what she used to do at *Mademoiselle* with what she
now wanted to say. She combined words and photographic images in aggres-
sive patterns, reminiscent of political posters from the first half of the century,
restricting her colors to red, white, and black. These works have the appearance of a tabloid or magazine cover, but they make thoughtful and critical

Figure 17.1 Barbara Kruger, *It's A Small World But Not If You Have To Clean It*, 1990. (Photographic silkscreen on vinyl, 143″ × 103″. Mary Boone Gallery, New York.)

statements. An example of this work is *It's A Small World But Not If You Have To Clean It*, 1990 (see Figure 17.1), a photographic silkscreen on vinyl measuring 143″ × 103″. In this image, a woman wearing 1950s hair and clothing styles looks through a magnifying glass, showing us an enlarged version of her eye. The words "It's a small world" run across the image like a magazine title. The words "but not if you have to clean it" run at the bottom of the image, in a small type size, reminiscent of the attempt at a tantalizing lead-in to an article in a magazine. Kruger's image makes a wonderfully straightforward and humorous statement of how things look different from the other person's point of view, in this case perhaps the traditional housewife, cleaning all day while her husband is out mastering the world. Of course this story-within-a-picture is a stereotype, but that is Kruger's point; that the media gives us stereotypes in the form of carefully constructed images, and it is up to us to recognize the stereotypes and turn them back upon themselves.

Kruger's *Untitled (We Don't Need Another Hero)*, 1987 (see Figure 17.2), was installed as a billboard in cities all over the world. In this work a little girl, wearing the hairdo and fashions of milk ads of the 1950s, points her finger in awe at the bicep of a little boy. The words "We Don't Need Another Hero" cross over the image, however, turning it into a humorous critique of male dominance, muscle culture, and militarism.

Figure 17.2 Barbara Kruger, *Untitled (We Don't Need Another Hero)*, 1987. (Photographic silkscreen on vinyl, 108 3/4" × 157 3/4". Mary Boone Gallery, New York.)

Kruger does with her work what all great artists have done: she gives drama to everyday life and helps us to consider its importance. At the Geffen retrospective, Kruger showed her most recent work dealing with issues of the body. In one room of this massive installation, the viewer walked into a dark room where video projections of three faces confront her. Each of the faces fills its screen from floor to ceiling, taller than the viewer. Each of them is engaged in a monologue, in everyday language, criticizing something about you (the "you" they are addressing, which is perhaps us). Your hair, your clothes, the way you look, the way you are. It is a monologue not unlike what you might hear on a talk show, in a schoolyard, or from an acquaintance or family member.

It is upsetting, although possibly also humorous, to hear these critical monologues. You are in a big room, in public, with sound and image that is everywhere around you. And this is Kruger's point. These monologues about how we look, how we are, with reference to cultural conventions of fashion and behavior and attractiveness, are everywhere around us. They are in our heads. In 1920 when James Joyce was trying to document everything that was going on consciously and unconsciously in his character's mind in the novel *Ulysses*, the subjects were politics, religion, ethnicity, water distribution, high society, friends, word play, the look of the ocean, and a hundred other things in the world. Today it is different; there are *image*-world things all around us, that overwhelm us, and paralyze some of us into a state of constant worry about how we appear. Unfortunately many of these paralyzed people are children.

Barbara Kruger is a leading example of what contemporary artists do, and how contemporary art has changed. Artists take *ideas* as their starting point; they form *strategies* for getting those ideas across; and they find *materials* to embody those ideas. Cindy Sherman (b. 1954) is another leading artist whose ideas are concerned with the representation of women and the body in culture, and how those representations create limiting roles for women. Her strategy comes from her fascination with movies and the women in them.

Sherman became known for her *Untitled Film Still* series, in which she took photographs of herself in the roles of women in film of the 1940s and 1950s. Her characters are the innocent ingenue reaching for a book in the library, the teenager lying back on her bed, the working girl arriving in the big city (*Untitled Film Still # 21*, 1988. See Figure 17.3), the girl coming home alone at night on a cold dark urban street (Sherman, 1990). These are the characters of film noir, of Marilyn Monroe and Doris Day films.

Sherman's *Film Still* characters have in common the idea of the vulnerable woman, an idea that exists inside the film culture rather than in social reality (Gaines, 1998). And this is Sherman's point. She shows us what is

Figure 17.3 Cindy Sherman, *Untitled Film Still #21*, 1988. (Silver gelatin print, 8″ × 10″. Metro Pictures, New York.)

plausibly a film still, an 8×10 glossy like we used to see in theater windows, so as to give us a "still" moment, a moment to stop and consider the way that women are portrayed in films. Her strategy is enhanced by our knowledge that she had to go to elaborate lengths with makeup, costuming, set design, lighting, and composition to allow herself to become all of these roles.

By emphasizing the effort involved (hiring a model would not have had the same impact) she lets us in on just how contrived these roles are. We question the "reality" of the vulnerable librarian, or the lost shopgirl, and wonder how the thousands of images like these that we have grown up on have effected us. How have they effected how we think of women? And how would we represent women, and men, differently than these images, if we were making the films?

Lorna Simpson (b. 1960) also asks us to look again at how women are represented in the media. In her photographic/text work *Twenty Questions (A Sampler)*, 1986 (See Figure 17.4), Simpson shows us the backs of the heads of four African-American women and under them places the labels "Is She Pretty As A Picture" "Or Clear As Crystal" "Or Pure As A Lily" "Or Black As Coal" "Or Sharp As A Razor"? Simpson gives us a critical statement through both the photographs and the words. The photographs show us the women, but they don't show us. They put us in the position of not looking at the women, not finding out who each of them is as an individual. In this way Simpson

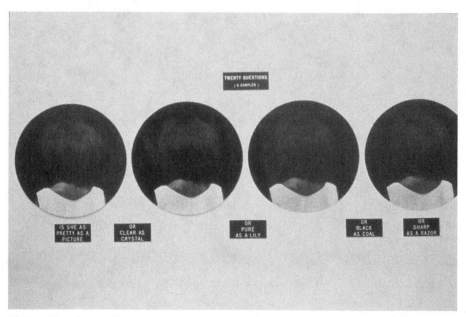

Figure 17.4 Lorna Simpson, *Twenty Questions (A Sampler)*, 1986. (Sean Kelly Gallery, New York.)

gets across the larger point that U.S. society depersonalizes the African-American woman, seeing her as a type rather than as an individual.

The words Simpson chooses make a further statement. Each is a cliché. Each says something so stereotyped as to say nothing of substance. Instead they say something about the nature of stereotypes themselves. Stereotypes are a means of concealment, of disinformation. Media stereotypes construct a view of a person, and they give us a label that tells us what to think about that view of a person, but their final effect is to hide the person's inner life from us rather than to bring us closer to that inner life.

Simpson, Sherman, and Kruger share a brilliance of imagination in finding strategies to convey the content of their works. Kruger moves us viscerally with her large-scaled installations, Sherman connects us to the movie heritage that has been part of our lives, and Simpson uses irony to show us the damaging shortcomings of stereotypes.

These artists also exemplify the way that art has broadened its use of materials, Kruger working with sound and painted walls, Simpson with text, and all three artists with photography. Many other artists search for virtually any material, and any form of *installation* (arrangement of a total space), that will convey what they want to say. Kiki Smith has dedicated most of her work to

Figure 17.5 Jenny Saville, *Hyphen*, 1999. (Oil on canvas, 104″ × 144″. Gagosian Gallery, New York.)

the body as a subject, using resin, ceramic, metal, and many other materials to convey ideas and issues related to the body. By using diverse materials, artists like Smith make the statement that traditional categories of materials (oil painting, marble sculpture, charcoal drawing) are less important than the ideas that the work represents.

At the same time, painting continues to be an important form of addressing ideas of the body. In England, Lucien Freud and Jenny Saville are figurative painters who continue the modern commentary on the body that has continued from Picasso and Frida Kahlo through Alice Neel and Francis Bacon. In Freud and Saville (*Hyphen*, 1999. See Figure 17.5) intense seeing and drawing combines with contemporary concerns for issues such as marginalized body types and "unflattering" views of the body. By looking at the body in ways that the popular media does not, Freud and Saville return to us the sense that we can think for ourselves and make up our own minds about the nature of the body.

Issues of the Body and the Elementary Art Curriculum

Many of the works of contemporary artists are addressed to the adult as viewer, and to an adult's experience with life and with the media as a context. But the principles underlying the works I have mentioned are very relevant, and very adaptable, to the needs of children. In this concluding section I would like to summarize some of the key points in the approach of contemporary art to the body, and then suggest some implications for the elementary school curriculum.

First, the emphasis of contemporary art is more on *ideas* than appearances.

Second, ideas are formed through *thinking*, writing, discussion with others, and study of ideas in other subjects, from history and psychology to biology and physics.

Third, the artist consciously thinks of a way to *involve the viewer* in thinking about the idea of the work. Another word for this process is a strategy.

Fourth, the artist searches for *materials* that convey the idea. The materials can take any form.

Fifth, the artist takes some *point of view* in her or his work. The art encourages people to think differently rather than reproduce what is already and everywhere out there.

In a school, these ideas could mean that children would value their own thinking as a starting point for an art project. Children are already taking in conceptions of the body through the media, so it is especially important that schools give children the opportunity to form their own ideas within a positive context. Children could learn about the body through anatomy, through biology, through nutrition, through exercise, through photography and art history, and many other pathways to come up with their ways of thinking about the body.

Children could learn about stereotypes. Many excellent curriculum materials on stereotypes convey this idea, and can lead to a study of stereotypes in magazines and on television. Children can learn for themselves about how many different kinds of people there are, people that stereotypes do not convey, and about how many different kinds of people are healthy and happy.

Children could apply their growing knowledge to critical discussions (yes, children do enjoy critical discussions) about what they see in the media and in works of art. By sharing their ideas with others they find out that they have their own idea, and they learn from other children's ways of seeing at the same time.

Children can also learn ways of thinking about a person without thinking about the body. Poetry is an excellent means to form images of the self that focus on emotions and convey a sense of self without focusing on the physiological or physiognomic. In this way children can build a positive self-concept that is an alternative to the media imagery and the habit of negative self-criticism that media imagery can initiate.

Children could make installations to convey their poetic images using materials that no one had ever thought of before. Children can learn more about what words mean, how computer graphics can be used to place precisely the words and feelings of words that they want to include in their installation.

Children can think of strategies for suggesting ideas to viewers, to involve viewers in thinking about ideas, without spelling out every bit of the idea.

The contemporary artist and the child are not living in different worlds. Each is living in a complex social reality, and each needs to find a way to make art work for them within that reality. The art they find may not look on the outside like the art of a century ago, it may look unfamiliar, and it is very likely not to meet with immediate approval. But the purpose of art remains to find the deeper beauty, the beauty on the inside of each person, the insistence that we are not trapped by any limiting or demeaning way of seeing ourselves. Contemporary artists are making some important inquiries into issues of the body, and these inquiries hold promise for education as well.

References

Barthes, R. (1981). *Camera lucida.* New York: Hill and Wang

Benjamin, W. (1968). The work of art in the age of mechanical reproduction. In *Illuminations* (pp. 219–244). New York: Harcourt, Brace and World.

Berger, J. (1977). *Ways of seeing.* New York: Penguin Books.

Gaines, C. (1998). *Content and form comics.* Los Angeles, CA: Charles Gaines.

Gudis, C. (1989). *A forest of signs: Art in the crisis of representation.* Cambridge, MA: MIT Press.

Linker, K. (1990). *Love for sale: The words and pictures of Barbara Kruger.* New York: Harry N. Abrams, Inc.

Nadaner, D. (1985). Responding to the image world: A proposal for art curricula. *Art Education, 37*(1) 9–12.

Rorimer, A. (1989). Photography-language-context: Prelude to the 1980s. In C. Gudis (Ed.), *A forest of signs: Art in the crisis of representation* (pp. 129–154). Cambridge, MA: MIT Press.

Sherman, C. (1990), with intro. by A. C. Danto. *Untitled Film Stills.* New York: Rizzoli.

Sontag, A. (1978). *On photography.* New York: Farrar, Straus and Giroux.

CONCLUSIONS AND FURTHER QUESTIONS

1. Describe what Nadaner means by the terms "good information" and "bad information." How can we determine good from bad information? Why is it important to teach children about these differences?

2. Why is it important for children to understand how concepts of the self and body images are formed? In what ways can a critical examination of media images help students understand these concepts?

3. Nadaner writes, "artists take *ideas* as their starting points; they form *strategies* for getting those ideas across; and they find *materials* to embody those ideas." Discuss the ideas, strategies, and materials of one of the artists that Nadaner discusses in this chapter. How is this connected to the approaches that teachers use?

4. Describe the five key points that Nadaner presents as the approach of contemporary art to the body. How are each of these points related to the elementary classroom?

5. What is the relationship between studying artworks such as those presented in this chapter and other forms of visual culture that represent the body? In what ways can we use the work of contemporary artists to intervene in the production of limiting images of the body?

RESOURCES AND SUGGESTIONS
FOR FURTHER READING

Terry Barrett. *Criticizing photographs.* Mountain View, CA: Mayfield Publishing Co., 1990.

Susan Bordo. *Unbearable weight: Feminism, Western culture, and the body.* Berkeley, CA: University of California Press, 1993.

Susan Bordo. *The male body: A new look at men in public and in private.* New York: Farrar, Straus and Giroux, 1999.

Jane Brettle & Sally Rice (Eds.). *Public bodies/private states: New views on photography, representation, and gender.* New York: St. Martin's Press, 1994.

Zdenek Felix & Martin Schwander (Eds.). *Cindy Sherman: Photographic work 1975–1995.* London: Schirmer Art Books, 1995.

Lawrence Gowing. *Lucien Freud.* New York: Thames and Hudson, 1982.

Amelia Jones. *Body art/performing the subject.* Minneapolis, MN: University of Minnesota Press, 1998.

Barbara Kruger. *Remote control: Power, cultures, and the world of appearances.* Cambridge, MA: MIT Press, 1993.

Barbara Kruger. Pictures and words. New York: Inner-Tube video, 1996. (28-minute videocassette)

Barbara Kruger. Exhibition catalogue. Los Angeles & Cambridge, MA: Museum of Contemporary Art & MIT Press, 1999.

Suzanne Lacy (Ed.). *Mapping the terrain: New genre public art.* Seattle, WA: Bay Press, 1995.

Nicholas Mirzoeff. *An introduction to visual culture.* London; New York: Routledge, 1999.

Rebecca Schneider. *The explicit body in performance.* London; New York: Routledge, 1997.

Cindy Sherman: Retrospective. Exhibition catalogue. Museum of Contemporary Art, Los Angeles and The Museum of Contemporary Art, Chicago. New York: Thames and Hudson, 1997.

Lorna Simpson, & Sarah J. Rogers. *Lorna Simpson: Interior/exterior, full/empty.* Columbus, OH: Wexner Center for the Arts/The Ohio State University, 1997.

A world of art. Works in progress: Lorna Simpson. Oregon Public Broadcasting production in association with Oregon State University for the Annenberg/CPB Project. S. Burlington, VT: Annenberg/CPB Project, 1996. (26-minute videocassette)

Deborah Willis. *Lorna Simpson.* San Francisco & New York: Friends of Photography; Distributed Art Publishers, 1992.

Beryl J. Wright, & Saidiya V. Hartman. *Lorna Simpson: For the sake of the viewer.* Chicago, IL: Museum of Contemporary Art, 1992.

CHAPTER 18
QUESTIONS AND EXPLORATIONS

1. What is the relationship between religious freedom and freedom of expression (for example, artistic freedom)? How do these freedoms relate to public elementary schooling?
2. Find an example of a religious work of art. Describe why you think the object is religious. Why is it an artwork? In what ways does the object function as religious? In what ways does it function as an artwork? How do these two contexts help you understand and interpret the object? Are there any contradictions between these two contexts? Any similarities?
3. Would you consider using a religious work of art in an elementary classroom? Why or why not? What issues would an artwork such as this raise?
4. Describe the differences and commonalities between teaching religion and teaching about religion. Is there religious content that you consider to be inappropriate to teach about in a public school setting?
5. What is the relationship between religious beliefs and identity? Would you describe yourself as a religious person? How might this affect your understanding of artworks based on religious subject matter?
6. Do schools have an obligation to teach about religion? If so, what religions should be taught about?

Concerning the Religious in Art Education[1]

Paul S. Briggs

Educators at all levels, and particularly elementary educators, (both specialists and generalists) often leave unexamined the religious content of art or refuse to talk about religious art objects, even those of the recommended classroom canon (Freedberg, 1989; Parks, 1994). By doing so these educators are participating in a self-defeating campaign that undermines the development of a more substantial and encompassing art world for artists, educators, and students.

Attention to art content, that is, the discussion of the meaning of works of art, has recently been considered usual classroom practice (Wilson, 1997; Clark, Day, and Greer, 1987). In addition, art that expresses personal religious sentiment with clearly recognizable subject matter[2] has begun to be endorsed by the contemporary art world (Wilson-Lloyd, 2000). Despite these changes most elementary educators are reluctant to discuss the religious content of artworks that they show in the classroom. This is an iconoclasm[3]of omission, due, in most cases, to teachers' fear that they may be seen as proselytizing or denigrating the religious beliefs of another (Oreskes, 1989).

Yet these omissions are also the result of a repression of response. We fear that our emotions, and our beliefs, may enter into our discussion of the images and somehow taint the critique (Freedberg, 1989). This is true not only of religious imagery, however other potentially emotionally charged issues such as race, gender, sexuality, violence, and democracy are becoming accepted as content for discussion in the classroom. Religion as content for classroom discussion is not yet included. Religion, however, as a cultural practice, continues to nurture presuppositions about politics, education, race, and gender.

Education of Artist and Audience

Elementary art education is, by its very nature, a general art education, for at this level there is rightly no attempt to distinguish the future artist from those students who primarily will become viewers of art and both receive the same artistic preparation (Wilson, 1997). Indeed, it is difficult to know which children may go on to study art at the college level with the intention of becoming an artist.

In addition, general education is increasingly leaving unexamined many of the great ideas of Western civilization (Wilson, 1997). Youth graduate from public schools never having discussed ideas such as virtue and vice, temperance, good and evil, necessity and contingency, religion, or the various conceptions of God, creation, and evolution (e.g. see Adler, 1952). There is little opportunity for dialogue and debate around the salient religious content that has shaped much of Western literature, art, and culture. Many young adults leave school with no sense of the role that religion has played in the development of aesthetic ideas.

Children who go on to become students of art at the college level will most likely receive occasion in their education to fully reflect upon an array of issues including those surrounding religious artistic expression. Others may never get an opportunity to examine these ideas. The result is a disproportionate number of people in the audience of the art world that do not understand art (Eaton, 1988) and cannot tolerate religious art that does not concur with their own religious conceptions and beliefs. In addition, response to contemporary religious art during the past fifteen years is indicative of a public audience who lacks an understanding of the ways that meaning is constructed and communicated in the visual arts. Such an understanding is necessary to appreciate personal visual responses to religious experiences (Bolton, 1992; Dubin, 1992, Cloud, 1999). Negative response to contemporary religious art, then, is sometimes due to an unwillingness or inability to understand contemporary art, disagreement with religious content, or a reaction to both the artwork and the content.

Contemporary Religious Expression

Several contemporary controversies have centered on artworks depicting religious content that offended persons who apparently believe that religious experience should only have limited forms of artistic expression. Andres Serrano's *Piss Christ* in 1985, and more recently Chris Ofili's *The Holy Virgin Mary* in 1999, caused more than a stir when viewed by public audiences. Audience protests to both works of art prompted city officials to threaten, if not actually cut, funding for the arts at some level. One of the primary figures who led the attack and the debate that almost led to the elimination of the National Endowment for the Arts (NEA) in the late eighties was Republican Senator Jesse Helms of North Carolina. His reasoning is instructive.

Jesse Helms knows what he likes. At his home in Arlington, a Virginia suburb of Washington, the Senator has oil paintings of North Carolina scenes: a man sitting at a table with his hands folded in prayer over a Bible, a summer home once owned on Lake Gaston and a snowy scene of a pier. "The self-proclaimed, self-anointed art experts would scoff, and say, 'Oooh, terrible,' but I like beautiful things, not modern art," Senator Helms said, "I can't even figure out that sculpture in the Hart Building," he added, speaking of an Alexander Calder mobile of metal clouds and mountains that is in the newest Senate office building (Dowd, 1989, p. A1).

Helms admits he likes "beautiful things." As described, these beautiful things are traditionally represented scenes, in a traditional medium. It must be noted that the one image with religious content portrays a traditional representation of religious subject matter. Helms also makes it clear that he does not like modern art, and further reveals a source of his frustration when he states that he can't even figure out a Calder sculpture. He does not like art that he does not understand. Given the passion with which people often hold to religious beliefs it is not surprising that he might respond even more negatively to religious imagery that he cannot comprehend. Beauty, it seems, is in the ideology of the beholder.

Education is supposed to bring about new understandings and fresh relationships between ideas. It should broaden a student's perspective. Schooling in history, science, and mathematics should give learners the ability to deepen interpretations of, for example, law, democracy, technology, logical reasoning. Education in the arts should allow students the freedom to explore the profound and varied aesthetic choices of groups and individuals in literature, performance, and visual art. Currently, the NEA, funding for the arts, and public spaces for art risk having budgets cut or discontinued, and closed (Hughes, 1995) because there is an audience of civic leaders and their constituents whose art education did not prepare them to approach works of art that employ novel and unique ways of expressing personal religious experience. The injustices done to the art world due to an inattention to religious content are far reaching, and this neglect subsequently undermines art education.

In addition, America's religious heritage has instilled a mistrust of spontaneous religious art (Cubberley 1934; Briggs 1995). Art as a subject is seen as a sort of creative recess and easily comes under suspicion when students explore ideas that are controversial. Art teachers often steer students away from dealing with subject matter that involves strong content while popular culture uses this same *taboo* content ostentatiously.

New conceptions of traditional Western religious ideas cannot be developed in a context of iconoclastic aesthetic intolerance. It is crucial that we develop approaches for discussing the religious content of art objects at the elementary level. There are many ways to express one's religious beliefs or lack thereof and America's laws protect that right. Whether this expression is accomplished in a place of worship, on a canvas, or using a lump of clay, all are free to express their personal religious experiences. Yet many of our rights and freedoms are limited, not by laws, but by fear and intolerance. Students who are not engaged in discussions about alternative visual expressions of religious sentiment at the elementary level may become resistant to and possibly intolerant of non-traditional modes of religious expression.

Art History and Religious Objects

Most of us would agree that the majority of Western art objects from antiquity to our present time had as their inspiration a religious belief (Gombrich, 1995). A great number of these works were an attempt to concretely represent profound conceptions of deity. Whether that conception was of a supernatural being, or a superhuman individual invested with god-likeness, or a polytheistic array of beings, art served to clarify conceptions of the supernatural. These objects functioned more as religious objects rather than objects of art. Their use for ritualistic or didactic purposes in a community differed greatly in intention from contemporary individual expressions. Considered sacred due to their function in enabling the religious to participate in worship, and to apprehend deity (Giakalis, 1994), the modern idea of these pieces as art is insufficient.

The designation of these objects as art is conventional and convenient for art historical purposes. Yet these inextricable religious connections, even in more recent works, receive a superficial critique, or they go unexamined by art educators. For example, rarely, if at all, in the elementary classroom is Thomas Cole's *Oxbow* (1836) discussed as a debate over God's intention for natural resources, nor is Mark Rothko's *Ochre and Red on Red* (1954) explained as a "quest for the religious sublime" (Hughes, 1997, pp. 15, 18). More often Cole's work is simply explained as an example of American landscape painting and Rothko's study as Color Field painting. The latter treatments are correct but fall short of conveying the depth of purpose and spiritual concern that drove each artist.

It should be impossible to avoid religious content when dealing with many works of art. For example, teachers and students have to discuss Jewish religion and Christian translations of the Hebrew Bible to know why Moses has horns in Michelangelo's marble sculpture created for the Tomb of Julius II, 1513–1515. To avoid such a discussion in these cases is no doubt due to an ongoing iconoclastic heritage (Kibbey, 1986; Dillenberger, 1984).

The Egyptian era known as the New Kingdom is a prime example of the influence of religion on art. The monarch during this period, Akhenaten, due to his conception of deity, transformed the appearance of art objects even though there had been an established aesthetic for several centuries. Ancient Egyptians were a polytheistic people. Akhenaten made one prominent deity, Aton, the sole God during his reign, and became an iconoclast. He persecuted priests who maintained rituals of the former religion and attempted to change linguistic designations to represent his monotheism disfiguring earlier creations (Microsoft Encarta, 1998). His religious ideas did not live on after his death, but his influence on the aesthetics of Egyptian art were far reaching (Janson, 1995). Though this era and the study of Egyptian art and culture is popular in elementary schools this important fact about the period is seldom discussed.

Any brief survey of Classical Greek and Roman sculpture reveals its content source to lie in polytheistic mythological beliefs. These works, due to their ideal realism, are often heralded as among the world's most beautiful works of art (Gombrich, 1995) and nearly every marble likeness (and temple) is devoted to the reflection on and worship of one of many deities. This context is very seldom considered as Gombrich notes:

> We too often forget . . . that people prayed before them, that sacrifices were brought to them amidst strange incantations, and that thousands and tens of thousands of worshippers may have approached them with hope and fear in their hearts—wondering, . . . whether these statues . . . were not really at the same time gods themselves. (p. 84)

To fully explain these objects some knowledge of Greek mythology and religious ideas are needed. Teachers might include the reading of an excerpt from Homer's writings, since his *Iliad* and *Odyssey* serve as the foundation for later treatments of Greek myths.

In the general classroom students may begin learning about Greek history and mythology as early as the second grade and an interdisciplinary approach to studying this history and art could make connections between the structure in this mythology, its conception of deity as human in form and sensibility with the form of Greece's religious art.

The culture and history of Greece and Rome are often studied simultaneously. One reason why this is so is also rarely mentioned. Most of what remains of the magnificence of Greek sculpture are Roman copies of Greek originals. Though many of our western ideas of ethics, democracy, art, and literature are derived from Greek mythology, most of the originals were smashed by Christians after the triumph of the Church (Gombrich, 1995). As did Akhenaten, Judeo-Christian traditions centered worship in the appeasement of one God as opposed to many (Flusser, 1988).

In the East, Islamic[4] and Buddhist traditions also affected the development of art forms through the forbidding and embracing of images respectively. Religion's profound effect on the course of artistic development is too significant to be left untaught.

Both Greek and Egyptian artistic religious imagery was varied and imaginative. Traits associated with certain animals were often transferred to gods and humans using literal visual combinations. Besides the obviously beautiful human-bodied gods, Greeks also had Satyrs, Centaurs, and the Minotaur, all half-beast, half-human forms. Egyptian gods ranged from cat deities to a plethora of half-beast, half-human gods to symbols such as Akhenaten's sun disk. A discussion of the symbolism of these beings could address important moral ideas as they did for ancient Egyptians and Greeks.

The Hebrew Bible forbade the use of images, and the Hebrew religion is credited with one of the first and most enduring expressions of iconoclasm— Moses' destruction of the golden calf during the Exodus of the Israelites from Egypt (Freedberg, 1989). Later adherents to the Judeo-Christian faith point to this example as reasoning for pure, that is, imageless places of worship. Still the Hebrew religion was not lacking in visual imagery (Goodenough, 1953), nor was the prohibition strictly enforced at all times as can be seen in the temple at Dura-Europos. This temple employed even human art forms as didactic visual aids to worship (Gombrich, 1995).

Early Christian art also employed a more varied and creative repertoire of images and symbols. The griffin, dragon, gargoyles, oxen, lions, lambs, two headed phoenixes, and fish are among other real and imaginary beasts that adorned objects for use in sacred rituals and many holy texts (Ferguson, 1961). Even after the Church divided into its eastern and western expressions, a rich symbolic imagery was developed that is retained by both Orthodox and Catholic traditions to this day (Barasch, 1992). Christian imagery declined only after the Protestant Reformation and the rise of and the expression of Christian fervor that became known as Calvinism, named after its zealous leader John Calvin. Calvin (1559/1983) prohibited nearly all images. Calvin's ideas were transplanted to America with the Puritans. They, like the Hebrews, the Egyptians under Akhenaten, and the Church as far back as the third century, denied for others the religious freedom they had sought to obtain.

The Church grew continually more iconoclastic, eventually strictly regulating and limiting religious imagery and placing value in words alone (Kibbey, 1986). This was especially true of preaching for the Puritans (Lloyd-Jones, 1987). As a result, the rich imagery of the early Church is all but forgotten by contemporary Christians. Although Americans grew to become, for the most part, religiously eclectic people (Ahlstrom, 1972), today there are Protestant Christians who continue to believe that Catholic and Orthodox Christians are idol worshipers. Narrow perspectives such as this may be broadened through the study of the role of religion in art, and the inclusion of art in teaching about religion at the elementary level. From these few examples it is evident that the use of religious objects and the religious practices of different cultures and groups are inextricably linked.

Conclusion: Parameters of Image Selection

A myriad of visual religious expressions can be studied in diverse cultures, including African, Islamic, native American, and Hinduism among others, using much of the art that is shown regularly in elementary classrooms. The history of art is becoming more inclusive of non-western images and objects. Indeed, America, an immigrant country, is fast becoming home to populations that embrace faiths not affiliated with the prevailing Judeo-Christian heritage. It should be accepted that a plurality of faith and beliefs must allow for a plurality of expression even when that expression is visual. It follows that the plurality of beliefs, and varying degrees of assent to dogma within present day Judeo-Christian faith, must also allow for a range of visual expression for these personal religious experiences (Barstow, 1999).

Not all works of art are appropriate for young students either because the content is so esoteric that it is inaccessible to youngsters or because the visual nature of the work may be too strong depicting, for example, explicit sexual practices or extreme violence. But others should be used as exemplars such as the various versions of Anselm Kiefer's *Ways of Worldly Wisdom: Arminius's Battle*, (n.d.), or his *Resurrexit*, (1973).

If one doubts the ability of youth to explore issues of theology, race, history, and heroism, tune into Saturday morning or weekday afternoon animated cartoons and try to follow the various layers of plot, meaning, or sort out the transmutations of characters that are sometimes evil but at other times are good. Comic books take liberties unexplored by television. Sometimes the imagery in them is dark, the language brusque, and the content unsettling. Examples from popular culture may even shed light on traditional religious ideas that may otherwise be unfamiliar to or difficult for youth to grasp from visual clues they have not yet mastered. Most superheroes and heroines used to derive their powers primarily from biologically or ontologically morphing with animals. These days they get power from animals and various contemporary technologies or a combination of the two. Many of these ideas are borrowed from scientific and/or ancient religious ideas. What students understand about these characters can be used to facilitate the study of Assyrian-Babylonian Rhytons, or the animal symbolism of the evangelists in the illuminations of the Book of Kells, or Egyptian gods. It may seem this would be a belittling comparison. Yet some ideas, when presented visually or using different visual strategies, may simply become developmentally appropriate when animated or cartooned. Our interpretation of and/or response to images may change depending on the medium or visual principles used to convey specific subject matter.

There is an added possibility that ideas may be trivialized when borrowed and abstracted from their source, be that an original visual, oral, or written context. Take for example one contemporary religious work, Andres Serrano's *Pieta*—a photograph of a woman clad in a black hooded robe passionately holding a large fish, her hand inside the gaping wound in its side. This image cannot be fully appreciated without knowing that the early persecuted Christians, who designated themselves as "fishers of men," had as part of their iconography the *ichthus* (Greek for fish) as a hallowed symbol of Christ (Institute of Contemporary Art, 1994). One may view the replacing of Jesus with a fish a trivializing visual metaphor. In contrast the little plastic stick-on fish symbol many Christians place on the back of their cars may seem terribly inadequate as a symbol of the passion of Christ. Can parameters be set for what would be legitimate interpretations of this event? And which of these representations, if either, should be outside these parameters, and which could possibly be used to teach students the atrocity of punishing someone for expressing their religious beliefs?

If future audiences are educated to "figure out" or appreciate contemporary works of art, the parameters for religious imagery and therefore personal religious expression through the arts will be broadened. They may also be able to experience some of this work as religious art, as modern icons, and as art that transports its viewers from worldly concerns to spiritual contemplation. Many receive healing, hope, transformation, conversion, and rapture during such contemplation induced by viewing an image. Censoring specific content as too incendiary can cause much of the content in art to be left untaught. This view renders issues such as artistic representations of women as sexual objects a taboo subject for conservative modernists who may already be repressing as morally unacceptable the fact that looking at these images may cause arousal.

Obvious religious content of both Judeo-Christian and pagan expressions becomes unacceptable for liberals and conservatives for fear of being viewed as proselytizing. Yet this content and imagery is everywhere present in popular culture and youth are left to interpret these grand themes, disguised as insignificant plots and expendable lyrics, on their own. Is it educationally prudent to leave the teaching of good and evil to "Power Rangers" (FOX), the conception of supernatural beings to "Touched by an Angel" (CBS), the union of marriage to "Married with Children" (Columbia Tri Star), family relationships to "The Simpsons" (FOX), and the notion of justice and democracy to the various trials and cop and court shows that have in recent times become popular television? If one fears the possible mollification of content that takes place when ideas are represented differently than in their original conception, it might be more appropriate to refer to Dante's *Inferno* in his *Divine Comedy*, 1321, and Hieronymus Bosch's *Garden of Earthly Delights*, 1550, to learn about good and evil, Homer and Michelangelo to learn of supernatural humans and beings, Hera to talk about marriage, and Egypt to learn about justice, for these expressions have faithfully captured the imagination of audiences over many years.

We may even after some time be ready to view the work of Anselm Kiefer and Andres Serrano for dialogue about martyrdom (Barrett, 1994) and to Jolene Rickard's *3 Sisters*, 1989, to discuss spirituality, and Masami Teraoka to explore issues of race and sexuality (Cahan and Kocur, 1996). This sort of art is not easy to talk about, but it is preferable for students to be uncomfortable critiquing certain images than to be ignorant of the ideas, or comfortable with unacceptable content (Begly, 1993). When approached in this manner, art education is conceived as an empowering and transformative experience.

Endnotes

1. Wassily Kandinsky, *Concerning the Spiritual in Art* (1977, original 1911), was one of the first artist in modern times to explore the role of the interior life in artistic creation.
2. Earlier attempts at expressing religious or spiritual content by artists such as Kandinsky, Malevich, Rothko, et al., stressed the purity of the nonobjective as best able to communicate ethereal ideas.
3. Iconoclasm is derived from the Greek word meaning to literally break (*klastes*) and image (*eikon*). Today the term is often used to denote persons who seek to deconstruct tradition or ideas deemed unacceptable.
4. In later periods (14th–20th century) Islam also influenced the development of art in the West—during the Ottoman Empire which, in the 17th century, stretched from northwestern Asia to southeastern Europe.

References

Adler, M. J. (Ed.). (1952). *The great ideas: A syntopicon of great books of the Western world* (Vols. 1–2). Chicago, IL: Encyclopedia Britannica.

Ahlstrom, S. (1972). *A religious history of the American people.* New Haven, CT: Yale University Press.

Alighieri, D. (1980). *The divine comedy.* C. H. Sisson (Trans.) Manchester: Carcanet New Press. (Original publication 1321.)

Barasch, M. (1992). *Icon: Studies in the history of an idea.* New York; London: New York University Press.

Barrett, T. (1994). Editorial: Culture wars. *Studies in Art Education, 36*(1), 3–5.

Barstow, D. (1999, October 3). As culture warriors dig in, public at last sees the art behind the fuss. *New York Times,* pp. 33–34.

Begly, A. (1993, March 26). The tempest around Steven Greenblatt. *New York Times Magazine,* pp. 32–38

Bolton, R. (1992). *Culture wars: Documents from the recent controversies in the arts.* New York: New Press.

Briggs, P. S. (1995). *The influence of Unitarianism on the inclusion of art education in the common schools of Massachusetts, 1825–1870.* Unpublished doctoral dissertation, State College, PA: Pennsylvania State University.

Cahan, S., & Kocur, Z. (Eds.). (1996). *Contemporary art and multicultural education.* New York: New Museum of Contemporary Art and Routledge.

Clark, G. A., Day, M. D., & Greer, W. D. (1987). Discipline-based art education: Becoming students of art. [Special Issue]. *Journal of Aesthetic Education 21*(2), 129–193.

Cloud, J. (1999, October 4). New York's art attack: The culture wars finally hit the culture capital. *Time,* p. 64.

Cubberley, E. P. (1934). *Public education in the United States: A study and interpretation of American educational history.* Boston, MA: Houghton Mifflin.

Dillenberger, J. (1984). *The visual arts and Christianity in America: The colonial period through the nineteenth century.* Chico, CA: Scholar Press.

Dowd, M. (1989, July 28). An unruffled Helms basks in the eye of an arts storm of his own making. *New York Times,* pp. A1, B6.

Dubin, S. C. (1992). *Arresting images: Impolitic, art, and uncivil actions.* New York: Routledge.

Eaton, M. Muelder (1988). *Basic issues in aesthetics.* Belmont, CA: Wadsworth.

Eusebius Pamphilus (1989). The statue erected by the women having an hemorrhage. In C. F. Cruse (Trans.) *The ecclesiastical history of Eusebius Pamphilus* (Book 7, chap. 15, pp. 288–289). Grand Rapids, MI: Baker Book House. (Original work published about AD 325).

Ferguson, G. (1961). *Signs and symbols in Christian art.* New York, NY: Oxford University Press.

Freedberg, D. (1989). *The power of images: Studies in the history and theory of response.* Chicago, IL: University of Chicago Press.

Giakalis, A. (1994). *Images of the divine: The theology at the seventh ecumenical council.* Leiden, The Netherlands: E. J. Brill.

Gombrich, E. H. (1995). *The story of art.* (16th ed.). Englewood Cliffs, NJ: Prentice Hall.

Goodenough, E. R. (1953). *Jewish symbols in the Greco-Roman period.* (Vols. 3 and 7). New York: Pantheon Books.

Hughes, R. (1995, August 7). Pulling the fuse on culture. *Time, 146*(6), 60–68.

Institute of Contemporary Art (1994). *Andres Serrano: Works 1983–1993.* Philadelphia, PA: Institute of Contemporary Art, University of Pennsylvania.

Kandinsky, W. (1977). *Concerning the spiritual in art.* (M. T. H. Sadler, Trans.). New York: Dover. (Original work published 1911.)

Kibbey, A. (1986). *The interpretation of material shapes in puritanism: A study of rhetoric, prejudice, and violence.* Cambridge, UK: Cambridge University Press.

Lloyd-Jones, D. M. (1987). *The puritans: Their origins and successors.* Carlisle, PA: Banner of Truth.

Microsoft Encarta 98 Encyclopedia Deluxe Edition [Computer Software]. (1998). Redmond, WA: Microsoft.

Oreskes, M. (1989, July 27). Senate votes to bar U.S. support of 'obscene or indecent' artwork: Measure, backed by Helms, angers arts groups. *New York Times*, pp. A1, C18.

Parks, M. E. (1994). *The art teacher's desktop reference.* Englewood Cliffs, NJ: Prentice Hall.

Wilson, B. (1997). *The quiet evolution: Changing the face of arts education.* Los Angeles, CA: Getty Education Institute for the Arts.

Wilson-Lloyd, A. (2000, January 23). In a new millennium, religion shows its face. *New York Times*, p. AR 43.

CONCLUSIONS AND FURTHER QUESTIONS

1. What is religious artistic expression? What argument does Briggs present for having us pay attention to the religious content of artworks?

2. Does the expression of personal religious ideas and beliefs result in an art object or a religious object?

3. Why should religion and the representation of religious ideas in works of art be included in the elementary classroom?

4. Before you read this chapter, you described whether or not you would teach about a religious work of art in your classroom. Have your views on this changed? Think about how you would now approach teaching a work of art with religious content in your classroom.

5. Describe the relationships between religious ideas and popular culture that Briggs discusses.

RESOURCES AND SUGGESTIONS
FOR FURTHER READING

Diane Apostolos-Cappadona. *Art, creativity, and the sacred: An anthology in religion and art.* New York: Crossroad, 1984.

Earle J. Coleman. *Creativity and spirituality: Bonds between art and religion.* Albany, NY: State University of New York Press, 1998.

Jane Daggett Dillenberger. *The religious art of Andy Warhol.* New York: Continuum, 1998.

Mary Daly. *Beyond God the Father: Toward a philosophy of women's liberation.* Boston, MA: Beacon Press, 1985.

Ellen Dissanayake. *What is art for?* Seattle, WA: University of Washington Press, 1988.

Francis A. Eigo, (Ed.). *Imaging Christ: Politics, art, spirituality.* Villanova, PA: Villanova University Press, 1991.

Marija Gimbutas. *The language of the goddess: Unearthing the hidden symbols of Western civilization.* London: Thames and Hudson, 1989.

G. W. F. Hegel. *On art, religion, philosophy: Introductory lectures to the realm of absolute spirit.* J. Glenn Gray (Ed. & Trans.). New York: Harper & Row, 1970.

Suzi Gablik. *The reenchantment of art.* New York, NY: Thames and Hudson, 1992.

David Ray Griffin (Ed.). *Sacred interconnections: Postmodern spirituality, political economy, and art.* Albany, NY: State University of New York Press, 1990.

James Alfred Martin, Jr. *Beauty and holiness: The dialogue between aesthetics and religion.* Princeton, NJ: Princeton University Press, 1990.

Amalia Mesa-Bains (curator). *Ceremony of memory: New expressions in spirituality among contemporary Hispanic artists.* Sante Fe, NM: Center for Contemporary Arts of Santa Fe, 1988.

Amalia Mesa-Bains. *Grotto of the virgins: November 30–December 31, 1987.* (Exhibition catalogue). New York: Intar Latin American Gallery, 1987.

David Morgan. *Protestants & pictures: Religion, visual culture, and the age of American mass production.* New York: Oxford University Press, 1999.

David Morgan. *Visual piety: A history and theory of popular religious images.* Berkeley, CA: University of California Press, 1998.

Dawn Perlmutter & Debra Koppman (Eds.). *Reclaiming the spiritual in art: contemporary cross-cultural perspectives.* Albany, NY: State University of New York Press, 1999.

Andres Serrano; Works 1983–1993. Exhibition catalogue. Philadelphia, PA: Institute of Contemporary Art, University of Pennsylvania, 1994.

Mark C. Taylor. *Disfiguring: Art, architecture, religion.* Chicago, IL: University of Chicago Press, 1992.

CHAPTER 19

QUESTIONS AND EXPLORATIONS

1. Think about and look around your community. Find a building or an environment that you think is an example of good design and explain why you think the design is good. Find an example of a building or an environment that you think is poorly designed. Why do you think that the design is poor? What do your two examples have in common? How do they differ?

2. How do you interact with the built environment around you? How is the built environment similar and different from what we generally consider to be the "natural" environment?

3. Have you ever visited a historic monument? If so, describe the monument that you visited and what it taught you about history.

4. What types of events and people do we choose to commemorate through historic monuments? Who and what do we leave out of our commemorations?

5. How are historical monuments linked to everyday life, cultural identity, and memory?

Teaching Art with Historic Places and Civic Memorials

Joanne K. Guilfoil

Picture a young adult shopper moving past the friendly door-greeter at a local supercenter, only to confront a tall, dauntingly dark three-dimensional cardboard plea for donations to a memorial about World War II. Would such a young adult care enough to ponder the proposed design, much less contribute money for its construction? Should this or any existing historic site be considered appropriate art content for instruction in elementary curriculum?[1]

Built environments,[2] including civic memorials such as the Vietnam Veterans Memorial and historic sites such as Union Station in Washington, DC, and Ghirardelli Square in San Francisco, California, have recently been suggested as artworks for study in the elementary classroom. In addition, texts for art appreciation and humanities courses have begun to describe historic sites such as the Statue of Liberty in New York Harbor and Jefferson's Monticello in Charlottesville, Virginia (Benton and DiYanni, 1999). What can be learned through the study of the built environment and why should future elementary teachers be engaged in this learning? Through the study of these designed environments, we learn more about art, the world at that time, and ultimately about ourselves. In this chapter, the artwork in question is our built environment, which includes historic sites and civic memorials. Historic sites including civic memorials honor our collective past and inform our future.

The Power of Place

Why would someone build a gas station that looks like a teapot or tourist cabins that look like tepees? How do trails and roads influence the growth of cities? How does a familiar landmark link local history and ideas to national events? These and other issues are addressed in *Teaching With Historic Places*, a training workshop for educators and a partnership initiative between the National Park Service and the National Trust for Historic Preservation. The study of historic places is presented in interdisciplinary units that are rich in cultural diversity, visual literacy skills, and that have an emphasis on critical thinking. The National Register of Historic Places is the nation's official list of cultural resources worthy of preservation.[3] Over 61,000 properties are listed including districts, sites, buildings, structures, architecture, and archeological resources. These objects and places are historic and significant in American history, and contribute to an understanding of the historical and cultural foundations of our nation. The partnership provides educators with teaching resources in a lesson plan format[4] based on historic places from the National Register list.

For example, in a unit on the Knife River archeological site in South Dakota, students use American landscape paintings, maps, and reports from explorers, traders, archeologists, and anthropologists to gather information on the size and complexity of the 18th-century Hidasta and Mandan villages. In another unit, students investigate how the automobile influenced pop culture in a study of roadside attractions such as the Teapot Dome Service Station in Zillah, WA. This unit on roadside attractions includes readings and activities on topics such as representational architecture, visual evidence, designing a building, convenience versus aesthetics, form and fantasy in design, boosterism, and giant statues. Visuals for this unit include such sites as Paul Bunyan and Babe the Blue Ox in Bemidji, Minnesota, and the Wigwam Village No. 2 in Cave City, Kentucky. Study questions for the Paul Bunyan and Blue Ox giant statues investigate proportion and vernacular public art. Questions about the Wigwam Village number 2 (once there were seven!) explore the ethnic attitudes of the 1930s and how this site stereotypes native American cultures.[5]

A final question in the unit asks how the nomination for the Wigwam Village to the Register of Historic Places might have differed, had it been written by a native American. Students also learn about the nomination process through the inclusion of the necessary forms. Anyone may complete a nomination form for a place; the form uses much of the same historical information that is contained in an elementary social studies curriculum. Students learn that these sites were developed at various times and locations by many different kinds of people for various reasons. These cultural contexts greatly influenced the places as they were created, and contribute to our understanding of them now. Throughout the lessons, students are encouraged to examine and question the attitudes and ideas that helped shape the objects and places of study. Teachers are provided with the information included in the nomination forms, and are invited to draft lesson plans about a historic place for publication in the series.

The *Teaching With Historic Places* series uses buildings, sites, districts, structures, and objects in our environment as documents of our historical experiences and cultural expressions. With these units, students can study far-away places and discover the connections between these places and places in their own community. They also learn to work together to find ways to take care of places that have special meanings. One way is to investigate a site and the work of those who initiated preservation efforts of that historic site. Students also learn what makes a site historic, and that the process can and should include them. Interdisciplinary connections include language arts/writing, history/social studies, math, and science. In the following section, a few examples of teaching about and through the built environment are discussed.

George Washington's Mount Vernon Estate and Gardens

"Has Washington lost his relevancy during this age of super-computers and worldwide communications?" (Rees, 1999, p. ii). If the answer is yes, is it because his character is no longer understood or appreciated by Americans? Or is it because of the way he is typically presented in history class? Why not study Washington's former home Mount Vernon? How can we explore new ways of learning through the study of the built environment and make meaningful connections across the disciplines?

Due to the efforts of the Mount Vernon Ladies' Association, founded in 1853, Mount Vernon is almost unchanged from its appearance in 1799, the year of Washington's death. During his forty-five years as owner, George Washington tripled the size of the mansion, redesigned the grounds and outbuildings, and expanded the plantation to an 8,000-acre farm. The mansion provides an outstanding example of colonial architecture, and thus a look into privileged life during colonial Virginia, with a lookout to the majestic Potomac River. Architectural details include arched colonnades, palladian and oval windows, high columned piazza, parlors, upper and lower bed chambers, and the study where Washington wrote letters about the establishment of a federal government. The mansion houses more than 100 period objects including andirons, bisque porcelain figurines, as well as prints, pastels, landscape paintings, and portraits.

A Contextualist Approach

As a landowner and planter, Washington lived and worked in a world where slavery was part of the accepted order. However, over the course of his lifetime, his attitude changed and he ultimately emancipated his slaves (in his will) after his death. As he switched from tobacco to wheat farming and needed skilled labor, he realized the drawbacks and poor economics of enslaved labor. Washington also became aware of the humanity and emotions of the enslaved, and their ultimate despair upon being separated from friends and family. (Married couples did not always live together and work assignments sometimes required that a mother and her children live on a different farm than that of the children's father.) Near the time of the American Revolution, Washington resolved to never again purchase or sell a slave and by the end of his life he had decided that slavery had no place in the American democracy.

Mount Vernon has a cemetery used by slaves and free blacks that has as many as seventy-five unmarked graves. In 1929, the Mount Vernon Ladies' Association placed a stone marker at the Slave Burial Ground to commemorate the site. In 1983 a Slave Memorial was erected "in memory of the Afro-Americans who served as slaves at Mount Vernon . . ." (Rees, 1999, p. 109). The Slave Memorial was designed by architecture students from Howard University in Washington. It serves as a focal point for an annual commemoration by the Mount Vernon Ladies' Association and the Black Women United for Action. The Association, a private non-profit organization which still owns Mount Vernon, should be commended in its effort to preserve not only the historic objects, formal characteristics, and places of Washington's estate, but also the social memory embodied in these designs. Thus, restoration of the estate and gardens of Mount Vernon had to include restoration and narration of the lives of slaves who supported the luxury and style we still admire.

With a sound understanding of the social meanings expressed in a built environment, educators are better prepared to participate in discussions about historic landmark preservation (Hicks and King, 1999). Built environments are more than visual texts to be appreciated only for their visual qualities. They are also "action-guiding texts" which influence "the form and substance of our lives" (Hicks and King, 1999, p. 12).

Ellis Island and the Statue of Liberty

For many Americans, another historic landmark of interest is Ellis Island. This national monument is a symbol of the United States's immigrant heritage. The magnificently restored Great Hall, once a focal point of immigrant processing, also provides a narrative of the lives of third-class or steerage-class passengers who, after long, perilous, uncomfortable voyages, endured mandatory medical and legal examinations, just for a place to live. In the end, most immigrants were given permission to land. However, some were denied entry into the country and returned home on the next boat.

Ellis Island was opened as an immigration depot on January 1, 1892 and until 1954 processed some twelve million people fleeing hardship, persecution, or political unrest. As record numbers arrived in search of freedom and opportunity, the original three-acre island depot was expanded to 27 1/2 acres by dredging and depositing earth. On this new land, thirty-five additional buildings were constructed to process immigrants. As many as 5,000 people per day would be checked and questioned for three to five hours. The station facilities remained overburdened and inadequate until after 1924 when immigration quotas stemmed the tide. Later, when not used for processing, the station became a center for the detention and deportation of undesirable aliens. It also served as a hospital during both world wars and a training center for the U.S. Coast Guard.

Ellis Island was closed in 1954 and remained abandoned until 1965 when President L. B. Johnson placed it under the care of the National Park Service. He recognized the essential unity between the Statue of Liberty and Ellis Island as symbols for the dreams of freedom and opportunity in the United States. Both places are timeless visual expressions, and reminders of the courage and energy required of immigrants.

Just in time for the immigration depot's centennial in 1992, the Main Building was refurbished, in recognition of the significant role it played in United States history. A museum was constructed to tell the poignant stories of the immigrants who passed through its halls. The Immigration Museum features exhibits, restored areas, and education facilities. Galleries are filled with more than 2,000 artifacts, photos, oral histories, and music that tell what happened to the newcomers at the depot. Taped interviews, documentary films, videos, and audio tours in several languages explain in arresting detail and heartfelt emotion the anguish, fear, hope, and joy experienced by the immigrants who helped settle the United States. Ellis Island is a magnificently preserved monument to be admired in form and function, but also as a memorial to those who were processed and examined.

For educators, any discussion of arched windows, tiles, or vaulted ceilings would be incomplete without a genuine understanding of the world at that time and the reasons people left home seeking steady work and a decent living. Our country continues to grow every day, with immigrants coming from many regions of the world, still seeking freedom, opportunity, and a decent place to live.

A Place to Stand: Civic Memorials as Public Art

Americans have many memorials and monuments dedicated to the struggles to attain, maintain, or declare democracy. In fact, more than 100,000 monuments alone honor the Union and Confederate dead (Carnes, 1999). Are these art? Should these public art objects be considered content for elementary curriculum and instruction in art? If the answer is yes, it is because civic memorials provide more than visual texts to be appreciated only for their visual qualities. Civic memorials also tell us about us, as a people. They give us pause. They influence our lives, and serve as visual reminders of our past.

Public art is "notoriously ill defined and can be interpreted in a variety of ways" (Adams, 1997, p. 7). It is however, sculpture in the open air, or art in a public place that is owned and maintained by and for a community (town, city, or nation) rather than for a privileged few. It may be intended for environmental improvement, decoration, or to alter a place temporarily for an event. Or, public art can be used to symbolize civic pride, enhance people's experience of a particular environment, and trigger memories or associations. Civic memorials as public art become cultural investments that "contribute to local distinctiveness and create a sense of place or regional identity" (Adams, 1997, p. 7). Educators might ask, "How far should the artist be seen as environmental improver or cultural messenger? How much should the artist seek to stimulate, challenge, or disturb the public?" (Adams, 1997, p. 7). Just what is the part of "the public" in public art? Should the public have any say in the site or the design of public art? How have civic memorials been created in the past? What design policies should we follow in the future?

As in other public art projects, civic memorials can involve different approaches to design, development, and management. Some have developed from a very personal vision, such as Maya Ying Lin's original design for the Vietnam Veterans Memorial on the National Mall in Washington, DC. Built in 1982, dedicated in 1984, Lin's piece of funerary architecture with the deceased soldiers' names etched chronologically in black granite slabs expresses her personal reflection and private reckoning. This national civic memorial was funded with private donations. The constant controversies and eventual compromises of figurative additions by other artists in 1984 and 1993 only "brought her memorial closer to truth . . . that as a nation we still could not resolve the Vietnam War" (Guilfoil, 1997, p. 49).

Maya Ying Lin provides another very personal vision of our collective memory in United States history with the Civil Rights Memorial dedicated in 1989, in Montgomery, Alabama. Rather than a monument to suffering, it is a memorial to hope. It serves as a vehicle for reflection about the struggle for equality and freedom, and the forty people who lost their lives in that struggle. A black granite table with water flowing across the top, records those names, and the wall behind reflects a Bible verse often quoted by Martin Luther King, Jr.:

> *[We will not be satisfied]*
> *. . . until justice rolls down like waters and righteousness like*
> *a mighty stream.* (Amos, Chapter 5 Verse 24)

The building of some civic memorials are artist-led, while others are developed through inter-agency collaboration involving artists, local agencies, arts or government agencies. Sometimes, local communities are involved in generating design ideas, developing the memorial, and fund-raising. An example of a collaborative approach between designers, artists, and agencies can be seen in the Franklin Delano Roosevelt Memorial dedicated in 1997 in Washington, DC. Attributed to landscape architect and World War II veteran Lawrence Halprin (b. 1916), the design took forty years to initiate, negotiate with the federal government, and construct, requiring a design team of several artists and sculptors. Halprin's design, also of granite and water, is a tribute to the man Franklin Delano Roosevelt, his presidency, the Great Depression, World War II, and above all, the desire for peace, and prosperity.

A collaborative effort between a team of designers from the Pennsylvania State University and the American Battle Monuments Commission resulted in the hauntingly reflective Korean War Veterans Memorial also on the Mall in Washington, DC. The design process was difficult and confusing at times. There were disagreements between the two parties, resulting in struggles and lawsuits. However difficult, together they created a tribute to the soldiers and their courage; to fear, war, and above all, peace. As we view the slightly larger-than-life figures who stand as if on guard and moving, but frozen forever in that fearful place, we go back in time. As we move closer to view photographic images of soldiers etched on a granite wall nearby, we also see a reflection of ourselves and those haunting figures behind us. The intent was to "honor not war, but those the nation sent to war," and those who protected and preserved our way of life, our collective memory, our sense of place (McCarthy, Weber, and Hansen, 1995, p. 318).

These national civic memorials, and others that are in the planning stages, should be of interest to teachers. As mentioned at the beginning of this chapter, in almost any community the local WalMart store boasts a kiosk describing the National World War II Memorial. As with most civic memorials, money must be raised and the capital campaign goal in donations for this project is $100 million. Fund-raising efforts have involved veterans, corporations, and schoolchildren as solicitors and donors (Duffy, 1998). While the money is being raised, the American Battle Monuments Commission must obtain a construction permit from the Secretary of the Interior. Before a permit is issued, a "final" design must be approved and all funds must be on hand. Officials continue to debate the design of this memorial and its proposed location on the National Mall. Just imagine their discussions about design criteria, symbols, people, places, materials . . . to commemorate a global event! After construction of the memorial, the National Park Service then assumes title, control, and maintenance.

The proposed World War II Memorial is supposed to be designed to:

> honor all those who served and sacrificed in World War II—those who served in uniform as well as those on the home front! Recognizing World War II as a defining event of the 20th century, the memorial will educate future generations

> on the spirit, sacrifice, and commitment of the American people united in a just and common cause. (Hoffman, 1997, p. 55)

The memorial was supposed to be constructed at the Rainbow Pool site, at the east end of the Reflecting Pool between the Lincoln Memorial and the Washington Monument (Duffy, 1998). Dedication of the memorial was originally planned for Veterans Day, 2000 in Washington, DC. However, final approval of the World War II Memorial was delayed and hearings were scheduled into the fall of that year. At issue were the siting, the "final" design, and whether or not all parties including the general public could participate in those decisions.

In some cases, the local community, the national community, and the inter-agency collaborations deadlock over the design and proper location of a civic memorial. So goes the struggle to find the right place to mark Martin Luther King, Jr.'s contributions. The proposed site is close to where he gave his "I Have a Dream" speech, near the Tidal Basin and the Mall in Washington, DC. Some planners worry about noise from jet planes zooming over the head of King's statue. Others argue that an alternate location "would segregate memorials to black leaders and heroes," calling it "a back-of-the-bus-location" (Leonnig, 1999, p. A6). The planners and commissioners will need compromise or consensus, or the King memorial will remain in limbo too long and could become a forty-year project like the FDR Memorial. Congress, in 1996, gave formal authorization for the memorial to be located near the National Mall. Sponsors still need to locate a site, choose a design, and raise the expected $10 million for construction.

The design committee wants to create on the Mall a "path of leaders, where the words of Lincoln, FDR, and Jefferson will be combined with the words of King . . . where the son of a slave is placed in the same cityscape as the owner of a slave—which speaks volumes to how far America has come" (Leonnig, 1999, p. A6). The sponsors want King's memorial to be a "destination memorial—one you specifically trek to Washington to see, rather than one you pass on your tour" (Leonnig, 1999, p. A6). Even the chairman of the National Planning Commission realizes that "there is a tremendous amount of emotion wrapped up in anything having to do with monumental Washington" (Leonnig, 1999, p. A6). Of course, that is the nature of public art, especially civic memorials, which contain our collective and sometimes differing memories of social meanings.

A New Place

As we cross another threshold in history, imagine a new stone in Washington, DC, a national memorial to the enslaved that commemorates the toll of slavery and the hidden legacy of human suffering that helped to build this nation. Our local and national landscapes boast historic sites, monuments, and memorials that "astonish us with the struggle it took to declare that our democracy could no longer abide human bondage" (Carnes, 1999, p. 3). But we do not have even so little as a gravestone to honor those 10,037,000 Americans who suffered the institutionalized evil of American slavery, all the while contributing to the infrastructure and economy of the nation. Such a monument should occupy a conspicuous place on the National Mall. One design possibility suggests a structure incorporating bricks made by slaves, gathered from antebellum sites around the country. Such a monument could involve community efforts nationwide including schoolchildren and their families, who would help select, document, and transport the materials.

Perhaps students could participate with designs of their own as they ponder the colors of our nation's soil, the clay bodies available, and the hand prints and legacy of those who first made the bricks. Ponder the possible art education, social study, and the "awesome potential of the dedication ceremony" (Carnes, 1999, p. 3). Teachers and students could contribute more than money to a national civic memorial that descendants of the enslaved, fellow Americans, and visitors could see, touch, and reflect upon for generations.

Local Places

Some teachers may choose instead to begin at the local level, especially when urban-planning issues make the news. For example, in Kentucky, newspaper articles informed taxpayers in one community about "plans for using public money to pay farmers not to turn their pastures into residential subdivisions" (Baniak, 1999, p. A1). Less than a year later, those same taxpayers were informed about a "farmland preservation ordinance" designed to "preserve . . . rural area while allowing for future development" (George, 2000, p. A). With the purchase of development rights, local officials hoped to preserve signature horse farms and reduce urban sprawl. During the year, students from across the state were brought into the debate.

In another section of that same newspaper, high school students' artwork was featured honoring Preservation Week. The paintings, drawings, collages of historic buildings, building details, and landscapes were later printed as a calendar. One teacher viewed the project as "educating a future community" and another considered "perspective for a drawing technique and an architectural rendering" as "perfect for our curriculum" in art (Thompson, 1999, p. 18). The students echoed an interest in preservation and questioned urban growth in newspaper interviews and in their artwork. The students also learned that art and architecture are not created in a vacuum, but as part of the social world in which the objects are created.

Another program called *Protecting the Irreplaceable* invited students of all ages (primary, intermediate, secondary) to photograph and write about the importance of historic preservation, with copies sent to local decision-makers. This involved students at all age levels in discussions about protecting and preserving historic resources. These are only a few examples of ways to teach art with historic places. Civic memorials, historic places, roadside attractions, and even school buildings, as designed objects, are influenced by the time and place and social context in which they were created.

Your Work Place

When identifying regional historic sites, and local resources, remember your campus or school buildings. For example, in central Kentucky, the Blue Grass Trust for Historic Preservation marks significant structures, including college campus buildings and public schools, with its well-known and respected oval "BGT" plaque. Contact your local board of education and research the school facilities in your area. As a future teacher, help students identify particular materials, space, and details characteristic of a time period, architectural style, or design firm. Help elementary students discover the person, event, or place for which the facility was named. Learn to see your place of work with new eyes. Help your future elementary students appreciate their school building as a record of visual culture in place and time, rich with social memories and meanings. Teach them about the historic places close to home, and the objects, events, and people whose lives influenced those places.

While some elementary students may grow up to become designers, most will become citizens whose tax dollars pay for local and national projects. All elementary students will become community members who should know how familiar landmarks link local history to national events and a collective social memory. Teaching with historic places helps elementary students understand the social contexts surrounding the built environments and themselves.

Endnotes

1. Standard I of the NAEA standards for art teacher preparation on "Content of the Visual Arts" expects students to attain knowledge "of the context in which works of art have been created . . . including artifacts from a variety of cultures, periods, places, and styles" and knowledge of the "cultural context surrounding major artistic styles, historical periods, and the development of art from a global perspective." Teacher education programs should also provide "various methods and models of art criticism . . . aesthetic theories and philosophies of art to study functions and purposes of art from various cultures and differing contexts" (NAEA News, 1999, p. 11).

   In a recent study regarding teaching practices, one writer found an "overwhelming number of respondents" who used a curriculum "reflective of the national standards in art: the inclusion of art history, art criticism and aesthetics within a studio based curriculum" (Leshnoff, 1999, p. 12).

Even before the national standards for art teacher preparation were penned (NAEA, 1999), leading writers such as Laura Chapman (1985, 1994, 1998), Herberholz and Herberholz (1998), and Rosalind Ragans (1998) discussed built environments.

2. The built environment refers to any designed environment. All buildings, towns, bridges, monuments, parks, highways, and so on are part of our built environment.
3. A place (building, structure, or site) is considered "historic" as a result of a nomination process during which it satisfies three major criteria: (a) age (more than 50 years old), (b) integrity (fabric, building materials), and (c) significance (events, people, or design). A place may also be significant because of (d) what is *not* known, that is, its information potential (e.g., an archeological site). Sometimes we don't know what a place will tell us. Places are judged by their known categories (a–c) *and* their information potential (d). All of the above information is used by a nominee to explain the historic significance of a particular place. Rather than a collection of facts, the application is supposed to provide a "window to the past" that also illuminates the context in which the place was created which helps explain why it is significant. The list of historic places is also supposed to be a "teaching opportunity" that informs us about ourselves.
4. As part of the *Teaching With Historic Places* program, lesson plans have been prepared for listings such as Attu Battlefield, Aleutian Islands, AK; Andersonville National Historic Site, Macon County, GA; Manassas National Battlefield Park, Prince William County, VA; Knife River Indian Villages National Historic Site, Mercer County, ND; Taft Home, Hamilton County, OH; and roadside attractions in Minnesota, North Carolina, Kentucky, and Washington.
5. Ask for the unit called "Roadside Attractions" in the *Teaching With Historic Places* program. Ask for nomination forms to nominate a place in your community.
6. The creative, entrepreneurial, and generous qualities of this singular leader were reintroduced to the American people in 1999 with the George Washington Bicentennial. The event marked the life and death in 1799 of George Washington, as the nation faced the challenges of a new century.
7. This type of controversy is not new to civic memorials, and is the very reason that the general public, including school children, should be involved. Civic memorials, like public art are for everyone, for all time. The struggles over site and design are not just disagreements between designer and client. The differences of opinion reflect different value systems as well as different aesthetics. Just as in the effort to identify and preserve historic places, the effort to create a civic memorial as a "window to the past" becomes difficult as all parties seek to define the "what" and "why" of an object as a view to the past. Of course, the issue is which past, whose past, and how best to represent those memories.

References

Adams, E. (1997). *Public art: People, projects, process.* Sunderland, UK: AN Publications.

Amos. (1995). *The Holy Bible: Contemporary English version.* New York, NY: American Bible Society.

Baniak, P. I. (1999, May 12). Farmers want public money to save land; will taxpayers agree? *Lexington Herald-Leader,* pp. A1, A8.

Benton, J. R., & DiYanni, R. (1999). *Arts and culture: An introduction to the humanities.* Upper Saddle River, NJ: Prentice Hall, Inc.

Carnes, J. (1999, Fall). Editor's note: A place to stand. *Teaching tolerance 16,* p. 3.

Chapman, L. (1985). *Discover art.* Worcester, MA: Davis Publications, Inc.

Chapman, L. (1994, 1998). *Adventures in art.* Worcester, MA: Davis Publications, Inc.

Duffy, J. A. (1998, December 11). "WWII memorial is in a race against time." *Lexington Herald-Leader,* p. B10.

George, J. (2000, January 10). Spending public money to save private land. *Lexington Herald-Leader,* pp. A1, A6.

Guilfoil, J. K. (1997). *American architects.* Aspen, CO: Crystal Publications, Inc.

Herberholz, B., & Herberholz, D. (1998). *Artworks for elementary teachers: Developing artistic and perceptual awareness.* Boston, MA: McGraw Hill.

Hicks, L. E., & King, R. J. H. (1999). Mapping a sense of place: A contextualized approach to designed environments. In J. K. Guilfoil & A. R. Sandler (Eds.), *Built environment education in art education.* Reston, VA: The National Art Education Association, pp. 1–12.

Hoffman, N. L. W. (1997, April). Leatherneck line: World War II Memorial, *Leatherneck,* pp. 54–56.

Leonnig, C. D. (1999, September 10). Planners struggle over King memorial site: Process at impasse as each of 3 possible locations has opponents. *Lexington Herald-Leader,* p. A6.

Leshnoff, S. K. (1999, November). What is going on in elementary art classrooms? *Art Education, 52* (6), 6–12.

McCarthy, R. T., Weber, W. E., & Hansen, R. L. (Eds.). (1995). *Korean War Veterans Memorial: A tribute to those who served.* Paducah, KY: Turner Publishing Co.

NAEA News. (1999, February). NAEA standards for art teacher preparation. p. 11.

Ragans, R. (1998). *SRA art connections.* Columbus, OH: SRA McGraw-Hill.

Rees, J. C. (1999). *Mount Vernon commemorative guidebook.* Mount Vernon, VA: The Mount Vernon Ladies' Association.

Thompson, S. (1999, May 12). Art and soul of the bluegrass. *Lexington Herald-Leader,* pp. 18–20.

CONCLUSIONS AND FURTHER QUESTIONS

1. What is a built environment? Why is it important that we study the built environment? How does studying the built environment create possibilities for teaching across the curriculum?

2. What is a historic site? What is the significance of a historic place? What is the relationship between built environments and historic sites?

3. How does Guilfoil contextualize her description of Mount Vernon? Why is such a contextualization important?

4. In her chapter Guilfoil discusses the Ellis Island site and the Immigration Museum located there. Visit an Immigration and Naturalization Service (INS) office or visit the INS website, *www.ins.gov*. What does this communicate about the current process of immigration to the United States? How does this compare to reports in the media on immigration? How does this compare to Guilfoil's description of the Immigration Museum and the experiences of immigrants? What are your personal experiences with immigration?

5. Who is involved in making decisions about and planning for public monuments? What should the role of the public be in these decisions? How can public monuments help us understand the communities in which we live and teach?

RESOURCES AND SUGGESTIONS FOR FURTHER READING

Carol Becker. *Zones of contention: Essays on art, institutions, gender, and anxiety*. Albany, NY: State University of New York Press, 1996.

David W. Black, Donald Kunze, & John Pickles (Eds.). *Commonplaces: Essays on the nature of place*. Lanham, MD: University Press of America, 1989.

John Bodnar. *Remaking America: Public memory, commemoration, and patriotism in the twentieth century*. Princeton, NJ: Princeton University, 1992.

Victor Burgin. *In/different spaces: Place and memory in visual culture*. Berkeley, CA: University of California Press, 1996.

Edward S. Casey. *The fate of place: A philosophical history*. Berkeley, CA: University of California Press, 1997.

Edward S. Casey. *Getting back into place: Toward a renewed understanding of the place-world*. Bloomington, IN: Indiana University Press, 1993.

Judy Donnelly. *A wall of names: the story of the Vietnam Veterans Memorial*. New York: Random House, 1991. (Children's book)

Frances Downing. *Remembrance and the design of place*. College Station, TX: Texas A&M University Press, 2000.

Joanne K. Guilfoil & Allan R. Sandler (Eds.). *Built environment education in art education*. Reston, VA: The National Art Education Association, 1999.

Kristin Ann Hass. *Carried to the wall: American memory and the Vietnam Veterans Memorial*. Berkeley, CA: University of California, 1998.

Bob Italia. *Maya Lin: Honoring our forgotten heroes*. Edina, MN: Abdo & Daughters, 1993. (Children's book)

Suzanne Lacy (Ed.). *Mapping the terrain: new genre public art*. Seattle, WA: Bay Press, 1995.

Maya Lin. *Boundaries*. New York: Simon & Schuster, 2000.

Nadia Lovell (Ed.). *Locality and belonging.* New York: Routledge, 1998.

Freida Lee Mock. Maya Lin. A strong clear vision. Santa Monica, CA: American Film Foundation, 1995. (98-minute videocassette).

Richard Morris. *Sinners, lovers, and heroes: An essay on memorializing in three American cultures.* Albany, NY: State University of New York, 1997.

Julie H. Reiss. *From margin to center: The spaces of installation art.* Cambridge, MA: MIT Press, 2000.

Roy Rosenzweig & David Thelen. *The presence of the past: Popular uses of history in American life.* New York: Columbia University Press, 1998.

CHAPTER 20
QUESTIONS AND EXPLORATIONS

1. What is technology? What technologies do you use on a regular basis? How is your identity shaped by your use of technology? How is your understanding of technology shaped by your identity?
2. Should computer technology be used in the elementary classroom? In what ways should it or should it not be used? Explain and support your answer.
3. What ethical considerations are raised by the question of equal access to technology? Who determines what information we receive through technologies such as the Internet and television?
4. Is teaching a form of technology? Explain and support your answer.

Computer Animation
at an Apache Middle School:
Apache Children's Use
of Computer Animation Technology

Mary Stokrocki
with Marcia Buckpitt

What kind of choices do children make in their use of technology? What kinds of images do they construct? Why do they choose them? Are there differences in how boys and girls use computers? How does Apache children's ethnicity and gender influence the choices that they make? How can teachers help all students better their images, evaluate them, and become critically aware of the limits and stereotypes associated with electronic images?

In order to discover some answers to these questions, I spent three weeks learning computer animation with Apache middle-school children at a summer school program. The children taught me a great deal while I, along with their art teacher, encouraged them to develop their images and some criticality. Findings suggest that we cannot make assumptions that all boys or girls make certain choices. Differences like ethnicity and culture also affect what we do and how we think. This paper explores these questions and issues.

Context

McNary Elementary School is on the historical Fort Apache Indian Reservation in Arizona. The White Mountain Apache Tribe, who call themselves *N'dee*, meaning the people, inhabits 1.6 million acres of its ancient homeland (White Mountain Apache Tribe, 1997, p. 1). The White Mountain Apache descended from nomadic people who later settled and raised livestock and agriculture. The chief industries now are the timber mill, a re-manufacturing plant (parts of the Apache helicopter), the new Hon Dah Casino, and a large ski resort that is run by the Apache Tribe. The Apache consist of approximately 12,000 members, spread over nine tribal communities (e.g., Tonto, San Carlos, and Cibecue). Nearby is the Apache Cultural Museum, which preserves Apache traditions that include the corn dance, basketry, and female puberty ceremonies (White Mountain Apache Tribe, 1997).

McNary Elementary School is located in a forest of pine trees about four miles outside of a small working class community. The present building, erected in 1947, houses grades three to eight, the library, nurse's office, and computer room. The large computer room (45' × 22') contains eighteen Macintosh computers, one instructional GE model, two printers, a videorecorder, and a scanner.

Art teacher Marcia Buckpitt has been teaching part time in this school for seven years. She received her B.S. in Art Education, M.A. in Printmaking, and M.F.A. in Book Arts from the University of Wisconsin. She taught printmaking at Princeton University, the community college level, and has been self-employed as a graphic artist and illustrator of children's books for over fifteen years. Buckpitt offered computer art to interested students so she could learn more about the technology, inspire the students to tell stories (part of their oral history heritage), and experiment with art criticism inquiry tools. During the year, she incorporated such storytelling lessons as facial expressions, figure drawing, and landscape painting into a class storybook. Her principal supports the program and finds that "students love the technology and can develop their drawing abilities."

Approximately sixty students registered in the three-week summer school, although the small public school regularly enrolled 130 students. I focused on two classes through participant observation (Stokrocki, 1997), a sixth-grade class of seven females and three males and an eighth-grade class of five males and five females.

The program's purpose was to "give kids something educational and fun to do in the summer and keep them out of trouble" (personal correspondence, Guy Morris, Assistant Camp Director, June 21, 1999). Sponsored by the Apache Tribe, the summer school program included math, crafts, physical education, and computer art classes. On Fridays, the program included swimming, basketball camp, and a barbecue on the last day. The computer art program consisted of initial exploring of tools and menu choices, then making backgrounds, and finally designing animated characters and moving them.

What Choices Do Children Make in Their Use of Technology?

Throughout the course, students explored the many options in *Kid Pix* (Hickman, 1991). Initially their favorite tools were explosion and kaleidoscope techniques and stamps. Since quitting the computer program involved a bomb icon with accompanying sound effects, the boys always seemed to be blasting away. Later, one boy showed me the trick to freeze the design by using the option-control keys. He also learned to make a kaleidoscopic design by hitting the swirl paint tool and then the control-option key to enlarge it. He exclaimed, "Wow! It's like *Star Wars* hyperdrive!" *Kid Pix* enabled students to experiment with many patterns and special effects that were not possible with earlier computers and programs (Stokrocki, 1986). Some students were willing to teach others what they had learned.

The stamp tool enabled students to duplicate, enlarge, and adjust an array of premade images from the stamp menu. On one occasion, I photographed three girls in a row who copied a rainbow stamp. Two boys seated behind them had identical landscapes starting with fluffy clouds in the sky, sun in corner, mountains below, and pine trees. All these images came from the stamp menu. Popular stamps included trees, moon, and stars. Wilson and Wilson (1977) suggest that beginners learn to depict by copying popular and peer configurations. Teachers, however, also need to set up idea-generating assignments so that students can connect the technique to their own lives and experience.

What Were the Dominant Image Choices?

Nearly all students (18/20) made realistic landscapes, including mountains, trees or cacti, with either sun or moon. More confident students outlined backgrounds and filled in colored areas on the computer. Calvin, for example, created a simple mountainscape. He first chose a mountain stamp, enlarged it, and then printed several in a row. Then he drew a ground line, filled the area with brown paint, added a random spot pattern, and stamped roses along the bottom of the page. Next, he filled the sky with a dark purple color, overlapped a row of stamped clouds, and added several stamped lightning bolts. This piece was environmentally significant because it recalled the afternoon thunderstorms that the region experienced each day. Indeed, the Apache named one of their mountains "Thunder Mountain."

A second example was a desert road in perspective. Nicole started with the two receding lines that met at a vanishing point, filled the road with gray color, and drew a yellow dotted stripe over the road. Next she filled in the large desert areas with brown paint and colored in the mountains with brown. She then filled the sky with a brilliant red-orange color and added a yellow sun behind. The next day, I saw her paint five saguaro cacti of various sizes with shadows. One large cactus was on the left, which she identified in her interview as asymmetrical. She added color to cactus blossoms and parallel rib lines that bent with the cactus contour. The entire scene glowed as a sunset. The reservation is located in the higher elevations of Arizona. To get there, one must pass through long flat roads in the low desert areas. Arizona sunsets are spectacular.

Sunrise scenes were frequent with girls. One example shows a girl sitting with her back to the viewer, "looking at the sunrise." Navajo craft teacher Maye Hill remarked, "This sunrise picture reminds me of my painting as a girl." She used to paint herself looking into the sunrise. Apache teacher Jackie Lavender commented, "Sunrises are culturally related to the Apache girl's puberty change in the Sunrise Ceremony." The ceremony lasts for three days during which the girl actually runs towards the sunrise for blessings. Lavender continued, "If you face your door to the east, at sunrise all good things come into your house." (For more information on the Sunrise Ceremony, see Basso, 1970.)

The last assignment was for students to design animated characters. Some students designed their own animated characters. Jake (8th grade), for example, taught us how to use the *Kid Pix* Slide Show with his multiple cows. I mentioned that he didn't have to draw each cow separately, but could do the animation in a limited way. I prepared an example using his cow body. Buckpitt motivated all students the next day with her animation example, "Evening Walk." She directed, "In one frame without a background, draw the character body once, duplicate it; redraw the arms and legs, move the body slightly to the right, duplicate and redraw limbs. Cut and paste it into each background frame."

Fifty percent of the students tried to draw human characters frame-by-frame. Two students attempted to show an animated character receding in the distance. Exceptional was the work of Nicole, who added a man running down her desert road. In the first scene, the back of his head appears with the words "I need WATER!" In subsequent scenes, she drew the entire body progressively smaller from the rear view. A few students animated such animals as an ant and a dog with the help of the stamp tool.

Why Did Students Choose These Images?

Apache children, similar to all children, may select stamped images at first for convenience as they explore new toys or programs. Children who tend to lack drawing confidence respond better to simpler animation techniques, such as repeating stamps to show motion. Of the ten older students whom I observed, five students animated stamps, such as Noah who cut-and-pasted his ant to run from left to right.

They also select those images that are culturally important. The boys choose animal symbols that represent power and girls select those that transmit their sense of love [such as hearts or deer]. Some of these children are not pure Apache but racially-mixed. They are also highly influenced by popular media, even though they live in a rural setting, so their traditions are changing.

Apache children tend to reproduce themes that reflect their love of nature, such as running by a mountain, camping at a lake, and watching a sunrise. These themes suggest a continuance of their culture's belief and living relationship with Mother Earth (Schlessinger, 1993). This finding contradicts Gardner's (1980) preoccupation with spontaneous "free-drawing" from imagination and supports Wilson and Wilson's (1977) stress on the effects of themes from people's cultural environment. In fact, when I asked younger students to draw an imaginary creature, several children depicted a masked Apache crown dancer who represents a mountain spirit. Their imagination is full of traditional spirit images that would not seem inventive to Gardner.

The weather affects life in White River. It rains nearly every afternoon in June. In late summer, the monsoons can be ferocious. Children repond to the awesome power of nature that they worship. Noah made lightning move by simply removing and adding bolts. Lathena created twinkling stars by using the spiral tool. The nighttime sky in Apacheland is expansive and part of communal celebrations. For example, the Mountain Spirits Dancers, who protect the Apache, perform under the stars as part of the Sunrise Puberty Ceremony. The ceremony may be held every weekend in March (personal correspondence with Herb Stevens, San Carlos Apache Cultural Center, 7/17/00).

Apache children are fond of animals. They have household pets, especially dogs, but they are particularly fond of horses. In her scene, called "Nighttime Magic," Janine moved a horse stamp diagonally across the mountains and progressively made it smaller, until it disappeared into the sky. Horses are very special within Apache culture. LaVerne (1966) wrote about the spiritual status of horses as guardians as well as friends among the Apache.

Even though students were not directly asked to tell stories and class time was too short, several student animations resembled stories. Most significant in this study is the fact that Apache children do not depict animated stories in the sense of developing a plot or showing intense activity. They construct a setting with time or weather change or a character walk. Such structures tend to be cyclic and the forces of nature would fall under the natural rhythm theme, according to Wilson and Wilson (1983). Whereas most non-native people tend to interpret these themes and structures as simple actions, many native Americans regard a walk through nature or the rise and fall of each day as a life-affirming relationship.

The Influence of Ethnicity and Gender

In this section, I present my exploratory findings, including tentative gender differences and cultural content issues. These are discussed in comparison to other studies. My findings suggest that we cannot make assumptions that all boys or girls make certain choices. Differences such as ethnicity and culture also affect what we do and how we think.

Boys seemed to play more computer games [such as "Snood"] and to experiment more with computer programs and special effects than girls did. They also initiated video music more often. Wohlwill and Wills (1987) mention that boys respond more to video games than girls do. Colbert (1996) suggests that teachers tend to show boys more about how to use technology, but that girls need the same technical information and direction as well. The result of this is that boys gain more technical skills at earlier ages.

Perhaps in these cultural groups, girls are taught to be more rule dependent than boys are. Apache girls, similar to other girls of the same age, may depend initially on stereotyped images, such as teddy bears, bows, roses, and stars from the stamp tools for cards or signs. Some girls however tended to patiently finish their complicated assignments (such as the example discussed earlier of a diminishing figure, drawn frame-by-frame, running in the distance). They also seem to depict human figures better than boys do and prefer symmetrical arrangements.

The Apache are a matriarchal society. Preserving traditions demands patience, cooperative work, and attention to details. Women are responsible for transmitting cultural images, such as clan symbols, as well as crafts, including burden basketry. Such techniques are laborious but intricate. Therefore, many female students are keen reproducers [copiers] and inventive in combining details.

The older boys refused to draw animated figures because drawing is time consuming. Some preferred to animate stamps and others raced ahead to the slide show routines. This finding supports Freedman's (1989) discovery that boys often initiate their own computer experiences and give more attention to movement. In a gifted summer program in Indiana, Caucasian boys who were more experienced with computers behaved similarly in an earlier study (Stokrocki, 1986). Boys tend to explore more challenging computer functions (Wohlwill and Wills, 1987). They also tend to make different thematic choices, such as team sports (Wohlwill and Wills, 1987).

Yet several Apache boys preferred non-competitive activities, such as camping, trucking, and hunting scenes. I discovered that Apache boys seem first loners and then they develop teams when necessary.

Finally, the Apache will fight to maintain their land, especially the mountains, which they believe are sacred. In this study, nearly every background contained a cherished landscape. Forest fires rage nearly every summer, due to lightning or careless tourists. The Apache are vigilant watchers and fighters. Perhaps Apache children excel in reminding us of our lost horizons.

Culture and other social factors affect and influence the development of who our students are and what they create. In order to make connections to their lives and make learning more meaningful, Mesa-Bains (1996) points out that "experience and text = meaning" (p. 32). She feels that we must relate assignments or art works to our students' lives. Teachers need to consider what kinds of artwork give students ideas for personal experience expressions. How do we find out about our students? One possible way is to do local oral history research. Another way is to ask children to draw what they like to do or something imaginary. When I earlier asked these Apache students to draw their preferred activities, they depicted mostly outdoor events such as camping, swimming, fishing, and playing with pets. Favored pets were cats, dogs, and horses.

We also can now show students computer art examples from older Apache children (Caddo, 2000). In this locally published manuscript, several Apache mountain spirits (popularly called crown warriors) appeared. "Such an image sparked students to action as Internet warriors, a positive rather than a passive identity image" (personal correspondence with Chris Kitzmiller, Cibecue High School computer teacher in another Apache tribal town, 5/11/00). Finally, teachers can relate learning to popular culture and allow students to discuss familiar animated films.

What Does Computer Art Technology Mean to Native American Children?

Computer training is important for native American students so that they can directly communicate with the world. Computers arrived in Apache schools through a federal grant. "The Apache student must bridge two worlds, persevere a cultural past, and go forward into a high tech world," according to Kitzmiller at Cibecue High School (Caddo, 2000). Computers also break student isolation and community desperation from economic pressures, alcohol, and family dysfunction (personal correspondence with Kitzmiller, 5/11/00).

Many Apache students in this school have had computer training since the third grade, but computer art or animation programs were never offered before. The novelty of special effects definitely motivates students and results show that they initially may copy each other's schema or use premade stamp images. They need guidance on how make a new schema by combining several stamps, such as the young boy who created "Electric Man" with a light bulb head, windmill hat, lightning arms, and saws for feet. The persistent use of premade stamps suggests that computer graphics has become the art of arranging supplied images, often programmed by others (Hubbard and Boling, 1983). This study supports Chia and Duthie's (1993) claim that how children learn to make computer art is as important as what they learn. In this summer school study, the relaxed atmosphere helped children to explore tools, special effects, and image possibilities at their own speed. Apache children resent learning in school by drill or force (Basso, 1971).

On the other hand, Koscielecki (2000) warns, "This peculiar cult and fetishism of electronic equipment results from intellectual immaturity of a 'young artist' . . . the easiness of getting an average result may lead to intellectual passivity and idleness" (p. 2). Therefore, teachers still need to introduce and insist on some design guidelines, such as repeating colors or using a variety of [stamp] size, to help children grow in their representation abilities.

Ideally, teachers should spend at least one week explaining and practicing the techniques with students. Some teachers prefer to have students learn techniques simultaneously while generating ideas for creation. Similar to many students, some Apache students are independent learners, while other students need individual guidance to help them generate meaningful images and keep them on task. Still other students, who have difficulty reading directions, need videotaped step-by-step procedures on how to draw a human schema and make it move, and how to store files, because their reading skills are poor.

Teachers can ask children to talk about what they did and talk about the work of others through storytelling. A simple story can consist of a character, a setting, and a changing phenomenon. This initial talk story can act as a review, a kind of in-process appraisal. Students can work with each other to suggest ways to finish classmates' stories. Students also could continue the story in a different art medium as well. At the White Mountain Middle School, for example, the Apache art teacher encourages students to tell stories through drawing and photography (Schlessinger, 1993). Later these images can be scanned and manipulated on the computer with a supplementary plot and resolution. An entire class can work in groups, to animate a segment for a longer animated story. They could together decide on the story, characters, plot, and actions. Students could assume various roles, such as animators, background designer, editors, and so forth. Animation can be considered a form of visual storytelling.

Attempts at art criticism in a three-week summer program tend to be exploratory and students' answers were short. Time constraints, a lack of experience with art criticism, and poor writing skills limited the reflective abilities of these Apache middle-school students. Older student assistants can be helpful in such a setting. In Apache tradition, talk takes time to translate and to gain trust (Basso, 1971). From their history of negative experiences with white people, native people are hesitant to share their ideas with them (Schlessinger, 1993).

Teachers should design art activities that can help develop students' critical thinking skills so that they will not have difficulty talking about their own work or the work of others. Teachers should encourage students to critically review images they encounter on the Internet and other electronic and popular culture sources and guide students by asking questions to enable them to look deeper into the work. Critical thinking helps students to recognize the stereotypical and push beyond it. When teaching animation, another way to encourage criticality is to direct students to rate animation examples that they find based on criteria they establish to determine levels of quality from low to high and explain their reasoning. Students need to be challenged and learn that computers are tools for creative work, not an end in themselves.

References

Basso, K. (1970). *The Cibecue Apache.* New York: Holt, Rinehart, and Winston.

Basso, K. (1971). To give up on words: Silence in Western Apache culture. In K. Basso, K. & M. Opler (Eds.), *Apachean culture history and ethnology* (p. 153). Tucson, AZ: Anthropological Papers at the University of Arizona, #21.

Caddo, B. (2000, Spring). *Dishchii'bikoh Cibecue: The crown edition.* Cibecue, AZ: Locally published manuscript.

Chia, J., & Duthie, B. (1993). Primary children and computer-based artwork: Their learning strategies and context. *Art Education, 46* (6), 23–26.

Colbert, C. (1996). Issues of gender in the visual arts education of young children. In G. Collins and R. Sandell (Eds.). *Gender issues in art education* (pp. 60–69). Reston, VA: National Art Education Association.

Freedman, K. (1989). Microcomputers and the dynamics of image making and social life in three art classrooms. *Journal of Research on Computing in Education, 21* (3), 290–298.

Gardner, H. (1980). *Artful scribbles: The significance of children's drawings.* New York: Basic.

Hickman, Craig. (1991). *Kid Pix and Slide Show: User's guide.* Novato, CA: Broderbund Software Inc.

Hubbard, G., & Bolling, E. (1983). Computer graphics and art education. *School Arts, 83* (3), 18–21.

Koscielecki, S. (2000). *Dilemmas of the contemporary plastic arts education.* Unpublished paper presented at the 5th InSEA European Conference in Posnan, Poland.

LaVerne, C. (1966). *They sang for horses: The impact of the horse on Navajo and Apache folklore.* Tucson, AZ: University of Arizona Press.

Mesa-Bains, A. (1996). Teaching students the way they learn. In S. Cahan & Z. Kocur (Eds.). *Contemporary art and multicultural education* (pp. 31–38). New York: New Museum of Contemporary Art & Routledge.

San Carlos Apache Cultural Center. (No date). San Carlos Apache Cultural Center. Author. Available on-line: http://www.carizona.com/super/attraction/san_carlos.html.

Schlessinger, A. (Exec. Prod.). (1993). *Apache* (videorecording). Bala Cynwyd, PA: Library Video Co.

Stokrocki, M. (1986). A qualitative interpretation of a microcomputer graphics course for gifted and talented adolescents. *Art Education, 39* (1), 44–47.

Stokrocki, M. (1997). Qualitative forms of research methods. In S. La Pierre & E. Zimmerman (Eds.). *Research methods and methodologies for art education* (pp. 33–55). Reston, VA: National Art Education Association.

White Mountain Apache Tribe. (1997). Home Page. Available on-line: http://www.itcaonline.com/Tribes/whitemtn.htm.

Wilson, B., & Wilson, M. (1977). An iconoclastic view of the imagery sources in the drawings of young people. *Art Education, 30* (1), 5–11.

Wilson, B., & Wilson, M. (1983). Themes for graphic narratives of American, Australian, Egyptian, and Finnish children: Tales from four cultures. *Journal of Multicultural and Cross-cultural Research in Art Education 11,* 63–76.

Wohlwill, J., & Wills, S. (1987). A study of elementary school children's computer graphics. *Visual Arts Research, 13* (1), 1–13.

CONCLUSIONS AND FURTHER QUESTIONS

1. What context does Stockrocki establish for the school at the beginning of the chapter? Why is it important for us to know this?
2. What types of gender and cultural differences were seen by Stockrocki in the use of computer technology, both in terms of the content of the work that the students produced and the ways in which the students used the technology?
3. How did the students' identities emerge in the class? What did we learn about students' culture through the works that they created? What ideas and images did the students carry into their classroom with them? Why is it important for teacher to understand this?
4. Describe the ways that reading this chapter has affected your thoughts about using computers and technology in the elementary classroom.

RESOURCES AND SUGGESTIONS
FOR FURTHER READING

AAUW Educational Foundation Commission on Technology, Gender, and Teacher Education. *Tech-savvy: Educating girls in the new computer age.* Washington, DC: American Association of University Women Educational Foundation, 2000.

David Bell & Barbara M. Kennedy (Eds.). *The cybercultures reader.* London; New York: Routledge, 2000.

Cynthia Cockburn and Susan Ormrod. *Gender and technology in the making.* London; Thousand Oaks, CA: Sage, 1993.

Digital divide: teachers, technology, and the classroom. Princeton, NJ: Films for the Humanities & Sciences, 1999. (Four 57-minute videocassettes.)

Keith Grint & Rosalind Gill (Eds.). *The gender-technology relation: Contemporary theory and research.* London; Bristol, PA: Taylor & Francis, 1995.

Richard Holeton. *Composing cyberspace: Identity, community, and knowledge in the electronic age.* Boston, MA: McGraw-Hill, 1998.

Timothy V. Kaufman-Osborn. *Creatures of Prometheus: Gender and the politics of technology.* Lanham, MD: Rowman & Littlefield, 1997.

Joseph Migga Kizza. *Ethical and social issues in the information age.* New York: Springer, 1998.

Arthur & Marilouise Kroker (Eds.). *Digital delirium.* New York: St. Martin's Press, 1997.

Richard A. Lanham. *The electronic word: Democracy, technology, and the arts.* Chicago, IL: University of Chicago Press, 1993.

Peter Lunenfeld. *Snap to grid: A user's guide to digital arts, media, and cultures.* Cambridge, MA: MIT Press, 2000.

Melanie Stewart Millar. *Cracking the gender code: Who rules the wired world?* Toronto, Canada: Second Story Press, 1998.

Devon G. Peña. *The terror of the machine: Technology, work, gender, and ecology on the U.S.–Mexico border.* Austin, TX: CMAS Books, 1997.

Virginia Driving Hawk Sneve. *The Apaches.* New York: Holiday House, 1997.

Clifford Stoll. *High tech heretic: Why computers don't belong in the classroom and other reflections by a computer contrarian.* New York: Doubleday, 1999.

Jennifer Terry & Melodie Calvert. *Processed lives: Gender and technology in everyday life.* London; New York: Routledge, 1997.

Sherry Turkle. *Life on the screen: Identity in the age of the internet.* New York: Simon & Schuster, 1995.

Michael Wessells. *Computer, self, and society.* Englewood Cliffs, NJ: Prentice Hall, 1990.

Section III
Pedagogical Strategies

Introduction

Pedagogy can be understood as a relationship based on dialogue, "a transformation of consciousness that takes place in the interaction of three agencies—the teacher, the learner and the knowledge they together produce" (Lusted, 1986, p. 3). As a result of the exchange, students and teachers may begin to think differently and move to new places in learning and teaching. Pedagogy can be informed by different theories and as a result different approaches emerge with different emphases. For example, feminist pedagogy is theoretically informed by feminist theory. Critical pedagogy is based in critical theory and in some cases, influenced by Freire's liberatory pedagogy. There are different pedagogical strategies offered in this section and the theories behind them are more obvious in some chapters than in others. Needless to say, all chapters contain theoretical frameworks. Pedagogy is a theoretically informed practice of teaching. The use of the word pedagogy also carries with it ideas that the pedagogy is a critical approach to teaching and that those who engage in it believe that pedagogy carries with it a hope for social transformation through education. As such pedagogy is very much tied to the ideas contained in the first two sections regarding the inclusion of social, political, and cultural issues in the curriculum.

In Section I the emphasis of the chapters was on presenting and understanding a number of theoretical frameworks that can inform our teaching of art at the elementary level. In the chapters in Section II the authors stress the importance of doing our own investigative research on works of art to prepare us to walk into our classrooms with meaningful content for teaching and learning. In this section the authors introduce different pedagogical strategies to use with children as a means of teaching a variety of content. They present lesson ideas, units of instruction, and practical examples of teachers, students, and community members participating in a variety of art activities such as art criticism, aesthetics, studio production, integrated learning, working with an artist-in-residence, building a community network, and creating a large-scale puppet production.

As you will find in the following chapters, pedagogical strategies are not methodologies or sets of rules to be followed. It may also be practical to recognize that the approaches to issues and ideas in the following chapters vary in their level of integration with other subject disciplines. Much of the content found in contemporary art requires pedagogical strategies that will help children uncover meaning that makes sense both within the context of their lives and in relationship to the world outside the classroom. Content determines what kinds of questions to ask, what information is available, how we construct meanings, what kinds of activities or projects can evolve from it, approaches to understanding and interpreting artworks, and links to other subject areas.

Continuing from Sections I and II, the authors in this section put into practice some of the ideas that were explored in the first two sections. These include the study of artworks that contribute positively to students' lives, the connection of learning to the lives of students and real-life issues, ways to critically look at sources within visual culture as content for study, the study of art in the contexts of culture and everyday life, the building of community relationships, and strategies to teach children to think critically. In addition, authors in this section include issues of the body as content for study, the building of interdisciplinary connections within the elementary curriculum, and the creation of units of instruction around themes of human experience. They also include the cultural identities of students in the learning process, discuss ways to link learning to the world outside the classroom, consider art learning in non-school settings, and move teaching and learning to the level of social action.

Julia Marshall discusses strategies for developing an art curriculum using cultural artifacts as sources for critical inquiry. Marshall presents three lessons modeled on the contemporary art practices of using research as a strategy for art making and objects as artifacts for study. Students investigate common manufactured objects that represent everyday experiences and find meaning in them. Students take on the roles of cultural anthropologists and cultural critics by asking questions in order to understand these objects as forms of material culture and as expressions of the culture in which they live. In these lessons, students learn about themselves as contributors to and creators of culture.

Through art criticism, students construct meaning and contribute to our understanding of works of art. Terry Barrett presents a strategy for interpreting art and offers teachers some practical suggestions and guiding principles for classroom use. Barrett maintains that if we do not interpret artworks we are ignoring them. By participating in art criticism with a group of learners, students build life-skills of listening, observation, and articulation. He explains the difference between personal and communal interpretations and why both are necessary for understanding a work of art. He describes interpretation as an ongoing dialogue where differences have room to co-exist.

Issues of difference in relation to age is a community-interactive interdisciplinary thematic unit that Doris Guay develops for an elementary curriculum. Guay suggests an integrated learning approach that joins issues/information found in elementary texts and uses contemporary artworks to extend learning. Guay shows us how the content of contemporary art can open a space for a deeper study of the human condition in relation to issues and provoke a more critical engagement with aspects of issues not included in textbooks. She points out that children are well-aware of issues in everyday life, exposed to them through sources at home, the media, as well as their textbooks at school. Guay positions students as makers of social change.

Through the investigation of postmodern art and issues, Melody Milbrandt also positions students as agents of social change. She uses postmodernism as a framework for content and selecting contemporary artists for a socially engaged art curriculum. Through the study of contemporary artist Maya Lin and her design of the *Vietnam Veterans Memorial* in historical, social, cultural, and aesthetic contexts, Milbrandt connects real-life issues with DBAE practice so that students build deeper understandings about life through art. Fifth-grade students engaged in extended discussions about aesthetic issues and social concerns which, Milbrandt suggests, better prepares them to function with awareness and understanding in today's society.

Karen Keifer-Boyd introduces us to sensitive perceptions of the environment through the work of ecofeminist artist Lynne Hull and her approach to environmental installation art as a form of political activism to raise consciousness about ecological issues. Keifer-Boyd relates the experiences of working with Hull as an artist-in-residence to inspire teachers to develop interdisciplinary lessons that explore our relationships with the earth and all living things. She provides strategies for teaching environmental installation art, concepts of ecofeminism through science and site-specific sculpture at the elementary level, and offers Web sites for further exploration of environmental issues, artists, and activities that teach creative and critical thinking.

Elizabeth Reese applied the theoretical concept of hypertext to real communities by combining it with narratives to develop a teaching strategy that links individuals, communities, and local organizations through art. As an alternative to traditional educational practices that maintain one dominant perspective, Reese presents an approach in which diverse learners contribute memories, experiences, and information to the creation of knowledge. Reese describes how children and facilitators engaged and evaluated social and political issues in relation to their own lives, the local community, and the larger world through dialogue, interpreting artwork, and art making activities.

Mary Adams combines community and social issues with art to develop an interdisciplinary project having to do with drug and violence prevention. The project, a large-scale puppet production organized by Adams, involved the efforts of students, parents, teachers, community members, and local businesses. Performed by students, the songs and script have been professionally recorded and these tapes are available for public use. The script and soundtrack have also been posted on their own Web site, moving social action well beyond the school community.

B. Stephen Carpenter and Billie Sessions suggest that elementary teachers can extend art learning and its significance by expanding the study of works of art that are being studied in the art classroom to include three-dimensional works. Using a content-based inquiry approach, teachers can explore meanings in works of art through tasks that require skills already being developed in the elementary classroom, shifting away from art making as an exclusive approach to the study of art. Sessions and Carpenter promote the study of three-dimensional works of art in general, and clay specifically, and walk us through a content-based investigation of the issues and meaning of a contemporary ceramic artwork, offering activities suggested by the content of the work.

Mary Ann Stankiewicz teaches fifth-grade gifted students how to read works of art, specifically a three-dimensional artwork, through various contexts in order to find meaning. As part of an instructional unit on multicultural art that fits within the fifth-grade curriculum and introduces a critical component to learning, Stankiewicz selected a work by Lorna Simpson, a contemporary African-American artist, for study and discussed the different contexts of the artwork with students. Students take on the role of cultural critics, working individually, in pairs, and in groups, to investigate the work in relation to critical cultural values, beliefs, and issues. Students participate in a dialogue that connects art to life for more meaningful learning.

Reference

Lusted, D. (1986). Why pedagogy? *Screen, 27* (5), 2–14.

CHAPTER 21

QUESTIONS AND EXPLORATIONS

1. Choose an object that is familiar to you and that you know well. Describe and tell the various stories that you associate with this object.
2. What differences exist between what we typically call "everyday objects" and "artworks?" Why are there these differences?
3. Do you see "everyday objects" or "artworks" as being more important? Which type of object is personally more important to you? Which type of object is more important to our culture? Why do these differences occur?
4. What would be the consequences of blurring the boundaries that exist between everyday objects and artworks?
5. The Museum of Modern Art in New York City has various pieces of Tupperware on display as examples of "good design." Does the context of the museum change the meaning of this Tupperware from that which you might have in your kitchen? Why or why not?

Exploring Culture and Identity Through Artifacts: Three Art Lessons Derived from Contemporary Art Practice

Julia Marshall

Perhaps the greatest challenge in teaching is creating lessons that provide engaging and tangible entryways into exploring complex ideas. Art lessons and artmaking offer such entrances that are active, multi-modal, and motivating for young people. Artmaking challenges students to think, imagine, and visualize, and then act upon ideas in inventive and personal ways. In this chapter I discuss specific strategies for developing art curriculum and present three lessons that challenge students to explore, think, and create, using processes and ideas that originate in contemporary art practices and draw from current trends in general education.

In my practice as an artist and art educator I have developed an approach to curriculum writing that is grounded in a few fundamental concepts that challenge conventional thinking in lesson development. These concepts are:

1. Curriculum development, like art, requires creative processing. Lessons are generated in many artistic ways: they give form to complex ideas, they catalyze thought, they allow for interpretation and active involvement on the part of the viewer/participants, and each lesson represents an aesthetically shaped experience comprised of presentations, exercises, reflection, and closure. As a cluster or sequence of these experiences, the curriculum also has aesthetic qualities (order, coherence, and form) as well as other characteristics emblematic of contemporary art (open-endedness, improvisation, and an evolving nature).

2. Developing lesson ideas is similar to generating ideas for artwork. Idea generation in art lessons mimics art idea generation in that both employ creative strategies and originate in observation and questioning.

3. As in much contemporary art, the fundamental goal of art lessons is engendering critical thinking about issues and ideas of social and personal consequence. In introducing the essential ingredients of imagination, fantasy, and subjective interpretation to the thought process, artmaking is a compelling way of catalyzing personal investment and engagement while deliberating significant ideas.

4. Art lessons are most meaningful when they connect to a student's world. A meaningful lesson derives from prior experience and evolves from there to the creation of new knowledge, experience, and a deeper understanding of life.

5. The primary task of art education lies not in preparing consumers of culture but in developing and enabling creators of culture.

6. Art lessons should be in alignment with postmodern, contemporary art practices, and be concept-based or, even better, process-based. In a postmodern lesson, ideas and processes drive the art lesson and the artmaking, with materials and techniques in a supporting role.

There are three specific concepts originating in contemporary art practice that are embodied in the lessons presented here: (1) process: artmaking is employed as a form of inquiry or research, (2) medium: common cultural artifacts are utilized as sources or mediums for critical inquiry and artmaking, and (3) intent: consciousness and understanding of critical issues such as identity and culture constitute the purpose of artmaking.

Artmaking as Research

The art processes in the lessons discussed in this chapter come directly from models in contemporary art inspired by research in the humanities and social sciences in areas such as anthropology, sociology, and cultural studies. Many contemporary artists have found research a rich and rewarding way of developing ideas of consequence. Making research a strategy for artmaking expands the boundaries of content to include issues outside the artist's direct experience, affords a way of making art informative and full of content, and often presents alternative formats for art. Contemporary art that is based in research is challenging and refreshing as it often resembles journalism, cultural studies, or scientific research more than conventional art forms. In this hybrid of art and other disciplines, process leads the product to new forms that are often derived from the aesthetics of other areas of scholarship.

In engaging research, artists have tapped into a significant concept that lies at the intersection of art and learning: all artmaking is essentially a form of research. As such, it presents a method of inquiry that entails gathering information, the interpretation of findings, and the creation of a response or product. Artmaking, when seen as research, represents knowledge construction and the creation of understanding and meaning that is organic and evolving. What makes artmaking especially noteworthy as research is the creation of an art form that embodies both concept and process and serves as a springboard for more thought and learning.

Essential to the concept of art as research is the notion that all artmaking is a learning experience. This concept has one very positive implication for art education: framing artmaking as learning focuses attention away from the qualities of the product (Does it work? Is it beautiful?) to the nature of the process (What did we learn? How did we learn it?). Artmaking as learning also confirms the significance of subjective knowledge, knowledge that we create or discover personally through our senses, intellect, and experiences.

Artifacts as Sources of Investigation

In using lessons that are centered in everyday objects and students' experiences with them, teachers can encourage children's curiosity about their world, while bringing classroom art practice closer to the methods, purposes, and content found in much contemporary art, especially art that touches on cultural studies, criticism, and commentary.

In applying research methods as an artmaking strategy or process in the classroom, inquiry into common objects also encourages children to examine their own knowledge, experience, and attitudes. Inquiry of this sort generates a myriad of artistic responses that have an interdisciplinary, unconventional, and contemporary art aesthetic reminiscent of science projects or text and image research reports.

Investigating and "unpacking" common manufactured objects provides a rich source of ideas for research-based lessons. As content for lessons, common objects represent receptacles or manifestations of concepts, memories, stories, and cultural practices. As such, they are artifacts. Csányi (1999) states, "Man-made [sic] objects are always expressions of ideas, which means that artifacts can also be interpreted as systems of organized rules of behavior" (p. 301). Artifacts represent especially direct entryways into cultural inquiry and criticism for they are often ordinary, familiar, multiple, and integrated into everyday life. Artifacts provide keys to the workings of culture and the values of a people. They mediate culture, shaping the way people think, and pass on ideas and values to each other and to the next generation. Going beneath the surface of an object can reveal its meaning, the ways it mediates thought, and the world view it embodies.

Using artifacts as subjects of research invites children to explore something that is familiar to them that speaks of everyday, often unexamined, experience. In looking at cultural objects, students become "anthropologists" and critical analysts of culture, learning to question the objects around them, to find meanings in them, and to understand them as cultural expression (or metaphors for cultural properties). In doing so they discover and reveal the culture in which they live. By extension, students reveal themselves as cultural beings, participants, and embodiments (and subsequently critics) of culture. This notion is compatible with the postmodern concept of the culturally located and constructed individual.

It is also important to consider the dialectical relationship between culture and artifact. As noted above, artifacts shape the way people think. People, in turn, create artifacts (and culture). In exploring the dialectical relationship between culture (and the people who are part of it) and artifacts, children can come to understand that they, too, can contribute to their culture through the making of images.

Exploring contemporary visual culture, which is evidenced in all visual representations (artifacts, popular images, and art), is another important component of this kind of lesson. Through examining artifacts, children can come to see that artifacts (and popular images) are designed with intent, often convey messages, and have aesthetic qualities. In these ways, artifacts have much in common with art and often the lines between the two are blurred. Comparing and contrasting artifacts with objects and images designated as art challenges children to examine and construct their own concepts of art and to explore the intersection between art and everyday visual culture.

Generating Artifact-based Lessons

In artmaking and in lesson generation the process begins with observation, looking around, and paying close attention. Drawing and keeping notebooks, journals, and sketchbooks are strategies that are used by artists to collect and refine observations. Teachers can utilize sketchbooks for recording lesson and unit ideas. Sketchbooks also are useful for students as they gather ideas for their own artwork. For finding artifacts, my advice to teachers is to look around their homes or explore common places such as grocery and hardware stores, malls, or specialty shops. Look for objects that have many layers of content that are easily accessible and meaningful to children such as common toys, stuffed animals, packaged foods, and household objects and tools. To get a good idea of child culture go to child-appropriate movies or watch children's programming on television and observe what objects your students collect or carry around with them. The goal is to find objects that generate inquiry leading to critical awareness of contemporary culture and identity within culture. Many commercial commodities based on children's programming are excellent mediums for this inquiry.

Learning Through a Cycle of Making and Questioning

An artifact-based inquiry lesson often has four steps: (1) thinking through and "unpacking" the artifact, finding its meaning and implications; (2) researching other artifacts that are similar in form and concept at home, at school, in magazines or books, or in the neighborhood; (3) making new objects/artwork inspired by the artifact and ideas which surfaced in the discussion and research; and (4) reflecting upon the process and product. Step one involves group brainstorming and discussion among students and teacher. Step two includes keeping a journal of drawings and lists of objects and images. The third step, the artmaking component of the project, provides the opportunity to take these ideas and transform them into personal expression manifested in artforms that lead to further evolving ideas. In step four, students discuss the process they have experienced and ask further questions, this time focusing on the art product and its connection to the original artifact.

Although not all art-inquiry lessons must include the production of an art piece, students do learn through hands-on experiences and art lessons present excellent opportunities for learning this way. One crucial key to learning through artmaking is the engagement of imagination. Active involvement in artmaking that challenges the student to take the information gathered and apply it imaginatively encourages the student to distill concepts, shape them into metaphors, find connections, and make sense of ideas. This gives the subject of the lesson personal meaning to the artist and generates a deeper understanding of it.

Questioning is as fundamental as making to the learning process and also represents a form of imaginative thinking. Curiosity and imagination go hand in hand; one engenders the other. Also, puzzling and questioning are engaging, enjoyable activities for children (Battin, 1995; Matthews, 1994) and as anyone who is close to children knows, most kids are curious and ask lots of questions, often about serious subjects. This questioning frequently resembles play. As play, inquiry can work on many levels (social, cultural, personal, and historical) and presents a "play structure" for discovery and the construction of knowledge. As a location for playing with ideas and hypotheses, research in the form of questioning becomes engaging, imaginative, improvisational, and open-ended, creating an evolving process of learning for both children and teacher.

Questions for "unpacking" the artifacts could include: "What is this object?" "Where did it come from?" "Who made it?" "What do you do with it?" "What does it remind you of?" "Who or what does it represent?" Questions such as these can also be used to examine the artforms the children create in the lesson because artforms, like the generative cultural objects that began the process, embody ideas and are manifestations or remnants of experience (the process). The analysis of the children's work is similar to a traditional art critique in which students examine their art. However, it differs in the questions asked, the focus, and the goal, which are to investigate the art product not as an isolated aesthetic object but as a step in critical inquiry.

Encouraging students to come to their own conclusions, without answers dictated by the teacher, is crucial to learning through playful inquiry and dialogue. To do this, the teacher acts as a guide and facilitator asking questions, leading brainstorming sessions, gathering answers from the children, and gently leading the dialogue in multiple directions that fulfill the objectives of the lesson.

My advice to teachers in facilitating art discussions and lessons is to do what artists do; follow the trail, look for the implications, and see where the artifact leads the conversation. Brainstorming with children and developing cluster maps of connections between the artifact and related concepts, objects, activities, practices, places, peoples, etc., works well for expediting the thinking and questioning process and generating ideas for art and research.

The process of cyclical questioning and doing described above constitutes an art lesson informed and inspired by processes of contemporary artists/researchers. It is firmly based on process rather than product. It also presents a form of inquiry-based learning where children learn through finding answers themselves, where knowledge is revealed through "problem posing" or "problematizing" a situation (Freire, 1973). When extended to multiple art lessons evolving around a theme, the lessons become project-based learning (Katz and Chard, 1995). Art-research lessons, therefore, represent a convergence between concepts in progressive general education and contemporary art.

Making the Connection with Examples from Art

Using examples of artwork to illustrate an idea or demonstrate a technique is a time-honored method of conveying the content of an art lesson. In the traditional model, art examples are shown at the beginning of the lesson. However, if a lesson is to be centered on an inquiry into common artifacts, it makes sense that art examples, if to be shown at all, be introduced during the process as part of the research or after the projects are finished as validating examples.

In this approach, the process of artmaking, rather than an art idea or an art product provides the model. Four artists who use artifacts as entry points to examine culture and identity, or focus on objects as metaphors of culture are:

1. Fred Wilson: Wilson selects and arranges thematic exhibits in museums using those institutions' collections. His work addresses museum curatorial practices and biases, especially as these convey narratives of race and culture. (See Corrin, 1994).

2. Catherine Wagner: Wagner's crisp, clear, "objective," black and white photographs depict objects, tools, and specimens from science labs and school rooms, revealing the practices taking place in those environments and the values inherent in those practices. (See Homburg, 1996; Tucker and Morris, 1988).

3. Mark Dion: Dion arranges objects, tools, and specimens from science laboratories in tableaus that resemble actual labs. The subject of many of his installations is the culture of science. (See Corrin, Kwon, and Bryson, 1997).

4. Candy Jernigan: Jernigan's work consists of collections of miscellaneous debris arranged as souvenirs or specimens that serve as evidence of the moments in her everyday life. (See Dolphin, 1999).

Three Model Artifact-based Lessons

Lesson #1: Investigating a Souvenir

This lesson incorporates a simple cultural object as a catalyst for inquiry and interpretation. It builds a critical dialogue on culture, souvenirs, and art, and involves "unpacking" a souvenir. Any visually interesting and depictive souvenir would do, but for this example I use a souvenir snowdome of Chicago.

A snowdome with a miniature model of Chicago inside is an example of a pop-culture object harboring potential lesson ideas. This small object represents a simple fantasy depiction of Chicago but it also serves as a cultural expression and a souvenir of experiences in the city. For the person who collected it, it has memories and stories embedded in it. For the person who observes it as a cultural object, it is a playful illustration of one way that popular culture packages the desire to collect, fantasize, and remember. In this object, Chicago becomes a place now isolated, sanitized, miniaturized, fetishized, and secured. Because snowdomes are so common and inexpensive, Chicago becomes a subject of kitsch. How this transformation of image from the real thing to a cultural icon or souvenir occurs is a promising area to pursue with children and can catalyze critical thinking about culture, the creation and mediation of objects, and the desire to consume and own.

Here are some questions that could lead the discussion toward these ideas:

1. What does the object look like? (Describe it.)
2. What do you think this object is?
3. What is inside the object?
4. Is the city inside different from a real city? How is it different?
5. Why do you think the city is inside the object?
6. How does this object make you think about the city inside of it?
7. Is this object interesting or beautiful to you?
8. If you visited this city would this object be more interesting, beautiful, or more fun to look at?
9. How do you think a person would come to own this object?
10. Why would the owner want to have it? Why would he or she like it?
11. What do people do with objects like this?
12. Why do people make objects like this?
13. Have you seen objects that are similar to this? What are they?
14. Do you think this object is a work of art? Why? If not, why?

The discussion that evolves through these questions could be followed by scavenger hunts at home where children search for and collect souvenirs and bring them to school for display. Students could set up a "museum" and write descriptive labels for their souvenirs that incorporate the stories behind them. More discussion and investigation of visual and popular culture could evolve from critiquing these objects as artifacts and as museum pieces.

Lesson #2: Exploring Meanings in Personal Artifacts

This lesson is designed to generate critical inquiry into identity through memory and associations with an object of personal significance. It is a lesson in which research explores what students already know and feel, providing insight into a child's knowledge, experience, and sentiments. The lesson also involves collaborations in groups of two and challenges students to look into the commonalties between objects, thus tapping into cultural concepts and the meanings embodied in them. The lesson culminates in collaborative art projects.

The lesson begins with each student choosing an artifact that has personal significance for him or her. Each student will then examine his or her artifact through "interviewing" it or asking it questions. Some questions for the "interview" could be: "What are you?" "Who made you?" "What place did you come from?" "What do you do?" "How long have you been with me?" "What memories do we share?" "Why are you special to me?" Students write down the answers to these questions and further examine the objects by drawing them and paying close attention to details.

In groups of two, students discuss the commonalties or differences between their objects. They look for a common theme of likeness or difference, finding a relationship between their objects. Exploring the common theme that they have found, each group creates an artpiece that expresses that theme. Making a shared artwork provides a process by which ideas evolve far beyond the ideas plumbed from the original objects. Artpieces can take any form: a sculpture, a painting, a poem, an installation, a video, or a performance.

Introducing pop artists and postmodern artists who isolate and use familiar objects to comment on culture such as Jeff Koons, Andy Warhol, Haim Steinbach, Claes Oldenberg, and Fred Wilson, could enhance the lesson and connect it with contemporary art practice. Fred Wilson's work with cultural artifacts is especially relevant here as he focuses on the relationship between objects in constructing revealing narratives about cultural practices and values.

The discussion that follows could explore these additional related concepts:

1. Defamiliarizing the familiar or functional in order to "see" an object or artifact in a new light, becoming aware of its formal, physical properties such as shape, color, texture, materials, image, and details.

2. Finding and interpreting connections (similarities and differences) between objects and seeing how these connections reveal insights into history and culture. This is the most crucial concept as it is the connections between the artifacts that most reveal underlying themes and meanings.

3. Exploring the intersection between the personal and the cultural and seeing how artifacts represent personal and communal experience in time and place.

4. Process: Observing how collaboration and dialogue create shared meaning in examining and developing concepts. Creating a concept-generated object in a format and materials that enhance meaning, insight, and understanding.

Lesson #3: Exploring Multiple Approaches to an Artifact

In this project, students come to understand a common artifact in depth by researching the object, observing it closely, writing about it, and transforming and reinterpreting the artifact in multiple images. Research and play are combined to reveal information that students may or may not know previously about an artifact. Student inquiry and image-making could culminate in an artist's book or an installation/exhibition of texts and image.

Begin the lesson with a discussion of research as an inquiry that evolves through multiple questions and steps. Each student then chooses an artifact to explore. Together as a class, brainstorm questions to ask about the artifacts. Some questions could be: "Where did the artifact come from?" "Who made it?" "What is it made of?" "Why was it made?" "How was it made?" "Does it do anything?" "What does it do?" "Is it useful?" "Where can you find artifacts like this?" "What is its significance?" "What does it mean to me or to others?"

Brainstorm sources of information and suggest that students explore the object in many ways. Some possibilities are: looking on the internet for information, looking for similar artifacts in the encyclopedia, finding a definition for the artifact in the dictionary, searching in magazines for images of the artifact, interviewing store owners where these artifacts are sold, interviewing family and friends about their views, uses, and knowledge of the artifacts. Students collect texts and images. They can also study the artifact by drawing it, photographing it from different angles (in use and in different places), sculpting it in various materials, and making collages or paintings of it. These images can be inspired by the information students have gathered or be playful explorations of form and function.

Images and text can then be organized into books or installations. One possibility is to arrange objects and images in an installation and create a book of explanatory text and research findings to accompany the display.

Connections with contemporary art can be made by introducing the work of artists who develop their work through multiple explorations of concepts embodied in artifacts. Catherine Wagner's photographic examinations of schools and science laboratories are excellent examples of following a theme through multiple images of artifacts in their environments.

To conclude the lesson, the class views the completed works and considers how exploring one object in multiple ways and playing imaginatively with it reveals and enhances the meaning of the object. Through discussing the process, they can investigate the commonalities and differences between scientific or anthropological inquiry and artistic inquiry. Through making and reflecting, they can experience an intimacy with an artifact and its meaning that research and artmaking engender.

Conclusion

This is a particularly good time for rethinking and reconfiguring art education. We are witnessing promising and inspiring trends in contemporary art and in general education that can inform and shape our educational practices. In general education, we find inquiry-based, problem-posing approaches to learning that challenge students to think, constructivist theories of knowledge that suggest that learning begins with what learners already know, and hands-on learning by doing that functions as multi-modal strategies for teaching and learning. In contemporary art we see artists pushing the boundaries of art, approaching the content and processes of art as researchers, and incorporating models for artmaking from disciplines outside the arts. Contemporary art offers rich resources and models for radically reshaping and updating art education as it presents new processes (that emphasize the learning at the core of art), hybridized forms (that allow for multiple and fresh modes of expression), sources of content (that arise from disciplines outside of art or from real world issues and ideas), and goals (that are educative, journalistic, and/or scholarly). In tapping contemporary art practices and using these methods and ideas, educators can highlight the linkages between the many ways humans shape and come to know the world. They can also make art lessons more engaging and perhaps more relevant to children. I hope the lessons and curriculum strategies presented here will contribute to this endeavor.

References

Battin, M. (1995). Cases for kids: Using puzzles to teach aesthetics to children. In Moore, R. (Ed.) *Aesthetics for young people* (pp. 89–104). Reston, VA: National Art Education Association.

Corrin, L. (1994). *Mining the museum: An installation by Fred Wilson.* New York, New Press.

Corrin, L., Kwon, M., & Bryson, N. (1997). *Mark Dion.* New York: Phaidon.

Csányi, V. (1999). The social roots of creativity. In Montuori, A. & Purser, R. Ed. *Social creativity*, Volume 1 (pp. 289–313). Cresskill, NJ: Hampton Press.

Dolphin, L. (1999). *Evidence: The art of Candy Jernigan.* San Francisco, CA: Chronicle Books.

Freire, P. (1973). *Pedagogy of the oppressed.* New York: Continuum.

Homburg, C. (1996). *Art and science, investigating matter, Catherine Wagner.* Seattle, WA: Washington University Gallery of Art.

Katz, L., & Chard, S. (1995). *Engaging children's minds: The project approach.* Norwood, NJ: Ablex Publishing.

Matthews, G. (1994). *The philosophy of childhood.* Cambridge, MA: Harvard University Press.

Tucker, A. W., & Morris, W. (1988). *American classroom: The photographs of Catherine Wagner.* Houston, TX: The Museum of Fine Arts.

CONCLUSIONS AND FURTHER QUESTIONS

1. What might Marshall mean by the term "child culture?"
2. What is an artifact? What does the study of artifacts reveal? How are artifacts linked to everyday life, cultural identity, and memory?
3. Describe each of the four steps found in artifact-based lessons as outlined by Marshall.
4. Take the object that you chose to examine before you read this chapter. Using Marshall's questions that she asks about the snowglobe from Chicago, work through as many of her questions as are appropriate to your object. What did you learn about your object through doing this? In what ways is your understanding and description of your object

different from the description that you wrote before reading this chapter?

5. How does the collaborative process change the nature of the discussions that we have in classrooms?

6. Discuss why shared meanings are important. How might you make these part of your classroom?

RESOURCES AND SUGGESTIONS
FOR FURTHER READING

Michel de Certeau. *The practice of everyday life.* Steven Rendall (Trans.). Berkeley, CA: University of California Press, 1984.

Leah Hager Cohen. *Glass, paper, beans: Revelations on the nature and value of ordinary things.* New York: Doubleday/Currency, 1997.

James Deetz. *In small things forgotten: The archaeology of early American life.* New York: Doubleday, 1977.

Joanna Sofaer Derevenski. *Children and material culture.* New York: Routledge, 2000.

Margaret J. M. Ezell and Katherine O'Brien O'Keeffe (Eds.). *Cultural artifacts and the production of meaning: The page, the image, and the body.* Ann Arbor, MI: University of Michigan, 1994.

Michel Foucault. *The archaeology of knowledge and the discourse on language.* A.M. Sheridan Smith (Trans.). New York: Pantheon Books, 1982.

Michel Foucault. *Power/knowledge: Selected interviews and other writings, 1972–1977.* Colin Gordon (Ed. & Trans.). New York: Pantheon Books, 1980.

Henry A. Giroux & Peter McLaren (Eds.). *Between borders: Pedagogy and the politics of cultural studies.* New York: Routledge, 1994.

W. David Kingery. *Learning from things: Method and theory of material culture studies.* Washington, DC: Smithsonian Institution Press, 1996.

Daniel Miller (Ed.). *Material cultures: Why some things matter.* Chicago, IL: University of Chicago Press, 1998.

Henry Petroski. *The evolution of useful things.* New York: Vintage Books, 1992.

Thomas J. Schlereth. *Material culture studies in America.* Nashville, TN: The American Association for State and Local History, 1982.

Thomas J. Schlereth. *Material culture: A research guide.* Lawrence, KS: University Press Kansas, 1985.

Penny Sparke. *As long as it's pink: The sexual politics of taste.* London; San Francisco: Pandora, 1995.

Christopher Tilley. *Metaphor and material culture.* Oxford, UK; Malden, MA: Blackwell Publishers, 1999.

CHAPTER 22

QUESTIONS AND EXPLORATIONS

1. What is the job of a critic?
2. There are many different types of critics such as journalistic critics, academic critics, and movie critics. How many kinds of critics can you think of? What are the differences and similarities between different types of criticism?
3. What is art criticism? What forms does criticism usually take? Where might you find a piece of art criticism?
4. Read two examples of art criticism taken from different types of sources. What information did you learn from reading each of these pieces? How did the two pieces of criticism differ? Who is the intended audience of each form of criticism?
5. What does it mean to interpret art? What are the differences and similarities between art criticism and art interpretation?

Interpreting Art: Building Communal and Individual Understandings

Terry Barrett

This chapter provides a general understanding of what it means to interpret art, practical suggestions to engage learners in making interpretations, and some guiding principles to direct their interpretive thinking. When we interpret works of art, we open worlds of meaning and experience for ourselves and for those who hear our interpretations. Unless we interpret works of art, the fascinating and insightful intellectual and emotional worlds that artists make visible for us will be invisible to us. By carefully responding to works of art through inquiring and telling and listening, people build nurturing communities engaged in active learning about art and life.

What It Means to Interpret Art

To interpret is to respond in thoughts and feelings and actions to what we see and experience, and to make sense of our responses by putting them into words. When we look at a work of art, we think and feel, move closer to it and

291

back from it, squint and frown, laugh or sigh or cry, blurt out something to no one or someone. By more carefully telling or writing what we see and feel and think and do when looking at a work of art, we build an understanding of what we see and experience by articulating in language what might otherwise remain only incipient, muddled, fragmented, and disconnected to our lives. Donald Kuspit, a philosopher and art critic, says that the interpreter's most difficult task is just that: "to try to articulate the effects that the work of art induces in us, these very complicated subjective states" (in Van Proyen, 1991, p. 19).

When writing or telling about what we see and what we experience in the presence of an artwork, we build meaning, we do not merely report it. Marcia Siegel, a dance critic, says, "words are an instrument for thinking" (in Meltzer 1979, p. 55). To demonstrate this to students, I engage them in what some English teachers call "quick-writes." I show them an artwork and ask them to put pencil to paper and write about it for a designated amount of minutes, maybe five or seven or ten, without stopping, editing, or censoring. When they have done this they see that they do have something to say about art and that in the saying they understand the art and their reactions to it better. If they share what they have written, we all gain insights into the work and to one another and have first responses to the work upon which to build more slowly, carefully, and thoughtfully.

To interpret is to make meaningful connections between what we see and experience in a work of art to what else we have seen and experienced. Richard Rorty, the philosophical pragmatist, says that "reading texts is a matter of reading them in the light of other texts, people, obsessions, bits of information, or what have you, and then seeing what happens" (Rorty, 1992, p. 105). *Texts* means paintings as well as poems. *Seeing what happens* means examining what connections we can make between a painting, a dance, or a poem and our relevant experiences of books we have read, pictures we have seen, music we have heard, emotions we have felt in situations we have lived or heard about from others. Some of these connections are meaningful and worth pursuing toward greater knowledge and insight about ourselves and the world; other connections are less worthy and we let them fade away.

To interpret is to make something meaningful for ourselves and then, usually, to tell another what we think. In telling our interpretation we hear it in our own words, and we have the opportunity to obtain responses from others about what we see, think, and feel. Others' responses may be confirming or confounding. When they are confirming, we are reassured in our understanding; when they are confounding, we are given opportunity to further explore our interpretive response or to elicit differing interpretive thoughts from the ones who are confounded.

Telling is valuable to others as well as for ourselves. In successfully telling our interpretation to another, we enlarge that person's understanding of the artwork that we are telling about, the world as we understand it, and ourselves. Not to interpret a work of art in its presence is to ignore it, leave it meaningless, and pass it by as if it were dumb and with nothing to offer. For many aestheticians, to look at a work of art and not interpret it is not to see it at all (e.g., Danto, 1981).

When interpreting art of the historical past, we can seek to know what it meant to the people who saw it in its time, and we can also make it meaningful for ourselves in the present. With art of another culture, we can learn from the outside how it functioned within that culture. We can also see what knowledge and beliefs and attitudes we share with that culture and how we differ from it. Interpreting art of the present and of one's own culture is often simpler because it is generally more immediately accessible just because it is of one's time and place. When teaching interpretation, I often begin with contemporary American art and recent art of the West before using art of times and places distant from those of most of my students.

Some Simple Methods

On the basis of knowledge of art and education, I select works of art that I think are important for students to know about. I also select works that they are developmentally ready for and in which I predict they will be interested. No matter the age or the art, I show the images to groups of students, ask them questions, listen to their responses, and ask further questions (Barrett, 1997). If I am showing works to a whole class in a classroom, I use large poster reproductions or photographic slides or images projected from the Internet. Sometimes I break the whole class into small groups and give them reproductions torn from calendars or on postcards or on websites at computer terminals. I like to have both print reproductions and slides of those reproductions so that I can project large images that the whole class can easily see. If I am dependent on reproductions in classrooms rather than original works in museums, the reproductions must be of high technical quality and shown in good viewing conditions. It is essential that everyone can comfortably see what I am showing.

Carefully formulated questions are essential for productive inquiry (Jacobs, 1997). Of all works of art, I ask two generic questions that guide interpretation, phrased during the ensuing discussion in many different ways: "What do you see?" and "What does it mean?" These two questions are commonly referred to as descriptive and interpretive. Descriptions and interpretations are intertwined and overlapping. They form a hermeneutic circle. We describe what we want to interpret, we interpret what we have described, and we only know what to describe because of the interpretive questions we are trying to answer. To further a speaker's thought, and to remind all of us that claims ought to be grounded in evidence, I sometimes interject a third question, "How do you know?"

I also formulate more specific guiding questions for the work of individual artists. For example, after initial interpretive observations of William Wegman's photographs of dogs, I ask, "Are these about dogs or about people?"

To challenge inquirers to formulate concluding generalizations about many of René Magritte's paintings after we have examined them individually, I ask students to write a paragraph beginning with the phrase "The world of Magritte." I formulate my questions and my assessment of student responses, in part, on the basis of what I know, through direct observation and scholarly study, to be important about the work of Wegman (1990, 1982) and Magritte (Gablik, 1970; Hammacher, 1995; Meuris, 1994), or the work of any artist we are viewing.

During the discussions I constantly reinforce listening skills as well as skills of observation and verbal articulation. If respondents are not listening to one another and are not building on each other's insights, then we are not building a community of inquirers and are losing the benefits of many individual insights that could contribute more knowledgeable and comprehensive understandings.

Some Principals to Guide Interpretation[1]

Interpreting Art Is Both a Personal and Communal Endeavor

We can think of interpretations as having two poles, one personal and individual, and the other communal and shared. A satisfactory interpretation is located in both poles but may lean more strongly toward one pole than the other. A personal interpretation is one that I have formulated for myself after careful thought and reflection. It is an interpretation that has meaning to me. I may have accepted it from another, or embrace it with some modifications. Most importantly, the interpretation has meaning to me and for my life. A communal interpretation is an understanding or explanation of a work of art that is meaningful to a group of interpreters with common interests. Through the world of art scholarship, we often receive communal interpretations of works of art that have been initially formulated by individuals, revised by others, reformulated, and then passed on to us in a history of art text by Janson (1999), for example, or in a gallery talk by a curator, or in a comment by a professor in an art class.

Personal Interpretations

Although aestheticians embrace both the individual and communal poles of interpretation, some aestheticians position themselves closer to personal interpretations than to communal understandings. According to the French phenomenological philosopher of interpretation, Paul Ricoeur, for example, *an interpretation is incomplete until the interpreter has meaningfully appropriated the significance of the work for his or her own life* (in Bontekoe, 1988). Rorty (1992) would seem to agree with this position, believing that *there should be no difference between interpreting a work and using it to better one's life.* Rorty argues that a truly inspired interpretation is one that causes one to rearrange one's priorities and purposes in life.

After viewing Magritte's paintings, an elderly woman participating in an interpretive discussion of paintings by Magritte provides an example of an interpreter who was able to make meaning for herself that could change her life. She wrote,

> Magritte's works often seem to be of someone looking in on life from the outside, not as a participant. As a widow, I often feel that way. It's sometimes hard to make myself participate. It's often simpler to stay inside, behind walls, behind a curtain—isolated. Life should not be a picture you view. You must put yourself in the picture.[2]

Children readily make personal interpretations of what they see and experience. When reading a draft of this chapter, my wife gave me a compelling example of a young child who was able to make interpretations very personal. She was his teacher in a Montessori school in Florida.[3]

> I took my class to the beach. One boy was especially fond of the sea. He drew many pictures of the sea. I had art books in the classroom—my college art history texts as well as contemporary books of art. He loved to look at art of the sea. He was an excellent swimmer. I watched him for more than a half-hour do this: he laid down at shore break. His body was limp. He relaxed and let his body do as the sea did. Like a jellyfish caught at shoreline, he moved as ebb and tide. It was one of the most graceful and peaceful movements I have ever seen. I asked him later to tell me about it: he said he watched the water and wanted to feel it, to be it, to draw it, and to write a story about it. Today he is a practicing architect.

Alisha, a second grader, wrote this personal interpretive response to an expressionistic painting of a large monkey sitting in a rain forest, *The Mandrill* by Oscar Kokoschka.

> I liked *The Mandrill*. Because when he [the visiting critic] showed the picture to us it felt like I was in the jungle and I could hear the birds chirping. And I could hear it moving. I liked the purple on his fingers. And I could smell the fruit he was eating. I could hear the waterfall coming down. I thought it was neat. It looked like the artist did it fast and a little bit slow. The mandrill looked neat because it looked like I was like right there with him. I just felt like I could see what he was eating. And I could eat with him. I just like it so very, very, very, very much!

Alisha wrote her paragraph after examining and talking with her classmates about the Kokoschka painting and three other paintings by 20th-century artists. I facilitated that discussion as a guest critic. Following that forty-five minute session, Alisha's teacher[4] asked her class as a group to orally recall from memory the four paintings we had discussed, and then to each individually pick a favorite, write about their feelings in seeing it, and illustrate their writing. Alisha's paragraph is personal and it is informed by her classroom community. It is personal in that she tells us how much she likes the painting and how she felt when looking at it. It is communally inflected in that when she saw it in a group and heard others' comments about it, she likely noticed and recalled features of the painting because of her peers' comments.

Although personal interpretations clearly are valuable, and some theorists argue that a personal connection is essential for an interpretation, a personal interpretation can be too personal for purposes of art education. An interpretation that is too personal is one that is so subjective and idiosyncratic to the interpreter that the art object of interpretation cannot be recognized in the interpretation by those who hear the interpretation and see the work. Such an interpretation may reveal a lot about how and what the interpreter thinks and feels but fails to reveal anything about the art object being interpreted.

Communal Interpretations

Personal, individual interpretations can and should be informed by knowledge of the artwork from other persons and sources. Works by renowned artists such as Wegman and Magritte and Kokoschka receive many carefully considered interpretations by the artists themselves, art historians, curators of art who exhibit the works, and art critics who have written about those exhibits. The art of Wegman and Magritte is also the subject of thought by interested viewers outside of the artworld. The French philosopher Michel Foucault (1983), for example, was intrigued by Magritte's use of words in his paintings, and although Foucault did not often write about art, he was moved to write a short book about a painting by Magritte, *This Is Not a Pipe*. When children interpret Wegman's photographs of his Weimaraners, those children who have dogs as pets have knowledge about and insights into the photographs that children without dogs lack. When a scholar reads an interpretation of a Magritte painting written by another scholar, and when a child hears an interpretation of a Wegman photograph told by other children, and when the scholar and the child reflect on those interpretations and include insights from them into their own interpretations, they become part of a community of interpreters. By joining this community, they have opportunities to expand and deepen their individual interpretations and understandings of art and life, as well of those of the members of their community.

The Encyclopedia Britannica Online (2000) offers a communal interpretation of the work of Magritte:

> Magritte, René (-François-Ghislain). Belgian artist, one of the most prominent Surrealist painters whose bizarre flights of fancy blended horror, peril, comedy,

and mystery. His works were characterized by particular symbols—the female torso, the bourgeois "little man," the bowler hat, the castle, the rock, the window, and others.

It is a succinctly articulated, comprehensive, two-sentence interpretation likely culled from volumes of scholarly Magritte interpretations.

Interpreters of young age can also offer communal interpretations. The following is by Luke, a nine-year-old, who wrote it after participating in a group-discussion about paintings by Magritte that I facilitated with him and his classmates.[5]

> Magritte's mind is about things in common. He likes views out of a building or house. He likes perspectives. He likes to have round objects in his paintings. Optical illusions are another thing he puts in his art. He likes to make you think about his paintings. One piece of evidence of that is his titles. He does not give titles that really give any clues. Some of his art is a little fantasy, like in terms of how it looks. But most of his art is realistic.

Luke's interpretation is communal in the sense that it is synthesized from insights and observations he gained from hearing his classmates talk about the paintings, as well as by his own observations and articulation.

An interpretation that is wholly individual and personal, if such a thing is even possible, runs the risk of being overly idiosyncratic, to the point that if one heard the interpretation one might not be able to see any connection between it and the artwork about which it is an interpretation. An interpretation that is wholly communal runs the risk of irrelevance to the individual interpreter. If the viewer receives an interpretation that has no bearing on his or her life, knowledge, and experience, it is not a meaningful interpretation for that viewer, and in a sense, no matter how accurate it may be, it is not an interpretation for that viewer at all.

Shared communal interpretations and individual personal interpretations are not mutually exclusive ideas. Interpretations that are both individual and communal are understandings of works of art that are personally meaningful and relevant to the viewer's life, informed by others' interpretations of that work, and can be meaningfully held by the community of interpreters who are also interpreting the same art.

Any Work of Art Can Support Many Different Interpretations

There can be as many interpretations of a work of art as there are purposes for interpreting that work (Rorty, 1992; Stecker, 1995). Foucault's interpretation of Magritte's painting is written especially for those who are interested in philosophy of language and signification. The widow's interpretation of Magritte's paintings is for a group of her fellow docents in an art museum.

Luke's interpretation is for his classmates in a grade school. Historical scholars seek to understand how Magritte's work fits within Surrealism and how
Surrealism intersects with 20th-century art. A psychological interpretation
might seek connections between Magritte's paintings and psychoanalytic theories of Sigmund Freud, Magritte's contemporary.

Each of these interpretations serves different purposes and different audiences, and each will be assessed by those audiences according to the purpose of the interpretation and the audience's interests. Foucault's interpretation
does not exhaust the linguistic meanings of Magritte's painting. The widow's
personal interpretation does not exclude other personal interpretations.
Luke's interpretation will further more interpretations from other children.
Scholars will continue to interpret Magritte's work even though, and because,
many scholarly books have already been written about that work. When we
hear or read a stunningly insightful interpretation from a third grader or a
leading scholar, we should pause and delight in it and absorb it, but we
should not abandon the interpretive endeavor. Good artworks invite interpretations and good interpretations invite further interpretations. Good interpretations invite us to see for ourselves and continue on our own (Eaton, 1988,
p. 120).

Interpretations Are Not So Much Right or Wrong, Rather They Are More or Less Meaningful and Insightful

The goal of interpreting is not to seek one, true, eternal interpretation of a
work, but rather to construct interpretations that are insightful, original, interesting, provoke new thoughts, expand meaningful connections, and so forth
(Hampshire, 1966). Although there is no single true interpretation of a work
of art, some interpretations are better than others because they are more insightful, better grounded in historical fact, better argued, more responsive to
what can be seen in the work, more inclusively explanatory of the work's
complexities, and more convincing. One can judge the adequacy of an interpretation (Hirsch, 1967; Eaton, 1988, pp. 104–123), by testing its coherence,
correspondence, and completeness. Coherence: the interpretation should
make sense in and of itself independently of the artwork being interpreted.
Correspondence: it is not enough that the interpretation makes sense in itself,
it must also account for what can be seen in the artwork, and it ought to fit
the historical circumstance of the artwork. Completeness: the interpretation
should account for the complexity of the artwork and not ignore or omit significant aspects of the work being interpreted.

Thus, *any* interpretation is not a good interpretation, no matter how well-
meaning and hard-working the interpreter. Luke's interpretation of Magritte's
work is better than some interpretations offered by his classmates because
Luke's interpretation corresponds to what we can observe in the work, it's comprehensive, and it's inclusive. I know this, as a teacher, because when I read

Luke's words I can meaningfully apply them to what I can see in Magritte's paintings. Luke offers evidence for his interpretation. I also know that Luke's interpretation is a good one because it fits within communal interpretations of Magritte's work. Further, Luke seems to have personally engaged with Magritte's paintings. From Luke's written paragraph, we can see that he wants to think about Magritte and the paintings, and Luke seems to own his interpretive insights and conclusions.

Conclusion

When interpretive occasions with groups of learners are successful many good things are happening. Learners are engaged in thinking and talking about art in which they are genuinely interested. Through examining that art and their thoughts and feelings about it, they are learning about the world and their responses to it. Individual students are building individual understandings, and they are also telling them to their classmates, who are listening. Students who actively and respectfully listen to one another are learning that there can be many different responses to the same thing or event. They are learning that one's insight can build on and respond to another's, and that eventually a group of interpreters is able to construct a shared understanding of what they see, and all interpreters leave the session with meanings relevant to their own lives.

Endnotes

1. For more principles of interpretation, see Chapter 4, *Interpreting Art*, in Barrett, T. (2000), *Criticizing art: Understanding the contemporary*. Mountain View, CA: Mayfield.
2. Docent training session, co-leader Susan Michael Barrett, Indianapolis Museum of Art, Indianapolis, Indiana, 1999.
3. Susan Michael Barrett, personal correspondence, January 15, 2000, about her experience at the Center for Education, Bradenton, Florida, in 1987.
4. Melissa Thayer-Webber, Devonshire Elementary School, Columbus City Schools, Columbus, Ohio, 1994.
5. Sands Montessori School, Cincinnati Public Schools, Cincinnati, Ohio, 1992.

References

Barrett, T. (1997). *Talking about student art*, Chapter 5, General Recommendations for Interactive Group Critiques. Worcester, MA: Davis.

Barrett, T. (2000). *Criticizing art: Understanding the contemporary*. Mountain View, CA: Mayfield.

Bontekoe, R. (1988). *Encyclopedia of aesthetics*. New York: Oxford University Press, 4:162–166.

Danto, A. (1981). *Transfiguration of the commonplace*. Cambridge, MA: Harvard University Press.

Eaton, M. (1988). *Basic issues in aesthetics*. Belmont, CA: Wadsworth.

Encyclopedia Britannica Online, René Magritte, http://search.eb.com/bol/ search?, January 28, 2000.

Foucault, M. (1983). *This is not a pipe*. Berkeley, CA: University of California Press.

Gablik, S. (1970). *Magritte*. New York: Thames and Hudson.

Hammacher, A. M. (1995). *René Magritte*. New York: Abrams.

Hampshire, S. (1966). Types of interpretation. In Kennick, W. E. (Ed.), *Art and philosophy: Readings in aesthetics*. New York: St. Martin's Press, 1979, pp. 200–205.

Hirsch, Jr., E. D. (1967). *Validity in interpretation*. New Haven, CT: Yale University Press.

Jacobs, Heidi Hayes. (1997). *Mapping the big picture: Integrating curriculum and assessment K–12*. Alexandria, VA: ASCD.

Janson, H. W. (1999). *History of art*, 5th ed. New York: Abrams.

Meltzer, I. (1979). The critical eye. Master's thesis, Ohio State University.

Meuris, J. (1994). *René Magritte*. Cologne, Germany: Benedikt Taschen.

Rorty, R. (1992). The pragmatist's progress. In Eco, U., *Interpretation and overinterpretation*. New York: Cambridge University Press, pp. 89–108.

Stecker, R. (1995). Relativism about interpretation. *Journal of aesthetics and art criticism*, 53(1), 14–18.

Van Proyen, M. (1991). A conversation with Donald Kuspit. *Artweek*, 5, September.

Wegman, W. (1982). *Man's best friend*. New York: Abrams.

Wegman, W. (1990). *William Wegman: Paintings, drawings, photographs, video tapes*, Kuntz, M., (Ed). New York: Abrams.

CONCLUSIONS AND FURTHER QUESTIONS

1. According to Barrett, what is the process of interpretation?
2. What is the relationship between interpreting and telling? Why is each of these important to our understandings of works of art?
3. What two types of questions does Barrett ask to guide discussions about artworks with students?
4. How can the interpretation help us understand the issues that are present in an artwork?
5. Interpretation can take place both individually and in a group. What are the benefits of communal interpretations? What are the benefits of personal interpretations? How do the two intersect?
6. How does Barrett suggest that we should judge interpretations of artworks?

7. Find an image of a contemporary artwork that interests you. Based on what you have read in Barrett's chapter, work through developing an interpretation. Describe what you learned during this process.

RESOURCES AND SUGGESTIONS
FOR FURTHER READING

Terry Barrett. *Criticizing photographs: An introduction to understanding images*. Mountain View, CA: Mayfield, 1990.

Michael Baxandall. *Patterns of intention: On the historical explanation of pictures*. New Haven, CT: Yale University Press, 1987.

Doug Blandy & Kristin G. Congdon (Eds.). *Pluralistic approaches to art criticism*. Bowling Green, OH: Bowling Green State University Popular Press, 1992.

Mihaly Csikszentmihalyi and Rick E. Robinson (Contributor). *The art of seeing: An interpretation of the aesthetic encounter*. Los Angeles, CA: J. Paul Getty Museum, 1991.

David Freedberg. *The power of images: Studies in the history and theory of response*. Chicago, IL: University of Chicago Press, 1991.

W. J. T. Mitchell. *Iconology: Image, text, ideology*. Chicago, IL: University of Chicago Press, 1987.

Griselda Pollock. *Differencing the canon: Feminist desire and the writing of art's histories*. New York: Routledge, 1999.

Mark W. Roskill. *The interpretation of pictures*. Amherst, MA: University of Massachusetts, 1989.

Linda Weintraub, Thomas McEvilley, & Arthur Coleman Danto. *Art on the edge and over: Searching for art's meaning in contemporary society 1970s–1990s*. Art Insights, Inc. 1997.

Useful sources for art criticism and interpretations include contemporary art magazines, journals, and periodicals such as *Art in America, ARTnews, New Art Examiner, Artforum, The Art Journal, Woman's Art Journal*, and *Flash Art*. Many of these are available in libraries.

In addition, good sources of journalistic art criticism include the *New York Times* (specifically the Friday and Sunday arts sections), *Newsweek, Time*, and *The Nation*.

CHAPTER 23

QUESTIONS AND EXPLORATIONS

1. In your experiences in school how was learning organized? For example, was the knowledge that you were expected to gain divided amongst a variety of subjects or was the knowledge integrated? How did the approach that was used help you understand the ways that knowledge is constructed? What might be the benefits and/or disadvantages of each approach?

2. Should the elementary classroom be a place where teachers use contemporary issues as a starting point for learning? Why or why not?

3. Explain what you see as the differences between an issues-based approach and a thematic approach.

4. What children's books and authors are you familiar with that deal with issues? Bring such a book to class to share.

5. What kinds of issues surface in contemporary elementary textbooks? What can contemporary art bring to the elementary curriculum?

The Dynamic Project, Contemporary Issues, and Integrative Learning

Doris M. Guay

If "everything is shaped by culture . . . [then] we . . . create our reality. We therefore contribute to it and can change it. This is an empowering way of living and of seeing ourselves in the world" (Staniszewski, 1995, p. 298). With knowledgeable and caring teachers, elementary age children can contribute to and cause change; teachers and children can together create a more positive reality that is based on the critical examination of community and social issues and the knowledge that individuals can make a difference in their world.

Contemporary popular media experiences provide even our youngest students with knowledge about technological innovation, scientific discovery, and both the ideal and darker sides of human nature. Elkind (1995) reminds us that children are exposed to much of the same public and private worlds as adults. They are exposed to images of the real and unreal, images that often distort the true stories of our environments.[1] Through popular media and conversations in their homes and schools, children become aware of many critical issues (i.e., prejudice, consumerism, disease, substance abuse, violence, environmental destruction) and the disturbing consequences of these issues in society. The media also exposes them to persuasive messages to consume and to images which covertly establish cultural values. These values, which I claim are often materialistic and prejudicial, need to be critically examined and counter-balanced. An important job for elementary teachers is to help children understand contemporary social, political, economic, psychological, and artistic issues. In addition, teachers should examine the genealogy of these issues, assess their impact on our communities, and realize that children can, as caring individuals, now and in the future, bring about the changes that make our world a more equitable place. Both children and teachers can be change makers (Giroux, 1992).

When we, as teachers, consider what should be taught in an art education curriculum, we frequently attempt to maintain what is perceived of as the innocence of childhood. Our choices for art curricula, because of the history of this field and the easy availability of quick how-to project books, often promote idealized, imaginative, or playful views of our world and suggest that art making should be used for enjoyment and therapeutic purposes. Non-art text and journal recommendations for integrating the curriculum frequently prescribe art as a form of decoration and illustration or superficially link art projects to the non-art curriculum in ways that honor neither the subjects nor the vast curiosity, mind power, and knowledge that children bring to the classroom.

In marked contrast to this, contemporary textbook series for elementary level children's literature and reading, social studies, science, health, and language arts curricula introduce issues of political, cultural, racial, age, and social difference, indifference, prejudice, and some of the less proud events and omissions in history. They address the body, disease, addictions, and abuse. Bringing the ideas found in contemporary art into the elementary classroom can open a space for deeper discussion of the human causes and human consequences of these issues, thereby creating an opportunity for meaningful and empathetic learning. The artist Elizabeth Catlett (Catlett quoted in Witzling, 1991) tells us that "true art always come[s] from cultural necessity" (p. 340) and that,

> Art will not create social change, but it can provoke thought and prepare us for change. Art can tell us what we do not see, sometimes what we do not want to see, what we do not realize about life, about sensitivity and crassness. What is ordinary may be seen as spectacular. What seems ugly may appear quite beautiful and vice versa. What seems trivial may become important depending on how it is presented by the artist. (p. 341)

Contemporary art brings us an awareness of and confrontation with today's issues. In this chapter I suggest bringing together the didactic, informative materials found in elementary texts with the stories, meanings, and messages of artworks and the questions, awareness, and concerns these raise. Such an approach brings about positive integrated learning that enables teachers and children to build a community of learners who not only care from a distance but engage with and extend into their environments to deal with issues and solve problems. This view of integrative learning promotes relationships of caring and hope through community engagement and real world experiences.

Integrated Learning

On a daily basis aesthetic images entice children to be discontented with what they have and to want more or different material goods, life styles, and personal appearances. The flow of images and narratives sets moral, material, and identity values while anesthetizing children (Chapman, 2000a) to the insidious destruction of personal critical thought and choice making. If we wish for our world, environment, and people to survive, students must learn to critically think, view, and discuss, to value self and not prejudiciously create "others." They need to become aware of biases, prejudices, and community concerns and to work with others to peacefully create needed change. Chapman (2000b) concluded that we and our students need some perspective on the civilization we're creating and the role of imagery in persuading us what to value, think, acquire, throw away, cherish.

Integrative curricula create empathetic relationships and real world understandings through comprehensive learning units that extend from the classroom into the community and the community into the classroom. Such learning engages the hearts and minds of elementary children in ways that help them make sense of life experiences and that help them develop understanding and empathetic, or as needed, oppositional, critical relationships with their environments. This form of integrated learning engages children in discussions of the serious, raises awareness of issues in today's world, and investigates the genealogy of these issues in history. It engages children cooperatively and collaboratively, allowing time for understanding to evolve.

Recognizing art as integral to the lives of people currently, historically, and culturally, equips teachers and children to work with the ideas and messages of artists, eliciting thought, understanding, and empathy. Using contemporary art as the core of, or as a catalyst for, integrative curriculum avoids the misconceived and antiquated, but continuing practices of making imitative school-art products that, when posted on bulletin boards or taken home, perpetuate a definition of art and art education that prevents true understanding and experience of art (Giles, 1999; Efland, 1976). Art projects that decorate, illustrate, or signify rote learning in non-art areas, or products that imitate the sacred and secular beliefs and customs of people of non-Eurocentric cultures, do little to help students to make sense of, or critically think about, experiences. They do little to give students a critical voice, to empower them to make change. In contemporary integrative practice, teachers understand art as a product of society and culture that communicates the values, experiences, and beliefs of people. They understand art education as a discipline that engages children's minds and hearts in meaningful inquiry and empathetic understanding. Children sensitively discovering, interpretively analyzing, and knowledgeably solving problems are our hope for the future.

A Planning Process

To integrate curricula in ways that honor art and non-art subject matter learning objectives and the human potential of children requires knowledge of art, the specific children's needs, curricula within a number of disciplines including art, and community problems, issues, needs, and concerns. Integrating curricula means designing rich, community-interactive, interdisciplinary thematic units that provide opportunities for discovery, delight, and learning. The tasks of planning for integrated curricula involve teachers developing questions that cause children to think about, analyze, and evaluate their experiences, whatever their source, and designing a framework for art learning and involvement with actual environments that extend experience and make community difference. In analyzing the integrative process that I used for many years in the Arts Impact schools in Columbus, Ohio, seven major steps or phases emerged:

1. Either the art and/or the elementary classroom teacher recognizes the needs for and possibilities of social/political action and human caring within the elementary curriculum.

2. Teachers search for, interpret, and research the contextual origin and functions of artworks and children's literature including stories and poems to inspire and extend personal and reading, science, social studies, or health textbook ideas. They design integrative learning possibilities that engage children in caring experiences of community.

3. Teachers brainstorm and plan together, each sharing resources and ideas. Each commits to planned learning actions with participating children. Each knows and understands the curricular concepts (big ideas) and conceptual questions with which the other teacher(s) will work.

4. The art and/or classroom teacher(s) present the "what if" idea possibilities inspired by the artworks and literature to the children and to community collaborators, asking them to consider the "what else" possibilities. Teachers, collaborators, and children extend ideas and plan learning actions.

5. Teachers and students organize, develop a matrix/time line, and make needed contacts for community interaction and action.

6. Teachers alone and together as a team follow planned learning experiences with the children.

7. Children and teachers, at the end of the lesson/activities, reflect and critique their accomplishments interpretively and plan for follow up.

The Integrative Curricula Planning Process

Once the experiences and needs of the children are assessed and it is determined that a broad, comprehensive, and integrative unit is desirable, teachers current with news events, critical texts, and professional literature readily recognize societal issues and concerns. Extending the list of those mentioned earlier, these can include habitat destruction, human loneliness and isolation, family change, injustice, intolerance, and inequity. Teachers also need to understand the diverse views and the political and economic interests that underlie many of the problems. Entry points and possibilities for art and non-art curricula overlap. In my research I found that issues in current elementary texts include: relating to people of different ages, races, genders, and socioeconomic classes; biases and prejudices; homelessness; family and belonging; the first peoples; the needs for community of diverse peoples; conservation of natural environments; rain forests, ecology, interdependence, recycling and cooperation; war, the depression, and industrial expansion (agriculture to industry); the human body, drugs, alcohol, tobacco, and AIDS. In the first grade social studies text, *I Know a Place* (Armento, et al, 1997), a unit is focused on "asking why." This is a core question for both teachers and children at every grade level. Teachers engaged in planning for integrative learning ask why the issues and problems exist and help each other understand their experiences of these issues, the children's experiences of these issues, and the possibilities for positive interconnected learning as understood by each team member.

Researching and Making Connections

When an art teacher works closely with an elementary classroom teacher, each researches areas of personal expertise. Each brings understanding as well as research and interpretive skills to the integrative-learning team. Research and interpretive study are needed to determine whether a work of art meaningfully interconnects with curricula ideas or concepts taught in the elementary classroom. Resources found, interpreted, and researched are shared informally and/or in a team meeting. This generates early excitement and provides hinges for more ideas.

Working alone on an integrative-learning unit is also possible. If the elementary classroom teacher works alone, he or she will find that art references such as very current art history texts, visual art anthologies, and the *Art Index* are invaluable resources for discovering art that extends unit ideas. Internet art resources and articles in both art education journals and art periodicals are also good sources. The art teacher working alone will find current children's textbooks and the teachers' guides for these, as well as helpful librarians specializing in children's books and library-search data bases. Searching demands time and persistence. The resulting resources and contextual information will, however, greatly inspire and extend teaching ideas.

Art educator Michael Parsons (1998) declares that all integration of art with other subject matter must be based on an interpretation of the art. Without knowledge of what the artwork means and how it functions, or of the interplay of art with the experiences and commitments of the artist, the ideas within the art integrative unit will remain shallow. Selected artworks and stories serve as references that engage our thought about issues of concern. They help tell cultural stories and they serve as catalysts for the children to communicate through art and story and to engage with local communities or global environments in service learning.

Brainstorming and Planning

Individual teacher research precedes collaborative planning. Early in the process written and oral communication among teachers provides direction and cohesion. Teacher guides to textbooks should be accessible to and used by the art educator. As children's literature and visual art resources are discovered, they may be recommended for purchase by the school library. Planning that takes advantage of a library's resources is especially productive. Planning begins with the question, "What do we want the children to learn?" and continues with questions such as, "Why is this important?" When learning objectives are chosen, the questions become: "How might children learn this?" "How might they engage with community in a meaningful way?" "How might children learn that they can make a difference through their engagement with art and community?" "How can they make a difference now?" Finally, teachers planning integrative units consider the question, "How will we know the children have learned, have thoughtfully pondered the ideas and realized that their actions can bring about change now and in the future?"

Bringing the "What-if" Idea to the Children and to Community Collaborators

Involving students, from the beginning, in a community-based project and sharing thoughts about possible engagements and learning outcomes is important to the planning process. Asking children to brainstorm ideas may seem surprising; however, I find that they share many great ideas and inviting their participation is most productive. A teacher may present a partial idea, which the children, through the brainstorming process, complete with great clarity and thought. "What if?" "Who has ever?" and "Why might?" are good discussion starters. Teachers do not need to control this process. They can listen, question, offer possibilities, and rely on the children to expand choices. This step empowers and encourages communication and problem solving. Introducing relevant artworks to this process helps children discover issues and problems and encourages further discussion. "Are there things we can do to make a difference in our community?" is the important question. A similar process can involve community collaborators separately or with the children. Discussing teachers' idea(s) with the children and community collaborators facilitates the elaboration and finalization of planning.

Organizing and Contacting

Once ideas are generated, solid learning objectives and teaching strategies must be formed, resources gathered. Some ideas may be more workable than others. During this step, teachers work on the development of broad learning questions that engage thought, experience, speculation, empathy, and imagination. Children may assist in making necessary contacts and may, as appropriate, also research art and other materials to enhance the unit. It is important at this stage of the planning process to also consider possibilities for culminating events and for public information to be executed at the end of the unit. School board contacts and community newspaper contacts may need to be made.

Following of Planned Learning Experiences

Commitment to the planned learning matrix/time line is an essential aspect of team teaching. A broad, multifaceted project requires extraordinary dedication that may cause stress. Honest discussion of concerns and stresses either one-on-one or as a team helps to resolve problems. It is not unusual to assist one another with resources or to modify the timeline of in-depth projects. Being understanding and remaining focused on the possibilities for in-depth learning that will ensue enables the team spirit to continue. When teaming with others, communication for coordination prevents many frustrations. Communication, in writing, person-to-person, even through quick phone calls, is key. Know all the team teachers' preferences for the mode of communication, times, and places and use them.

Reflection and Critique

A clearer perspective on learning is gained when time is set aside to talk about, write about, and communicate with the children about their art and their experiences. This phase of the integrative process asks teachers and children to reflect on their personal learning and accomplishments, and to consider the possibility of follow-up or related involvement. Reflection needs to be an honest endeavor. What has been accomplished? What could have been stronger? Were the objectives learned? The school community should be informed about the integrative community project. This may involve, for example, having children and teachers present their work at a school board meeting, or a photographic essay of the events mounted in the board of education building or the school office. Some school districts encourage or even require principals to invite newspaper coverage. Certainly, school newsletters could tell the children's learning story to parents.

An Example from Practice

If children contribute to society, learn through engagement with cultural problems, and critically think about community issues, art education will look and feel different from many of the familiar "school art" paradigms (Efland, 1976). The example that I write about in this section is designed to engage children for several weeks in the study of art and non-art subject matter through visual art, literature, and community service. I have included a number of ideas and possible avenues of involvement. Intended to model thought processes as much as to provide the reader with materials and references to take into the classroom, this unit is described through an introduction and contains suggestions for relevant artworks and children's literature.

The first-grade unit takes children to a nearby senior citizen home to communicate and learn stories about people who can be stereotyped as being on the fringes of society, often overlooked because they no longer contribute to the economy. In what ways can we learn from them, respect them, and celebrate them? The sample unit was designed to engage and raise the consciousness of children through artworks that pose questions about society's values, fictions, and norms. The unit, as Grossberg (1994) suggests, "proposes that [children] gain some understanding of their own involvement in the world and in the making of their own future" (p. 18). It was designed to provide a perspective and counterbalance to media representations that influence our worldview.

The Hands of Friendship: A First-Grade Unit

While some children live with and are cared for by grandparents, others live at a distance from and have little contact with people who are special in their lives but very much older than they are. Popular media often project an unrealistic picture of elderly people, portraying them as sarcastic, cynical, or helpless, or just as fictively, vivacious and carefree. Young children, meeting with residents of a senior complex and/or perhaps a group of invited neighbors of the school, are asked through this unit, to re-form images distorted through market driven advertising or by the multiplicity of visual misrepresentations employed by the entertainment industry. This unit is offered to promote intergenerational friendships and provide a life-world picture that challenges conventional media stories. Young children, partnered with a senior citizen, have the opportunity to learn about and from their partner. Seniors provide a true voice as children ask questions, listen, and share. The understandings developed through this unit can be extended to individuals and groups other than senior citizens.

A search for possibilities that might enhance and extend first graders' learning in several non-art subjects were important considerations in the development of this unit. For instance, first grade reading texts, *Here We Grow, The Very Thing,* and *Books! Books! Books!* (Aoki et al., 1993) all include relevant learning ideas. They provide units with themes that deal with friendship, growth (including aging), and differences. The *Your Health* series (Gibbons, Middleton, and Ozias, 1999) first-grade text considers factors that make each person unique and includes strategies for learning how to show respect and be friendly. A number of language-arts texts for the first grade emphasize skills in focusing attention and responding to a speaker by thinking about what has been said, asking questions, contributing ideas, and retelling what is in one's head. Asking "Why?", learning how to be a friend, and working together are emphasized in social studies units in the first-grade text, *I Know A Place* (Armento, et al., 1997). These objectives are all important to the art-understanding and communication objectives of this unit. Additionally this unit would aim to challenge children to revise their understanding of what it means to be older and to appreciate and value the processes of human growth and aging.

Possibilities for the Artworks Gallery

The use of many artworks rather than one or two open up many possibilities for learning about older people as seen through the eyes and minds of artists. The artworks below provide different entry points to discussions and interpretive viewing. *Buttons* (1982), a self-portrait by Elizabeth Layton tells us that she is a dynamic, strong, independent woman. In *Double Portrait of the Artist in Time* (1935), Helen Lundeberg reflects on her own growth and change. *Checkered House* (1943) and *Hoosik Falls, NY in Winter* reveal life memories of Grandma Moses who did not begin painting until she was in her seventies. Photographic portraits, one of *My Grandmother* (1976) standing in her kitchen, by Richard Hill, and another of an eccentric-haired *The Grandmother* (1987), by Meinrad Craighead, reveal artists' memories of their grandmother. In The *Banjo Lesson* (1893), Henry Ossawa Tanner reveals loving, learning, and relating; and, collective thoughts about aging are revealed by the stories and pictures of the performance works *Whisper, the Waves, the Wind* (1984) and *Crystal Quilt* (1986) by Suzanne Lacy. Other possible artworks include *F. K. Boston's* (1984), by Nicholas Nixon; *Self Portrait on Geary Street* (1958), by Imogene Cunningham; *Last Sickness* (1984), by Alice Neel; and *Box #122* (1988), by Lucas Samaras, which shows a form of an iconographic self-portrait box.

Possibilities for Integration of Children's Literature

Coco Can't Wait by Taro Gomi (1984) is a story about young and old sharing and appreciating each other. *Hattie and the Fox* by Mem Fox (1987) offers a message of doing something when one sees something that isn't right. *How Does it Feel to be Old?* by Norma Farber (1988) and *I Know a Lady* by Charlotte Zolotow (1984) are both delightful tales of children learning about and sharing the life-world of senior people. In one the child copes with the death of a senior friend. *Together* by George Ella Lyons (1989) shows how two friends can do anything together and *My Friends* by Taro Gomi (1990) shows how one can learn from friends.

Questions that could Guide Art Critical/Historical and Life-world Learning Through this Unit

In this unit, questions form learning objectives. Children and teachers work together to understand the answers to the objective questions throughout the unit. Strategies to teach toward the understanding of the answers are left to the expertise of each individual teacher. Questions may be used to assess the children's knowledge and experience. As important, during a unit, questions help children discover what they know or need to find out, and how their experiences, ideas, and opinions are shared with or differ from those of others. Questions set the stage for careful looking at works of art and for speculation about stories to be read. Both art-historical and critical inquiry are based on questions asked with and about the artworks in the gallery collected for the unit. Questions share discoveries and assess new experiences and learning. They are important during all phases of the integrative unit. The following are examples of question/objectives developed for this first-grade unit:

1. What does it mean to be a friend or have a friend? Can we be friends with someone who is very different from us? How can each of us be a friend?

2. Where does our thinking about people who are different from ourselves come from? How can we come to understand more about people who are different from ourselves or who live differently than we do? Why might this be important?

3. How can we make a difference in the life of another person? In what ways might people make a difference in our lives? Good differences? Bad differences?

4. Why is it important to tell our life-world stories and ask others to tell their stories? What might we learn when we do this? What stories do we have to share? What do we want to know more about? Do we like some of the same things as our senior partner? Some different things?

5. What are older people like in the television shows you watch? In advertisements? In what ways are our senior friend-partners alike and different from

television seniors? How can we tell their stories truthfully? What questions might we want to ask our senior partners in order to find out more about them?

6. What do artists, through the artworks in our gallery, tell us about people who are older? How are the older people in our art similar or different from us? From each other? If we could use our imaginations and walk into the artwork, what else might we see? What might we hear or smell? What might we ask the senior people we are with in the artwork?

7. What is Elizabeth Layton telling us about herself? Who are we inside? Outside? Why might Imogene Cunningham have surrounded her self-portrait with broken light bulbs? How does a sunny day make us feel? Why is Cunningham standing in sunshine?

8. What stories might *Checkered House* and *Hoosik Falls, NY in Winter* tell about Grandma Moses life-world? How is our life-world different?

9. What is Henry Ossawa Tanner telling us about people who are poor? What is richness and poorness? Why might this grandfather not have much money? What did he have that is very important?

Many questions are prompted by the teachers' critical inquiry and contextual research and the subsequent understanding of the artists' meanings and messages in the specific artworks chosen for the unit. Teachers formulate questions/objectives based on the needs of particular classes of children and the subject area being taught for integrative learning.

Possibilities for Engagement in Art Making

The children's initial visit to a senior partner could be facilitated by their creation of an iconic self-portrait box. This would be a work containing objects and pictures chosen by each child to tell personal stories. The self-portrait box references the box sculptures of any number of artists, including Lucas Samaras. It could be the children's means of introducing themselves. Through the children, seniors could also be introduced to Elizabeth Layton's self-portrait or to other portraits of senior people. The children could ask the senior about how they are similar to or different from the portrait shown. Children could tell their senior friends the stories they learned about the portrait and the things they discovered by looking carefully. As a studio project, the children's and the seniors, hands could be molded and plaster cast. The hands together could be displayed in many ways as a "hands of friendship" installation/exhibit. Art works depicting hands from prehistoric through Renaissance to contemporary times could be shared as the importance and meanings of hands are discussed. Returning to the classroom, children could create artist books retelling the stories they have learned about their senior partners. The books could be presented as gifts and conversation initiators during a subsequent visit. Any number of joint projects are possible, including creation of intergenerational murals, memory paintings, memory quilts, or even life size soft sculpture self portraits. Senior friends and children could find and share stories and meanings in works of art brought from the classroom gallery. Seniors could help children write the stories they discover together. Many senior complexes employ recreation directors or activity directors. This unit solicits their cooperation and possibly engages the seniors in shared art projects. A representative of the senior center, which could be one of the residents, should be included in all planning.

Art to Experience

Caine and Caine (1997) emphasize the need for students to acquire both "intellectual understanding and generate felt meaning" (p. 114). To encourage the integrative learning described in this paper, children engage in life-world experiences. They discover problems, ask genuine questions, and think about their own participation with others in creating a more equitable world. Artworks are the core of this learning. With their art, artists delight us and raise our understanding and conscience. They counterbalance popular media representations and misrepresentations. Artworks provoke thought and understanding as children consider them in the context of why the artist may have created them and what the artist may be communicating about their own world, their concerns, and their lives. When understanding of the historical, artistic, and cultural contexts of artworks and the life-world connections that teachers make with them is conveyed to elementary level children, they are encouraged to reveal their own thoughts and experiences. Through this process, children identify, challenge, and rewrite (Giroux, 1994) their representations of who they are, of culture, and of the ethics of need and greed.

Young children are capable of connecting to others and to the environment through stories and poems and the stories artists tell with their art. Older children are capable of understanding the motives behind cultural messages and to not only resist them but to work with others to create new/different ones. It is important that children imagine and work to realize the possibilities of a world that values other than material possessions and cultural practices that disrespect and destroy.

Conclusions

As Staniszewski (1995) states, "The most important artists of our time are visionary in that they continue to challenge us to see our world differently. . . . Artists prepare the mind and spirit for new ideas—new ways of seeing" (p. 289). The images and narratives of integrative curricula, when developed with an art core, initiate and foster thought, understanding, and problem solving, and communicate respect of others and the environment. Integrative curricula for contemporary education must be based upon "compelling ideas, meanings, and purposes" (Caine and Caine, 1997, p. 258). It must invite students to discover problems and create meaning through multiple sources of information including both artistic and real-world experiences. Teachers are choice makers for student learning. With integrative curricula that honor the meanings and messages of art and artists, images and narratives, imagination and possibilities, teachers join together to help students interpret and understand the multiple representations of culture, to communicate views of possibility in the world, and to make changes in their immediate world.

Endnote

1. The term environments is used comprehensively in this paper to include people, mass media, nature, and human-made entities.

References

Aoki, E.M., Flood, J., Hoffman, J.V., Lapp, D., Macias, A.H., Martinez, M., McCallum, A., Priestley, M., Roser, N., Smith, C.B., Strong, W., Teale, W.H., Temple, C., Tinajero, J.V., Webb, A.W., & Williams, P.E. (1993). *Reading/Language Arts Series*. New York: MacMillan/McGraw-Hill.

Armento, B.J., Klor de Alva, J.J., Nash, G.B., Salter, C.L., Wilson, L.E., & Wixson, K.K. (1997). *I know a place*. Boston, MA: Houghton Mifflin.

Caine, R.N. & Caine, G. (1997). *Education on the edge of possibility*. Alexandria, VA: Association for Supervision and Curriculum Development.

Chapman, L.H. (2000a, April). *Toward civic competence in art*. Paper presented at the meeting of the National Art Education Association, Los Angeles, CA.

Chapman, L.H. (2000b, April). *Arts of aesthetic persuasion in contemporary life*. Paper presented at the meeting of the National Art Education Association, Los Angeles, CA.

Efland, A. (1976). The school art style. *Studies in Art Education, 17*(2), 37–44.

Elkind, D. (1995). School and family in the postmodern world. *Phi Delta Kappan, 77*(1), 8–14.

Farber, N. (1988). *How does it feel to be old*. New York: Dalton.

Fox, M. (1987). *Hattie and the fox*. New York: Bradbury.

Gibbons, C., Middleton, K., & Ozias, J.M. (1999). *Your health*. Stockton, CA: Harcourt Brace.

Giles, A. (1999, Winter). School art versus meaningful artistically authentic art education. *N. A. E. A. Advisory*.

Giroux, H.A. (1992). *Border crossings: Cultural workers and the politics of education*. New York: Routledge.

Gomi, T. (1984). *Coco can't wait*. New York: Morrow.

Gomi, T. (1990). *My friends*. San Francisco, CA: Chronical Books.

Grossberg, L. (1994). Introduction: Bringin' it all back home—Pedagogy and cultural studies. In Giroux, H.A. & McLaren, P. (Eds). *Between borders: Pedagogy and the politics of cultural studies* (pp. 1–25). New York: Routledge.

Lyons, G. E. (1989). *Together*. New York: Orchard Books.

MacLachlan, P. (1980). *Through grandpa's eyes*. New York: Harper and Row.

Parsons, M. (1998). Integrated curriculum and our paradigm of cognition in the arts. *Studies in Art Education, 39*(2), 103–116.

Staniszewski, M.A. (1995). *Believing is seeing, creating the culture of art*. New York: Penguin Books.

Witzling, M.R. (Ed.) (1991). Elizabeth Catlett. In *Voicing our visions: Writings by women artists* (pp. 334–348). New York: The Women's Press.

Zolotow, C.S. (1984). *I know a lady*. New York: Greenwillow.

CONCLUSIONS AND FURTHER QUESTIONS

1. What is integrated learning? What is Guay's proposed framework for integrated learning? What should it prepare students for? In what ways is it different from other ways of approaching learning? Describe the ways that an integrated approach intersects with an issues-based approach?

2. What are some of the problems that Guay sees with the way art typically has been used in the elementary curriculum? How is this connected to perceiving children as innocent?

3. What possiblities emerge when the art teacher and the classroom teacher work together using such an approach? What can each bring to the relationship?

4. What does it take for students to be involved in an integrated approach? In what ways are students part of an integrated approach?

5. What are some of the issues that Guay thinks arise from using an integrated approach? Have you ever taught with or learned about any of these issues? Pick two examples from the list that Guay provides and discuss how you might use them in an elementary classroom.

6. How is an integrated approach to education related to ideas of community?

7. How does Guay redefine art and art education for teachers?

RESOURCES AND SUGGESTIONS
FOR FURTHER READING

Cecelia Alvarado (Ed.). *In our own way: How anti-bias work shapes our lives*. St. Paul, MN: Redleaf Press, 1999.

Doug Blandy & Kristin G. Congdon (Eds.). *Pluralistic approaches to art criticism*. Bowling Green, OH: Bowling Green State University Press, 1992.

Children's Book Press, San Francisco, CA publishes multicultural literature for children. They specialize in the publication of bilingual English and Spanish books and stories from Hispanic, native American, African-American and Asian-American cultures.

The *Conflict Resolution Consortium*, run by the University of Colorado, offers information on resolving disputes around a variety of potentially divisive issues. (*www.crinfo.org*)

Frances Ann Day. *Multicultural voices in contemporary literature: A resource for teachers.* Portsmouth, NH: Heinemann, 1999.

Louise Derman-Sparks, Carol Brunson Phillips, & Asa G. Hilliard III, *Teaching/learning anti-racism: A developmental approach.* New York, NY: Teachers College Press, 1997.

Express Diversity focuses on diversity with respect to disabilities for grades K–12. From VSA Arts in Washington, DC. (*www.vsarts.org/*)

Carmen Lomas Garza. *Family pictures.* San Francisco, CA: Children's Book Press, 1993.

Carmen Lomas Garza. *A piece of my heart/Pedacito de mi corazon. The art of Carmen Lomas Garza.* New York: New Press, 1994.

Gender Respect Workbook contains a number of great ideas on how to teach nonsexist behavior to elementary-age children. It is available from Childswork/Childplay (800–962–1141.)

Lucy R. Lippard. *Mixed blessings: New art in a multicultural America.* New York: Pantheon Books, 1990.

Alice McIntyre & Christine E. Sleeter. *Making meaning of whiteness: Exploring the racial identity of white teachers.* Albany, NY: State University of New York Press, 1997.

Sonia Nieto. *The light in their eyes: Creating multicultural learning communities.* New York, NY: Teachers College Press, 1999.

CHAPTER 24

1. What is meant by the idea of commemoration? What types of people, events, and ideas do we choose to commemorate? What do we leave out of our commemorations? What are some forms of commemoration? How do memorials help us form our cultural identities?

2. Have you ever commemorated a person, event, or idea? What form did your commemoration take? Why?

3. Choose an example of an object that has commemoration as one of its primary functions. Write a paragraph about the ways that the object communicates information about the subject that it is commemorating. How do you know that the object is commemorative?

4. What is the relationship between commemoration and history?

5. What is the relationship between commemoration and everyday life?

Elementary Instruction through Postmodern Art

Melody K. Milbrandt

Over the past decade contemporary art education has moved beyond the notion of art as purely recreational or decorative to a discipline based study of art (DBAE) that consists of studio production, art criticism, art history, and aesthetics. This comprehensive approach to the discipline of art encourages students with a variety of learning styles and strengths to participate and engage in art learning. Yet, there is no evidence to suggest that because students enjoy creating art, or even talking about art, that they necessarily view art as important to their lives in the "real world." Eisner (1988) suggests that "both curriculum and teaching should help students internalize what they have learned and relate it to life outside of school" (p. 29).

The challenge for educators today is to create supportive classroom environments and relationships that foster a high level of active intellectual inquiry about a subject. In art this means a shift in focus from the art product to include a more holistic focus on the artistic process as well. In contemporary art education, students should become engaged not only in producing works of art but also in constructing meaning behind the work. Thinking reflectively helps students gain a better understanding of how ideas evolve. Discussing how their art work relates to their life and society helps students view their own art work in a cultural context and develop a sense of identity as they gain an understanding of historical time. Discussing how their art work relates to their life, society, and time helps students view their own art work in a cultural context and connect scaffolds of learning across disciplines for more holistic and effective learning. Through art, students synthesize established knowledge, from a variety of disciplines and experiences, in the creation of new meaning.

Postmodern Art Content in Art Education

Postmodernism, as a critique of society, provides logical content for instruction that is personally and socially meaningful. Postmodern art raises current issues and problems that are connected to students' lives beyond school, making it favorable content for the development of critical thinking skills through in-depth discussions and exploration of meaning in art. As students examine the issues embedded in much postmodern art they may better understand the contemporary world in which they live. Through an investigation of contemporary art, important social issues may be addressed which prepare students to live as empowered responsible citizens.

Postmodern art, like contemporary life, reflects multiple, overlapping perspectives and values. Rather than mirroring a traditional linear, scientific, or modernist view of the world, postmodern art embraces a holistic approach that has been characterized as eclectic and sometimes chaotic. Many postmodern artists have rejected the modernist myth of the artist as a solitary hero and have instead defined themselves in the context of society. An understanding of the value of this relationship between artists and society may open doors for redefining the function of art in society and for redefining the role of art in education. Postmodernism may offer the means to move art education from a peripheral, somewhat elitist, modernist position to one that integrates and defines itself as interactive and relational.

Though the eclectic nature of postmodernism resists a single definition or label, it may be useful to consider as its major focus, critiques of society. Such critiques raise issues with viewers, often causing them to question or examine their cultural assumptions and biases. Some postmodern artists deconstruct or devalue dominant social attitudes, other reconstructivist artists work toward possible solutions to problems in contemporary society. In either case, postmodern art questions society and presents alternative views through art. According to the art historians, Wood, Frascina, Harris, and Harrison (1993), these social critiques cluster into three major areas: (1) a critique of class, race, and gender; (2) a critique of historical or autobiographical narrative; and (3) a critique of the myth of originality. A fourth critique, of ecological or social issues, also often arises (Gablik, 1991). These four critiques may serve as a framework for content and the selection of artists for building a contemporary art curriculum.

A Model for Teaching Elementary Art

Due to the need to meet district, state, and national standards that reflect a broad content area in the visual arts, it could be argued that an entire curriculum devoted to contemporary art may not be possible or desirable at the elementary level. Yet, the benefits of developing strategies for a socially engaged curriculum, through the study of contemporary art, are numerous. A model elementary art curriculum unit utilizing instruction to investigate the work of postmodern artists engages students in content learning that not only enlarges their knowledge of contemporary art but also positively influences their commonly held beliefs or attitudes regarding the function of art in society. Encouraging students to view art as a vehicle not only for personal expression or decoration but also as a means of providing social critiques of substance, may develop a new more sophisticated perception of the visual arts.

The following artists and artworks can provide examples for addressing postmodern art in an upper elementary curriculum unit of lessons:

1. A critique of class, race, and gender can be addressed through lessons about artists such as Maya Lin, a young Chinese-American woman who, at age 20, designed the *Vietnam War Memorial*, and endured much public criticism due to her Asian heritage, age, and gender.

2. A critique of historic/autobiographical narrative can be addressed through the work of Faith Ringgold and her storyquilts, such as *Tar Beach*. Ringgold uses the quilt media to express stories of her childhood in a traditional African-American woman's art form.

3. A critique of originality can be examined through Barbara Kruger's artworks such as *Buy Me, and I'll Change Your Life*. Kruger appropriates the style and images from the mass media and advertising to critique advertising and consumerism.

4. A critique of ecological and social issues is apparent in an installation called *Sea Full of Clouds, What Can I Do?* by Ciel Bergman and Nancy Merrill. The two women artists collaborated by collecting trash along the beach in Santa Barbara, and then created an interactive installation that conveyed the ecological dangers inherent in what they had found. Instead of a reception at the beginning of the exhibit there was a reception at the end of the exhibit and an open forum to discuss the environmental issues raised. Bergman and Merrill's installation emerged as community activism that involved people from all walks of life to address environmental concerns.

It is possible, and often probable, that artists' works deal with more than one critique. Yet, such an instructional structure allows teachers to present similar themes or topics for discussion in different contexts and from different points of view. In a postmodern curriculum, student learning may best be described as progressing in a spiral rather than in a straight line. Information and themes are periodically revisited in order to build in-depth knowledge and develop higher-level thinking skills.

Postmodern content, by its very nature, raises questions that involve the viewer in a search for meaningful connections to issues important for learning beyond the instructional context. Connecting real world issues to strategies in more traditional discipline based art education provides meaningful content for students to build deep conceptual understandings about life through art education.

A Narrative Lesson Example: Maya Lin

In this narrative account, a critique of historical narratives and issues of class, race, and gender overlap in a lesson based on Maya Lin and the *Vietnam War Memorial* presented to fifth-grade students. The issues surrounding the *Vietnam War Memorial* exemplify postmodern concerns. In this lesson, fifth graders first looked at the memorial, considered the context in which it was created, and discussed aesthetic issues, such as the importance of form and function. They identified other commemorative sculptures in our nation and community and then created their own commemorative artwork. The teacher began the lesson by explaining that memorials or commemorative art works were built to honor a person or event that our society deems important to hold in our collective memory. Such commemorative works are crucial for us as a culture because they help us remember and understand who we are by the values or actions we choose to honor.

After viewing slides of the *Vietnam Memorial*, the teacher explained that the designer, Maya Lin, was a young architecture student at Yale University when she submitted her proposal for the memorial to a national juried competition in Washington, D.C., in 1982. Maya Lin's design was selected from a blind review of 1421 entries. Eight male judges unanimously chose her design. Initially Lin's winning design was praised by the Commission of Fine Arts because it was apolitical and modernistic (*Current Biography Yearbook,* 1993). However, once Lin's gender, Chinese-American heritage, and undergraduate student status became known, a movement began to block the construction of the wall (Hess, 1983). While Maya Lin won the competition for her design and received the $20,000 in prize money, she was given little public recognition.

The art teacher led the class discussion about the initial negative public reaction to the *Vietnam War Memorial* by asking students their opinions of such questions as: "Why do you think there was a controversy surrounding the *Vietnam War Memorial?*" "Why do you think there was disapproval of Maya Lin's design?" "Why do you think Maya Lin was treated poorly by some people?" Students knew that the Vietnam War had been fought in Asia, and that it was an unpopular war, yet they were generally surprised that as a United States citizen, Maya Lin was publicly attacked for her Asian heritage. This led to a discussion of the nature of prejudice and the fact that it is often based in stereotypical myths.

After discussing the historical context of the *Vietnam Memorial* and the poor treatment of Maya Lin as a young artist, the teacher turned the discussion to the visual qualities of the memorial. The students discussed the visual qualities of the artwork and the emotions it communicated. The teacher asked, "Why do you think she use polished granite?" One student observed that because of the highly polished surface the viewer's reflection became a part of the memorial, overlaying the names of the dead or missing in action. Other students thought that the reflection added to the emotional impact of the work. One student commented, "Maybe it's very plain so we see only the names as the most important part of the artwork." Another suggested, "Maybe it looks dark to remind us of the graves underground," and another thought the memorial was "pointed to remind us that war hurts people." Most students thought the memorial communicated a sad or somber mood. The teacher reminded students of the aesthetic categories discussed earlier in the year and asked students to consider the best aesthetic stance for the memorial. After a brief debate of several views, students agreed that it was a good work of art from several aesthetic viewpoints. The students concluded,

> If we didn't know it was a memorial it would best fit the formalist category, because at first the artist seems most concerned with elements and principles of design. Since we know it's a memorial, then we know it has a function in society, so it might best fit into the functionalist category. It also has a strong emotional impact. Once you realize all the names on it for people who died, it is very expressive.

The teacher supported the students' reasons for their aesthetic judgments and the discussion continued. Other memorials located on the Washington Mall near the *Vietnam Memorial* were discussed. The teacher posed several more questions, such as "When Maya Lin's design was first revealed many people did not like it, yet today it has become one of the most visited memorials in our nation. Why do you think it took some people time to begin liking the memorial?" Several students commented that the memorial wasn't very pretty. They thought it was very plain, but it made people think about the number of people that were killed in the war. A couple of students had personally visited the monument. They thought it was more emotionally moving to see it in person, because the size and feeling as you walked along viewing the work was hard to convey in a photograph. They also noted that the visitors' response of leaving flowers or mementos at the wall heightened the emotional reaction to the work.

Next the teacher showed a slide of the *Tilted Arc* and explained that another artist, Richard Serra, made a sculpture that people didn't like, the *Tilted Arc*. One of the main reasons that many people didn't like it was because it caused them a lot of inconvenience in walking and it was a visual as well as a physical barrier. People complained so much that the city officials finally took the sculpture down. The teacher then asked, "What kinds of things should be considered when artwork is being installed in a public place?" "Should public art always make the environment more comfortable, pleasing, or uplifting?" "How important is the artist's intention or idea in a work of art?" "Should public art ever be censored?" "Why or why not?" Although most students agreed that artwork did not have to be "beautiful" to be a good artwork, they usually liked artworks best that looked "realistic" and "pretty." When the teacher reminded students that initially the public did not like the *Vietnam Memorial*, students agreed that sometimes, when an artist has a strong statement to make, it might take people a while to get use to it and accept it. In general, they also thought the public should have a voice in deciding what kind of art is exhibited in public places, and offered a variety of ideas about how to let people choose what their community displays.

Maya Lin's artwork was created as a memorial to American soldiers who died in Vietnam. The art teacher asked students if they remembered seeing any other memorials or commemorative artwork. Students responded with, "the *Washington Monument*, the *Lincoln Memorial*, the *Jefferson Memorial*." The teacher then asked them to name some of the other memorials they had seen in their own state and community. She reminded them that many small towns, including their own, had a war memorial of some sort on the courthouse lawn. Students quickly remembered other monuments in the area.

For the studio component of the lesson students were asked to make a commemorative cup from clay. The teacher explained that it could be a traditional cup with a handle, like a souvenir cup that they might purchase when they traveled someplace special, but they could also use broader definition of a "cup." For example, it could also be more like a trophy, or cup that might be awarded to someone special. In addition to being a cup in the sense that it could hold something, the teacher reminded students that their vessel also needed to be sculptural to communicate what it commemorates. The teacher reminded students that the commemorative cup should help us "remember someone special, or some special event or day of either personal or public importance." Students brainstormed a list of possible people and events that could be commemorated; all ideas were written on the chalkboard. The list included both famous people such as Abraham Lincoln, Amelia Earhart, Martin Luther King, Rosa Parks, Mark McGwire, Magic Johnson, and Christa McAuliffe as well as special people or events in their daily lives such as a favorite teacher, the principal, policemen, fifth-grade graduation, birthdays, and holidays. Students then drew a sketch of their sculpture and titled it. They worked on a variety of commemorative artworks including cups commemorating the work of Albert Einstein, their favorite baseball or football players or teams, favorite rock stars, their parents anniversary, a favorite pet, and their own accomplishment of high scholastic achievement. Several fifth graders in one class created cups that commemorated one of their classmates tragically killed earlier in the school year. In the spring these cups became part of a ceremony honoring that young student.

At the end of the lesson students wrote about what they had learned through the Maya Lin lesson. One student wrote that she learned she could "honor special events or people in her life through art." Another noted that he thought public art had a purpose, and it "didn't have to be pretty to catch someone's eye." A third student insightfully remarked that the most important thing that he learned from Maya Lin was that when creating art you "do what you believe in."

Conclusion

In lessons based on postmodern art there are many opportunities for students to make connections to the real world beyond the classroom. The *Vietnam War Memorial* was a monument that most students had heard of, if not personally seen; and prior to the lesson, few had heard of Maya Lin or the initial controversy surrounding the memorial. Although our culture has embraced the idea of honoring or commemorating a special person or event in our heritage through art, somehow students had not really viewed those monuments as "art." Perhaps this is a perception common to traditional public art. By looking at both commemorative art, not only on the national level but also at public art in their own town, and then creating their own personal commemorative art work, many students were introduced to a previously unrecognized function of art in society. In remembering something of personal importance to commemorate in their art, students gained an understanding of art as a means of bestowing honor, or making a person or event special. Students also discussed who decides what events or people are commemorated and who or what has been left out. Viewing art in its social context provides students with a much deeper understanding of not only contemporary artwork, but also of their own culture.

The characteristic of substantial conversation turned out to be a dominant component of this lesson. Students were engaged in substantial conversation about aesthetic issues, such as the relationship of form and function, artistic intention, and viewer response. Students were also involved in extended discussions about social concerns and had opportunities to reveal more of themselves through these discussions than in lessons with a predominant studio orientation. Some of the discussions mirrored "real world" biases already entrenched at the fifth-grade level.

These observations seem to suggest that in-depth investigations of the relationship between art and society better prepare students to function with awareness and understanding of contemporary society. As students investigate postmodern art and the issues addressed, the nature of discussion reached beyond technique and composition to touch on issues that students regarded as socially meaningful. Art and artists come to be viewed as contributing, active agents in contemporary society. In such lessons the long range goal is that students come to view not only art and art education differently, but also see themselves as responsible empowered agents of change in the reconstruction of a diverse, postmodern world. Intellectual standards may best serve humanity when they are taught through programs that build moral courage and connect, rather than distance, teachers and students to the most pressing problems and opportunities of the time (Aronowitz and Giroux, 1991). Through a study of postmodern art, art education may build programs that engage students in learning, with life as the content demanding critical investigation.

References

Aronowitz, S. & Giroux, H.A. (1991). *Postmodern education: Politics, culture, and social criticism.* Minneapolis, MN: University of MN Press.

Current Biography Yearbook, (1993). Annual, U.S.A.: H. W. Wilson, pp. 349–353.

Eisner, E. (1988). The ecology of school improvement. *Educational Leadership, 45* (5), 24–29.

Gablik, S. (1991). *The reenchantment of art.* New York: Thames and Hudson.

Hess, E. (1983, April). A tale of two memorials. *Art in America, 71,* 120–127.

Wood, P., Frascina, F., Harris, J., & Harrison, C. (1993). *Modernism in dispute: Art since the forties.* New Haven, CT; London: Yale University Press.

CONCLUSIONS AND FURTHER QUESTIONS

1. Why does Milbrandt suggest that we should study postmodern art? How does postmodernism relate to studying art in the elementary classroom? What is a postmodern curriculum? What is postmodern content?

2. Briefly describe the four critiques that Milbrandt discusses. How do these function as an instructional structure for teaching and learning?

3. On what different levels was commemorative art addressed in this chapter? How did the discussion of commemorative art relate to social and aesthetic issues?

4. Compare the *Vietnam Memorial* with another public memorial. What are the similarities and differences between the two? What groups of people are left out of each memorial?

5. How does the *Vietnam Memorial* compare to artworks such as Judy Chicago's *Dinner Party?*

6. Take the same commemorative object that you described before you read this chapter. Consider its commemorative function in terms of Milbrandt's discussion and write a brief paragraph that discusses the commemorative aspects of your object. As you write think about whether or not this chapter provoked any changes in how you see the object.

RESOURCES AND SUGGESTIONS
FOR FURTHER READING

Carol Becker. *Zones of contention: Essays on art, institutions, gender, and anxiety.* Albany, NY: State University of New York Press, 1996.

John Bodnar. *Remaking America: Public memory, commemoration, and patriotism in the twentieth century.* Princeton, NJ: Princeton University Press, 1992.

Judy Donnelly. *A wall of names: The story of the Vietnam Veterans Memorial.* New York: Random House, 1991. (Children's book)

Nina Felshin (Ed.). *But is it art? The spirit of art as activism.* Seattle, WA: Bay Press, 1994.

Kristin Ann Hass. *Carried to the wall: American memory and the Vietnam Veterans Memorial.* Berkeley, CA: University of California Press, 1998.

Bob Italia. *Maya Lin: Honoring our forgotten heroes.* Edina, MN: Abdo & Daughters, 1993. (Children's book)

Barbara Kruger. *Pictures and words.* New York, NY: Inner-Tube video, 1996. (28 minute videocassette).

Barbara Kruger. *Remote control: Power, cultures, and the world of appearances.* Cambridge, MA: MIT, 1993.

Suzanne Lacy. *Mapping the terrain: New genre public art.* Seattle,WA: Bay Press, 1995.

Maya Lin. *Boundaries.* New York: Simon & Schuster, 2000.

Kate Linker. *Love for sale: The words and pictures of Barbara Kruger.* New York: H.N. Abrams, 1990.

Freida Lee Mock. *Maya Lin: A strong clear vision.* Santa Monica, CA: American Film Foundation, 1995. (98 minute videocassette).

Richard Morris. *Sinners, lovers, and heroes: An essay on memorializing in three American cultures.* Albany, NY: State University of New York Press, 1997.

Julie H. Reiss. *From margin to center: The spaces of installation art.* Cambridge, MA: MIT Press, 2000.

Faith Ringgold. *Aunt Harriet's Underground Railroad in the sky.* New York: Crown, 1995. (Children's book)

Faith Ringgold paints Crown Heights. Chappaqua, NY: L & S Video, Inc., 1995. (28 minute videocassette).

Faith Ringgold. *Tar Beach.* New York: Crown Publishers, 1996. (Children's book)

Roy Rosenzweig & David Thelen. *The presence of the past: Popular uses of history in American life.* New York: Columbia University, 1998.

Robyn Montana Turner. *Faith Ringgold.* Boston, MA: Little, Brown, 1993. (Children's book)

CHAPTER 25

QUESTIONS AND EXPLORATIONS

1. Write a definition of ecoatonement. What might be some examples of an ecoatonement project?
2. Write a definition of ecofeminism. How does this term differ from the understandings that you have of the terms ecology and environment?
3. Find a variety of representations of nature (for example, written descriptions, photographs, memories, etc.). How do these representations come to construct our understandings of nature?
4. What is the relationship between the ideas of nature, ecology, and environment? What did you learn in school about each of these ideas? How does this learning intersect with your own experiences of and in nature, the ecology, and the environment?

Open Spaces, Open Minds:
Art in Partnership with the Earth

Karen T. Keifer-Boyd

Open Spaces, Open Minds:
Art in Partnership with the Earth

He tried to analyse this favourite theme of his—walking, different people walking to Norwich. He thought at once of the lark, of the sky, of the view. The walker's thoughts and emotions were largely made up of these outside influences. Walking thoughts were half sky: if you could submit them to chemical analysis you would find that they had some grains of colour in them, some gallons or quarts or pints of air attached to them. This at once made them airier, more impersonal. But in this room, thoughts were jostled together like fish in a net, struggling, scraping each other's scales off, and becoming, in the effort to escape—for all thinking was an effort to make thought escape from the thinker's mind past all obstacles as completely as possible: all society is an attempt to seize and influence and coerce each thought as it appears and force it to yield to another. (Virginia Woolf in *A Simple Melody*, originally written 1922–25, in Dick, 1985, p. 200)

Virginia Woolf expresses poetically the impact of environmental and societal surroundings upon our emotions and thoughts. Many artists are perceptive about their surroundings and seek, through their art, to express, nurture, or change their environment. Texas educators, like their counterparts elsewhere, recognize that sensitive perception to one's surroundings is and should be one of the four essential knowledge skills in art.[1]

This is the story of working with the ecofeminist artist Lynne Hull and her impact in a West Texas community that included university students, art teachers, children, preservice teachers, and scholars in several different fields of study.[2] This chapter also provides strategies for teaching environmental installation art in elementary schools.

Installation art has four key aspects. It (a) is site-specific; (b) engages viewer participation, often in multisensory ways using theatrical means; (c) is a synthesis of diverse materials, tools, and disciplines; and (d) concerns self and societal issues.[3] Hull is one of many installation artists who use their art as political activism to raise ecological consciousness.[4] She is concerned that birds and other wildlife use and value her art—a quiet political action honest to her aesthetics of place.[5] Lynne Hull, during her three-week residency at Texas Tech University's School of Art conveyed her purpose for creating art as follows:

> My sculpture and installations contribute to wildlife habitat, providing shelter, food, water, or space for other species, as ecoatonement for human encroachment. My work functions best on remediation sites, in the temporal interval between the beginning of reclamation and the full recovery of nature. Research and consultation with wildlife professionals and local communities is essential to project success. I began working from the observation that nearly all human actions are taken on behalf of human wants, needs, and desires, and from my theory that as the richest society in the history of civilization, we could afford to act on the needs of other species. If art is a cutting edge of civilization, couldn't this trans-species gesture be art? . . .
>
> While the concepts of "acting locally" and "inhabiting our place" have been embraced in both environmental and community arts arenas, with good reason, there are dangers involved in looking at environmental cycles from that limited perspective. The Swainson's Hawks who grace my roosts in Wyoming summers were dying of pesticides exported to Argentina—20,000 hawks died in two winters. Jaguar and Peregrine do not recognize the lines we draw on maps; to coexist we must accommodate accordingly. In many places the people governing those species are unable to protect them without our support; I feel we must "act locally AND globally."
>
> I take great delight from the existence of the other species with whom we share the planet, but I'm increasingly aware that the greatest challenge they face is the need for changing human values and attitudes toward conflicting rights, wants, and needs. Science daily offers new information, but do bar graphs and statistics lead to wisdom? It is the venue of artists, poets, philosophers to create the new myths, revise the stories, encourage the shifts in attitude we must have for all to survive in the long range. (Hull, 2000, January 20)[6]

Hull explained, "Our project [in Lubbock] was to take those homesteader forms—windmill, stock water tank, and hitching post—and convert them to sculptures for wildlife" (2000, February 6). (See Figure 25.1.) Hull noticed that anything on the flat Caprock landscape stood out for miles. While she normally uses natural objects in her environmental outdoor installations, she felt in this case the homesteader forms stood out on the *Llano Estacado*, the geographic name given by Spaniards to the area, which literally means, "staked plains." The purpose of the stock tank (an open tank of water used on ranches for livestock) in Hull's project is to provide auxiliary water and to have the floating sculpture contained in it as a rescue device for animals and birds that fall in the water and are unable to get out. She hopes that this will provide an example for local ranchers.

(a)

(b)

(c)

Figure 25.1 Wyman Meinzer Photographing Lynne Hull on **(a)** Windmill Bird habitat, **(b)** Stock Tank Floating Sculpture, and **(c)** Hitching Post Installation.

Because Hull designs her projects in consultation with wildlife profes-
sionals and local communities, the gallery director and I developed a set of
questions to guide our inquiry into an interdisciplinary study of art and environment.

- What key strategies could we utilize in making art that would illuminate ecological issues and effectively reach an audience? What audiences are the targets of
  such practices?
- Does an ecologically created work become art on the basis of the intent of the
  maker?
- What strategies of collaboration best focus the expertise and capacities of an
  artist, scientist, field-expert team?

Creating Environmental Art in K–12 School Situations

High school teachers in the area decided not to attend the art teacher's workshop on environmental art with nationally recognized artists, Lynne Hull and
Joe Walters, because they believed that environmental art would not help
their students prepare for *Scholastic Awards* and *Advanced Placement* (AP) port-
folio review.[7] Teachers under *AP* and *Scholastic* pressures follow modernist criteria articulated by Clive Bell from Roger Fry's lectures at Bloomsbury that
began in 1904. In 1913 "Clive, following Roger's ideas, articulated the idea of
'significant form' as the basis for all good art" (Marsh, 1995, p. 52). In the
mid-twentieth century, art critic Clement Greenberg refined the criteria further: "In formalist criticism, the criterion for significant progress remains a
kind of design technology subject to one compulsive direction: the treatment
of the whole surface as a single undifferentiated field of interest" (Steinberg,
1972, p. 79).

While formalism is the driving force of the high school art curriculum,
elementary school teachers who came to the teacher environmental workshop
found that what they learned was important to implement in their art curriculum and that it fitted their administration's urge to develop interdisciplinary
curriculum. Elementary art teachers, who worked with Lynne Hull, learned to
teach art inspired by Andy Goldsworthy's environmental art processes.[8] In
this art lesson students gather natural elements in the surrounding schoolyard
and place them temporarily on a canvas or neutral colored sheet to discuss
them in terms of their visual qualities and according to associations derived
from contemplating the elements and their combinations. The canvas helps
to isolate the elements from their context during the discussion to illuminate
their characteristics. The discussion is critical to sensitizing student perception. Then, either in teams or individually, students create a site-specific
sculpture with natural elements found at the site. The metaphorical "canvas"
is as large as the grounds, and the borders of the art extend to the end of one's

Figure 25.2 Environmental Sculpture Process and Creations.

line of vision. Students document their art with a digital camera, Polaroid camera, or through drawing. (See Figure 25.2 for examples of the environmental sculptures by elementary art teachers.)

Environmental Installation Art is Art of Place

There are views concerning what constitutes good art other than those based on the modernist and formalist aesthetic values of Fry, Bell, and Greenberg. Teaching only one set of aesthetic values in a multicultural society is limiting and excludes most of the world's population. For example, minimalist artist Carl Andre begins to explore an aesthetic that is based on place when he states, "the work is not put in a place, it is that place" (Holt, 1979, p. 171). Andre (1985) describes place in relation to art: "A place is an area within an environment which has been altered in such a way as to make the general environment more conspicuous" (pp. 189–90). The French poststructuralist Michael Foucault (1980) in his theory of historical discontinuity suggested that "a whole history remains to be written of spaces—which would at the same time be the history of powers (both of these terms in the plural)—from the great strategies of geopolitics to the little tactics of the habitat" (p. 149).

Photographer and Web artist, Esther Parada, practices Foucault's theory in her art in such works as *Transplant: A Tale of Three Continents* in which she explores the relationship between human interventions in the ecosystem and cultural power.[9] Art critic Lucy Lippard (1997) wrote that, "place is latitudinal and longitudinal within the map of a person's life" (p. 7). *Art of Place* for Lippard concerns the circumstances of one's context, an issue that elementary school children can explore by creating visual maps of their lives. Hull (2000) defines four distinct strategies for creating *Art of Place*:

1. Artists interpret nature, creating artworks to inform us about nature and its processes, or about environmental problems we face.
2. Artists interact with environmental forces, and create artworks affected or powered by wind, water, lightning, and even earthquakes.
3. Artists re-envision our relationship to nature, and propose new ways for us to co-exist with our environment.
4. Artists reclaim and remediate damaged environments, restoring nature in artistic and often aesthetic ways.

Cultural feminists involved with ecological issues have developed art in partnership with the earth; that is, ecofeminism. By the 1970s, some eco-activists, eco-theorists, environmental artists, and cultural feminists began to revalue women's culture and practices. They sought to consciously create new cultural values that would embrace and honor the values of caretaking and nurturing. They believed that the dominant culture's devaluation of natural processes was due to valuing power as control, domination, and competition. They affirmed and celebrated the embeddedness of all the Earth's peoples in the multiple webs and cycles of life. This valuing of difference emerged as a Postmodern ideology. Ecofeminism integrates peace, feminist, and ecology movements. Ecofeminist politics seek to invoke new stories that acknowledge and value the biological and cultural diversity that sustains all life. Ecofeminism embraces not only women and men of different races, but also all forms of life—other animals, plants, and the living Earth itself. By evoking societal earth-friendly transformations, artists that create new images of living with the Earth are an integral part of the ecofeminist movement. Ecofeminists consider the arts to be essential catalysts of change. Characteristics of ecofeminist art include that it is:

1. A participatory, socially interactive framework for art, often of long-term involvement.
2. A process denoting life cycles and interrelationships, rather than products of a permanent nature.
3. Created to raise energy, evoke visions, and to alter states of consciousness.
4. Focused on specific questions of local, ecological, and social transformation rather than on beauty, ownership, and economic gain.

Ecologists, humanists, feminists, peace workers, and others believe that we should educate youths and engage ourselves in socio-ecological responsible action: "Our call to action, our call to nonviolent transformation of society is based on the belief that the struggle for disarmament, peace, social justice, protection of the planet Earth, and the fulfillment of basic human needs and human rights are *one* and indivisible" (Kelly, 1989, pp. ix–x).

Green Criticism, an art-criticism model sensitive to concept of place, judges the value of art based on the artist's intent, the materials used, the processes employed, and the work's relation to its location. According to art critics who favor ecofeminist art, the ultimate criterion for judging "good art" is the degree to which the viewer is invited to take a pro-active, ecological stance. Specific questions for elementary school children to consider are: Where did the materials originate? Are the materials biodegradable? Were any species exploited in the production of the materials applied in the art process? Does the artwork contribute to the place in which it resides?

Questions to Ask Prior to Building Environmental Sculptures

When Lynne Hull develops her ideas she asks questions about the local ecosystem. Prior to coming to Lubbock, Texas, to create a work of art she asked,

> Playa Lake—what is the basic ecology, what species does it support, what's the main plant and animal community? What is the water depth fluctuation and [in] what seasons is that effect? I gather it has a perimeter size fluctuation as well? Are there species of concern in the area? Where does it stand on the Partners in Flight inventory of migratory bird stopovers? . . . What is the administrative structure of the lake and whom do we have to convince about what we want to do as the project evolves? What would you say are the biggest wildlife issues in the area? What would you like the public to be more aware of? What is the water quality, and what are the nutrient sources on the playa lake? If we wanted to add some

aquatic plants with our floating structure, which ones would contribute and clean up the water? Where would we find some to gather? (Hull, 1999).

A biologist, the gallery director, and I answered some of the questions with the knowledge that we had from observing playa lakes near our homes. We found out that there was much more to playa lakes than meets the eye.

Playa Lake Research

Lynne Hull landed in Lubbock expecting to build a floating sculpture on a playa lake for a perch and shelter for birds. We found dried cracked mud, dead plants, and no water in the playa lake. (See Figure 25.3.) We sought a playa lake expert, David Haukos, a U.S. Fish and Wildlife specialist. He takes K–12 science classes to a playa site to teach young people about the unique and important role of playa lakes in providing water in West Texas. On the *Llano Estacado*, some 20,000 playas exist. Playa lakes, except those that are artificially kept filled, dry up and fill on an irregular basis. They need to dry to open the earth's cracks to allow the water deep into the huge Ogallala Aquifer, otherwise rain on the Caprock flows across and not into the earth. The playa lakes refill the Ogallala Aquifer, which provides water from Texas to Nebraska.

Figure 25.3 Playa Lake Drawing by Kate Knochel.

We had an inspiring and educational walk in the dry playa lake. David Haukos described how the drying of playa lakes helps to stimulate a greater biodiversity than in those kept filled.

Area Species Research and Ceramic Playa Creatures

David Haukos described a previous experience of standing in a playa lake during a downpour. Within two hours the parched, seemingly barren earth filled with amphibians, insects, and birds. The creatures that emerged included toads, turtles, lizards, snakes, water beetles, and shrimp.[10] David explained that playa lake experts argue over whether these creatures arise from deep in the earth or travel from afar to start a life in the newly filled playa lakes. The story captured our imagination as we stood in a seemingly lifeless place. Lynne decided to use playa lake clay mud (see Figure 25.4) to create these creatures that appeared during the rains. By placing the human-created clay creatures in the dried cracked mud we were reminded of the life that would appear. When the life forms that these clay animals symbolized appeared, the clay artworks would be buried in the mud due to the rains, per-

Figure 25.4 Playa Mud Photos by Kippra Hopper.

haps to emerge again during the dry season. A group of ceramic students researched the playa lake's life forms, dug the playa lake's dried clay, and used it to form representations of the absent creatures.[11]

Drawing: An Essential Process in Creating Environmental Sculptures

Lynne Hull encourages students to develop their drawing skills. Her drawings serve as presentation tools to gain support for her proposals. To actualize her environmental sculptures, Lynne presents her drawings (see Figure 25.5) to obtain permission for land or water uses, to reuse or borrow materials, or to find a means to move large objects such as a windmill to the Lubbock site. Most importantly she uses her ideas expressed as drawings to gain the expertise and collaboration, and check the scientific validity of the project with biologists, ornithologists, agriculturists, landscape architects, plant and soil specialists, welders, machine operators, photographers, artists, and many others involved with the site-specific project.

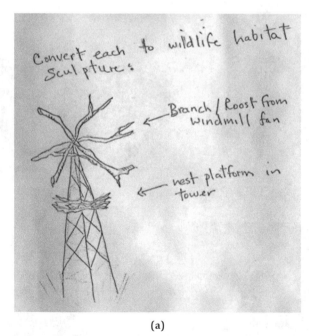

(a)

Figure 25.5 Lynne Hulls Drawings for the Playa Installation: **(a)** wildlife habitat sculpture,

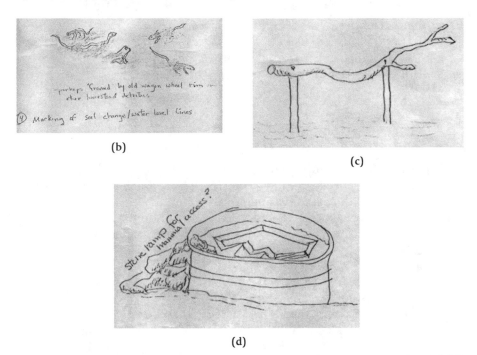

(b)

(c)

(d)

Figure 25.5 (continued) **(b)** playa lake creatures, **(c)** hitching post perch, and **(d)** stock tank floating sculpture.

Andrew Martin who teaches drawing at Texas Tech University's School of Art invited Hull to visit his class. Andrew proposed that Lynne Hull lead a discussion generated by a brief overview of environmental artists and of her work. He asked Lynne Hull to discuss four issues with his drawing students:

1. How environmental artists translate responses to particular ecological issues or problems into works of art.
2. Lynne Hull's approach to nature as an artist as well as her ideas about human relationships and responsibility toward the environment.
3. Research strategies and suggested sources for information.
4. The role drawing plays in Lynne Hull's development of ideas and execution of the actual works.

Elementary teachers could develop art lessons based on these four issues for their students. For example, teachers could develop WebQuests for children in which students visit selected sites on environmental art projects and then draw a plan for a place that they believe needs improvement.[12]

Documentation

Lynne Hull documents her work through photographs and poetry. Below is Lynne Hull's poem about the Lubbock playa installation.

TEXAS TEXT

Enormous Llano sky, endless Llano plains
Grasslands stretch to edge of earth, centuries of horizontal, only the flow
    of water reaching up to sky and down to aquifer
The homestead brought change, structures stand out on the land:
    windmill, hitching post, stock tank, stark against horizon line
We could convert
    Subvert
Forms, echoes for use by wildlife, atone for habitats lost under plow and
    pump
Bring back the birds if not the bison
So we built as they did, dug holes as they did, raised a windmill as they did
Now sculptures, like every life form on the llano, waiting, waiting
    For rain

The biologist told
Of standing in the dry playa in a storm
Seeing, feeling, the water rush in
In an hour, toads came singing
In two hours, snakes came winding
Where do they come from and go?
So we took the playa bottom, earth to clay to creatures
Bringing back animal presence, even in the dry.

People in Texas range widely as the plains
The art professor with passion for birds
The bird professor with passion for honesty
    In art or chess or π
Whose ranch pays him off in more days of hard work
The educator who can't let her students be contained
    constrained
By ivory tower or gallery walls
The Latina artist who loves Chiapas and weeps for it as I do
The agency biologist who needs, besides science, soul bonds to the land
The rancher whose life which never finds the need to leave the county
(and Texas has small counties)

The photographer who drives 40,000 miles in a year, mostly in Texas
The students open to radical art and avant-garde ideas
but closed to dried cranberries after a hard day's work
Two women who share their legacy of this place
Their love of the canyons,
Their wisdom to value the ground that they stand on
Sunlight on grasses and a coyote killed crane
    We all listen to country and western but sometimes
    An aria blows in on the wind

(Hull, 2000, February 3)

Undergraduate students in my art criticism course decided to produce a documentary video about their experience working with Lynne Hull to create the playa installation. The voice-over narratives flow from one student's statement to the next while video images dissolve into student drawings. (See Figure 25.6 for an example of one of the student's drawings.) Below are some excerpts from the students who spent two or more hours outside of class working with Lynne Hull.

> When she leaves West Texas, visiting artist Lynne Hull will take with her memories of open spaces, great skies, playa lakes—what she calls vertical water cycles . . . Hull has emerged as a major ecofeminist artist who believes that creativity of artists can be applied to helping solve real-world problems. She hopes that in seeing her work, people also will realize that that they, too, can take actions to honor other species. . . . (Kippra Hopper)

> Dr. David Haukos [described that when] the rains come this playa just blossoms into this pool of life. Dormant plant seeds start to germinate and animals appear. . . . Lynne's art is mainly for the benefit of animals and the environment but it serves as a really important visual reminder to humans of the presence of the other species that are around us . . . (Susannah Noles)

> The materials we used were found objects or donated and that we were recycling or reusing things, to me, added another layer to the ecological responsibility that was such an important part of the project. It's good for kids to learn how and why to use what they have and reuse what they can. (Elizabeth Mott)

I noticed that no one referred to the installation as ecofeminist art. After the three weeks with Lynne Hull a student asked why there was the need for the feminist label when ecological art seemed an accurate label. This question opened students' minds as they discussed their ideas and beliefs about what feminism meant to them and they heard a range of different views. I described different types of feminism and the idea that ecofeminism referred to a belief in and desire for a nonhierarchical world of caring. Lynne Hull's art exemplified this belief.

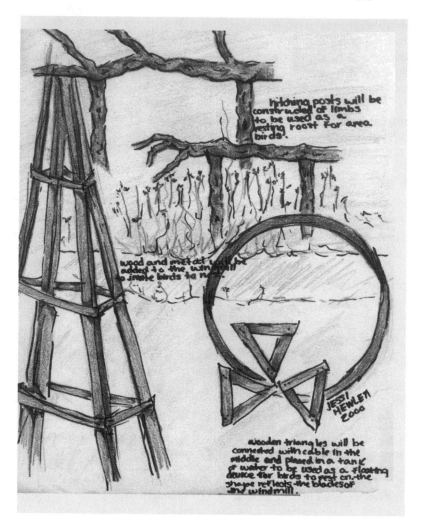

Figure 25.6 Jessi Hewlett's Drawing of the Playa Installation Elements.

Elementary art teachers might open themselves to the concept of ecofeminism by reconsidering the scientific classifications of life forms. Typically scientists describe the lowest life forms as cells without a nucleus (e.g., bacteria) and describe multi-celled creatures as more advanced and complex. Bacteria are necessary to digest food and plants need bacteria to grow. We are part of a system that depends on bacteria. Caring for symbiotic relationships within a specific place is at the core of ecofeminist art. Art projects that explore symbiotic relationships will evoke comments like those from my students in which they expressed awakened perception of and greater respect and responsibility for their environment.

Art in Partnership with Earth

Go outside and find a spot of nature. Draw the features and life forms that stand out to you. Learn how it changes over the year and reflect on its past history. Consider how it is connected to you and to other local life forms. Is there harmony in the site between these species? What would help balance the needs of all the species that share that space? Create a sculpture that reflects the essences of the place and that is an ecoatonement.[13]

Endnotes

1. Perception is the first of four Texas Essential Knowledge and Skills for Fine Arts basic strands. See *http://www.tea.state.tx.us/teks/117–001n.htm#117.1.*
2. In the Lubbock playa lake project Hull created a habitat for migrating birds. I asked students in my art criticism course to document some aspect of Lynne Hull's work on the bird habitat installation through interview, observation, and/or dialogue. Some of the documentation is posted on the course Web site at *http://www.art.ttu.edu/arted/syllabi/3365.html.*
3. These factors are according to Shwu-Huoy Tzou who conducted extensive research on installation art created between 1960 and 1999 for her dissertation that I directed and which is in process. The title of her dissertation is *Cultural-specific and international influences on and critical perceptions of five Asian installation artists: Gu Wenda, Yanagi Yukinori, Xu Bing, Miyajima Tatsuo, and Choi Jeong-Hwa.*
4. See my web site at *http://www.art.ttu.edu/arted/syllabi/3365eco.html* for a bibliography on many artists dedicated to raising ecological consciousness.
5. An "aesthetics of place" refers to a belief that art should respond to the place where it is exhibited. This is achieved by being of the materials and forms of the place and/or responding to the societal and environmental concerns of the place.
6. See Hull's Web site at *http://www.wecsa.com/ecoart/pages/about.html* and the Green Arts Web site at *www.artswire.org/greenarts.*
7. I initiated this artist residency to help the people of Lubbock understand, appreciate, and protect their unique high desert environment. North Carolina artist Joe Walters shared the gallery space with Lynne Hull. Lynne exhibited documentation of the playa lake site bird habitat sculpture while Joe created an installation of natural forms (leaves and animals) that denied their proper size in relation to each other to call into question the hierarchical categories that place humans above nature. The combination of artists reached a range of audiences and aesthetic values.
8. Teachers also learn about Lynne's process of art making and may model her approach and develop a long-term, well-researched, interdisciplinary, and collaborative art project.
9. See Parada's Web site with links to her art at *http://www.rtvf.nwu.edu/Homestead/eparada/desc.html.*
10. See the Native Range Research Site list of species that live in Lubbock's playa lakes at *http://www.rw.ttu.edu/ppna/Flora&Fauna/herps.html.*

11. David Haukos, the playa lake expert, assured us that we would not harm the ecosystem if we used some of the playa mud for sculptures from a place in the playa that was used to gather soil samples for research.
12. For Web resources on environmental artists and WebQuest templates and descriptions of how to teach critical and creative thinking with well-designed WebQuests go to *http://www.art.ttu.edu/arted/syllabi/3365.html.*
13. I thank Lynne Hull, Kippra Hopper, and Ernest Boyd for their insightful feedback on this chapter.

References

Andre, Carl. (1985). Carl Andre. In D. Ashton (Ed.), *Twentieth-century artists on art* (pp. 189–90). New York: Pantheon Books.

Dick, S. (Ed.) (1985). *The complete shorter fiction of Virginia Woolf.* New York: Harcourt Brace Jovanovich.

Foucault, M. (1980). The eye of power. In C. Gordon (Ed.), *Power/knowledge: Selected interviews and other writings 1972–1977.* Brighton, UK: Harvester Press.

Holt, N. (1979). Discussions with Heizer, Oppenheim, Smithson. In N. Holt (Ed.), *The writings of Robert Smithson,* (p. 171). New York: New York University Press.

Hull, L. (2000). About eco-art. *Lynne Hull: Environmental artist* [Online]. Available *http://www.wecsa.com/ecoart/pages/about.html* [2000, February 19].

Hull, L. (*EcoartHull@cs.com*). (2000, February 6). Thanks, video. E-mail to Karen Keifer-Boyd (*KarenKB@ttu.edu*).

Hull, L. (2000, February 3). Texas text. [unpublished exhibition documentary poem].

Hull, L. (*EcoartHull@cs.com*). (2000, January 20). Statement to share. E-mail to Karen Keifer-Boyd (*KarenKB@ttu.edu*).

Hull, L. (*EcoartHull@cs.com*). (1999, December 11). Lubbock eco. E-mail to Karen Keifer-Boyd (*KarenKB@ttu.edu*).

Kelly, P. (1989). Foreword. In J. Plant (Ed.), *Healing the wounds: The promise of ecofeminism* (pp. ix–xi). Philadelphia, PA: New Society Publishers.

Lippard, L. R. (1997). *The lure of the local: Senses of place in a multicentered society.* New York: The New Press.

Marsh, J. (1995). *Bloomsbury women: Distinct figures in life and art.* New York: Henry Holt.

Steinberg, L. (1972). *Other criteria: Confrontations with twentieth-century art.* New York: Oxford University Press.

CONCLUSIONS AND FURTHER QUESTIONS

1. What do we mean by the term "nature?" In what ways are our understandings of nature shaped and changed by our interactions with artworks such as those created by Hull?

2. With specific reference to the work of Hull discuss ways that art can function as a form of ecoatonement.
3. In what ways is Hull's work connected to a specific understanding of place?
4. Describe the various ecological perspectives that arise in Hull's work.
5. In this chapter Keifer-Boyd writes about the differences between ecofeminist art and ecological art. What are some of these differences? Why is it important to use the words "ecofeminist art" to describe Hull's ideas and work?
6. How does this chapter encourage you to think about ways that you could raise issues from ecofeminist and ecological art in your teaching? What types of actions and works could you and your students engage in?

RESOURCES AND SUGGESTIONS
FOR FURTHER READING

Arnold Berleant. *The aesthetics of environment.* Philadelphia, PA: Temple University Press, 1992.

Arnold Berleant. *Living in the landscape: Toward an aesthetics of environment.* Lawrence, KS: University Press of Kansas, 1997.

Clearing and *Green Teacher* magazines offer teachers a variety of K–12 environmental education resources, many of which are written by teachers. (*www.teleport.com/~clearing* and *www.web.net/~greentea*)

Peter Davis. *Ecomuseums: A Sense of place.* Leicester, UK: Leicester University Press, 1999.

Michel Foucault. *Power/knowledge: Selected interviews and other writings, 1972–1977.* Colin Gordon (Ed. & Trans.). New York: Pantheon Books, 1980.

Suzi Gablik. *The reenchantment of art.* New York, NY: Thames & Hudson, 1992.

Green Brick Road (GBR) is a non-profit organization offering resources and information for students and teachers of global and environmental education. (*www.gbr.org*)

Nicola Hodges. *Art and the natural environment.* London: Academy Group Ltd., 1994.

Jeffrey Kastner (Ed.). *Land and environmental art.* London: Phaidon, 1998.

Suzanne Lacy (Ed.). *Mapping the terrain: New genre public art.* Seattle, WA: Bay Press, 1995.

Barbara C. Matilsky. *Fragile ecologies: Contemporary artists' interpretations and solutions.* New York: Rizzoli, 1992.

Carolyn Merchant. *Earthcare: Women and the environment.* New York: Routledge, 1996.

Carolyn Merchant. *Radical ecology: The search for a livable world.* New York: Routledge, 1992.

Barney Nelson. *The wild and the domestic: Animal representation, ecocriticism, and western American literature.* Reno, NV: University of Nevada Press, 2000.

Project Learning Tree is a K–12 environmental education program that is administered by the American Forest Foundation and the Council for Environmental Education. (*www.plt.org*)

Julie H. Reiss. *From margin to center: The spaces of installation art.* Cambridge, MA: MIT Press, 2000.

Alan Sonfist (Ed.). *Art in the land: A critical anthology of environmental art.* New York: Dutton, 1983.

Erika Suderburg (Ed.). *Space, site, intervention: Situating installation art.* Minneapolis, MN: University of Minnesota Press, 2000.

Karen J. Warren (Ed.). *Ecological feminist philosophies.* Bloomington, IN: Indiana University Press, 1996.

Michael E. Zimmerman. *Contesting earth's future: Radical ecology and postmodernity.* Berkeley, CA: University of California Press, 1994.

CHAPTER 26

QUESTIONS AND EXPLORATIONS

1. Think about reading information on the World Wide Web. What types of relationships emerge between the various forms of knowledge that you encounter? What reading strategies do you use to read information on the web?

2. Have you created knowledge or concept webs? How do these webs help create connections between various forms of knowledge? In what ways are they similar to the World Wide Web? In what ways do they differ?

3. In what ways do you construct knowledge? How does narrative help you construct knowledge?

Investigate and Re-Envision Teaching Strategies: Linking Individuals, Communities, and Organizations Through the Visual Arts

Elizabeth B. Reese

Introduction

In February 1999, a visual arts pilot-program was initiated in the heart of a Corpus Christi, Texas barrio. Named collaboratively by the participants and facilitators, *Drop-In Art Adventures: Be Cool to Draw!* was held Tuesday and Wednesdays after-school in a community activity center for youth ages 7–12. The program was facilitated by three organizations. They include the Fighting to Rid Gangs in America Foundation (hereinafter referred to as the Foundation): a non-profit organization that provides prevention and intervention services for at-risk youth; *artconnects:* a local organization that facilitates programs which connect communities, organizations, education, and technology through the visual arts; and finally, members of the K Space Studios and Gallery, a cooperative contemporary arts organization.

The premiere project of the pilot-program, *Connect to Community Through Art,* consisted of several inter-related components that culminated in experiences and exhibitions that involved a citywide web of participants and

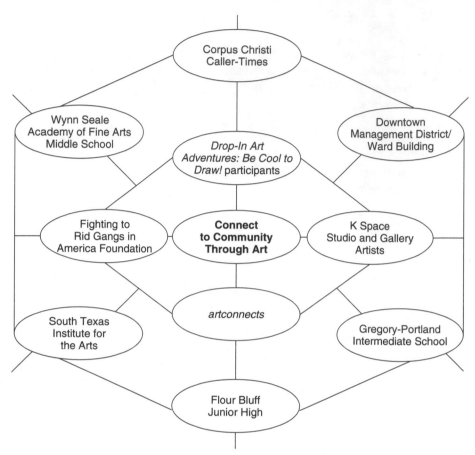

Figure 26.1 *Connect to Community Through Art* became a citywide web of cooperating individuals, communities, and organizations.

facilitators. In three months, the program grew from three youth, one facilitator, one exhibition location, and three cooperating organizations to more than 100 youth, 10 facilitators, 4 exhibition locations, and 9 cooperating organizations (see Figure 26.1). Based on this experience I examine how a teaching strategy can link a variety of individuals, communities, and organizations in several physical locations through the visual arts.

Investigate Teaching Strategies

In recent years, much attention has been drawn in education to learning that occurs beyond school boundaries. Understanding education in contexts broader than schooling has important implications for art education and calls for an examination of alternative venues, initiatives and strategies that facilitate artistic development, encourage aesthetic growth and promote reflection about the role and value of art in a society. (Irwin and Kindler, 1999, p. 1)

Schools and art museums undoubtedly are important places for people to learn about and through the visual arts. In recent years, however, there has been in increase in commentary that criticizes theories and practices used within these institutions. A number of these critiques are based on questions of teaching strategies that do not engage social and political factors (Garoian, 1999; Giroux, 1997; Lyotard, 1987; Roberts, 1997). Many educators still use traditional teaching methods that date back to the Enlightenment when knowledge was considered true by the "unanimity between rationale minds" (Lyotard, 1987, p. 73). This is a concern because the "rationale minds" that create this agreement are generally composed of the dominant culture and subsequently are not easily challenged by those outside this culture.

Educational practices that do not challenge the presentation of one perspective are questionable because the personal, social, and political memories, experiences, information, and knowledge of diverse learners may not be brought to bear on the creation of knowledge. Diverse learners may find such practices troublesome to employ because they can appear irrelevant to their lives and experiences. This is a problem because many students learn to depend more on structured learning environments for knowledge acquisition rather than on themselves to construct new connections to the world (Garoian, 1999; Illich, 1971). In the twenty-first century, it is time for educators to re-envision teaching strategies and the locations wherein such practices are available.

Re-Envision Teaching Strategies

Opportunities for learners to engage with diverse individuals and to examine disparate communities and organizations can legitimize their identity. Such experiences also can accentuate the unique social and political factors that make up different individuals, communities, and organizations. According to Giroux (1997), there are three key themes and issues that comprise these factors. The first concerns how the participants and facilitators perceive their experiences within their community and how they secure those perceptions. Second, the "system of attitudes and values that govern" how knowledge and information are developed, implemented, and evaluated must be considered (Giroux, 1997, p. 16). Third, how dominant societal beliefs, attitudes, and actions are produced, reproduced, and challenged.

In *Connect to Community Through Art*, the participants and facilitators engaged with and examined local and global social and political factors through the visual arts. The factors included violence, cultural differences, and stereotyping. In this manner, the visual arts were used to inquire into and express issues and concerns about community (Garoian, 1999). The visual arts were also used to challenge stereotypes and "to entertain differing points of view" (Garoian, 1999, p. 137).

The theoretical and practical dynamics of the World Wide Web—theoretically defined as hypertextual—in conjunction with a narrative form of education offered a framework for teaching and learning that emphasized the continuous engagement with and evaluation of social and political factors. Hypertext theories and practices enable individuals to explore, to connect, and to contribute information and knowledge (Aeseth, 1994; Landow, 1997). Theodor H. Nelson coined the term "hypertext" to denote a unique form of engaging with information and knowledge: non-sequential reading and writing that enables the free exploration of personally meaningful ideas that connect to one another (Aaseth, 1994; Landow, 1997). Like the independence a learner may experience when "surfing the web," educators can assist learners in exploring important social and political factors autonomously without the use of a computer.

Narrative forms of education advocate that educators, students, and others participate in critically examining that which is presented (Apple, 1995; Kincheloe, 1995; Roberts, 1997). In *Connect to Community Through Art*, "hypertextual narrative" strategies were useful teaching tools to re-envision how educators and learners can explore, connect, evaluate, and contribute to social and political factors within various learning environments through the visual arts.

Connect to Community Through Art as a Hypertextual Narrative

> Reconfigure teaching and learning in terms of the concepts of "links" and "networks" which have the power to redefine the roles of teachers, administrators, and learners. (Lankshear, Peters, and Knobel, 1996, p. 160).

Although hypertextuality is typically based in the "virtual" community of computers and the Internet, its theories and practices can be applied in "real" communities. Some individuals may already experience the world in this way. However, most educational programs are not developed, implemented, or evaluated using hypertextual narrative pedagogical strategies. Furthermore, many individuals may not actively consider exploring, connecting, examining, or contributing to social and political themes and issues.

To best describe how the strategy may operate with a group of elementary age youth, the four components of this approach—explore, connect, examine, contribute—are separated into individual stages. In reality, however, they tend to be inextricably linked. Therefore, the order in which the different activities appear is not meant to suggest a rigid recipe, but rather represents a strategy that can be employed as a nonlinear framework (see Figure 26.2).

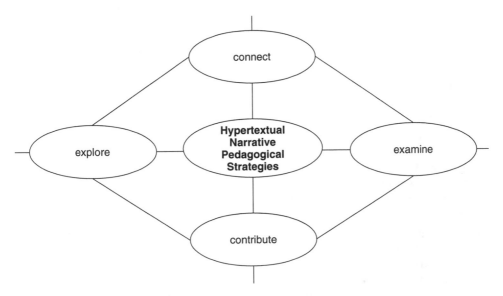

Figure 26.2 Hypertextual narrative teaching strategies can be used as a dynamic framework rather than as a static recipe.

Explore

> The pedagogical strength of generative themes and issues and the issues they provoke is that they emerge directly from student cultures and conversations and reflect "unresolved social problems" in classrooms and communities. Hence, they can stimulate and focus investigation around the relationship between personal life and larger issues, and provide genuinely "student-centered foundations for problem-posing." (Shor, 1992, 47, 55; also Freire, 1970; Shor and Freire 1987 in Lankshear, Peters, Knobel, 1996, p. 152)

In *Connect to Community Through Art*, the youth participants and the facilitators from the Foundation, *artconnects*, and K Space Studios and Gallery explored their perceptions about community, the systems or entities that govern how their perceptions are constructed, and the beliefs represented by these systems. Facilitators first invited youth to generate personally significant ideas and issues. School, family, teachers, hospitals, peace, violence, animals, church, and gangs were among the concepts that emerged. The youth then were asked to create an image that would depict their interpretation of a select concept. These images included sick people in a hospital, children playing on a playground, and a portrait of slain hometown *tejano* singer Selena. Participants were encouraged to discuss their drawings.

Next, the facilitators invited the youth to generate ideas about with whom, how, and where they might explore information about their community—both locally and globally. They suggested many sources, including television, radio, teachers, schools, parents, and newspapers. The facilitators also introduced the notion that artists could be important sources for information about issues, concerns, and events. To illustrate this possibility, the youth and facilitators went to see an exhibition at the Antonio E. Garcia Arts Education Center. The exhibition featured works of art by San Antonio artist, Joe Lopez.

The Garcia Center is the satellite space for the Art Museum of South Texas and is located two blocks from the Foundation's Romero Activity Center. Lopez's watercolors depict his memories and experiences of growing up in a barrio. The images include the *raspas* (ice cream) man, people dancing, *gallos* (large roosters), and many others.

Seeing his paintings on exhibition within a reputable art establishment empowered the participants to embrace their memories and experiences of their own community. This occurred because they saw themselves and customs from their own community within Lopez's paintings.

This exhibition was a valuable place to begin exploring how dominant beliefs and attitudes can control communities. A majority of the youth seemed surprised that these images were on exhibition in the Garcia Center. Their reactions were worth a thousand words as they exclaimed, "That looks *just like my* gallo" and "That's like my mom and pop dancing" and "I've seen that raspas man before!" When asked if they always identified with the art in the building they said "no." The youth indicated that they did not feel that their community was depicted in a positive manner within the images and narratives of the dominant culture.

Connect

> [Hypertext is] an open, far-flung, fluid, dynamic, networked, and radically connected space that comprises a burgeoning web of "worlds" within its overarching World. (Lankshear, Peters, Knobel, 1996, p. 167)

Documents created and published with HyperText Markup Language (HTML)—a programming language used for the WWW—may have links to and from them with the potential to be accessible to infinite number of readers and writers (Aeseth, 1994; Gaggi, 1997; Landow, 1997). Linking enables the reader to connect with and between texts in a nonlinear mode. This feature, constructing non-linear connections, is perhaps one of the most celebrated aspects of hypertext (Aeseth, 1994; Gaggi, 1997; Landow, 1997).

Connecting to intriguing information and knowledge can also be replicated without the use of the Internet. During *Connect to Community Though Art,* for example, the youth connected local and global perceptions, systems, and dominant cultural actions about violence and cultural differences.

With a surge of violent social and political events during the spring of 1999, the youth perceived several connections between local and global issues and concerns. Locally, these events included remembering Selena on the fourth anniversary of her murder, gang activity, and various personal experiences and memories of violence. Globally, these months were a time of extraordinary bloodshed around the globe including the Columbine tragedy and the "ethnic cleansing" in Kosovo.

The youth seemed to make strong connections to the "situation" in Kosovo. This was due to their personal experiences with people who evaluated them differently due to cultural differences. The youth also talked about how many gang fights stem from one group trying to prove that their differences make them better than the others. The participants related to dominating different people through violence as it occurred in their own local community. As shootings and murders were also a part of their personal memories and experiences, the youth supported the need to examine these problems in order to create more peaceful communities.

Examine

> To enable a narrative form of education, a museum [or community] can present the message that acknowledges its own nature—in other words, that is explicit about being not only a version but being the museum's [community's] version—then it does not exclude the possibility of alternative versions held by visitors [learners]. Second, if a message is presented in a way that allows for argument, complexity, or multiple perspectives, then it may begin to engage visitors [learners] in the process of evaluating it against their own perspectives. The result is a relation of shared authority, (Roberts, 1997, p. 145)

After the initial excitement about the WWW diminished, people became concerned about the quality, truth, and value of the vast amount of available information and knowledge. These concerns prompted questions about the validity of all published information: how does anyone know with certainty its truth?

Like any book, media story, art exhibition, newspaper article, issue, concern, or event, the information on-line requires careful examination by diverse individuals. Accordingly, the strength and importance of a narrative form of education is that it encourages and enables learners to examine different perspectives (Bal, 1997; Roberts, 1997). In its most general definition, a narrative can be described as a story, myth, poem, performance, drama, history, work of art, or other forms of communication that relates information about an idea through more than one viewpoint (Bal, 1997). Likewise, narrative teaching strategies promote the analysis of various versions of a possible story, event, or issue (Bal, 1997; Roberts, 1997). Similar to hypertext, narrative strategies empower learners and teachers to incorporate numerous sources and experiences to shape education into dynamic processes.

Narrative forms of education were engaged when facilitators encouraged youth to examine their perceptions and how they are developed and assessed. Youth also analyzed their actions both as individuals and as members of a larger community.

One afternoon, K Space artist Jimmy Peña brought the youth a print of his drawing, *Essuerzo*. The image depicts diverse individuals pulling several large ropes—like in tug-of-war. Different than typical games of this nature, the opposite side is not visible within the image. It is not obvious what or whom they are fighting against—or pulling toward them. The youth connected to the print of his drawing and it became the catalyst for examining perceptions and actions about differences.

Discussions began by comparing and contrasting Peña's drawing with the images and news about gang violence and "ethnic cleansing." In maintaining language appropriate to the elementary age level, conversations tended to evolve around whether or not people should "get along." Most of the youth claimed that everyone should "be best friends." Some of the older kids noted that people should at least be able to respect individuals' differences. Many participants said that they learned these values in school or at home—but a few acknowledged that they *could* learn these ideas from Community Centers and artists, like Peña.

The youth also discussed the fact that although the newspaper tended to include their community when bad events happened, there also were good events that took place. They became concerned that people in other parts of the community only associated their neighborhood with violence. This was a significant analysis because it demonstrated the need to question a seemingly reliable source of information, and brought to the foreground the idea that they could try to change the perceptions of others.

The next step in examining their perceptions was to discuss actions, both those of dominant cultures as well as of their own. Again, trying to keep language age-appropriate, participants and facilitators discussed the events in Kosovo in terms of "getting rid of" or hurting people who are different, but not explicitly talking about murder and rape. The youth felt that the actions definitely were wrong. One even made the analogy that it would be like getting rid of one of the facilitators because she was Anglo. They then examined what actions might provide more positive outcomes for disagreeing individuals to engage. They suggested that people come together and struggle for what is right—as depicted in Peña's drawing. The youth next revealed their beliefs through their own drawings. Alongside the youth, the facilitators also created images.

These images—created on newsprint donated by the local newspaper, with charcoal, crayons, markers, pens, and pencils—were simple illustrations filled with significant meanings. For example, one seven-year-old girl created a landscape that featured pink, yellow, and blue stick figures holding hands. In the clouds she wrote, "Be best friends! Never fight!" Peña drew two large hands—each a different color—about to engage in a handshake.

The facilitators spoke with the youth about the importance of their beliefs and values—that their images on the newspapers' newsprint were as important as the stories we read about in the newspaper. "If that's true, then we should be in the newspaper," one child joked. Humor aside, everyone agreed that this would be a great way to contribute the youths' messages to existing systems.

Contribute

> This hypertextual dissolution of centrality [one perspective], which makes the medium such a potentially democratic one, also makes it a model of a society of conversations in which no one conversation, no one discipline or ideology, dominates or founds the others. (Landow, 1997, p. 89)

In addition to the seemingly limitless navigational choices, in an ideal hypertext individuals also write their own information and knowledge within an existing or new document (Gaggi, 1997; Landow, 1997). As the reader has now become a writer, he or she can contribute to other documents (Gaggi, 1997; Landow, 1997). Indeed, one of the most exciting aspects of the WWW and of hypertextuality is the opportunity for individuals to contribute information and knowledge.

There were two ways that the youth and facilitators decided to contribute their beliefs and values. First, their drawings—participants' and facilitators'—were exhibited in several locations. The spaces included the Romero Activity Center and two downtown locations. One downtown location was obtained through the cooperation of the Downtown Management District (DMD), an organization that works with merchants and the city to make the area a more desirable destination. The DMD arranged for the availability of several street-level, large display windows of an abandoned retail store in a fairly visible location. These windows became filled with visuals from each week's activities: related newspaper articles, photographs of the project in progress, and the drawings. Additionally, one window displayed a large web of images and text that described the project.

The second downtown location was the K Space Gallery. This was the site for the celebration of the processes and results of the project. The Gallery typically exhibited the contemporary works of art of locally, regionally, and nationally recognized artists. During *Connect to Community Through Art*, however, the space featured drawings, paintings, sculptures, collages, and tiles created by the youth participants, adult facilitators, Joe Lopez, and most of the

K Space artists. The art was displayed in groups according to social and political issues and concerns—such as Kosovo or school violence—with all images treated with equal importance. That is, the images created by adult artists were not separated or given special treatment. The facilitators agreed that this was important not only in terms of democratizing systems that govern, but also in order to demonstrate the importance of each individual's message.

In an attempt to continue the hypertextual narrative strategy, visitors to the K Space Gallery were encouraged to explore, connect, examine, and contribute to the exhibition through an interactive draw-and-display activity. Visitors were encouraged to make their own drawings on newsprint on a table covered with newspaper in the middle of the Gallery. The drawings were hung on a designated wall also within the Gallery.

The second method used to disseminate the issues and concerns of youth and facilitators was through the assistance of the media, particularly of the local newspaper. This occurred as *artconnects* arranged to have photographs of the project in progress printed several weeks in a row in a section that featured community members in action. *artconnects* also worked with a staff writer to cover the project just prior to the opening. This resulted in a feature article that included commentary by the youth and facilitators, information about the project and celebration, and several photographs. As a result of this article, a local television station came to the celebration with cameras, and taped and televised the event with several interviews. Thus, the youth not only explored, connected, examined, and contributed to social and political events as reported by the local newspaper, but they also *became* the news.

Concluding Comments

There were numerous positive aspects of using hypertextual narrative strategies in *Connect to Community Though Art*, including linking individuals, communities, and organizations through engaging and evaluating social and political factors. One of highlights of this project was when individuals, like teachers in area schools, or organizations, like the DMD, stepped forward and asked if they could participate. Also noteworthy was the fact that many youth seemed to feel empowered by—proud of—their personal and cultural differences.

There also were, however, several aspects of this project that the participants and facilitators found problematic—but not impossible to solve. Although many people supported—and indeed were surprised—by the youths' engagement and evaluation of serious issues and concerns, many also felt concerned that these youth already had enough problems to think about. In subsequent projects, there has been an attempt to balance serious issues with positive ones.

Additionally, very few youth were able to attend the celebration or ever visit the downtown locations. To remedy this problem, facilitators agreed that parents and families should be more actively involved, that the project could be made available on-line, and that the Garcia Center could be a site for collaborative exhibitions. Since the culmination of *Connect to Community Through Art,* the three original facilitating organizations have submitted grant applications and obtained funds to develop, implement, and evaluate these concerns and the new ones that emerge each week.

Suggestions for Adaptation and Additional Exploration

Educators and learners can adapt and build upon hypertextual narrative strategies to match the unique needs and resources available within their classrooms and communities. Indeed, there are infinite possibilities. One suggestion is to empower learners to explore the social and political factors of a topic before new information is presented. Students then can construct connections to artists who investigate similar content through their works of art.

Invite the youth to share their discoveries. Try exploring and examining how individuals relate and respond to the information or experiences similarly and differently. Identify links among and between the students' findings. Ask learners to create visual responses to their discoveries.

Additionally, students can web or map their findings and responses on paper, on an overhead projector, and on a computer. It also is interesting to physically link individual students based on their ideas using yarn or ribbon.

References

Aeseth, E. J. (1994). Nonlinearity and literary theory. In G. P. Landow (Ed.). *Hypertext/Theory* (pp. 52–86). Baltimore; London: The Johns Hopkins University Press.

Apple, M. W. (1995). *Education and power.* 2nd Edition. New York: Routledge.

Bal, M. (1997). *Narratology: Introduction to the theory of narrative.* 2nd edition. Toronto, Canada; Buffalo; London: University of Toronto Press.

Freire, P. (1970). *Pedagogy of the oppressed.* New York: Continuum.

Gaggi, S. (1997). *From text to hypertext: Decentering the subject in fiction, film, the visual arts, and electronic media.* Philadelphia, PA: The University of Pennsylvania Press.

Garoian, C. R. (1999). Understanding performance art as curriculum text: The community-based pedagogy of Suzanne Lacy. In *Performing pedagogy: Toward an art of politics* (pp. 125–157). New York: State University of New York Press.

Giroux, H. A. (1997). Schooling and the culture of positivism: Notes on the death of history. In *Pedagogy and the politics of hope: Theory, culture, and schooling* (pp. 3–34). Boulder; Oxford, UK: Westview Press.

Illich, I. (1971). Learning webs. In *Deschooling society* (pp. 72–104). New York; London: Harper & Row.

Irwin, R. L. & Kindler, A. M. (Eds.) (1999). Art education beyond school boundaries: Identifying resources, exploring possibilities. In *Beyond the school: Community and institutional partnerships in art education* (pp 1–4). Reston, VA: National Art Education Association.

Kincheloe, J. (1995). Meet me behind the curtain: The struggle for a critical postmodern action research. In P. L. McLaren & J. M. Giarelli (Eds.). *Critical theory and educational research* (pp. 71–89). Albany; New York: State University of New York Press.

Landow, G. (1997). *Hypertext 2.0: The convergence of contemporary critical theory and technology.* Baltimore; London: The Johns Hopkins University Press.

Lankshear, C., Peters, M., Knobel, M. (1996). Critical pedagogy and cyberspace. In H. A. Giroux, C. Lankshear, P. McLaren, & M. Peters (Eds.). *Counternarratives: Cultural studies and critical pedagogies in postmodern spaces* (pp. 149–188). New York and London: Routledge.

Lyotard, J-F. (1987). The postmodern condition. In K. Baynes, J. Bohman, & T. McCarthy (Eds). *After philosophy–end or transformation?* (pp. 73–94). Cambridge, MA; London: MIT Press.

Roberts, L. (1997). *From knowledge to narrative: Educators and the changing museum.* Washington, DC: Smithsonian Institution Press.

Shor, I. (1992). *Empowering education.* Chicago, IL: The University of Chicago Press.

Shore, I., & Freire, P. (1987). *A pedagogy for liberation: Dialogues on transforming education.* South Hadley, MA: Bergin & Garvey.

Author's Notes

The author would like to thank Chelisa Herbrich and Amy E. Lewis for their editorial support and advice on this paper.

This paper is drawn from Chapters Two and Five of the author's in-progress dissertation, titled *Exhibitions and Hidden Narratives: Transforming Traditional Art Museum Pedagogical Practices through the Construction of Hypertextual Narratives.*

CONCLUSIONS AND FURTHER QUESTIONS

1. Reese argues that we must re-envision teaching strategies. What are the three key themes and issues (based on Giroux) that she states we must incorporate? How has each of these issues affected your conceptions of yourself as a teacher?

2. Describe what is meant by hypertext. What four hypertextual narrative strategies does Reese present? Give a brief explanation of each strategy and discuss the similarities and differences between them.

3. Why does Reese suggest that these hypertextual narrative structures are useful? In what order should they be used?

4. How is community conceptualized in this chapter? Describe the relationship between the community and the museum.

5. How can differing narrative structures help us reconceptualize our understanding of knowledge and the role of the museum and the community in the construction of knowledge?

RESOURCES AND SUGGESTIONS
FOR FURTHER READING

Carol Becker. *Different voices: A social, cultural, and historical framework for change in the American art museum.* New York, NY: Association of Art Museum Directors, 1992.

Susan A. Crane (Ed.). *Museums and memory.* Stanford, CA: Stanford University Press, 2000.

Douglas Crimp, *On the museum's ruins.* Cambridge, MA: The MIT Press, 1993.

Carol Duncan. *Civilizing rituals: Inside public art museums.* New York: Routledge, 1995.

Nina Felshin (Ed.). *But is it art? The spirit of art as activism.* Seattle, WA: Bay Press, 1994.

George E. Hein. *Learning in the museum.* New York: Routledge, 1998.

Ellen Cochran Hirzy, (Ed.). *True needs, true partners: Museums and schools transforming education.* Washington, DC: Institute of Museum Services, 1996.

Ivan Karp, Christine Mullen Kreamer, & Steven D. Lavine (Eds.). *Museums and communities: The politics of public culture.* Washington, DC: Smithsonian Institution Press, 1992.

Lucy R. Lippard. *Lure of the local: Senses of place in a multicentered society.* New York: New Press, 1998.

Ronald W. Neperud (Ed.). *Context, content, and community in art education: Beyond postmodernism.* New York: Teachers College Press, 1995.

Jane Remer. *Beyond enrichment: Building effective arts partnerships with schools and their communities.* New York: ACA Books, 1996.

Lynda H. Schneekloth & Robert G. Shibley. *Placemaking: The art and practice of building communities.* New York: Wiley, 1995.

Stephen E. Weil. *A cabinet of curiosities: Inquiries into museums and their prospects.* Washington, DC: Smithsonian Institution Press, 1995.

CHAPTER 27
QUESTIONS AND EXPLORATIONS

1. What interdisciplinary approaches to education have you used (either as a student or a teacher)?

2. How does the concept of interdisciplinarity help us approach issues in the elementary classroom?

3. Have you ever been involved in a school project that involved people from your local community? Explain.

4. As a teacher would you consider modifying your curriculum or involving yourself and/or your students in a project initiated by another teacher? Explain.

5. Should schools and/or individual classes become involved in projects that move them outside the physical boundaries of the school? Why or why not? Should teachers involve community members from outside of the classroom in class projects?

6. Whose responsibility is it to teach children about alcohol and drug prevention? When should teachers involve themselves and their students in drug and alcohol prevention?

7. Where can you go in your local community for assistance in school/classroom projects? What type of materials, supplies and support can be obtained from the community? How can teachers gain this type of support?

8. Should art at the elementary level concentrate on individual projects? What are your views on collaborative art projects? Have you ever collaborated on a project? Describe your experiences of the collaborative process.

Interdisciplinarity and Community as Tools For Art Education and Social Change

Mary Adams

In the global village in which we all live, communication and the sharing of ideas are but a mouse-click away. Community, once defined by physical boundaries, can now be defined by such parameters as commonality of interest regardless of proximity. Today, ideas exist not only in the context of books and discussion but also in the dynamic context of cyberspace. It is here that author and reader can interact and author and author can combine ideas by means of Internet links.

As an elementary art educator in the Youngstown, Ohio City School System, I have, since 1998, been pursuing an ongoing interdisciplinary project. Written and developed with much input from Youngstown West Elementary urban school children in grades three through six, *We Have Poipus!* is a puppet show having to do with drug and violence prevention and with having a purpose in life. This project has also involved technology and other educators from our district, as well as the local community. Initially conceived from a visual arts perspective, the project is grounded in social issues and was easily integrated with other subject areas.

I believe having a sense of purpose and believing that others also have purpose is an essential premise upon which humankind must draw for a healthy well-ordered society. We live in an increasingly violent world. I believe that this is due largely to a lack of belief in purpose, which can be translated into valuing other human beings as well as oneself. The meaning of our having a purpose is inexorably linked to an appreciation of differences among people. Aside from a common purpose to co-exist with others in the world, it would seem that each of us also has a unique purpose of our own for being here.

Violence in our schools has become an issue for national alarm. Safety measures in existing schools are stepped up and new schools being constructed are equipped with greatly increased security and surveillance devices. It might be expected, due to socioeconomic factors, that children from the inner city and crime-infested neighborhoods would have more of a propensity for violence, however violent behavior is in no way endemic only to urban situations. In recent years, school shootings and threats of shootings that have occurred in suburban and outlying districts are tragic indications of the omnipresence of potential violence.

Crime and violence associated with drug addiction continues to be a problem that threatens the everyday lives and safety of children and communities everywhere. All we have to do is turn on the evening news, read the newspaper, or experience in our own neighborhoods incidents of drive-by shootings, drug related murders, or acts of violence committed against other people in relation to drug abuse. But criminal drug abuse is not the only problem.

Although alcohol and tobacco are legal they are no less problematic. Tobacco has proven to be our most imminent health hazard for young people. To quote from an anti-tobacco web site,

> [A]s you read this, somewhere a child is trying tobacco for the first time. Every day 3,000 children in the United States will begin what for many will become a lifelong addiction. Subsequent mortality from tobacco (400,000 deaths per year) is annually greater than that from drug abuse, AIDS, suicide, homicide, and motor vehicle accidents combined. (www.tarwars.org)

While in many ways the remediation of society's ills may be beyond the scope of what we as educators can logistically take on, viable attempts at preventing problems through reaching our children, our future, are not beyond our scope and must not be neglected. I believe an interdisciplinary approach to education is the most promising tool upon which we, as educators, may call.

Studies have shown that interdisciplinary approaches to education have a synergistic effect, i.e., the end result is more than the sum of the parts. By teaching such basic disciplines as reading, writing, mathematics, science, social studies, health education, career education, art, theater, music, and physical education in a manner that interrelates, the student leaves with a deeper understanding of the subject matter than had he or she been taught each of these subjects separately. Peter P. Cebulka III has made documentation supporting the benefits of this approach to education as well as specific areas of help easily accessible on the Internet. "The Extensive Annotated Bibliography of Integrated Curriculum" which he compiled in 1998 can be found at (http://web54.sd54.k12.il.us/district54/lts/pbl/resources.htm) and is well worth taking a look at.

An Interdisciplinary Approach: We Have Poipus!

The following is an explanation of how this ongoing project, the production of the *We Have Poipus!* puppet show, which was initiated as an art class project and evolves around visual art, has developed as an interdisciplinary project and has grown to involve students, teachers, parents, and community members in activities whose scope extends well beyond the art classroom. It is only to be expected that not all disciplines can be an integral part of every "interdisciplinary" project. On the other hand, it can be too easy for teachers to stay within the insular world of the classroom. When we deal with social issues we begin to move beyond the walls of the classroom and into the community.

Art initially was, and still is, the main discipline involved in *We Have Poipus!* Art served as the inspiration and catalyst for the other disciplines, which have become a part of the production. Art inspired the writing of the script and songs contained therein. Other disciplines became a part of the process and end product as a result of the hands-on art process.

Although the puppets designed for the Youngstown production of *We Have Poipus!* are extremely complex and large, any puppet, even one as simple as the type that a kindergarten student could create, would be suitable for classroom use of the *We Have Poipus!* script and/or soundtrack. The puppets we are currently working on are designed to capture and maintain the attention of a large audience in a sizeable auditorium. Our goal is to produce a permanent professional production, which will travel from school to school within our district as well as beyond. A production as ambitious as this would more easily be accomplished with the help of an art supervisor who could generate financial and administrative support for the undertaking. In systems where a visual arts advocate and coordinator does not exist this kind of undertaking could serve as a good supporting argument for the creation of such a position.

One aspect that has made this project so appealing to audience members, in particular to children, is its visual and auditory components. The fact that popular culture (cartoons, TV shows, commercials, etc.) relies on visual imagery to get messages across is testimony to the impact imagery has on the psyche and the mind. Visual images play an extremely important role in illustrating and clarifying ideas and associations with words. Just as the use of language must be adapted to fit the intended audience, so also must the use of visual imagery be adapted. This is so crucial that the recent historic tobacco settlement forbids the use of cartoon characters in the marketing of tobacco products because of the strong appeal that cartoons have to children. The American Medical Association has a "Fact Sheet about Kids and Tobacco Advertising" on the web that states:

> "Old Joe," the cartoon camel used to advertise Camel cigarettes, is as familiar to six-year-old children as Mickey Mouse. A study found that 91 percent of six year olds not only recognized the Old Joe image, but were able to correctly link him with cigarettes. This was the same recognition level measured for the Disney icon. (http://www.ama-assn.org/special/aos/tobacco/fact.htm.)

The larger-than-life puppets we are creating for *We Have Poipus!* are actually colorful three-dimensional cartoon characters. We are subverting the efforts of corporations such as those found in the tobacco industry by, in effect, using cartoon characters to help children stay off cigarettes and other drugs.

Further evidence of the importance of the impact of visual imagery can be found on the web at *http://tobaccofreekids.org/*. This site is particularly chilling. At the top of the page there is a number stating how many kids have become regular smokers in the current year. Under this is a number stating how many will eventually die from their addiction. If you visit this site now and then go back again after reading the rest of this chapter you will see that the numbers have increased. The good news is that, as stated on the previous site, "school-based tobacco-use prevention programs in the United States have had consistently positive effects" (*http://www.ama-assn.org/special/aos/tobacco/ fact.htm.*).

Visual images in the classroom include images in popular culture as well as books, reproductions, and the artwork children create. In addition, art in the elementary classroom need not be viewed as "make and take" activities stressing individual projects but can be communal efforts around social issues like Youngstown's *We Have Poipus!* puppet show. It is important to choose social issues that relate directly to students' lives and to approach issues on levels that they would understand.

There are many approaches that can be used with varying degrees of impact. Creating a puppet show is an excellent means of reaching students because of the many elements involved such as visual, auditory, and use of movement. Students' writing of a script will result in ownership of the ideas. The positive use of peer pressure, which is also a part of this project, can be used to enhance learning of any kind and to affect behavioral outcomes for the betterment of the class. When ideas are discussed and translated into a creative form (written or an artwork) as a group effort, the positive forces of peer pressure take hold as a group consensus evolves pertaining to the issues. This can lead to individual commitment to the ideas being explored. The physical involvement of speaking the parts and operating the puppets results in identification with the characters.

When attempting to implement social change it is best to involve as many different disciplines as possible. While one child might respond most strongly to art, another child might respond most strongly to music. Likewise, there are students who relate just as strongly to the other disciplines. Music, like art, seems to have a broad appeal and helps make a production more entertaining, be it a puppet show or any other type of effort. In our production there are three original songs that students sing. Students rehearsed the songs and were taken to a professional recording studio along with the student actors to record the script and lyrics as the pantomime performance soundtrack.

For our show the puppets pantomime to the soundtrack. The puppets being constructed for the Youngstown production of *We Have Poipus!* are uniquely designed semi-marionettes fashioned from *papier mâché*. There are a total of twenty-one different puppets operated from below by students as they propel themselves around the stage on specially made carts. The carts upon which the puppets are mounted are equipped with a small table that holds the script. Students follow the script and operate the mouth and arms as they also move the cart about to make the puppets appear to walk. Each puppet has its own cart, and each puppet disassembles for easy storage and transportation.

An interdisciplinary approach to education, with its benefits exemplified by this Youngstown project, is further illustrated in the writing of the script. Art teachers and elementary classroom teachers need to reconsider their subject area boundaries for a more fluid approach to teaching that reframes limited definitions of art and the disciplinary boundaries that usually keep teachers and school subjects apart. As an example, in the *We Have Poipus!* puppet show, writing was the next step as we created the puppets. It became easy to write the script when one creative process, that of art making, flowed into the next or became a springboard into writing.

Students helped write the script, which was completed in a relatively short time. The writing was a dynamic process in which the students also named the characters/puppets as suggested by their features and characteristics. This in turn modified the development of the script and also affected the design and construction of the puppets and the set. For example, the name "Fireball" evolved as a result of painting one of the characters fire-engine red. (To add visual interest and to avoid any racial implications the puppets are every color on the color wheel.) Fireball implies shortness of temper—a perfect clue for a character in the play who originally has a poor disposition but develops into someone who learns to control his own behavior and emotions. Creating characters and script to be used as tools for learning is an exciting approach to helping students learn appropriate social behavior as well as other subject matter.

Health issues that are taught through art, music, and drama are the prime focus of *We Have Poipus!* It is hoped that students taking part in any production of this play or even just reading the script or listening to the soundtrack will learn about and make good choices to avoid drugs. Through art and song, children focus on the before and after effects of taking drugs and can clearly and dramatically see the differences over time (which flies by so quickly) between those who have made healthy choices and those who have not.

Just as important is the focus on mental health. It is essential for human well-being to know that each and all of us are an important part of the universe. We all play a role. Because we are all unique we are even more important. As Father Time says, in the play, "there is only one like each of us so we must use our gifts and talents wisely." It is indeed joyous for the characters in the play to learn that they have purpose, or as they call it, "poipus!" It is also joyous when they realize that what they have seen—their future lives—was not reality but a vision. They rejoice when they realize that they can still make right choices. The happy ending is that they all do choose to make right choices and to live their lives with "poipus!"

Character development in the writing of a play is more dramatic if accompanied by the opportunity for students to use different kinds of voices. For example, in *We Have Poipus!* the mocking voice of Green Meanie, the rickety old voice of Father Time, Leonardo Da Snozzio, who speaks with a voice box, the exasperated Fireball, and the other-worldly voice of the Decision Maker provide many opportunities for students to develop acting skills while enjoying the opportunity to ham it up.

The use of technology also enhances student interest in a project. The prospect of having their own voices used in a professionally-made recording and immortalized online, as well as an intense interest in the play itself, resulted in virtually every student in the school desiring to have a part. Students practiced reading the script freely, on their own time, and with a depth of understanding, which was clearly indicated by their dramatic interpretations. Auditions were held during art class and students ranging from grades three through six tried out for sixteen speaking parts. Because student interest was so intense, we had two students share the part of the narrator. As with much of the production, this was an idea generated by the students.

There are direct connections to cause and effect in the play as children realize that drugs lead to crime and violence. There is a breakdown of society starting with the basic unit of society—the family. Venus, who took drugs, has an abnormal child who is taken from her because of her drug problem. Likewise, there is a sociological study showing the downfall and demise of other characters. Fermento, who used to drink wine down at the park, later in life lives in a cardboard box. Fireball becomes part of the penal system because of his short fuse, and Mousetrap, the drug dealer, is shot and killed.

Student involvement in a project of this scope also includes having students become aware of numerous career opportunities. A project such as this could spur interest in careers such as becoming a playwright, an actor, being the voice for an animated cartoon, singer, art director, ad writer, producer, operating a recording studio, and a computer expert. Teachers, likewise, expand their horizons and are able to form many contacts who can serve as liaisons in bringing a project such as this to completion.

Teachers cover a lot of ground in what they do on a daily basis but they cannot be expected to be able to do everything. Teachers use many skills when taking on a creative project, be it large or small. Depending on the project, skills needed may include organizational abilities, communicative skills (verbal and written), public relations, research, networking, negotiating, and grant writing. It is important to build community support in order to get the help we need. Teachers can and should tap into the expertise of other teachers and community members. Teachers may not have to be experts in everything but it is important to be organized and resourceful! When teachers from different disciplines share ideas and work together with the community, remarkably effective and interesting events and projects like Youngstown's can take shape.

With a project this big it is best to involve as many children and interested educators in a school system as possible. Art educators Anita Groubert, Tresa Kurz-Hedrich, and Judith Szabo, who teach in other schools within the Youngstown School District, responded by making scenery with the help of their students, ranging from elementary to high school. West Elementary's music specialist, Marcia Miot, agreed to work with a group of students who would sing the songs in the script.

Any project that teachers take on may require skills beyond their expertise in teaching. With school budgets being as they are, it is helpful to be able to secure as much donated help as possible. Family members may be a good source of help. In our case the production involves twenty-one larger-than-life puppets, a 24-foot stage and elaborate scenery which required carpentry skills. My husband, Bill, designed the framework and operating mechanisms for the semi-marionettes. He also designed and made the 24-foot stage that disassembles into 4-foot by 8-foot sections and built the twenty wooden carts upon which the puppets will be mounted. My mother, Cathryn Burke, gladly helped with some of the puppet construction.

In addition, it is absolutely essential to have the support of parents in a project such as this. They need to understand what you are trying to achieve and why it is important. Parents readily cooperated when I needed students to stay after school. They gave permission for their children to have parts in the play. Other parents gave of their time and talent and offered helpful suggestions. For example, when I needed someone to help design Mousetrap's shifty eyes, which could be operated from below, Leonard Williams, a father of one my students, took on the challenge.

In the spring of 1999, a major break came when, through networking with teachers in my building, I met Maxina Gohlke owner of Ytown PC-HELP. Maxina, a parent from West, is a self-taught computer expert who has given generously of her time helping students and teachers in our school building work with computers. She agreed to donate her services as the webmaster for a web site I wanted to set up for The Steel Valley Art Teachers Association. This site would feature the *We Have Poipus!* puppet show. Because I believed the script could help children make good choices, the script was placed on this web site, www.svata.org, for public use in September 1999 even though the actual play production still had not taken place. Maxina also agreed to be the webmaster for www.wehavepoipus.org. We have recently placed an entire soundtrack along with the original music on the Internet at both these locations, making the script and soundtrack, as well as construction information for the carts, puppets, and stage, available worldwide.

Social issues affect and involve everyone. In order to make a difference it can be quite beneficial to move beyond the school arena into the community. Businesses and other organizations often are mindful of community problems and are more than willing to offer services or make donations. In our case donations from local businesses such as Carter Lumber of Boardman, Moss Brothers of Austintown, and Star Supply of Youngstown came in the way of materials needed for construction of the puppets and stage. Our local YWCA was willing to provide a space for us to continue working on this project throughout the summer of 2000. Interested educators Mary Ann Allgood, Becky Meredith, Linda Smith, and Nora Lewis helped work on the puppets with children at the Youngstown YWCA. I have recently spoken with personnel from The Oakland Center for the Arts, a local arts company that presents dance productions, musicals, dramas, concerts, and children's programs and have enlisted their help.

Friendships and bonds develop when working together for a good cause. People I hardly knew at the time are now good friends—like Pauline Hruby who originally typed the script and all the separate parts and Mary Ann Kalinich who retyped the script for the Internet. Our school secretary, Fran Blevins, always willing to lend a helping hand, typed numerous documents for this project. Mrs. Mary Allgood, the mother of one of my colleagues, made curtains.

Networking with other teachers can help you find other excellent resources. For example, with little effort I learned of Richard Wilmitch, of Rix

Mix Sound Ideas Recording Studio who does professional recording for the Youngstown Schools various music programs. He did much of the recording and the musical arrangements at a nominal fee, which was paid for by West Elementary's Parent Teacher Organization. When transportation to the recording studio seemingly became an obstacle, with a little networking I learned of another teacher who had received help from The Western Reserve Transit Authority. WRTA, our local public bus company, provided trolley transportation at no charge.

Some of the funding for supplies and a recording of the students singing came from a special fund Youngstown Schools had available for drug prevention activities. However, due to financial difficulties of the city school system, money for extra projects has not been available. The art program has seen cutbacks, which have affected the timely completion of this project. Despite the setbacks, I am continuing to pursue the project because I believe it is worth doing. I have seen how students relate to the script and have witnessed how the larger-than-life *papier-mâché* puppets capture the attention of children and adults alike. The script, combined with the puppets, will result in a production that will hold the attention of children at every grade level as well as adults.

The original recording of West Elementary students was done under my direction. Given the age of the students, the time frame we were working with, and the fact that for the most part we did not have the benefit of any persons trained in theatre, we produced an excellent recording. However, Donna Downy, a drama teacher in the Youngstown School System, has agreed to help us obtain a second reading of the script under her direction using older students more experienced in theatre. This will be a project for the 2000–2001 school year. This year there will be time allotted in the schedule since drama is a regular class at her building. This is important because elementary teacher schedules are very tight with many different tasks that need to be accomplished in a school year. It is also important that we get the best quality reading possible since our intentions are to promote this project heavily and to use the recording repeatedly with many different audiences.

After completing a project, or perhaps even before it is brought to completion, as we are doing with *We Have Poipus!*, it is important to promote the project. Accessibility with regard to projects involving social issues is imperative if teachers also want to reach audiences or interested individuals beyond the school or local community. Having a web site is an effective way to use the technology of the Internet. Once on the Internet it is important to advertise the web site location and content. We also made our professional recordings, audiotapes, and CDs available to the public. Videotape is another medium to consider for public access and/or promotion. Other means of promotion may include participation in school, county, or state sponsored events. We prepared a display of the puppets explaining this project for the Educational Hall at the Canfield Fair, one of the largest county fairs held in the USA.

Other ways to promote your project can be found by scanning your local newspaper for articles related to what you are doing. As a result of an article I came across in our local paper, I sent the script and soundtrack to The Ohio Teen Institute for the Prevention of Alcohol and Other Drug Abuse for their use. This is a training program sponsored by the Ohio Department of Alcohol and Drug Addiction Services. I am hoping that participants who are required to implement a drug prevention program in their home school district or county will make it known that this resource is available for anyone who would like to use it.

It is also possible to find appropriate organizations through the telephone directory that may be interested in what you are doing. I have sent the script and soundtrack to the Family Recovery Center, a non-profit organization located in Lisbon, Ohio, which serves Columbiana County and the surrounding area, as well as to the Mahoning County Chemical Dependency Programs, Inc. for their prevention program.

In some cases it might be advisable to seek expert legal advice. In our project I had some concerns with regard to whether this script might be misinterpreted as teaching religion. I consulted Attorney Robert Lev, who assured me that the right to free speech does give teachers and students the right to write a play such as this and to write about it afterwards. Although *We Have Poipus!* in no way attempts to teach religion, it does embrace commonly held principles of accountability, the need to appreciate and respect the universe, the importance and value of each individual, the importance of self-respect, and the need to give back—to do some good. The Decision Maker, who is a messenger in the play, could be likened to any messenger from world religions or mythology. The play is entertainment, but it allows for private philosophical exploration and reflection while embracing commonly held beliefs and principles. However, it would be advisable for teachers to obtain permission from their administration or Board of Education before using this script.

It does not matter if there are other programs in your district that address the same social issue that you would like to explore. Although there are a myriad of other drug prevention programs for students of all ages, many of which Youngstown Schools subscribe to, I believe this program has potential to reach children in significant and different ways than the other programs. Unlike any other programs of which I am aware, the format of this program is an entertaining puppet show written and developed with much input from the students themselves on a district-wide basis. Performance of the puppet show will be by students from the various buildings as the show travels from school to school within our district and beyond. From informal observation, I strongly believe that student involvement at these levels has already resulted in a personal commitment and ownership to the ideas in the play, which evolve around the concept that we have purpose, to a degree that is statistically significant if not staggering.

Evaluation of your project's success should be based on observable and measurable criteria. I believe that *We Have Poipus!* has been highly successful as an ongoing project because of the intense interest that students have shown in it. The following two examples are indications of the interest students have shown. One student who is bused in for the gifted program returned to West Elementary School where I teach, instead of attending another school within the system, specifically so she could continue to take part in the puppet show. Another student who is now in seventh grade and no longer attends West, came to see me recently and told me other former West students were singing *Tic Toc*, one of the original songs from the play, while riding his bus. These incidences and others have led me to believe that this puppet show can have significant impact on young people. It is my sincere hope that this script and project will be widely used to the benefit of a multitude of children.

References

American Academy of Family Physicians, *Tar wars: A partnership in youth education* [Online]. Available: *www.tarwars.org* October 23, 2000

American Medical Association, *Fact sheet: Kids and tobacco advertising* [Online]. Available: *http://www.ama-assn.org/special/aos/tobacco/fact.htm* October 23, 2000

Campaign for Tobacco-free Kids, *Tobacco vs. kids: Where America draws the line* [Online]. Available: *http://tobaccofreekids.org/* October 23, 2000

Cebulka III, Peter P., *The extensive annotated bibliography of integrated curriculum* [Online]. Available: *http://web54.sd.54.k12.il.us/district54/lts/pbl/resources.htm* October 23, 2000

CONCLUSIONS AND FURTHER QUESTIONS

1. What are the differences between integrated and interdisciplinary learning? How does each of these approaches to knowledge help us work with issues in the elementary classroom?

2. Describe the various groups and people that helped create and produce *We Have Poipus!* In what ways did such broad involvement help the project?

3. How did the puppet production reach out to audiences beyond the classroom? What did the students create?

4. When and how should a teacher approach community members and local businesses for assistance on school/classroom projects?

5. What kinds of skills are necessary for a teacher taking on creative projects with her/his students? Should money and resources be in place before taking on a large-scale project?

6. What kinds of interdisciplinary learning are possible with a production such as *We Have Poipus!*

RESOURCES AND SUGGESTIONS
FOR FURTHER READING

Carol Becker (Ed.). *The subversive imagination: Artists, society, and social responsibility*. New York: Routledge, 1994.

David Currell. *Learning with puppets*. Boston, MA: Plays, Inc., 1980.

Trevor J. Fairbrother. *In and out of place: Contemporary art and the American social landscape*. Boston, MA: Museum of Fine Arts, 1993.

Nina Felshin (Ed.). *But is it art? The spirit of art as activism*. Seattle, WA: Bay Press, 1994.

Cedric Flower & Alan Jon Fortney. *Puppets, methods and materials*. Worcester, MA: Davis Publications, 1983.

Rita L. Irwin & Anna M. Kindler (Eds.). *Beyond the school: Community and institutional partnerships in art education*. Reston, VA: National Art Education Association, 1999.

Suzanne Lacy (Ed.). *Mapping the terrain: New genre public art*. Seattle, WA: Bay Press, 1994.

Peter McIntyre. *Puppets with a purpose: Using puppetry for social change*. New York; Penang, Malaysia: United Nations Children's Fund; Southbound, 1998.

Ronald W. Neperud (Ed.). *Context, content, and community in art education: Beyond postmodernism*. New York: Teachers College Press, 1995.

Jane Remer. *Beyond enrichment: Building effective arts partnerships with schools and their communities*. New York: ACA Books, 1996.

Lynda H. Schneekloth & Robert G. Shibley. *Placemaking: The art and practice of building communities*. New York: Wiley, 1995.

Scott Cutler Shershow. *Puppets and "popular" culture*. Ithaca, NY: Cornell University Press, 1995.

CHAPTER 28

QUESTIONS AND EXPLORATIONS

1. When you hear the word "art" what types of objects and activities do you think of? When you hear the word "craft" what types of objects and activities do you think of? What are the similarities between these two terms? What are the differences? What would happen if we blurred or erased the distinctions between the two words?
2. Describe any experiences that you have had making three-dimensional objects. Are these experiences different from those that you have had when working in two-dimensions? In what ways? In what ways are they similar?
3. In your elementary school art experiences what types of objects did you make? How much did you study three-dimensional works as compared to two-dimensional works?

(Re)Shaping Visual Inquiry of Three-Dimensional Art Objects in the Elementary School: A Content-Based Approach

B. Stephen Carpenter II and Billie Sessions

While elementary art teachers continue to seek ways to adequately include historical or cultural information in their instruction, many find it difficult to do so without trivializing the content. Some believe they are neglecting artmaking experiences when they attempt to include historical, critical, or philosophical content. But these are not the only alternatives for art-related instruction in the elementary curriculum, and the art classroom is not the only location in the school in which works of art can be studied. Starting with the same works of art that are studied in the art classroom, elementary classroom teachers can extend the significance of art instruction by engaging their students in content-based inquiry of works of art. We understand that elementary classroom teachers often feel uncomfortable attempting artmaking activities with their students. However, they are well prepared to help students explore the practical, expressive, and symbolic content of art objects through tasks that require reading, comprehension, synthesis, questions, and responses to information and ideas in a variety of subject areas.

In this chapter, we intend to provide a theoretical foundation along with practical suggestions for implementing a content-based approach to studying three-dimensional art objects with elementary students. When we use the term content, we are referring to the explicit and implicit meanings conveyed in a work of art. Content-based instruction places this information at the center of student learning activities. Our approach shifts away from an exclusively production-centered (i.e. art making) form of instruction into, for example, historical, cultural, aesthetic, and social issues that can be found within and/or related to the object.

As a way to explore these issues, students can make critical interpretations of works of art. Critical interpretations require students to identify issues or meanings they believe the work conveys, by connecting specific visual characteristics of the work with similar characteristics they find in other objects, experiences, or information. In this way, content-based instruction attempts to engage students in serious inquiry about important content that is relevant to works of art. Works of art manifest information that can instruct us about the world and about the experience of making art (Albers, 1999). Therefore, the most important student interpretations are those in which students connect meanings they find in works of art to information found in classroom instruction and to their own personal experiences. Students and teachers using a content-based curriculum can explore information and contemporary issues such as diversity, multiculturalism, gender, and the environment.

As educators deeply interested in the possibilities and contributions of art objects to the education of elementary students, we find it interesting that most attempts to diversify the selections of artworks used in the classroom rarely mention sculpture or ceramics. In the following we will discuss possibilities for a content-based approach to three-dimensional works of art in general, and the use and study of clay specifically.

Why Three-dimensional Artworks?

Compared to the critical study of two-dimensional artworks such as paintings, drawings, collages, and various approaches to printmaking, the study and creation of three-dimensional artworks at the elementary level has been very limited. Reproductions available as art instructional resources overwhelmingly depict two-dimensional artworks, but three-dimensional works of art such as sculptures, ceramics, and assemblages can also inspire meaningful study. Children use three-dimensional objects as they play. Blocks, trucks, dolls, twigs, and cardboard boxes are often an important part of their manipulated worlds. The interplay of three-dimensional materials allows children to know their world in ways that two-dimensional materials do not and cannot. Through in-depth investigations of three-dimensional objects, elementary students can successfully make connections to issues in their own lives, as well as content relevant to the larger school curriculum and life outside of school.

Clay as Substantive Education

Because ceramic objects have functional, historical, ritual, aesthetic, global, and social value, and because clay is connected with the earth, fire, and water, they hold a unique position in both the art and craft worlds. Since the 1960s, ceramics has become more securely positioned in the world of fine art, but ceramics education has not become more securely positioned within the world of art education (Williams, 1988).[1] Ceramics in schools is typically not viewed as a significant educational component and its status remains peripheral and tenuous in the field, most likely because of its long perceived second class status as an artform within the fine art world, specifically in relationship to painting, drawing, and sculpture. Given its global heritage, clay artworks have a longer and more extensive history than that of (Euro-American) fine art. Although "clay is an ageless medium with boundless possibilities for art education" (Higby, 1988, p. 66), it is often only included in textbooks as a means to approach history. The availability of reproductions of contemporary clay artworks in elementary textbooks is even more limited.

Ceramic artworks could provide relevant educational experiences through content-based instruction (Brewer, 1992; Clark, 1987; Levin, 1988; Lynn, 1990; Sessions, 1999). Many elementary school ceramics programs are vestiges of outdated, erroneous rationales for teaching clay (DeMuro, 1992; Hill, 1988; Ropko, 1977). In short, there is no clear sense of the educational roles, values, or possibilities of ceramics in art education in today's schools.

As an entry into meaningful discussions about important issues of social, cultural, and historical importance, ceramic vessels and artifacts reflect educationally rich content such as technological developments, rituals, traditions, cultural values, economic conditions, systems of production, social status, and historical events. Three-dimensional artworks, including ceramics, can be placed within historical and cultural frameworks and can be investigated for their utilitarian and technical significance (Barringer, 1996; Hartman and Musial, 1987). What would a content-based approach to learning about three-dimensional clay objects at the elementary level look like? What other issues would need to be considered if three-dimensional works were studied by elementary students in this way?

A Content-based Approach to Instruction

Two visual diagrams illustrate how a content-based approach to inquiry about three-dimensional artworks can be achieved. Ceramic objects can be studied for their content through a variety of lenses. If a ceramic object were to be placed in the center of a curriculum web like that shown in Figure 28.1, many questions could be asked about the object, such as: Where, when, and how was it made? What was its intended use? Who made it? How was it decorated and fired? What are its "roots"? Does it have a special meaning to the society in which it was made? And lastly, What is its relationship to other handmade artifacts? These questions cover general circumstances that all ceramic objects share.

The second model (See Figure 28.2) pares down the complexity of Figure 28.1 to three more essential areas of content: technique, context, and concepts. Students who use this approach to reveal the content of an artwork might explore specifically how the work was created (technique), the influential social and cultural events relevant to that work (contexts), and the philosophical implications of the content of the work (concepts).

These two diagrams can help elementary teachers organize and assess the types of content present in three-dimensional artworks.

How might elementary students use these charts to explore the wooden assemblage sculptures of Beverly Buchanan (See Figure 28.3) created in the 1990s? Buchanan is known for creating wood and found-object sculptures in the form of shacks. These shack sculptures are also made of scrap metal, bottle

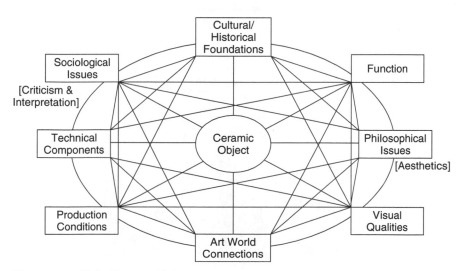

Figure 28.1 Eight Contextual Arenas

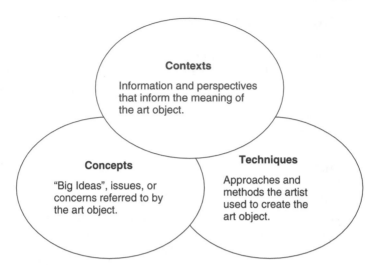

Figure 28.2 *Three Essential Areas of Content*

Figure 28.3 Beverly Buchanan, *Richard's Home*, 1993

caps, and other found objects. Through her work, elementary students might explore such sociological *concepts* as class, social status, history, and memories. For example, they could learn about how people's wealth sometimes influences how they are treated, what they can buy, and where they can live. They can also discover how souvenirs, stories, and historical records are all means of remembering people, places, or events from the past. With respect to cultural and historical *contexts*, students should explore how Buchanan's sculptures establish a sense of place and time. They might investigate the kinds of people who comprise our society, the places they inhabit, our perceptions of these people, and the types of houses that represent aspects of our culture. Exploring the *technical* components of her work, students might note how her craftsmanship looks laid-back or casual and that she uses found wood and other objects. Such observations should inspire students to ask questions like, "Why did she make it look like this?" or "Why doesn't she make houses that look like the one I live in?" Through a content-based approach led by classroom teachers, students can develop connections to content in other subject areas, such as social studies, geography, history, and language arts. Depending on the grade level, elementary students could write interpretations or record their interpretations of the artwork on video or audiotape. They could read books related to cultures and artists who influenced the works they are studying. Through these types of activities students gain a sense that some skills, abilities, and information are important to several subject areas or their everyday life outside of school.

A third approach to content-based inquiry is to have elementary students interpret art objects for their literal and metaphorical content (Carpenter, 1996). Literal content is often rather obvious and easily identified. For example, in terms of its literal content, Buchanan's work, *Richard's Home*, is a wooden sculpture of a house that appears to have been sturdy at one time but is now old and falling apart. A literal interpretation of this work would include a clear and detailed description of what the work looks like and how it is constructed. Metaphorical contents of artworks function in much the same way that metaphors function in language. In language, metaphors are a symbolic way of using one thing with certain qualities to stand for, or to describe, another thing. So, because *Richard's Home* looks like it is old and falling apart, it could be a metaphor for something else with those same qualities, such as a family or a neighborhood.

It is common practice for teachers to ask their students to respond to the symbolic qualities of works of art that they have made and that made by artists. Unfortunately, many elementary teachers do not typically build upon basic responses of their students (Geahigan, 1998). Merely noting that one of Buchanan's sculptures looks like it is unfinished, run-down, or falling apart, can be an important first step in developing a meaningful interpretation of her work. Initial interpretations like these should serve as points of departure for future episodes of in-depth critical and aesthetic inquiry. By requiring students to point to specific qualities of her work and to explain how she was able to make the sculpture look old or falling apart, such as her use of weather-beaten wood instead of new wood, importance and credibility would be added to the initial student interpretations. Students could also explore how some old objects, like antiques or fossils, are seen as valuable whereas other old and poorly maintained objects, such as rusty bicycles or broken toys, are not. Elementary teachers should also "provide opportunities for students to test and revise their hypotheses through interacting with works of art in the presence of other interested viewers" (Geahigan, 1998, p. 302). Teachers could have students read excerpts of critical writing about the works they have discussed and then revisit their own written responses in the following class sessions, revising or adding to what they had written based on their new knowledge of the artworks. Limits and criteria should be offered to help students build upon their basic responses, such as encouraging the inclusion of adjectives, metaphors, quotations from critics or art historians, and thoughtful questions.

Like works created in other media, some ceramic artworks address important issues of today's world, such as pop culture, diversity, gender, ecology, race, religion, environment, ethnicity, war, drugs, nuclear energy, colonialism, and equal rights. In varying degrees, these issues are accessible to elementary students. In the following section, we use the work of Adrian Saxe (1986) to illustrate the complexity of a content-based approach to three-dimensional artworks.[2]

Vessels of Cultural Diversity and Interdisciplinary Knowledge

As has been the case in other areas of art and society, postmodern issues such as pluralism, contradiction, and politics have influenced the aesthetics of the ceramics world over the past several decades. Studio pottery is currently more exuberant, experimental, and eclectic than ever before. At the same time, it is also conservative and upholds a rich decorative and functional tradition. The tension between these extremes, combined with the diversity of work currently being produced, give contemporary ceramics a special flavor and interest. (Dormer, 1994, p. 12). Social and political commentary as subject matter is also present in contemporary ceramics (Failing, 1995, p. 4). In short, contemporary ceramics in America reflects a multicultural, pluralistic society in which influences, techniques, and self-expression come from every period, civilization, culture, and geographic location (Deller, 1992, p. 29).

Clay works by North American ceramists like Adrian Saxe reflect many of these characteristics. Simultaneously, his works illustrate the inherent relationship shared among all ceramic vessels throughout history in his use of various glazes, clay bodies, symbols, and decorative techniques associated with the ceramics of specific world cultures. Because his works contain elements of an aesthetics of pluralism, politics, contradiction, and diversity, Saxe has been called a "global potter" (Knight, 1991), and his work has been called the exemplar of postmodern ceramics (Collins, 1993). As such, his works offer students rich opportunities to interpret and support their interpretations by making connections to other artworks, events, examples of visual culture, and new and unfamiliar situations.

Saxe's work deals with several seemingly disparate elements brought together in one cohesive work. Study of his work demands a critical investigation of the historical, social, and political references of the visual elements. For example, his *Untitled Covered Jar on stand with Antelope Finial (Garth Vader)* 1986, (See Figure 28.4) is typical of Saxe's style of the late 1980s. A careful observer notes his use of an antelope or ibex, a fleur-de-lis (a symbol of French monarchy), mechanical-looking gears, various gilt buttons and charms, a Buddhist bell shape used as the body of the jar, and an unconventional pedestal modeled to resemble lava or raw clay. Through a serious investigation of these symbols students can uncover intentionally "hidden meanings," such as possible correlations between power and wealth, how artistic success is determined, and relationships between nature and culture

Figure 28.4 Adrian Saxe, *Untitled Covered Jar on stand with Antelope Finial (Garth Vader)*

imbedded within this work. For example, students could begin to uncover how certain symbols can imply wealth or materialism, such as Saxe's use of gold (a precious, expensive metal) as the color for the fleur-de-lis and the dozens of bracelet charms, buttons, and medals that adorn the body of the work. Students could also discuss the placement of the antelope (a symbol of nature) in the center of the two mechanical gears (symbols of machinery and industrialization) and how this presentation seems to comment on a relationship between products of nature and those from "civilized" culture.

Advanced elementary students might question issues related to the commercial artworld by examining the implications of the title of the work, a combination of the names of gallery owner Garth Clark, (Saxe's dealer and friend), and the powerful bad guy from Star Wars, Darth Vader. The truly multicultural combination (Collins, 1993) of these seemingly random images offers points of entry to themes like ornamentation, kitsch, and aesthetic value. Teachers could lead their students toward further interpretations of these symbols and others used in Saxe's numerous works. Students could also be directed toward investigating how the issues presented in interpretations of Saxe's work manifest themselves within contemporary culture. Who determines which clothes, skateboards, celebrities, music videos, or games are "cool"? How do students, teachers, and parents make determinations about what movies, imagery, hairstyles, or clothes are acceptable? Through these and similar questions, students explore how instances of ornamentation, kitsch, and visual preferences are viewed and perpetuated in contemporary artifacts and popular visual culture.

Although his works are based on his diverse understanding of and deep interest in history, cultures, and symbolism, many viewers find themselves speechless due to the visual complexity or seemingly arbitrary combination of symbols and objects found in many of Saxe's works. The conceptual content of his work has equally drawn the attention of critics. Commenting on *Untitled Covered Jar on stand with Antelope Finial (Garth Vader)*, Collins (1993) states "within this whole the components engage in complicated forms of cross-talk or, more precisely, encourage the viewer to fill in the contexts alluded to and in the process experience the polyphonic dissonance of different styles and institutions that constitute contemporary cultural life" (p. 135).

In Saxe's work, elementary students can engage in historical exploration, metaphorical interpretations, and the design and execution of their own eclectic contemporary vessels. First, students should view and discuss reproductions of works and sources that have influenced the creation and meaning of Saxe's works. Among the possible examples are various versions of the fleur-de-lis, Sèvres porcelains, images of Louis XIV, Buddhist bells, and ancient Chinese ceramics. Next students should view reproductions of Saxe's vessels and make visual and conceptual connections between his work and the collection of images they just viewed. They should pay attention to the ways in which handles, lids, bodies, feet, spouts, and knobs are represented.

They could begin to discuss what the symbols might mean separately and what they mean when arranged together in one work.

Depending on their cognitive developmental level, the teacher might share with students what various critics have said about an artwork they are studying, or the students themselves might read excerpts from critical essays written about an artist's work. Next, students might revisit works by Saxe, or view related works of art, and construct interpretations that reveal their literal and metaphorical meaning. The antelope situated atop many of Saxe's works typically invites students to explore the literal and symbolic use of this and other animals in work from the Arts and Crafts movement (1870–1920), the Art Deco style (1920s and 1930s), in other clay artworks (Charleston,1968; Nelson, 1971; Speight, 1995), and in fables from various cultures (such as Aesop's Fables).

Another attribute of Saxe's works that encourages elementary students to make literal and metaphorical connections to other artworks is his use of gold as a decorative device. For example, some students make literal connections to the gilt decorations on French Baroque porcelains, antique clocks, or other cultural objects they have seen or heard about, such as gold watches, gold records, or the pot of gold at the end of a rainbow. Other students make metaphorical connections, such as asking whether Saxe is trying to make his work a kind of trophy with his use of gold, such as when a rock star is awarded a gold Grammy award, or the way a painting is meant to seem more important when it is placed inside a gold frame. Students can also be encouraged to create drawings of Saxe's works and the symbols he employs. Students can create a list of visual symbols and their meanings for use in these drawings.

Collages made from magazine cut-outs can supplement written interpretations of three-dimensional artworks. To create these collages, students could be instructed to select magazine images that serve as literal and metaphorical parts of their vessels. A student creating a collage depiction of a teapot might use an image of a spout from a teapot, a coffee pot, or even a watering can as a literal spout of her vessel. The same student might wish to metaphorically convey that the teapot would hold expensive tea. In this case, she might cut out images of coins and paper currency and arrange them to form the body of the teapot. In other words, by using images of money to depict the part of the teapot that holds the tea, the student would metaphorically be assigning the attributes of money to the beverage. With the assistance of the art teacher, upper-level elementary students could create actual ceramic vessels. The focus of such an assignment should be for students to create a vessel in which they use symbols to metaphorically represent themselves, their culture, or an aspect of their world. For example, a student might comment on the shift toward computers in our society as the primary means of communication by creating a vessel that depicts a laptop situated on top like a finial, a mouse and cable as the handle, various pencils and pens decoratively attached to the body of the vessel, and a stack of books as the pedestal. A strong conclusion to such an activity would be to ask students to write about another student's work for the purpose of uncovering literal and metaphorical content.

Conclusion

In this chapter we have advocated the examination of three-dimensional artworks with an emphasis on ceramic artworks. At the same time, we understand that the availability of adequate resources for these objects is limited. Textbooks, exhibition catalogs, journals, and similar publications are excellent sources for critical and historical information about three-dimensional art. These sources also provide visual examples of artworks, both historical and contemporary. Large poster reproductions of three-dimensional artworks are available from a few sources—such as Shorewood Prints. The American Craft Museum, for example, offers slide reproductions and several videos that focus on contemporary artworks. Among the concepts of the eight slide sets are: *The Object as Statement*; *Political Ceramics: Social Issues*; and *Political Ceramics: War*. These concepts are rich with issues and ideas for elementary students to explore in a content-based curriculum.

By studying objects made by living sculptors, content-based instruction posits a more direct link to the lives of the students because, through these works, artists often make visual references to our contemporary lives and issues. In these situations, teachers should encourage students to seek information about the works and the artists, in journals and other forms of popular culture media. Teachers should also help students link the artist's production methods and ideational concerns. If living artists have created the objects under investigation, teachers might assist students in contacting the artist for an interview. Through these contacts, reflecting on the artist's intentions, and comparing these intentions with interpretations given by critics and students, can enhance criticism and interpretation.

We believe that the potential of a content-based exploration of three-dimensional art objects has not yet been articulated in art education literature, and accordingly, substantive learning by elementary students in this area remains marginalized. We hope that a remedy to this situation has been initiated.

Endnotes

1. In recent Euro-Western history, handmade daily-use objects such as pottery, weaving, jewelry, and furniture were labeled as craft and not considered to be "art." The makers of these objects were considered to be artists if they made fine art (e.g., sculpture, painting, drawing) and craftsmen if they made functional objects. This art/craft issue is not necessarily the case in other regions of the world

where art or craft objects are not labeled as such, and handmade objects for daily living or rituals are often held in higher esteem than decorative items.
2. The authors would like to thank elementary art teacher Lisa Langston (Virginia Beach, Virginia) and her students whose content-based investigations of Adrian Saxe's works support some of the content of this chapter.

References

Albers, P. (1999). Art education and the possibility of social change. *Art Education, 52* (4), 6–11.

Barringer, M. (1996). The shape of ceramics history. *Studio Potter, 24* (2), 17–18.

Brewer, T. (1992). The effect of contrasting instructional strategies on seventh-grade students' ceramic vessels. *Studies in Art Education, 34* (1), 18–27.

Carpenter II, B. S. (1996). A meta-critical analysis of ceramics criticism for art education: Toward an interpretive methodology. *Marilyn Zurmuehlin Working Papers,* National Art Education Association (NAEA), pp. 107–114.

Charleston, R. (Ed.). (1968). *World ceramics.* Secaucus, NJ: Chartwell.

Clark, G. (1987). *American ceramics.* New York: Abbeville.

Collins, J. (1993). Adrian Saxe and the postmodern vessel. In M. Drexler-Lynn (Ed.). *The clay art of Adrian Saxe,* Los Angeles County Museum of Art, Los Angeles, California & Thames and Hudson, New York. pp. 121–146.

Deller, H. (1992). Preserving the foundation. *Studio Potter, 20* (2), 28–29.

DeMuro, T. (1992). Making a case for clay in art education. (Doctoral dissertation, Columbia University Teachers College, 1992). *Dissertation Abstracts International, 53,* (11A), 3779.

Dormer, P. (1994). *The new ceramics: Trends and traditions.* London: Thames & Hudson.

Failing, P. (1995). *Howard Kottler: Face to face.* Seattle WA; London: University of Washington Press.

Geahigan, G. (1998). From procedures, to principles, and beyond: Implementing critical inquiry in the classroom. *Studies in Art Education, 39* (4), 293–308.

Hartman, R., & Musial, J. (1987). *Navajo pottery.* Flagstaff, AZ: Northland.

Higby, W. (1988). Viewing the launching pad: The arts, clay, and education. *Studio Potter, 16* (2), 66–68.

Hill, J. (1988). An historical analysis of and speculation about the value of clay working in American education (Doctoral dissertation, Columbia University Teachers College, 1988). *Dissertation Abstracts International, 49,* (09A), 2507.

Knight, C. (1991). The global potter. *Los Angeles Times.* 24 November, Calendar section.

Levin, E. (1988). *The history of American ceramics.* New York: Abrams.

Lynn, M. (1990). *Clay today.* Los Angeles, CA: Chronicle Books.

Nelson, G. (1971). *Ceramics: A potter's handbook.* New York: Holt, Rinehart & Winston.

Ropko, A. (1977). An introductory secondary school ceramics curriculum model derived from four contemporary value education sources (Doctoral dissertation, University of Maryland, 1977). *Dissertation Abstracts International, 38* (11A), 6476.

Sessions, B. (1999). Ceramics curriculum: What has it been? What could it be? *Art Education, 52* (5), 6–11.

Speight, C. (1995). *Hands in clay.* Mountain View, CA: Mayfield.

Williams, G. (Ed.). (1988) A case for clay in art education [Monograph]. *Studio Potter, 16* (2), 17.

CONCLUSIONS AND FURTHER QUESTIONS

1. Why do Carpenter and Sessions advocate that we look at three-dimensional works of art in the elementary classroom?

2. What do the authors mean by content in art? What is content-based instruction? Why should teaching in the elementary classroom be content-based? How does content-based instruction link to other areas of the curriculum?

3. Describe each of the three approaches to content-based instruction that Carpenter and Sessions suggest.

4. What is the difference between the literal and metaphoric content of a work of art? What type of information does each form of content help us to understand?

5. Find an example of a three-dimensional work of art. How does each of the approaches suggested in this chapter help you understand the object? What are the literal and metaphoric meanings of the artwork?

RESOURCES AND SUGGESTIONS
FOR FURTHER READING

Andrew Benjamin (Ed.). *Sculpture: Contemporary form and theory.* London; Lanham, MD: Academy Group, 1997.

Color and fire: Defining moments in studio ceramics, 1950–2000. (Exhibition catalgogue.) Los Angeles; New York: Los Angeles County Museum of Art in association with Rizzoli International, 2000.

Cross-references: Sculpture into photography. James Casebere, Bruce Charlesworth, Bernard Faucon, Ron O'Donnell, Sandy Skoglund, Boyd Webb. (Exhibition catalogue.) Minneapolis, MN: Walker Art Center, 1987.

Jonathan Fairbanks & Angela Fina. *The best of pottery.* Rockport, MA; Cincinnati, OH: Quarry Books; North Light Books, 1996.

Angela Fina & Christopher Gustin. *The best of pottery, volume two.* Gloucester, MA; Cincinnati, OH: Quarry Books; Distributed by North Light Books, 1998.

Jan Greenberg & Sandra Jordan. *The sculptor's eye: Looking at contemporary American art.* New York: Delacorte Press, 1993.

Frances Hannah. *Ceramics.* New York: E.P. Dutton, 1986.

Home and the world. Architectural sculpture by two contemporary African artists: Aboudramane and Bodys Isek Kingelez. (Exhibition catalogue.) New York; Munich: Museum for African Art & Prestel, 1993.

Peter Lane. *Ceramic form: Design & decoration.* New York: Rizzoli, 1998.

Peter Lane. *Contemporary porcelain: Materials, techniques and expressions.* London: A & C Black, 1995.

Sarah Rogers-Lafferty. *Body & soul: Aspects of recent figurative sculpture.* Cincinnati, OH: Contemporary Arts Center, 1985.

Harriet F. Senie. *Contemporary public sculpture: Tradition, transformation, and controversy.* New York: Oxford University Press, 1992.

Traditions and transformations: Contemporary Afro-American sculpture. The Bronx Museum of the Arts, February 21–May 27, 1989. (Exhibition catalogue.) Bronx, NY: The Bronx Museum of the Arts, 1989.

Virginia Watson-Jones. *Contemporary American women sculptors.* Phoenix, AZ: Oryx, 1986.

John C. Welchman, Isabelle Graw, & Anthony Vidler. *Mike Kelley.* London: Phaidon, 1999.

Useful sources for examples of contemporary ceramic work and sculpture include the following periodicals: *Ceramics Monthly, The Studio Potter, Ceramic Review, American Ceramics, Canadian Ceramics, American Craft, Craft Arts International, Sculpture Review, International Sculpture,* and *Sculpture.*

CHAPTER 29
QUESTIONS AND EXPLORATIONS

1. Choose a work of art or an object that you are familiar with. How many different contexts for understanding can you place the object in? How do the different contexts intersect and support each other?
2. Discuss whether or not a work of art can mean different things in different contexts. What determines the meanings that we give an artwork?
3. Are there any differences between the ways in which we interpret works of art and the ways in which we interpret everyday objects and visual images? Why or why not?
4. How do students learn to "read" visual images and artworks?

Three: Reading Lorna Simpson's Art in Contexts

Mary Ann Stankiewicz

We can *read* works of art, not simply in terms of an alphabet and grammar of sensory and formal qualities, but for meaning and understanding. Thoughtful investigation of individual works can encourage student questions that, if we take time to model better ways of responding, can stimulate more critical and creative thinking. Some works of art are better than others for encouraging such investigations. Lorna Simpson's photographic work is grounded in semiotic theory, in the notion that images communicate by means of association with other images, texts and contexts. She deliberately creates works that engage our curiosity, that encourage us to take time and puzzle out possible meanings. Knowledge of Simpson's life, of the body of her artwork, of critical writings on her work, and of patrons who have supported her work provides one set of contexts for interpretation. Knowledge of American society, issues of wealth and power, and racial and gender inequalities provide even broader contexts. With guidance, elementary students can begin to explore not only art world issues, but also life world issues as they find meaning in works of art.

I used *III*, a multiple, three-dimensional work of art by Lorna Simpson, to help gifted fifth-grade students learn how to read works of art in various contexts. Barrett (1990) suggests that contextual information can help viewers develop a sound interpretation of a photograph (or other work of art). Unless one knows something about an art object, it is difficult to find meaning in it. Without supporting evidence to connect an artwork with some context or contexts, the viewer can only speculate; there are no grounds, no evidence to support an interpretation. Barrett distinguishes three types of contextual information: internal context, original context, and external context. The viewer learns about a work's internal context by attending to its "subject matter, medium, form, and the relations among the three" (Barrett, 1990, p. 77). The original context for a work includes knowing where, when, and how it was made, knowing about the artist, her biography, and her other works, knowing about the social and art worlds in which the work was created. Finally, external context, according to Barrett, "is the situation in which a photograph is presented or found" (p. 79).

III was presented to the students as a real artwork, not a reproduction, brought into their classroom for their interpretation and as the focus of the last lesson in a three-part instructional unit on multicultural art. Using actual art works instead of reproductions helps students understand the physicality of the work and gives them the opportunity to learn that art exists in more than two dimensions. In this chapter I discuss Simpson's work in relation to three contexts: the external context of the unit on multicultural American art; the original context of the artist's life and work and the patrons who commissioned *III*; and finally, a range of external contexts, some of which provide lenses through which Simpson's artwork can be interpreted.

Context I

For several years I had volunteered as a Picture Person at my daughters' school, a public magnet school for gifted students in grades 2–12. Picture Person programs are found in many schools around the United States. Sometimes supported by PTAs or PTSOs, these programs provide volunteers who introduce students to art reproductions, engage them in discussions about art works, artists, and art concepts, and, like museum docents, encourage what used to be known as art appreciation. My background as a professional art educator set me apart from many Picture Person volunteers, but also enabled me to treat the experience as an opportunity for action research.

When my older daughter was in fifth grade, I was asked to teach three Picture Person lessons to her class. Since I already knew that fifth graders would study American history in social studies, I decided to focus on American art. Rather than introduce traditional exemplars of American paintings by Homer, Eakins, or Stuart, I decided to use works by traditional and contemporary artists that would introduce a critical understanding of the increasing diversity of American culture.[1] As artist and educator Amelia Mesa-Bains (1996) points out, schools "have become the front line in this demographic revolution" (p. 31).

I planned the lessons around three big questions:

- Why do people make art?
- How do people look at art?
- How can we interpret one work of visual art?

Although these questions focus on understandings important to art, they have the potential to open dialogue on relations between art and life. Humans make art to meet physical needs for food, clothing, and shelter, to mark individual identity, group membership, and important life events (Chapman, 1978). We can respond to works of art as aesthetic objects, set apart from daily life, or as cultural texts to be interpreted. When we look at artworks as cultural texts, we investigate them in relation to values and beliefs—personal and social, traditional and controversial. Looking at works of art in the contexts of controversial issues can motivate students to engage both minds and hearts, developing habits of critical thinking and problem solving (Cook, 1984).

The third lesson in this unit used reproductions by African-American artists as a context for *III* by Lorna Simpson. After briefly discussing how these artists addressed the issue of racial identity, we looked at the work by Lorna Simpson. I asked the students to study it carefully, then, after I removed it from sight, to write a thorough description of it, a description that would help anyone who was absent that day to visualize it.

III is a wooden box 13.5 inches long, 5.25 inches wide, and 2.25 inches high. The Roman numeral has been printed on the cover, which slides into a groove near the top of the box. The wood has been stained a warm golden brown. Before sliding the cover out, I asked the students to speculate about what the box might contain. One student guessed cigars, perhaps because the box is constructed like a wooden cigar box. Inside the box, the students could see a 1/4 inch thick piece of creamy off-white felt with the image of a wishbone lithographed on it above the words:

Wish #1

Wish #2

Wish #3

When I lifted the felt out by the two rounded corners at the lower edge, an even thicker bed of felt was revealed. This 3/4 inch piece of felt fit snugly into the box. Three wishbone shapes had been cut into it, running the length of the box. One wishbone rested in each space. The top wishbone is made of white unglazed clay, the second of translucent, almost colorless rubber, and the third of a cold, somewhat heavy, black metal. Information printed under the cover lists the components of this work as: wood box and felt with ceramic, rubber, and bronze wishbones.

After students wrote their descriptions, we compared them, developing a comprehensive description. Now it was time to move into the role of cultural critic, speculating with the students about possible meanings of *III* by thinking about the work in relationship to information about the artist, their earlier discussion of the reproductions by other contemporary African-American artists, and their understanding of our culture—games or holiday rituals involving wishbones, stories that include three wishes, current political events. The students worked in pairs to develop their interpretations, referring to a list of eight clues passed out before they began to write statements about the original context of the work. (See Figure 29.1)

CLUE #1—Lorna Simpson was born in Brooklyn, New York, in 1960. She studied photography at the School of Visual Arts in New York, then moved to California. She got a Master of Fine Arts degree from the University of California at San Diego in 1985.

CLUE #2—Lorna Simpson is an African-American woman artist. She uses her personal experiences and the experiences of other African-Americans to get ideas for her work.

CLUE #3—She often makes works of art with several parts, three or five or more sections. Sometimes each part is almost the same as the others; sometimes each part is different.

CLUE #4—Lorna Simpson works with images or pictures in her works of art. Sometimes words tell part of a story. Sometimes, the words make the viewers ask questions: How do these words and pictures fit together? What is this artist telling us?

CLUE #5—Lorna Simpson believes that people use their knowledge of games and stories to make sense out of puzzling pictures. Her works of art sometimes remind viewers of stories they have heard, of games they played as children, or of current events.

CLUE #6—Lorna Simpson makes works of art that do not look handmade. They look like they are made by machines not by hand tools. They look like they could have been made in a factory, mass-produced like shoes or other things we buy in stores.

CLUE #7—Lorna Simpson wants people to think about the art she makes and to ask questions about what they see and about the world we live in. She doesn't give us answers.

CLUE #8—Lorna Simpson's photographs of people often focus on parts of their bodies, a back or neck or part of a face. Sometimes she uses fragments of bodies with parts of sentences in her art.

Figure 29.1 Handout prepared for the fifth grade-students with information about Simpson as contexts for interpretation.

We discussed the various interpretations, noticing how different people attended to different aspects of the work or put it into different frames. As we began to shape a joint interpretation, I explained that this object had been commissioned as a multiple work of art to be sent as a holiday greeting. We talked about how this fact might influence an interpretation. We also talked about *III* as a work of conceptual art, designed by the artist to make people think and speculate.

We discussed the implications of the materials from which the wishbones had been made—fragile fired clay, flexible rubber, unbreakable bronze. The ceramic wishbone in our box is broken; I asked the students if they thought it might have been planned that way. Why might someone send you a wishbone that had already been used up? What about the two wishbones that could not be broken? Finally, students wrote three wishes, connecting our investigation of Simpson's artwork with their own dreams and desires.

Context II

Original contexts include Lorna Simpson's life, her body of professional work and the themes her work explores, as well as the art patrons who commissioned *III*. Born in Brooklyn in 1960, Lorna Simpson was an only child. Her father, a social worker, and her mother, a medical secretary, often took Lorna to museums and the theater (Wolf, 1994). Her interest in photography began when she sent away for a free camera, a special offer on the box of tissues she was using for a bad cold. She took her first photography course in high school and received a BFA in photography from the School of Visual Arts in New York in 1982. During college, she interned in the education department of the Studio Museum in Harlem. Three years later she completed her MFA in Visual Arts at the University of California in San Diego. That same year she received the first of many grants and awards, an Arts Management Fellowship from the National Endowment for the Arts, and held her first one-person exhibition. Simpson quickly became "one of the most closely watched conceptual artists working" in the 1990s (Sadowski, 1999). At age thirty, she had a one-person exhibition at New York's Museum of Modern Art.

As an undergraduate, Simpson documented people in New York's streets and subways through black and white photographs. Dissatisfied with the appearance of objective truth, which concealed historical and cultural meanings, she used her graduate school years to explore ways of making art related to her experience as an African-American woman and broader issues of African-American history. Like other late twentieth century artists such as Barbara Krueger, Jean-Michel Basquiat, and David Wojnarowicz, Simpson has combined images with text. She creates visual puzzles that raise questions about men and women, black and white, power, skin color, the body, language, games, myths, and stereotypes. Although, at first glance, Simpson's artworks may seem to be cool, distanced recordings of people, objects, and body parts treated as objects, tensions exist between verbal and visual texts and the external contexts of feminist and African-American critiques of American culture.

One of the first works in what has come to be regarded as Simpson's characteristic style was *Gestures/Reenactments* (1985).[2] A row of six photographs shows portions of an African-American male's torso, clad in a white t-shirt and light-colored pants. Seven rectangular boxes of text beneath the row of photographs seem to tell a story or parts of several stories about the pictures. Art historian and critic Linda Nochlin has written that Simpson uses an "intellectually complex interweaving of text and image to construct an individual in terms not merely of his body, but of his relationship to the wider community of family and friends" (1995, p. 91).

Between 1986 and 1992, Simpson worked with images of women, parts of their bodies, or braids of hair. The woman, photographed from the back or from the neck down, often wears a shapeless white shift. *Neck Lines* (1989) combines three vertically oriented photographs of a Black woman's neck and the scalloped edge of her white shift with two black blocks of white text.[3] The first block of text contains the words necktie, neck & neck, neck-ed, neckless; the second: necking, neckline, necklace, breakneck. Reading images and text together suggests sexual differences between men and women as well as the history of lynchings of African-American men for alleged rapes of white women.

While many of Simpson's works have been read by art critics as sophisticated critiques of gender and race relations, objectification of the female body, patriarchy, the power ascribed to science, and social issues such as violence, other works require knowledge of children's games. For example, *Placques* (1986) presents four oval photographs of hands—in a fist, flat with palm outward, with the first two fingers raised and separated, then with one hand covering the other. The rectangular block of text above the row of pictures lists three words: rock, paper, scissors. The text below states: "it was impossible to make sense of the natural order of things being dark and heavy-handed" (Wright and Hartman, 1992, p. 59). Children will recognize the game but can also discuss prejudice, social hierarchies, power relations, and competition, bringing their own experiences to the process of interpretation.

In 1993, Simpson collaborated with Kim Petro, a glass artist, on an installation about wishing. Two hundred glass wishbones hung on a gallery wall above photographs of broken wishbones. Repeated along the wall was the text: "Clearly, if you got what you wished you know you'd end up wanting another wish" (Wolf, 1994, p. 58). Explaining Simpson's work for young readers, Wolf connects this piece with human desire and rituals of wishing on stars and with pennies tossed in fountains.

Simpson has continued to challenge definitions of photography while exploring controversial issues. During the mid-1990s, she tried printing photographs on felt, a material that, unlike glossy photographic paper, absorbs light. Toward the end of the 1990s, she began to explore moving images during a residency at Ohio State University's Wexner Center for the Arts (Simpson and Rogers, 1997). These works continued her interest in large-scale photographic images, in narrative, the ways words and pictures can complement or comment on each other, and issues of intimacy and distance. Part of the support for Simpson's residency in Columbus came from the Peter Norton Family Foundation, established by Peter Norton, who with his wife Eileen commissioned *III*. The Norton Foundation is one of several private art foundations established in southern California within the past two decades to support the visual arts but also to memorialize the donor's name (Heartney, 1992).

The relationship between artist and patron is rarely explored in art classes but can lead into discussions about relationships between the art world and social issues. Eileen and Peter Norton, a former computer software publisher, were recognized as major collectors of art produced by young Southern California artists during the 1980s. In 1988, the Nortons began sending out a holiday greeting commissioned through requests for proposals from artists (Smith, 1991). Their extensive mailing list grew out of Peter Norton's contacts with artists, museum trustees, and others. The first commissioned work was a series of audiotapes for the Nortons' answering machine by Marc Pally.

In 1990, the Nortons stirred controversy by commissioning three different works by three different artists. Those on the mailing list were asked to choose whether they wanted a religious greeting, a secular greeting, or the third work—suitable only for adults—commissioned to recognize the Day Without Art, December 1, set aside to remember art world victims of AIDS. The project stimulated debate over whether the Nortons should have given the money directly to AIDS research and patient care, or to homeless shelters or other charities, rather than gratifying their egos. However, one commentator pointed out that not only were the Nortons enhancing the careers of the artists they selected, but that the project stimulated discussion about AIDS, racism, and religion through the use of art (Carlson, 1991).

In 1994, the Nortons commissioned a work from Lorna Simpson. *III*, created in an edition of 5,000 was the result. A greeting-card photograph enclosed with the work reveals that the Nortons are a multiracial family and describes Simpson's work as both "an investigation of the issues of race and gender" and a "meditation on wishing." Knowledge of the Norton family's relationship with *III* as the patrons who commissioned the work combined with knowledge of themes and concepts explored in Simpson's other works can help us interpret this work more fully.

In our society, some people are wealthy enough to give away wishes. Like the genies in folk tales, they have the power to grant requests to those who ask. But, again as in the stories we read to children, not all wishes are fulfilled. Some wishes might be easily granted, like the ceramic wishbone, but may be ephemeral, only gratifying the recipient for a short time. Other wishes, like the rubber wishbone that bends easily but never breaks, may never be granted. Racial inequalities in American society guarantee that many wishes made by African-Americans will remain unfulfilled, just as the blackened bronze wishbone will never break without strong force or structural change. But, just as human beings continue wishing on each new evening star, so we must continue to critically examine our society, questioning racial, ethnic, and gender inequalities.

Context III

External contexts for Lorna Simpson's artwork spread out like ripples from a pebble thrown into a still pond. The fifth-grade students and I talked about the work as a holiday gift, connecting the closed box with unopened presents and recalling eager anticipation and speculation about what might be inside. Many students were familiar with classical Greek and Roman mythology. They compared *III* with Pandora's box; perhaps evil would fly out when we opened it and hope would linger inside. Once we had opened the box and seen the wishbones, the children shared their stories about wishing on turkey or chicken bones. We learned that different families had different traditions regarding such rituals. What each of us considered the "right way" to wish was foreign to others. All the students were familiar with traditional stories incorporating three wishes, such as Aladdin and the Magic Lamp or The Fisherman and His Wife. We might have extended the connection between visual art and literature further by writing stories about what might happen to someone who received *III* as a gift and tried to use the wishes.

The responses of art critics to Lorna Simpson's work constitute another external context. Many critics have used semiotic concepts and theories to interpret Simpson's work. Semiotic theory developed from work by the American philosopher Charles Sanders Peirce. He distinguished three types of sign systems: a) iconic signs where the sign resembles the thing it stands for, like the silhouettes of children on a school crossing sign; b) indexes where the sign indicates the presence of the object it points to, for example, snow is an index of cold winter weather; c) true symbols where the sign has an arbitrary relationship to the object or idea it stands for (Richter, 1989). The wishbones in *III* are true symbols; their relationship to the concept of "wishing" is culturally determined, a convention within certain groups that share particular beliefs and customs.

I might have explored the context of art criticism further by giving the students brief quotations from critic's writings, appropriate to their reading level, then asked whether they agreed or disagreed with what the critics said and why. My intent in this lesson, however, was to move beyond knowledge about art and to engage the students in a search for meaning, making a bridge between art and life. Therefore, I placed *III* in an educational context of teaching thinking skills. Sternberg (1994) argues that asking questions is an excellent way to develop intelligence and thinking skills. While schools are usually focused on the teacher as the questioner and the student as the one who must provide answers, Sternberg argues that children need to *mediate* their environment, that is, to make sense of the world by *asking* the questions. Parents and teachers who respond to those questions at higher levels, by encouraging children to find a response from an authority, by considering alternative explanations, by considering not only explanations but how to evaluate their adequacy, or by actually doing what needs to be done to evaluate an explanation, support analytic and creative learning.

Perkins (1994) argues that looking at works of art, either actual art objects or their reproductions, offers an excellent opportunity to build thinking. He explains that works of art offer sensory anchors, concrete objects or images, which can be referred to during discussion or which can exemplify aspects of otherwise abstract concepts. Second, the work of art offers instant access—it is right there so you can check statements against visual evidence. Third, art works invite personal engagement. The fifth graders could connect with *III* on many different levels and discuss it in relation to personal experiences. Fourth, artworks appeal to emotions as well as intellect. Recent research on thinking suggests that when our emotions are engaged, thinking is reinforced. As Perkins writes: "In an atmosphere of heightened affect, the dispositional side of thinking seems more at home" (1994, p. 85). Fifth, a work of art engages several sensory modalities and, as a system of signs, may function in multiple ways. Finally, as I have been demonstrating throughout this paper, works of art exist in multiple contexts, they have many connections. To quote Perkins again,

> Art tends to be multiconnected. We can find links with many things—social issues, aesthetic concerns, trends of the times, personal commitments, even science and mathematics sometimes. Art is generally richly connected culturally and historically. (1994, p. 86)

Endnotes

1. The school's collection of older printed reproductions was limited to the usual range of European-trained, white, mostly male painters, but I had access to colored reproductions from the Multicultural Art Prints Series (MAPS) copublished by the Getty Education Institute for the Arts and the J. Paul Getty Museum and distributed by Crystal Productions. The MAPS sets I used included: Selected American-Indian Artifacts: Chumash, Hopi, Hopi-Tewa, Lakota, Navaho from the collection of the Southwest Museum, Los Angeles; African-American Art from the permanent collection of the California Afro-American Museum Foundation; Women Artists of the Americas from the collection of the National Museum of Women in the Arts; and Mexican-American Art from the collection of the National Museum of American Art, Smithsonian Institution. The URL for Crystal Productions is: <<www.crystalproduction.com>>.

2. A reproduction of this work can be found in Wright & Hartman, 1992, p. 10.

3. See Wright & Hartman (1992), p. 42, or Wolf (1994), p. 53.

References

Barrett, T. (1990). *Criticizing photographs.* Mountain View, CA: Mayfield.

Carlson, L. (1991, February 7). The personal gesture. *Artweek, 22,* 19.

Chapman, L. H. (1978). *Approaches to art in education.* New York: Harcourt Brace Jovanovich.

Cook, K. K. (1984). *Controversial issues: Concerns for policy makers.* ERIC Digest No. 14. (ERIC Document Reproduction Service No. ED 253 465)

Heartney, E. (1992, January). The new patronage. *Art in America, 80,* 72–79 & 129.

Mesa-Bains, A. (1996). Teaching students the way they learn. In S. Cahan & Z. Kocur, (Eds.), *Contemporary art and multicultural education* (pp. 31–38). New York: The New Museum of Contemporary Art & Routledge.

Nochlin, L. (1995, March). Learning from "Black Male." *Art in America, 83,* 86–91.

Perkins, D. N. (1994). *The intelligent eye.* Santa Monica, CA: The J. Paul Getty Trust.

Richter, D. H. (1989). *The critical tradition.* New York: St. Martin's Press.

Sadowski, P. (1999). *Lorna Simpson and Carrie Mae Weems.* [On-line]. Available: *www.arts.usf.edu/~ooguibe/afroam21.htm.*

Simpson, L., & Rogers, S. J. (1997). *Lorna Simpson: Interior/exterior, full/empty.* Columbus, OH: Wexner Center for the Arts/The Ohio State University.

Smith, R. (1991, February 7). Eileen and Peter Norton art collectors. *Artweek, 22,* 19–20.

Sternberg, R. J. (1994). Answering questions and questioning answers. *Phi Delta Kappan, 76*(2), 136–138.

Wolf, S. (1994). *Focus: Five women photographers.* Morton Grove, IL: A. Whitman.

Wright, B. J., & Hartman, S. V. (1992). *Lorna Simpson: For the sake of the viewer.* Chicago, IL: Museum of Contemporary Art.

CONCLUSIONS AND FURTHER QUESTIONS

1. How does a cultural critic approach a work of art? How does this form of criticism differ from other types of criticism?

2. What is semiotic theory? How does semiotics help us understand and interpret works of art? How does Simpson's artwork reflect semiotic theory?

3. Describe each of the contexts that can help us interpret works of art. Why does Stankiewicz argue that we should look at a number of contexts within which we can place the work?

4. Choose an artwork that responds to an issue that you think is important. Develop an interpretation of your artwork based upon the contexts that Stankiewicz has suggested. How did an understanding of these various contexts aid our interpretations?

5. Based upon the interpretation that you have written, develop your understandings of the work into ideas that you could use in the

elementary classroom. How would you link this learning to the lives and experiences of your students?

6. How does a contextual approach help students create knowledge and meaning?

RESOURCES AND SUGGESTIONS
FOR FURTHER READING

Terry Barrett. *Criticizing art: Understanding the contemporary.* Mountain View, CA: Mayfield, 2000.

John Deely. *Basics of semiotics.* Bloomington, IN: Indiana University Press, 1990.

Julia Kristeva. *Desire in language: A semiotic approach to literature and art.* Leon S. Roudiez (Ed.); Thomas Gora, Alice Jardine, & Leon S. Roudiez (Trans.). New York: Columbia University Press, 1980.

David Lidov. *Elements of semiotics.* New York: St. Martin's Press, 1999.

Charles S. Peirce. *The essential Peirce: Selected philosophical writings.* Nathan Houser & Christian Kloesel (Eds.). Bloomington, IN: Indiana University Press, 1992.

Charles S. Peirce. *Peirce on signs: Writings on semiotics.* James Hoopes (Ed.). Chapel Hill, NC: University of North Carolina Press, 1991.

A world of art. Works in progress: Lorna Simpson. Oregon Public Broadcasting production in association with Oregon State University for the Annenberg/CPB Project. S. Burlington, VT: Annenberg/CPB Project, 1996. (26 minute videocassette)

Hugh J. Silverman (Ed.). *Cultural semiosis: Tracing the signifier.* New York: Routledge, 1998.

Linda Weintraub, Thomas McEvilley, & Arthur Coleman Danto. *Art on the edge and over: Searching for art's meaning in contemporary society 1970s–1990s.* Litchfield, CT: Art Insights, Inc., 1997.

Deborah Willis. *Lorna Simpson.* San Francisco, CA; New York: Friends of Photography; Distributed Art Publishers, 1992.

Conclusions
and Other Thoughts:
Yes, the Witch can be Purple

Imagine a Kindergarten classroom humming with activity as students eagerly complete an assignment and apply color to a drawing. Peg carries her work up to the teacher's desk whereupon the teacher grades it. The teacher places a large black X across the image of a witch whose dress and hat have been colored purple. The teacher hands the paper back to Peg, leaning over to explain her action. "Witches," the teacher says matter-of-factly, "are not purple."

Even at age five, Peg was aware that this was not a valid assessment but she was unable to articulate her reasons for thinking this nor did she know what the alternatives were. Luckily, this incident did not hamper her creativity or her future in art, but it remained an indelible memory. Other people who might have experienced similar situations as a child might not have walked away unscathed.

Imagine yourself as the five-year old child in these circumstances. Now imagine yourself as the teacher. How would each of these perspectives affect your understandings of this purple witch?

Assessment in the Elementary Classroom

We open the final chapter of this book with this story because it raises a number of questions about teachers' assessment of students in art and the grading of artworks and interpretations. Many of us have experienced such seemingly arbitrary judgments put forward about our artworks. Sometimes these judgments were required by the structure of the school and systems of reporting, at other times they were opinions and conclusions that were unsolicited and perhaps unnecessary. In addition, the incident is significant to the teaching of art at the elementary level because it calls our attention to the complexities of assessment. We might ask, for example, why should teachers assess children's artwork? What are students expected to *learn* from the assignment, the activity, and the assessment? Why is this learning important? What is the relationship between the artwork, the interpretations and critical writings produced by the student, and the learning that has taken place? How do we measure this relationship? What is the relationship between learning and assessment? What criteria might we use for assessment? How should teachers grade a student's interpretation of an artwork? If students' works are based on issues such as identity and personal history, how do we grade the artworks that these students produce without seeming to assess their identities? What does assessment tell us? What color can a witch's clothing be?

In this chapter, we outline some of the salient issues regarding assessment in the elementary classroom. Our purpose here is not to provide specific strategies for assessment, but rather to suggest questions that teachers need to take into consideration as they work on developing approaches to assessment that are situated within the particulars of the students they are working with and the classroom, school, and community within which they are teaching.

We need to begin any discussion of assessment by developing a basic understanding of what we mean by the term. Donna Kay Beattie (1997) writes, "assessment is the method or process used for gathering information about people, programs, or objects for the purpose of making an evaluation" (p. 2). Assessment is also a form of measurement. Understanding *what* we are measuring and *for what purposes* are key questions that we must ask ourselves before developing any assessment strategy. Assessment should primarily be about measuring learning rather than measuring the products that students make. Assessment may also be understood as an evaluation based on certain criteria for the purpose of making a judgment or, in the case of much public schooling, assigning a grade. A judgment is based on particular criteria when we seek to measure what our students have learned or experienced, revealing for example, the achievement of content knowledge and/or certain skills. A judgment is supported by criteria that help us determine what students have learned through the ideas, issues, and materials that we have brought to class in order to prepare for the next steps in teaching and learning. As such, assessment may help us make determinations about our own teaching. Evaluation should also be based on what students have learned, knowing from what positions they started and looking to see where they have moved in their learning.

Assessment serves as an indicator of where we have been in order to help us decide where we will go. Beattie (1997) states that "effective assessment techniques can improve classroom instruction, empower students, heighten student interest and motivation, and provide teachers with ongoing feedback on student progress" (p. 2). Within such a context, *how* we assess our students becomes an important issue. There is no doubt in our minds that there are appropriate and inappropriate ways to assess student artworks and their interpretations of art. Assessment measures that are unrelated to the students' learning and to the content that is being taught are not effective forms of measurement. Examples of such forms of ill-considered assessment would include grading that is solely based on criteria such as effort and neatness rather than the content of the teaching and learning.

The complexity of the issues surrounding assessment could lead some teachers to avoid assessment. Admittedly, one of the challenging tasks we face as teachers in the elementary classroom is assessing student learning. However, a total disregard for assessment in art would be as inappropriate as assessment that is unrelated to the learning that has taken place, for it diminishes the possibilities that art learning brings to the elementary experience. Initially, many elementary teachers express discomfort with the idea of assessing children in art, yet at the same time they may not question the idea of assessing children in other subject areas. Teachers who feel this way are often supported by their own experiences in art as children, by their personal views about art and its role in the classroom, and by their constructed views about children. Yet, as Brent Wilson (1997) reminds us, "formal assessment validates a school subject; if students are not tested in a subject, then its importance to their education is questioned. If art is to take its place as a core subject in the elementary school curriculum, it is reasoned, then student learning must be assessed" (p. 156). If we accept the idea that art is an important part of the curriculum and that art can be learned, then art can and should be assessed. Evaluation is as important in teaching art as it is in other subject areas, however this does not mean that art should necessarily be assessed in the same way that other subjects are assessed.

Assessment in an Issues-based Curriculum

Throughout this book, we have read about some of the possibilities for art at the elementary level when teaching through an issues-based approach. This includes raising students' awareness and understanding of social issues, relating issues and classroom learning to everyday life, drawing from our own experiences to inform learning, and thinking about and working with art as a means of communicating with and connecting to the world outside the classroom. The approaches discussed in this book also ask students and teachers to develop personal responses to public issues and to think about alternative ways to see the world and participate within it. Teachers are challenged to explore conceptual frameworks for connecting learning across the curriculum and to develop a variety of means to grasp a concept or idea and to understand difference and our identities.

Strategies for measuring learning with regard to any of the above require thoughtful consideration. Terry Barrett (2000), in his discussion of art criticism, argues that "judgment is an important part of criticism, but not the most important" and that "a judgment without benefit of interpretation is irresponsive to a work of art and probably irresponsible" (p. 25). In an analogous sense, we need to understand what our students are learning and learn to interpret the responses that they give. Such considerations take us far beyond how neatly a student completed an assignment or an evaluation of the colors that a student used. When we ask students to bring their lives and experiences into their creative responses to projects, assignments, or critical discussions in art, we must expect their responses to cover a range of possibilities.

What does this mean with regard to assessing students in an issues-based art curriculum? If we think of assessment in terms that extend beyond the measurement of the successful completion of a particular assignment, then assessment becomes an ongoing process and dialogue to which students and teachers are committed. Art, within an issues-based curriculum, may be assessed using a variety of strategies that include question and answer, discussion, collaboration, worksheets or tests, the presentation of an art exhibition, developing scoring rubrics,[1] art portfolios, and journals. It means that the assessment is not solely focused on the outcome, the end product, or the artwork that the student has made but rather that it is about understanding what the child has learned.

Students come into our classrooms with varied life histories, identities, abilities, skills, and experiences. Keeping these differences in mind, we ask ourselves what happens to this range of possibilities if we exclusively focus on a singular definition and understanding of an end product? Sole attention or emphasis on end products, which present themselves in different forms, causes a shift in assessment to a universal set of criteria through which we can make judgments about the diverse products that our students have produced. For example, we might then seek to evaluate works based upon a set of formalist criteria by "objectively" examining each work. The content or meaning contained in the work becomes secondary or lost altogether. All that is considered important is how the work looks within a formal elements and principles of design framework. This would be similar to grading all writing assignments exclusively for grammar and punctuation but disregarding the content of the essays.

In some instances in the process of learning this type of evaluation may be useful but assessment should not remain fixed on a single aspect. An issues-based approach to the teaching of art requires different criteria for assessing the artwork of children. When projects or assignments are connected to the lives of our students, understanding and constructing meaning become very important components of the work. While formalist criteria may continue to be a valid consideration for assessment, they should not be the main focus or the only focus. Measuring what our students have learned about the issues at hand should be the main focus of assessment. Given the complexity of many of the issues that are being studied, this suggests that there will be no "right answer" to any given unit. Teaching and assessment in an issues-based curriculum should be an open exploration that can take into account and critically examine diverse viewpoints.

Our assessment strategies must take into account the differences among students and the kinds of learning that art makes available for each of our students. We must ask ourselves whether or not we are using assessment means that are equitable given the differences that exist amongst our students. As we develop assessment procedures we need to be wary of hidden biases that they might contain. We need to let go of the myth of "objective assessment" and

---

[1]Rubrics are scoring guides. See Donna Kay Beattie (1997) for an in depth discussion on different assessment strategies.

understand that knowledge is contingent upon a variety of cultural, social, and political contexts. It is therefore important to create approaches to assessment that are situated within the specifics of our classrooms, the lives and experiences of our students, our lives and experiences as teachers, and the communities within which we teach. Assessing student learning includes examining student achievement in tandem with the content of the curriculum and the pedagogical approaches used by the teacher. A more critical attitude towards assessment also involves questioning ourselves as teachers on *what* we are measuring when we assess our students and why this is important. We need to ask ourselves what we are learning from our students as they participate in our lessons and activities.

Finally, assessment should be embedded within the curriculum (Wilson, 1997). Such a framework for assessment is very different from thinking of assessment as a task that is to be completed after students have finished their work. Embedded assessment asks us to be continually involved in the process of assessment and suggests that assessment should be an integrated and active part of the process of teaching and learning. Such a view of assessment positions it as an important part of any unit of learning rather than a task that only takes place at the end of an assignment. An embedded approach suggests that developing assessment strategies be an ongoing part of curriculum planning. As we explore metaphors for curriculum, we also need to take into consideration the ways in which our teaching, learning, and assessment approaches are structured. When approached in this way, assessment has the potential to reveal individual learning, progress, or growth; the significance of particular content; and the effectiveness of pedagogical practices.

References

Barrett, T. (2000). *Criticizing art: Understanding the contemporary,* 2nd edition. Mountain View, CA: Mayfield.

Beattie, D. K. (1997). *Assessment in art education.* Worcester, MA: Davis Publications.

Wilson, B. (1997). *The quiet evolution: Changing the face of arts education.* Los Angeles, CA: The Getty Education Institute for the Arts.

List of Artists

Contemporary Art and Artists for Use in the Elementary Classroom

Many contemporary artists whose work engages with social, political, and cultural issues create works that cross these boundaries and divisions. In order to make this listing of artists easier to refer to, we give for guidance a brief list of the issues that each artist's work typically deals with. Since many of the artists produce work that encompasses several issues, and often involves the intersection of a group of issues, the listing is not definitive and you may find an artist's work relevant to other issues. All of these artists confront political and social inequalities and broad issues about the nature of contemporary art-making and representation in their work.

In addition, we suggest that you refer to contemporary art magazines such as *Art in America*, the *New Art Examiner, ArtForum,* and the *Art Journal* for ongoing sources of contemporary visual artists' works. These magazines also offer readers critical assessments of artworks and provide visual images that will be a useful resource to teachers.

We encourage you to begin developing a visual resource file of artists whose work interests you and addresses issues that you are teaching about in your classroom. Initially such a file could contain images of the artist's works, facts about the artist's life, and critical interpretations about the artworks. It could also record ways that you have used these issues and works in your classroom and examples of the works that students produced in response to the issues that you are teaching.

Finally, we would like to add a note of caution. As many of the authors in this text have argued, we need to look at the metaphors and ideas represented in the artworks that we are teaching with. The works of the artists listed below are complex, both in terms of the ideas that are being explored through the work and the way in which the work has been made. We would argue that the purpose of looking at such works is to develop metaphors that help us understand difficult issues, not to use the works as starting points for imitation. In other words, these artworks should not serve as examples that children will try, in a simplified way, to reproduce. Instead teachers and students can use the artwork to understand ways of approaching an issue and, from this starting point, develop their own understandings and interpretations of the issue.

Acconci, Vito. The body and gender.

Ackroyd, Heather and Dan Harvey. Genetic engineering, technology, and the environment.

ACTUP. Health and illness (specifically AIDS), the body, and sexuality.

Anderson, Laurie. Technology, the body, and gender.

Antin, Eleanor. Gender, the body, and representation.

Arbus, Diane. Representation and identity.

Azaceta, Luis Cruz. Health and illness (specifically AIDS), the body, and sexuality.

Baca, Judy. Public art, race, ethnicity, gender, class, immigration, and labor conditions.

Basquiat, Jean Michel. Race, particularly representation of African-Americans.

Bearden, Romare. Race, particularly the representation of African-Americans.

Biggers, John. Race, particularly the representation of African-Americans.

Birch, Willie. Race, particularly the representation of African-Americans.

Bleckner, Ross. Health and illness (specifically AIDS), the body, and sexuality.

Bourgeois, Louise. Gender and representation.

Burgin, Victor. Gender and representation.

Burson, Nancy. Technology, identity, ethnicity, and representation.

Cattlett, Elizabeth. Race and gender.

Chicago, Judy. Gender, women's history, and women's experiences.

Chin, Mel. Public art, site-specific art, the environment and ecology.

Christo and Jeanne-Claude. Public art, site-specific art, and the environment.

Coe, Sue. Human and animal rights.

Colescott, Robert. Race, gender, and representation.

Cooday, Jesse. Race, gender, and representation.

DeMaria, Walter. Public art, site-specific art, the environment and ecology.

Denes, Agnes. Public art, site-specific art, the environment and ecology.

Dougherty, Patrick. Public art, site-specific art, the environment and ecology.

Dove, Toni. Narrative structure, technology, and the body.

Durham, Jimmie. Race and representation.

Edelson, Mary Beth. Gender, spirituality, and female power.

Escobar, Marisol. Gender and representation.

Flack, Audrey. Gender, representations of beauty, and female power.

Frey, Viola. The body and identity.

Fusco, Coco. Gender, race, ethnicity, and representation.

Garza, Carmen Lopez. Autobiography, personal history and memory, and ethnicity.

Mihail, Karl S. and Tran T. Kim-Trang. Technology and the body.

Min, Yong Soon. Representation, race, ethnicity, and stereotypes.

Morimura, Yasama. Representation, race, ethnicity, gender, and popular culture.

Mujeres Muralistas. Public art, race, ethnicity, and gender.

Munoz, Celia Alvarez. Race, ethnicity, and gender.

NAMES Quilt. Health and illness (specifically AIDS).

Neel, Alice. Gender and the body.

Newton, Helen and Joshua Harrison. Public art, site-specific art, the environment, and ecology.

O'Grady, Lorraine. Gender, race, and the representation of black women.

Oursler, Tony. Technology and the body.

Paik, Nam June. Technology, representation, and the body.

Pindell, Howardena. Autobiography, race, and representation.

Piper, Adrian. Race, ethnicity, and gender.

Rainer, Yvonne. Race, ethnicity, class, and gender.

Rickard, Jolene. Race, ethnicity, and gender.

Ringgold, Faith. Gender, race, and representation.

Rosler, Martha. Gender, technology, and the body.

Saar, Alyson. Gender, race, and representation.

Saar, Betye. Gender, spirituality, race, and representation.

Saint-Phalle, Niki de. Gender, race, and the body.

Sanchez, Juan. Race and ethnicity.

Scott, Joyce. Race, gender, and representation.

Serrano, Andres. Spirituality, religion, and representation.

Sherman, Cindy. Gender, representation, art history, and the body.

Simpson, Lorna. Race, gender, and representation.

Sligh, Clarrisa. Race, gender, and representation.

Smith, Kiki. Gender, language, and the body.

Spero, Nancy. Gender and the body.

Stelarc. Technology and the body.

Tansey, Mark. Representation and the history of art.

Ukeles, Mierle Ladeerman. The environment, ecology, labor, and social responsibility.

Viola, Bill. Technology and the body.

Walker, Kara. Race, gender, and representation.

Weems, Carrie Mae. Race, gender, and representation.

Wilding, Faith. Technology, gender, and the body.

Wilke, Hannah. Gender, the body, representation, and health and illness.

Williams, Pat Ward. Race and gender.

Wojnarovicz, David. Sexual orientation and the body.

List of Contributors

Mary Adams has taught for twenty-nine years as an art educator and a regular classroom teacher. She holds a B.A. degree from Ohio Dominican College and two Master of Science in Education degrees from Youngstown State University. She has recently served as president of the Steel Valley Art Teachers Association.

Debra Attenborough is presently completing her Ph.D. in Education. Since 1992, she has been an instructor at Brock University in both the Graduate Faculty of Education and the Women's Studies Department. She is the author of numerous publications on arts education and women in art. Since 1981, she has been the Curator of Education at Rodman Hall Arts Centre in St. Catharines, Ontario, Canada.

Joyce Barakett is associate professor of Education at Concordia University in Montreal. Her recent research interests include the sociology of education, sociology and social psychology of gender, and critical consciousness and art and social typing in the classroom. She is co-author of *Sociology of Education: An Introductory View from Canada.*

Professor of Art Education at Ohio State University, Terry Barrett wrote *Criticizing Art: Understanding the Contemporary, Criticizing Photographs: An Introduction to Images,* and *Talking About Student Art.* He is former editor of *Studies in Art Education* and visiting scholar to The Getty, the Center for Creative Photography, the University of Georgia, and Colorado State University.

Flávia M. C. Bastos is an assistant professor of Art Education at the University of Cincinnati. She studied the community of Orleans, Indiana during her doctoral work at Indiana University. In Brazil, her home country, she worked with Paulo Freire and his collaborators.

Dr. Paul S. Briggs developed his theories concerning religion, popular culture, and art education while preparing teachers in the Massachusetts College of Art, Art Education Department. He is now putting his ideas into practice at the Storm King School, Cornwall-on-Hudson, NY, where he is Head of Visual Arts.

Marcia Buckpitt completed her M.F.A. in art at University of Wisconsin. She taught at Princeton University from 1976 to 1980. Her art and poetry is published, collected and shown throughout the world. Currently she is head of the art program and teaches art to Apache children at McNary School.

B. Stephen Carpenter, II is Art Education Program Director at Old Dominion University in Virginia. He holds a B.F.A. from Slippery Rock University, and M. Ed. and Ph.D. degrees from Pennsylvania State University. He exhibits ceramics and mixed-media artworks and has written on ceramics criticism, teacher education, and visual literacy.

Ed Check is an activist, artist and educator. Cofounder of the NAEA Lesbian, Gay, and Bisexual Issues Caucus, Ed currently teaches visual studies at Texas Tech University. Ed's research and art explores personal narratives about gender, sexual identities, art and teaching.

Kristin G. Congdon has taught art in a variety of settings, including public schools, correctional settings, treatment facilities, museums, and universities. She has a Ph.D. in art education from the University of Oregon, and has published extensively on the study of folk arts, feminist criticism, and community arts. She is a professor of Art and Philosophy at the University of Central Florida.

Paul Duncum is a lecturer in Visual Arts Curriculum in the Faculty of Education, University of Tasmania in Launceston, Australia. He has published widely in the areas of his research and teaching, which include mass media images of childhood, children's unsolicited drawing, and critical theory and art education.

Charles R. Garoian is Director of the School of Visual Arts and professor of Art Education at The Pennsylvania State University. He has performed nationally and internationally and his scholarly articles are featured in journals on art and education. His book *Performing Pedagogy: Toward an Art of Politic* is a State University of New York Press publication.

Yvonne Gaudelius is an assistant professor of Art Education and Women's Studies at The Pennsylvania State University. Her research and teaching interests include feminist pedagogy and feminist theory in the arts, especially in relationship to issues surrounding representation and the gendered body as well as issues surrounding the intersection of art, technology, and the body.

As an associate professor of Art, Doris Guay teaches a range of course work in the School of Art at Kent State University, Kent, Ohio. Her favorite course has been Art Education Professional Practices, a course that challenges senior-level art education students just prior to their student teaching experiences. For elementary education and art education majors, she teaches a course that integrates art education as a discipline with elementary curriculum. Dr. Guay's research focuses on instruction with a particular emphasis on instruction in art classrooms inclusive of special needs students.

Joanne K. Guilfoil is an associate professor of Art Education at Eastern Kentucky University. With Allan Sandler she coedited the book *Built Environment Education in Art Education* published in 1999 by The National Art Education Association.

Carol S. Jeffers is a professor of Art Education at California State University, Los Angeles where she teaches a variety of graduate and undergraduate courses in art and art education.

Karen Keifer-Boyd, Ph.D., an associate professor of Art at Texas Tech University, teaches and researches gendered and technological contexts to develop creative and critical discourse on the values embedded in visual culture. She received the Arts Administrator of the Year National Art Education Award for the Pacific Region in 1994.

Debra Koppman exhibits her work as a visual artist nationally and internationally. She teaches studio and theory in the Department of Arts and Consciousness at John F. Kennedy University in Berkeley, California, and works as an artist-in-residence at Sequoia Elementary School in Oakland, California, helping children transform their community.

Don Krug, an associate professor of Art Education, at Ohio State University, is senior editor of the *Journal of Multicultural and Cross-cultural Research in Art Education*. He has twenty-plus years of K–16 teaching experience and his research interests include the study of visual culture, curriculum and instruction, new technologies, and biodiversity.

Julia Marshall is assistant professor of Art Education at San Francisco State University where she teaches graduate and undergraduate courses. She holds an M.F.A. from the University of Wisconsin and an Ed.D. from the University of San Francisco. Her experience includes many years as an artist in elementary schools developing and implementing curriculum that integrates the arts with academic subjects.

Sara Wilson McKay is a clinical assistant professor at the University of Houston whose major research areas include: theories of vision and perception, cultural reproduction, and art and democracy. She is currently developing the Houston Area Visual Resource Center and forging new collaborations with area cultural organizations and schools.

Melody K. Milbrandt is currently an assistant professor of Art Education at the State University of West Georgia, Carrollton, Georgia. She previously taught art in the public schools (K–12) for eighteen years. Her research interests include addressing social concerns through art education, authentic instruction and assessment, and action research in the art classroom.

Susana Monteverde, Curator of Education at Blaffer Gallery, the Art Museum of the University of Houston advocates expanding the role art museums play in classroom practice and curriculum building. Most recently she established the conceptual framework and guided the design and construction of an innovative outreach effort, the Mobile Art Quest.

Dan Nadaner is a painter and professor of Art at California State University, Fresno. He is the author of numerous essays on critical theory, and is coeditor of the book *Imagination and Education*. He has worked with teachers for twenty years on innovations to education through art.

Andra Nyman is an associate professor at the University of Georgia where she teaches courses in issues and practices, art theory, art and cultural diversity, and research methodology. Her research interests include curriculum and instruction, cultural diversity, and art for students with special needs.

Formerly the Curator of Education for the Art Museum of South Texas, Elizabeth B. Reese is a freelance writer, educator, and consultant in art, art education, and art museum education. She is also the director of *artconnects*, connecting communities, organizations, education, and technology through the visual arts. Additionally, Reese is a doctoral candidate at the Pennsylvania State University.

Billie Sessions is an associate professor of Art and the Art Education Program Director at California State University, San Bernardino. She holds a B.F.A. and M.Ed. from Utah State University and a Ph.D. from The Pennsylvania State University. She frequently presents and publishes on ceramics curriculum and Bauhaus potter, Marguritte Wildenhain.

Peg Speirs is an assistant professor of Art Education at Kutztown University, Pennsylvania. Dr. Speirs taught K–12 art in a public school district in Ohio from 1985–1995. Her research interests include feminist art, theory, and pedagogy. Dr. Speirs is also a practicing artist.

Mary Ann Stankiewicz, associate professor of Art Education, at The Pennsylvania State University, is the author of *Roots of Art Education Practice* (in press) and many articles on art education history. She has coordinated art education programs at the University of Maine and California State University, Long Beach, and is a past editor of *Art Education*.

Marilyn Stewart is professor of Art Education, Kutztown University, Pennsylvania, author of *Thinking Through Aesthetics*, editor of Davis Publications's *Art Education in Practice* series, co-author of Davis's three-text middle school program, *Art and the Human Experience*, and author of *QuestionArte*, by Crizmac. A frequent speaker and consultant to numerous national projects, she was the Getty Education Institute for the Arts 1997-1998 Visiting Scholar.

Mary Stokrocki, professor of Art Education at Arizona State University, received her Ed.D. from Pennsylvania State University. She is a World Councilor for INSEA, The International Society for Education through Art and former President of USSEA, the United States Society for Education through Art.

Graeme Sullivan is associate professor in the Department of Arts and Humanities, Teachers College, Columbia University. His research interests include studies of artistic cognition and contemporary art practice. He is the senior editor of *Studies in Art Education* and the author of numerous published articles on art education.

Jay Michael Hanes and Eleanor Weisman are a husband and wife team who attempt to teach with a social conscience. Having a child of their own, they are moved by the

American Indian concept of making decisions while conscious of the effect on the next seven generations of children.

John Howell White is an associate professor of Art Education at Kutztown University. He researches historical, cultural, and philosophical relationships that affect teaching and learning. He is the recipient of the National Art Education Association's Manuel Barkin Award for a scholarly publication and a Getty Center for Education in the Arts Fellowship.

Originally from North Carolina, Mary Wyrick received a B.F.A. in painting with teacher certification at the University of North Carolina at Chapel Hill. She taught junior high school art and Spanish at a public school in Fayetteville, North Carolina. She received her Masters at Applachian State University in Boone, North Carolina and a Ph.D. in Art Education at The Pennsylvania State University. She now teaches art education at Buffalo State.

Shirley Hayes Yokley is associate professor of Art Education at Middle Tennessee State University in Murfreesboro, Tennessee. For five years, she was assistant professor in Art Education at Kent State University in Ohio. Dr. Yokley holds a Ph.D. in Art Education with a minor in Curriculum and Instruction from The Pennsylvania State University.

Photo Credits

Chapter 1   Page 30: Pamela Lawton; **p. 32:** Lori Don Levan, ©Lori Don Levan 1994; **p. 33:** Hugo Ortega; **p. 34:** Aphrodite Desiree Navab.

Chapter 8   Page 110: Elaine Cunfer.

Chapter 14   Page 181: TimePix; **p. 182:** Dr. Don H. Krug, "Visiting County Artist" Photo Don Krug; **p. 184:** Los Angeles County Museum of Art, Robert Rauschenberg (American, b. 1925–) "Earth Day" 1970, color lithograph, 52 1/2 × 37 1/2 inches – 133.4 × 95.3 cm. Los Angeles County Museum of Art, gift of The Sidney and Diana Avery Trust. Photograph copyright ©2000 Museum Associates/LACMA. ©Robert Rauschenberg and Gemini G. E. L./Licensed by VAGA, New York, NY; **p. 190:** Andy Goldsworthy, ©Copyright Andy Goldsworthy from his book "Stone" (Abrams); **p. 192:** Walker Art Center, Mel Chin "Revival Field" 1991, landfill, chainlink fence, six plant varieties, perennial and annual seeds, 60 × 60 ft. Mixed media installation, St. Paul, Minnesota. Sponsored by Walker Art Center and the Science Museum of Minnesota, in cooperation with the Minnesota Pollution Control Agency. ©Mel Chin; **p. 193:** Barbara Westfall, Daylighting The Woods, An Ecological Art Installation by Barbara Westfall.

Chapter 15   Page 204: David Heald/The Solomon R. Guggenheim Museum, Faith Ringgold "Tar Beach" (Woman on a Beach Series #1), 1988, acrylic paint on canvas bordered with printed and painted quilted and pieced cloth, 189.5 × 174 cm (74 5/8 × 68 1/2 inches). Solomon R. Guggenheim Museum, New York: Gift, Mr. and Mrs. Gus and Judith Lieber, 1988. Photo: David Health ©The Solomon R. Guggenheim Foundation, New York, FN 88.3620; **p. 207:** National Gallery of Art, Washington, D.C., Jacob Lawrence (American, born 1917) "Daybreak — A Time to Rest" 1967, tempera on hardboard, .762 × 610 (30 × 24); framed: .924 × 768. Anonymous Gift, ©2000 Board of Trustees, National Gallery of Art, Washington.

Chapter 16   Pages 214, 217, 218, 220, 221: Mary Wyrick.

Chapter 17   Page 229: Zindman/Fremont/Mary Boone Gallery, Barbara Kruger "Untitled" (It's a small world but not if you have to clean it) 1990, photographic silkscreen/vinyl, 143 × 103 in. Collection: Museum of Contemporary Art, Los Angeles. Courtesy: Mary Boone Gallery, New York; **p. 230:** Zindman/Fremont/Mary Boone Gallery, Barbara Kruger "Untitled" (We don't need another hero) 1987, photographic silkscreen/vinyl, 109 × 210 in. Collection: Emily Fisher Landau, New York. Courtesy: Mary Boone Gallery, New York; **p. 231:** Cindy Sherman/Metro Pictures, Cindy Sherman "Untitled Film Still #21" 1978. Courtesy of the artist and Metro Pictures, New York, NY; **p. 232:** Sean Kelly Gallery, Lorna Simpson "Twenty Questions (a sampler)" 1986, 4 × 24 inch diameter silver gelatin prints, 6 engraved plastic plaques. Courtesy: Sean Kelly Gallery, New York; **p. 233:** Robert McKeever/Gagosian Gallery, Jenny Saville "Hyphen" 1999, oil on canvas, 108 × 144 (274.3 × 365.8cm). Photo: Robert McKeever. Courtesy of Gagosian Gallery.

Chapter 25   Page 329: Wyman Meinzer/Karen Keifer–Boyd, Ph.D.; **pp. 329, 331:** Karen Keifer–Boyd, Ph.D.; **p. 334:** Kate Knochel; **p. 335:** Kippra D. Hopper; **p. 336:** Lynne Hull; **p. 337:** Lynne Hull; **p. 340:** Jessi Hewlett.

Chapter 28   Page 374: Bernice Steinbaum Gallery, Beverly Buchanan "Richard's Home" 1993, oil crayon on wood and mixed media, 78 × 16 × 20 7/8 in. Courtesy Bernice Steinbaum Gallery, Miami, FL; **p. 377:** Adrian Saxe, Garth Vader "Untitled" (covered jar on stand with antelope finial) 1986. Permission of the artist.

Index